Soviet Historians and Perestroika

Titles in the Series

NEW DIRECTIONS IN SOVIET SOCIAL THOUGHT
An Anthology
Murray Yanowitch, ed.

PERESTROIKA AND THE ECONOMY
New Thinking in Soviet Economics
Anthony Jones and William Moskoff, eds.

PARTY, STATE, AND CITIZEN IN THE SOVIET UNION
A Collection of Documents
Mervyn Matthews, ed.

THE SOVIET MULTINATIONAL STATE
Readings and Documents
Martha B. Olcott, ed.

SOVIET HISTORIANS AND PERESTROIKA
The First Phase
Donald J. Raleigh, ed.

Soviet Historians and Perestroika

The First Phase

Edited by

Donald J. Raleigh

M. E. Sharpe, Inc.
ARMONK, NEW YORK
LONDON, ENGLAND

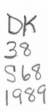
Library of Congress Cataloging-in-Publication Data

Soviet historians and perestroika : the first phase : an anthology /
   edited by Donald J. Raleigh.
        p.   cm.
     Articles translated from the Russian.
     Includes bibliographical references.
     ISBN 0-87332-554-0
     1. Soviet Union—Historiography—History—20th century.
   2. Perestroika. 3. Soviet Union—Politics and government—1985–
   4. Soviet Union—Intellectual life—20th century. 5. Historians—Soviet Union—History—20th century. I. Raleigh, Donald J.
   DK38.S68   1989   89-10724
   947'.0072—dc20   CIP

Printed in the United States of America

BB 10 9 8 7 6 5 4 3 2 1

*To Anya, Dasha, Vanya, Masha, Egor, and Adam
in the hope that they shall become friends*

Contents

Introduction

DONALD J. RALEIGH

The highly politicized Soviet historical profession responded sluggishly to Mikhail Sergeevich Gorbachev's calls for reform. Reverberations of the processes that have been recasting Soviet society since 1985 first became noticeable within the historical profession in 1987. By early 1988, however, it was clear that the reform-minded historians were not only on the offensive, but also in control of the prominent historical journals. The most sensitive issues in Soviet history had become topics of debate. Maverick historians, whose research had been fettered during the Brezhnev years, now published broadly and helped to shape the profession's future. To be sure, within the discipline opposition to reform continued, but it was more subtle and subdued. This transformation of the conservative Soviet historical profession is remarkable precisely because it represents systemic adjustment.[1]

Soviet historians responded cautiously to the call for change because the profession's intellectual integrity had been destroyed during the Stalin years, when historians became creators and defenders of historical myths. When Gorbachev came to power, the generation of historians trained during the Stalin period still predominated. The brief flood of revitalization that swept the discipline in the decade or so following the Twentieth Party Congress of 1956 taught historians an important lesson in caution: the limits of historical reassessment were never clearly spelled out by the party's factional leadership, but only became clear once revisionist historians were censured for passing beyond them.

A case in point is the Burdzhalov Affair of 1956–1957, when Eduard Nikolaevich Burdzhalov published two sensational articles on the role of the Bolsheviks in the February Revolution and, as assistant editor of the historical profession's major journal, *Voprosy istorii* (Problems of History), facilitated publication of materials that challenged orthodox interpretations within Soviet historiography. Dismissed from his editorial position and from his teaching post at Moscow University, Burdzhalov carried on his struggle and eventually published his exceptional study on the February Revolution of 1917.[2] Burdzhalov's book and several other revisionist accounts were published just before the Soviet invasion of Czechoslovakia in 1968. Afterward, S. P. Trapeznikov, head of the Science and Education Section of the CPSU Central Committee under Leonid Brezhnev, launched a crackdown in the cultural realm that sharply circumscribed what historical topics could be studied. Those independent sorts who sought to carry out their research in the spirit of the Twentieth Party Congress found it increasingly difficult to function professionally. Many of the nonconformists came under fire and suffered setbacks. The above scenario helps explain why historians responded warily to appeals for reform before 1987, but also why dissatisfaction with the status quo had existed long before Gorbachev came to power.[3]

The presence of reformist currents within the profession, then, helps explain why historians finally came around in 1987–1988. But there are several other reasons as well. First, Gorbachev's criticism of the Brezhnev regime's predilection for ignoring mistakes and failings in Soviet history, made at the January 1987 plenum of the Central Committee, amounted to a call for a candid reexamination of Soviet history. This same plenum retired Central Committee Secretary Mikhail Zimianin, who had upheld a conservative line in the key disciplines of history and philosophy, clearing the way for Gorbachev's protégé, Aleksandr Iakovlev,[4] who encouraged personnel changes and lamented prevailing conditions in academic institutions. Gorbachev himself set the tone for new appraisals of the past by informing the public of Stalin's role in the purges of the 1930s and of his responsibility for Soviet unpreparedness at the start of World War II. This signal by Gorbachev, as well as similar appeals by Iakovlev and others for honest writing about the past, altered the professional landscape: such authoritative statements made it possible to publish on topics that heretofore had been banned, and even drove opportunists to start giving lip service to restructuring.

A second consideration that helps us understand the transformation that occurred in the historical profession, though one that is difficult to assess with precision, is the constructive impact of Western influences and of Western historians, previously depicted as ideological opponents rather than as colleagues practicing the same craft. The public revelations about the Soviet past that now disoriented the Soviet people, all of which were known outside the country, exonerated Western writers. One of the significant changes of 1987 concerned the status of foreign historians. "Bourgeois historians" became "non-Marxist historians." It soon became fashionable to read them, cite them, and hobnob with them.

Finally, in February, following Gorbachev's address at the January 1987 plenum, the Soviet leader met with a group of prominent editors and instructed them that "there should not be any blank spots in either our history or our literature." Retirements and replacements swept across the media. The result was that historical themes and questions were now posed more audaciously than in the past in films, on television, in newspapers, and in Soviet literary journals.[5] The public affairs writers, or publicists (mainly writers, economists, and journalists), with amazing dispatch, and with greater autonomy from the party leadership than the historians displayed, raised critical historical issues. In so doing they deprived the historians of their audience, and also discredited them in the eyes of the public. In response, historians in general criticized the publicists, and also writers of historical fiction, for the ahistorical nature of much of the writing on historical themes taking place outside traditional forums. Certainly, though, some of them must realize they are in the publicists' and writers' debt for keeping the public's interest in history alive. In any event, the reform-minded historians now cited the challenge posed by the publicists as justification for their need to treat the past afresh.

And they have begun to do so. The purpose of this anthology is to illustrate the significant turnabouts that have transfigured Soviet historiography during the first phase of *glasnost'* and *perestroika*, which in terms of the historical profession, if not of society at large, lasted from the beginning of 1987 until the spring of 1988.

Why these chronological limits? Apart from a few interesting items appearing in newspapers and journals in late 1986,[6] there was no noteworthy reversal within the profession until early 1987. At the end of 1986, Iurii Afanas'ev, who has since emerged as one of the strongest voices of reform in the profession, was named rector of the Moscow State Institute of Historian-Archivists (after having been dismissed from his position at the Institute of World History). The speech he made upon his appointment, published in *Moskovskie novosti* (Moscow News) in early 1987, can be considered the "first direct challenge of the new trend against the academic elite of the conservative school."[7] Appropriately enough, this anthology opens with Afanas'ev's address.

The shock Afanas'ev sent throughout the Soviet intellectual community was magnified because the appearance of his text in *Moskovskie novosti* roughly coincided with the release of Tengiz Abuladze's acclaimed film *Pokaianie* (Repentance), a damning indictment of the Stalinist system. Further, in the first half of the year several novels and plays dealing with historical themes caused sensations.[8] That spring Afanas'ev's institute sponsored a series of public lectures on "The Social Memory of Mankind," presented by the reformers.[9] Not to go unchallenged, critics of the nonconformist views refuted the reformers, but in so doing they exposed their own intellectual poverty and prompted the revisionists to push even more for change.

By mid-1987 the impact of Gorbachev's appeal began to show even on the more orthodox elements of the profession. For the most part, personnel changes had not yet affected the leadership of research institutes, universities, and journals. But the appointment of Georgii Smirnov, a member of the Gorbachev camp, to head the Institute of Marxism-Leninism stirred the institute's heretofore monotonous publication, *Voprosy istorii KPSS* (Problems of History of the CPSU), to take on new life; it was transformed into a forum for perestroika.[10]

Conservative elements continued to oppose each incursion of the reformers, but were having a more difficult time reacting to their moral earnestness. Thus, a group of historians challenged Afanas'ev in the pages of *Moskovskie novosti*, suggesting he was too sympathetic to the unrehabilitated Leon Trotsky (see Part One of this anthology). In July, F. M. Vaganov, head of the Archival Administration, joined the fray, as did Politburo member Egor Ligachev.[11] This unresolved tension continued throughout the year, and remained unabated after Gorbachev's November address on the occasion of the seventieth anniversary of the October Revolution. Gorbachev's speech may well have been a compromise, or even a retreat, as some Western specialists have argued. It does evince elements of caution, and it distorts some burning issues by ignoring them or glossing over them. It must be stressed that both sides of the debate could find support for their positions in Gorbachev's presentation, which neither radically promoted historical revisionism nor curbed it. But the speech did once again place the country's history on center stage, and it deprecated the "administrative-command system of party–state management of the country."[12]

Haruki Wada and others have argued that the period from November 1987 through April 1988 was one in which the conservative Ligachev faction was on the offensive.[13] Boris El'tsin's dismissal as head of the Moscow party organization and the media's failure to publish his speech at the party plenum distressed intellectuals and pro-perestroika forces, especially since the old guard historians managed to elect their own to important posts within the Academy institutes and to membership in the Academy of Sciences itself at the very end of 1987. Moreover, Mikhail Shatrov's bold anti-Stalin play *Onward, Onward, Onward!* came under fire.

Despite such manifestations of strength from conservative groups, however, the reformers also scored some successes. Military historian D. Volkogonov published a crushing exposé of Stalin in December 1987.[14] In February 1988 Nikolai Bukharin was rehabilitated. How the party leadership treated him was a test case of vital significance; the rehabilitation opened the Pandora's box containing the remaining taboo topics. Throughout the country local civic groups collected funds to erect a permanent memorial to the victims of Stalinism. In early 1988 the prominent Academy of Sciences institutes of World History and History of the USSR replaced their old-line directors with ones more supportive of reform. More important, the premier historical journal, *Voprosy istorii*, appointed a new editor, A. A. Iskenderov, who immediately purged the editorial office of materials accepted by the previous editors and proceeded to alter the publication's contents and format. The second issue of the journal under Iskenderov's editorship carried a stunning roundtable discussion, perhaps the freest the profession had had to date.[15] Soon, dramatic shifts became noticeable in the important publication *Istoriia SSSR* (History of the USSR), which began to publish exciting material as well.

In retrospect, it is clear that by the spring of 1988 the reformers had won the upper hand. But this was not evident at the time. The publication in *Sovetskaia Rossiia* (Soviet Russia) of what *Pravda* was later to condemn as a manifesto of the

anti-perestroika forces—a letter by a Leningrad chemistry teacher, Nina Andreeva, entitled "I Cannot Betray My Principles"—aroused fears among the
nonconformists. *Pravda*'s condemnation of Andreeva's letter was slow in the
coming and this created a period of nervous anticipation among the intelligentsia.
When it did appear, the *Pravda* statement prompted a torrent of public support for
perestroika,[16] and gave the reformers a critical edge prior to the opening of the
Nineteenth Party Conference (June 1988), which declared to the Soviet people
that there could be no restructuring without glasnost' and greater legality.

This then, is the chronology of the documents found in this collection. In
selecting materials for the anthology, I have sought to demonstrate how the
historical profession first responded to the new climate. The articles show the
evolution of the historians' reaction, from Afanas'ev's first salvo in early 1987 to
the roundtable discussion published in *Voprosy istorii* in the spring of 1988. I
have made every effort to include items that treat the writing of history in the
Soviet Union in the broadest sense, and have avoided selections that focus on
specific historical questions. Later volumes in this series will document the
evolution of views on those volatile issues that have been discussed since mid-
1988: the New Economic Policy, the rehabilitation of Bukharin and of the Left
and Right Oppositions, collectivization and industrialization, Stalin and Stalinism, the 1930s, Soviet foreign policy, the international communist movement,
World War II, the Khrushchev and Brezhnev years, the nationalities question, and
the writing of history in the national republics.

This volume is divided into five parts. Part One includes items that demonstrate the tensions within the profession at the start of perestroika, and the first
calls for writing history in a fresh way. The documents in Part Two illustrate how
specific directives from the party leadership prompted serious discussions on the
state of the profession. Of the two selections in Part Three, the first is an early
response to the problem of rewriting the history of the Great October Socialist
Revolution, whereas the second article indicates that true change was coming to
an important corner of Soviet history that had been crudely whitewashed over the
years. Part Four presents some representative items belonging to the world of the
publicists, which vividly show how far they have gone in treating sensitive
issues. The final section consists of excerpts from the roundtable discussion held
in January 1988. It is an excellent barometer of the changes that had come to the
profession since the first stirring in 1987. Some of the participants are among
those who lost earlier battles, and many of them belong to Gorbachev's generation such as V. P. Danilov, I. Ia. Froianov, N. N. Bolkhovitinov, A. P. Novo-
sel'tsev, V. I. Startsev, P. V. Volobuev, and others.

Since the reformers surged ahead in mid-1988, stunning developments within
the profession have continued to amaze foreign observers. Historians are now
discussing such painful issues as the meaning of socialism and whether or not
Soviet society can be considered socialist. As history textbooks in use became

totally discredited, education authorities suspended the required history exam in Soviet secondary schools. On June 10, 1988, *Izvestiia* announced that "even the best and most inquisitive teachers . . . presented the history of our homeland in a monstrously distorted and unrecognizable form," while Afanas'ev quipped that there was not "a single page [of the official text] without a falsification."[17]

What the future will bring is anyone's guess, for the long road to freedom is fraught with dangers. Besides, we know very little about the Soviet historical profession. As this volume goes to press the Soviet people are glued to their television sets, intoxicated by the proceedings of the opening of the Congress of People's Deputies. The journal *Novyi mir*, edited by Sergei Zalygin, has begun to publish excerpts from Aleksandr Solzhenitsyn's *The Gulag Archipelago*. In the meanwhile, the deteriorating economic situation threatens to undermine the success of glasnost', as does nationalist ferment, dramatic developments in Eastern Europe, and obstruction from elements of the omnipresent and ineffectual Soviet bureaucracy, fighting to defend its vested interests. On the historical front, the proponents of reform continue to battle against opposition from within the profession and against those who fear that the truth will undermine the party's authority. To date they have not produced book-length manuscripts based on empirical data. They also face a hostile population that holds them accountable for lying about the past. Unfortunately for the pro-perestroika forces, the public does not discriminate between the historians of integrity and the majority of conformists belonging to the profession.

The tasks facing Soviet historians are indeed formidable, but the fundamental reversals that have been accepted so far carry moral authority and entail real changes in the way that history is approached, written, discussed, and taught. There are strong grounds for optimism, providing the political and economic situation remains stable. As Afanas'ev said, "Of course the path before us is a difficult one. If we wish to truly change our society, however, we must tread this path without hesitation. Only new historical studies, free of ideological dogma, can help us in reconsidering our past in all its enormous complexity, in liberating ourselves once and for all from Stalinism, and in reconstructing our social identity. Perestroika and historical knowledge need each other."[18]

I am pleased to recognize the support of Patricia A. Kolb, executive editor at M. E. Sharpe Inc., Publisher, for her invaluable advice in bringing this project to fruition. I received much appreciated research assistance and clerical help from Kathy S. Transchel, who served as my editorial assistant for *Soviet Studies in History* during the 1988–89 academic year, from which many of the items included in this anthology were selected. Several articles published in this collection originally appeared in the Summer 1988 issue of *Soviet Studies in History*, ably edited by William B. Husband. Paul H. Vivian shared with me his vast knowledge of the current ferment in Soviet historiography. Andrew Lewis commented on an earlier draft of the preface and carefully prepared the index. I am grateful to

Soviet colleagues who called my attention to the most stimulating literature pouring out of the Soviet Union today and encouraged me to complete this endeavor. Finally, I wish to thank Karen and Adam.

Notes

1. Apart from the sources cited in the notes that follow, several other attempts to assess the current ferment in Soviet historiography may be noted. See, for instance, Dev Murarka, "Recovering the Buried Stalin Years," *The Nation* (October 24, 1987), pp. 443, 447–51, and "A New Revolution in Consciousness," *ibid.*, (October, 31, 1987), pp. 486–90; Ben Eklof, "Glasnost' and the Historians," *Radical Historians' Newsletter*, no. 56 (November 1988), pp. 1, 7–8; Thomas Sherlock, "Politics and History under Gorbachev," *Problems of Communism*, vol. 37 , nos. 3–4 (May–August 1988), pp. 16–42; part two of Stephen Wheatcroft's article cited in note 9, "Steadying the Energy of History and Probing the Limits of *Glasnost'*: Moscow, July to December 1987," *Australian Slavonic and East European Studies*, vol. 1, no. 2 (1987), pp. 57–114; and Lewis H. Siegelbaum, "Historical Revisionism in the USSR," *Radical History Review*, no. 44 (1989), pp. 32–61.
2. For more on the Burdzhalov Affair, see the introduction to my translation of Burdzhalov's book, *Russia's Second Revolution: The February 1917 Uprising in Petrograd* (Bloomington, 1987), pp. ix–xxii.
3. See Jerry Hough, "Gorbachev's Consolidating Power," *Problems of Communism*, vol. 36, no. 4 (May–June 1985), p. 34.
4. For a discussion of an important address made by Iakovlev on April 17, 1987, see R. W. Davies, "Soviet History in the Gorbachev Revolution: The First Phase," *The Socialist Register* (1988), pp. 40–41.
5. The pro-reform newspapers include *Moskovskie novosti*, *Sovetskaia kul'tura*, *Literaturnaia gazeta*; the most reform-minded journals are *Novyi mir*, *Druzhba narodov*, *Ogonek*, *Iunost'*, *Neva*, and even such unlikely ones as *Argumenty i fakty* and *Nauka i zhizn'*.
6. I have in mind here an article by Iurii Afanas'ev in *Kommunist*, vol. 14 (1985), pp. 105–16.
7. Haruki Wada, "Perestroika and the Rethinking of History in the Soviet Union, 1986–88," in *Facing Up to the Past: Soviet Historiography under Perestroika*, ed. Takayuki Ito (Sapporo, 1989), p. 39.
8. See, for example, Aleksandr Bek's *Novoe naznachenie*, Boris Mozhaev's *Muzhiki i baby*, Vladimir Dudintsev's *Belye odezhdy*, Anatolii Rybakov's *Deti Arbata*, and Mikhail Shatrov's play, *Brestskii mir*.
9. See Stephen Wheatcroft, "Unleashing the Energy of History, Mentioning the Unmentionable and Reconstructing Soviet Historical Awareness: Moscow, 1987," *Australian Slavonic and East European Studies*, vol. 1, no. 1 (1987), pp. 107–108.
10. For the significance of this development, see my introduction to the vol. 27, no. 3 (1988–89) issue of *Soviet Studies in History*, pp. 3–5.
11. See F. M. Vaganov and A. N. Ponomarev, "Ne idealizirovat', no ne dramatizirovat' . . . ," *Sovetskaia kul'tura*, July 4, 1987, p. 6, and *Sovetskaia kul'tura*, July 7, 1987, p. 2. For a discussion of these attacks, see Wada, "Perestroika and the Rethinking of History," pp. 43–46.
12. The speech was not as disappointing as some Kremlin watchers pronounced. For a brief but pertinent discussion of Gorbachev's speech see Mark von Hagen, "History and Politics under Gorbachev: Professional Autonomy and Democratization," *The Harriman Institute Forum*, vol. 1, no. 1 (November 1988), pp. 2–3. Also informative is

R. W. Davies, "Changing Official Views of Soviet History," *Detente*, no. 11 (1988), pp. 12–13. For a misreading of the speech see Jiri Hochman, "The Soviet Historical Debate," *Orbis* (Summer 1988), pp. 369–83.

13. Wada, op. cit., pp. 48–58. See also Ben Eklof, *Soviet Briefing: Gorbachev and the Reform Period* (Boulder, 1989), pp. 29, 42.

14. See *Literaturnaia gazeta*, December 9, 1987, p. 13.

15. A discussion of the roundtable can be found in Hans-Joachim Torke, "The History of Pre-Revolutionary Russia in the Current Debate of Soviet Historians," in *Facing Up to the Past: Soviet Historiography under Perestroika*, ed. Takayuki Ito (Sapporo, 1989), pp. 97–109.

16. The Nina Andreeva letter was published in *Sovetskaia Rossiia*, March 13, 1988, p. 3. The denunciation in *Pravda* is found in "Printsipy perestroiki: Revoliutsionnost' myshleniia i deistvii," April 5, 1988, p. 2. Although there was much speculation over whether or not Nina Andreeva was a real person, recent newspaper articles featuring her introduce her to skeptical readers and seek to explain what prompted her to write her manifesto. See, for example, *Sovetskaia molodezh'*, April 4, 1989, p. 3.

17. The *Izvestiia* article and Afanas'ev's statement are cited in William B. Husband, "Rewriting Soviet History Texts: The First Phase," in *Facing Up to the Past*, p. 85.

18. Iu. Afanas'ev, "Perestroika i istoricheskoe znanie," *Literaturnaia Rossiia*, June 17, 1988, p. 9.

Soviet
Historians
and
Perestroika

Part One

GIVING CLIO A FACE-LIFT

The Soviet historical profession did not don the mantle of perestroika and glasnost' until early 1987. At that time the burning issue was still whether or not the discipline would truly reject the old way of doing things or merely give lip service to M. S. Gorbachev's plans for restructuring Soviet life and society. In part, the agenda was set by a lively, much talked about exchange in the pages of the newspaper, *Moscow News*, which in 1986 emerged as a leading champion of reform. Debate was sparked by publication in the paper of an article by Iu. N. Afanas'ev, who had recently become director of the Moscow State Institute of Historian-Archivists. The appearance of Afanas'ev's letter caused a special stir because it coincided with the January 1987 Plenum of the CPSU Central Committee, at which Mikhail Sergeevich Gorbachev called upon historians to fill in the "blank spots" in history and to reassess Soviet history, mistakes and all.

A specialist on French history, Afanas'ev, in his own words, has been studying "bourgeois historiography" for twenty years. From this vantage point he assails the unhealthy state of the Soviet historical profession. His trenchant exposure of the propagandistic nature of Soviet historical writing complements his appeal for sweeping change "so as to learn to teach new generations of Soviet people to think and act in a new way." Announcing that historians, too, were awakening from their slumber, Afanas'ev chides the status quo historians by suggesting that the "propaganda of success" that was called history in the Soviet Union happens to be bad Marxism.

Afanas'ev was not to go unchallenged. The rebuttal by four historians, all of whom teach party history at institutes of higher education in Moscow, carries added weight because it had the blessing of F. M. Vaganov, head of the Central Archival Administration, who was soon to come under fire by Soviet historians for his unwillingness to improve the unsatisfactory state of affairs in regard to archival access. Vividly revealing the head-on clash between the forces of reform and the defenders of the existing state of affairs, the rebuttal takes umbrage at Afanas'ev's suggestion that Soviet historical science had become "stagnant" and was "lagging" behind the present-day world level. The authors also seek to cast Afanas'ev in the role of a bad Marxist. Undoubtedly bolstered by Gorbachev's speech at the January 1987 Plenum of the Central Committee, Afanas'ev took on his opponents with aplomb, exposing their failure to understand the very essence of perestroika. With the benefit of hindsight it appears that Afanas'ev came out the winner in this debate, for today defenders of the former status quo would be far less likely to identify themselves publicly.

Soviet historians had good reason to be critical of the state of the profession long before Gorbachev had come to power. S. L. Tikhvinskii's report to the General Assembly of the Academy of Sciences Division of History in October 1986 offers some insights into the dissatisfaction that was extant prior to the onslaught of glasnost'. A member of the Presidium of the Academy of Sciences and deputy chair of the Section of Social Sciences, Tikhvinskii, in his address, presents one of the first responses, appearing in the pages of Soviet historical journals, to the challenges posed by the new leadership. Tikhvinskii's report attempts to bridge the abyss between the proponents of reform and the status quo. Presenting his critique of the profession in the language of the Twenty-seventh Party Congress, citing both Gorbachev and the more conservative E. K. Liga-chev, Tikhvinskii discusses problems of the profession such as unattractive sala-ries, unsatisfactory work conditions, slow-paced promotion from the lower ranks, etc. Above all, he acknowledges the need to create a healthy moral and psychological climate, and attacks breaches of professionalism. Finally, he re-proaches the antihistorical character of some of the publicists' writing appearing in Soviet journals and newspapers. In so doing, he tacitly admits that Soviet historians had been dilatory in responding to the new climate.

Party historian V. A. Kozlov in his essay "The Historian and Perestroika" also addresses the fact that Soviet readers turn to belles lettres and public affairs writing, instead of to history, for knowledge of the past and present. The rich and varied writings of publicists in the Soviet Union by 1987 had done a great deal to pose critical moral questions that needed to be answered honestly before true reform could succeed. Kozlov is critical of this writing because even though it often serves as an antidote to twisted official histories, it does not always deepen and promote historical consciousness. Calling for the writing of history in a new way, cleansed of its "distortions, omissions, and unoriginal commentaries," Kozlov appeals to the profession to meet the public's need for honest history as soon as possible. It must be emphasized that this is a party historian writing in a party journal, *Voprosy istorii KPSS* (Problems of History of the CPSU). Pub-lished in mid-1987, Kozlov's sophisticated, fresh essay demonstrates that real shifts had come to the profession.

The Energy of Historical Knowledge

Iu. AFANAS'EV

Professor Iurii Afanas'ev, D.Sc. (History), has recently become rector of the Moscow State Institute of Historian-Archivists. The following excerpts from his speech at the Academic Council give an idea, we believe, of the problems facing historians today—both researchers and teachers.

Intellect and talent needed

What is the best way of coming to understand the present with the help of the past, and the past with the help of the present? Life is taking such a turn that it is vitally important for us, professors and lecturers, to ponder these questions again so as to learn to teach new generations of Soviet people to think and act in a new way.

This is an exceptionally dramatic task, especially considering that stagnation phenomena have been stockpiled of late in the higher school, as it was pointed out at a recent All-Union Conference of Heads of Social Science Departments.

I am a historian, which is why I shall try to demonstrate this, using material from the area of knowledge that is closest to me. I shall leave aside the enumeration of achievements. Of course, we have had and still have brilliant humanitarians, there are successfully functioning sectors and chairs, very good books are sometimes published, and so on. But, nevertheless, I would primarily use the word stagnant to characterize the state of domestic historical science which in many respects is lagging behind the present-day world level. I, as someone who has devoted twenty years now to studying non-Marxist historiography, cannot afford not to make comparative evaluations, though it's a risky undertaking, as you know.

There exists the unquestionably asserted view that our social science cannot in any respect be lagging behind the non-Marxist, bourgeois one. And inasmuch as in our country any, say, historian already by the right of his having been born in the Soviet land, in the higher education cradle is recognized as "Marxist" and nothing else, it appears thereby that any book we publish is not only methodolog-

Moscow News, 1987, no. 2 (January 18–25), pp. 8–9. English text © 1987 by "Moscow News." The translation has been edited for clarity. Reprinted with permission.

ically but also in its main contents higher than the books published "by them." Machine tools and footwear not necessarily, but humanitarian research studies already at the stage of their conception acquire a kind of Marxist-Leninist quality seal. Alas! In real life everything is much more complicated. After all, to learn by rote, like a verse, something about "law-governed change of socioeconomic formations," and so on and so forth, and even the thesis that "Marxism is not a dogma but a guide to action," does not yet mean to be a Marxist. This, as we know, calls for hard work, intellectual courage and subtlety, scientific talent, and fresh ideas and approaches that have not yet been tested by anyone (except logic and facts). In short, there is a need for enormous efforts to be up to the lofty name of a Marxist historian of the late twentieth century.

Many important sections in the field of historical science have in effect been fading away, whole epochs have not been covered by research studies, and sometimes we have one or two specialists for whole centuries and countries. The social mission and the vast possibilities for building up historical knowledge are realized on a very small scale in our country.

The most interesting and captivating topics

It has to be admitted that in our country, the land of the October Revolution, many problems bearing on the historical experience of winning power by the Russian proletariat, defense of the Revolution, and socialist construction are yet to be studied. I would like to dwell on this question in greater detail in these first days of the incipient jubilee year, bearing in mind Lenin's behests on this score: attention must be focused on questions that are yet to be solved. The scientific studies of the history of the October Revolution, the teaching of these problems, and the new way of posing them are called upon to refresh the atmosphere at the higher school. It is on these problems that we should set up a "zone of high intellectual tension" first and foremost.

In the past one and a half or two decades the impulse given by the party decisions of 1956–1961 began to run low and damp down, and a decline set in in studying the history of the October Revolution.

This was due to many reasons. I shall point out two of them: methodological and social.

It will be recalled that in the mid-1960s we started extensive studies and discussion of the problems involved in the methodology of history: interesting books were published, pointed articles appeared on these problems, and a discussion was resumed on the so-called Asiatic mode of production. Historians and philosophers turned to the richest arsenal of Marx, Engels, and Lenin, whose historical-methodological concept became a subject of serious study. It stands to reason that not everything in the publications of that time was impeccable, mistakes were also made, there were also cases when some statements by the participants in the discussion were declared fallacious or even "non-Marxist" through misunderstanding (or, rather, simply through lack of knowledge). In those conditions the elaboration of the methodological problems of history had to be continued with even greater intensity; instead, however, it was simply discontinued by forcible intervention.

Once again the servile cowardice of scholarly bureaucrats made itself felt. The point is that in the course of the discussions historians began to show that world history was much more complicated, diversified, and variegated than it was customarily presented in our standard textbooks on history and philosophy, and even in some "learned" works written following the well-known hyperschematic "five-member" scheme of the historical process rooted in Stalin's work *On Dialectical and Historical Materialism*. The bureaucrats began to worry—after all, they could not allow the scheme to be broken. And the search for the truth was discontinued.

The methodological quests that unfolded in the latter half of the 1960s and the early 1970s also touched on the historiography of the October Revolution. Historians began, for example, to pay more attention to the objective assessment given by Lenin to Russia's development up to the moment of the Socialist Revolution. There is no need to speak in detail about the special importance—methodological and practical—of this problem. After all, it was very difficult to build socialism in Russia, the most backward among the major capitalist countries. Until the early 1970s historians still managed to stick to this position. However, the attempt that was made to approach the posing, clarification, and then investigation of these questions, notably on the basis of the problem of multiplicity of economic forms, was artificially cut short here as well. From that moment on it was believed that the character of socioeconomic development prior to the October Revolution belonged to the questions that were "solved by science," so that any disputes on that score were out of place. As a result, our historiography still has no considerable work enlarging upon Lenin's thesis that "while the development of world history as a whole follows general laws, it is by no means precluded, but on the contrary, presumed, that certain periods of development may display peculiarities in either the form or the sequence of this development."

Placed on the agenda therefore is the problem of the peculiarities in Russia's capitalist evolution in comparison with the sequence in which the capitalist formation was shaped in countries of the first echelon of bourgeois development. The task facing researchers, as we see, has been considerably compounded. But the game is worth the candle. We have long been speaking about a party of the new type that first appeared in our country, about the new type of bourgeois-democratic revolution, and about the peculiarity of the processes in contemporary developing countries. Having elaborated the problem of capitalist evolution in Russia, we could get a deeper insight into the problem of the general and the particular in world history, and on this basis also draw more realistic practical conclusions.

The second reason for the stagnation should be seen in the effects of the old, compressed stratifications which weighed heavily on researchers' thought since the 1930s.

This was facilitated by the circumstance that we felt the reassuring effect of broader notions not only about the state of our science, but also about the current phase of society's development—in which, as it followed from "theoretical" generalizations, no room was left for fundamental contradictions, ideological antagonisms, and serious contrasts. This is what actually happened on the surface, but going on underneath were processes that later gave grounds for a bitter, alarming conclusion: we have poor knowledge of the society we live in.

Our biggest theoretical (and practical) mistake perhaps was that we at times forgot about the revolutionary (and hence inevitably extremely difficult, danger-filled, and, if you like, excruciating, sometimes tragic) character of the path we had dared to follow. There arose the unacknowledged conviction that once we had gotten on the rails, and received the initial world-historical impulse, in the future our system would roll smoothly from achievement to achievement, from one victorious stage to another, from good to better. As if this does not call for the greatest strain of efforts, flexibility, and self-denial; as if the "demonic force of ignorance," inertia, and self-interest had already disappeared among particular individuals and groups of the population.

After the April 1985 plenum of the CPSU Central Committee we had to rethink the notion of "existing" or "real" socialism—in the form it is now being used by our philosophers and propagandists. This amounted to a truly intellectual and essentially revolutionary endeavor. And this, in its turn, called for reviving our hopes, our labor efficiency, and our ability to be true to ideals. The question is, of course, not about verbal and parade-type "ideals," not about toadyism or the designation of exact deadlines for universal happiness, but about the ideals of sober-minded people who are fully aware of their own imperfections, of all the immense difficulties of the path which we reembark upon, and the sources and wellsprings of inertia.

It may seem that this recent period is far removed from the traditional concerns of the servants of Clio. But this is not so! The stereotyped thinking about present-day conditions in our society, molded to the tune of exuberant reports and bureaucratic optimism, have brought and, alas, still continue to bring an inverse pressure to bear on our historical studies. The pulse of the life of the past was hardly felt in them; from an instrument of knowledge, history began to turn into a servant of the lopsided "propaganda of success," into apology for whatever had already been achieved. In this condition it certainly cannot assist in the great cause of our society's restructuring.

It is easy to see this, for instance, upon opening any of the latest standard textbooks on the history of the CPSU. These textbooks are a peculiar "mirror" of our science on the party's history.

They have been written by large bodies of authors and not everything in them is of equal value. But on the whole these outwardly solid, stately publications are written lifelessly, dryly, and monotonously. Mikhail Gorbachev's words, which I believe have a direct bearing on these textbooks as well, sounded as a bitter but fully justified reproach to all of us. "A paradoxical picture has taken shape. The most interesting and thrilling topics in scientific learning today—the individual and society, the laws governing human development, the contradictions, the struggle of classes, the building of a new world, the aspiration of humanity to the ideal, the spiritual quests and disillusionments, the gaining of the truth, and the heroism of labor creativity—are all quite often made to be something boring, official, and formal."

The textbooks present a one-sided, crippled picture of many events in the actual history of the CPSU, while they pass over many other things simply in silence. They have still not overcome, and sometimes directly reproduce, Stalin's scheme of the victory of the October Revolution and socialist construction in the USSR—a scheme that is far from the truth.

Educate by the truth

Take at least the question of Lenin's last letters and articles as they are presented in some of our textbooks.

A sufficient number of pages are devoted to the summary of the last letters and articles. But only one or two actually deal with Lenin's plan. The rest are stuffed with cut-and-dried banalities about the epoch of humankind's transition from capitalism to socialism, the beginning of a "world revolution," the outlook for a transition to socialism by bypassing capitalism, about the main contradiction of the epoch, and so on and so forth—that is, with things Lenin said nothing about (with few exceptions) in his "testament." The integrity and structure of Lenin's plan are not shown. Even less fortunate are the characterizations which Lenin, in his last letters, gave of the leading members of the Central Committee. They are divorced from the presentation of his plan and shifted into the section describing the Twelfth Congress of the CPSU. They are quoted one-sidedly, with all the positive characteristics [Lenin] attributed to would-be opposition members deleted and only the negative ones remaining.

Can all of this awaken a young person's keenness of mind and charge him with that energy of historical knowledge which is so necessary today for our society's comprehensive renewal? Of course not. The poor student who comes under the barrage of Stalin's definitions—"variety of Menshevism," "Menshevik deviation," "anti-revolutionary group," "agents of the kulak class," and so on—has to expend his intellectual capabilities mainly on learning labels by rote. On the other hand, he is not in a position to get down to the essence of theoretical disputes and concepts in building socialism or to compare the road of socialism in the USSR with that of building socialism in other countries. Here, truly, is where we have not the tree of life but a telephone pole! Yet, given high-quality, honest, and profound presentation of the material, this history can and must evoke a feeling of the deepest interest.

*   *   *

The spring that began in our society in April 1985 is felt in every sphere of life. Historians, too, are awakening from their slumbers—regrettably, too slowly so far. But, according to the laws of nature, a spring is an inexorable phenomenon; the spring of socialist creativity is not something transient.

Apropos of Iu. Afanas'ev's Article

At the beginning of this year, Moscow News *carried excerpts from the speech which Professor Iurii Afanas'ev, rector of the Moscow State Institute of Historian-Archivists, made at the Academic Council. Almost immediately, MN editors received a telephone call from Professor F. Vaganov, head of the USSR Chief Archives, who said that he considered the publication of these excerpts to be a mistake. Professor Vaganov was invited to express his own views in our weekly. Three months later, however, Professor A. Nosov came to the MN office, bringing with him a letter signed by four Soviet historians. The letter, he said, had been agreed upon with Professor Vaganov. Frankly, we don't quite understand why the four scholars took such a cumbersome path. Surely, the editors would have in any case treated their letter in all seriousness, even if there were no reference to the head of the USSR Chief Archives. Below we publish the letter in full, with nothing changed in it. Since many of the questions raised in the letter are addressed to Professor Iurii Afanas'ev, we deemed it necessary to acquaint him with the letter so that he would have an opportunity to reply.*

The appearance of Professor Iu. Afanas'ev's material, "Energy of Historical Knowledge," in *Moscow News* (no. 2, January 11, 1987) cannot but be welcomed by non-Marxist historiographers, cannot but puzzle and bewilder the young students of history, and arouse the indignation of the older generation of Soviet scholars engaged in the study of the history of the CPSU and the USSR. What's it all about? Why has this unscientific, sensational, and opinionated material caused such a small ruckus? If one looks into its content and intent this will become clear.

Essentially, Iu. Afanas'ev is calling upon historians to revise the historical road covered by the Soviet people over the past seventy years, the road traced by the historiography of the USSR and the CPSU. It appears, according to Iu. Afanas'ev, that Soviet historical science is "stagnant" and in many respects "lagging behind the present-day world level" (p. 8).

What "world level" does he mean, and what branches of science? (Perhaps some auxiliary branches of historical studies?) Hasn't the author realized as yet the contrast between Marxist and bourgeois methodology in historical science? And doesn't he know about the Leninist principle of partisanship in science? Restructuring does not mean destruction; it means construction, an ascent to new

Moscow News, 1987, no. 19 (May 17–24), p. 11. English text © 1987 by "Moscow News." The translation has been edited for clarity. Reprinted with permission.

heights in historical science. In this ascent we draw upon the best in the historiography of the CPSU and the USSR. And there is much to draw upon, indeed. Iu. Afanas'ev believes that during the past fifteen to twenty years, the historians' impulse began to "run low and damp down" in studying the history of the October Revolution. But how, then, can one explain the appearance, precisely in that period, of some very outstanding scientific works, among them two books of the third volume of the multivolume edition of the history of the CPSU, three volumes of *The Great October Revolution* by Academician I. Mints, the monographs by V. Anikeev, A. Sovokin, I. Petrov, and S. Murashov (the work by the latter has been translated into Spanish), and hundreds of other books and articles. These works, published on the centenary of Lenin's birth and on the fiftieth, sixtieth, and seventieth anniversaries of the Great October Revolution, expound the Leninist (and not Stalinist) concept of the October Revolution and the Bolshevik party's Leninist strategy and tactics in the revolution, and demonstrate the international significance of Leninism and of the October Revolution's experience. During that same period, many scientific conferences and discussions were held, including criticism of the "new trend" in historical science led by P. Volobuev.

The books present thousands of heroes of the October Revolution. At the same time they, and some other works, criticize the stand taken during the revolution by Trotsky (to "wait" for the Congress of Soviets, Lenin argued, would be "*utter idiocy, or sheer treachery*"), and by Kamenev and Zinov'ev, who informed the enemy about the Central Committee's decision on an armed uprising. Their anti-Leninist stand during the October Revolution was leading straight to the formation of a Trotsky–Zinovi'ev bloc aimed at frustrating Lenin's plan of socialist construction. In this connection we deem it necessary to draw attention to Iu. Afanas'ev's strange and fallacious stance in appraising the party's Leninist general course of building socialism.

He regrets that the textbooks on the history of the CPSU "have still not overcome, and sometimes directly reproduce, Stalin's scheme of the victory of the October Revolution and socialist construction in the USSR—a scheme that is far from the truth" (p. 9).

The author advanced a postulate, providing no proof or arguments, the reason being that he has none. The CPSU Program adopted by the Twenty-seventh Party Congress says that following the winning of political power by the working class, the victories on the Civil War fronts, and the rout of foreign military interventionists, the party set about implementing Lenin's plan of socialist construction. "Relying on the enthusiasm of the masses, repulsing the attacks by right-wing and leftist opportunists, and strengthening its ideological, political, and organizational unity," the program says, "the party undeviatingly pursued the Leninist general line aimed at building socialism." It was this Leninist plan of socialist construction and its implementation, and not some nonexistent Stalinist "scheme" of the revolution, that Soviet historians wrote about in their works.

As is known, Trotsky was the only person in the party who laid claims to his own scheme of the revolution. But it is also commonly known that our party rejected, resolutely and irrevocably, these claims aimed at substituting Trotskyism for Leninism.

Iu. Afanas'ev regrets that the textbooks on the history of the CPSU treat Lenin's "Letters to the Congress" "one-sidedly," as he alleges. "All positive characteristics addressed to would-be opposition members have been deleted," he says. But everyone knows, just as Iu. Afanas'ev himself does, that in studying the history of the party our students make use, not only of the textbooks, but mainly of Lenin's works, among them "Letters to the Congress."

Iu. Afanas'ev mentions only Lenin's letters "To the Congress," passing over in silence the long and fierce struggle waged by Lenin and the party, before and after the October Revolution, against Trotsky and the Trotskyites on the questions of the character, the motive forces, and perspectives of the revolution in Russia, especially the victory of socialism in our country. This struggle began way back in 1903, at the Second Congress of the Russian Social Democratic Labor party. It flared up again in 1905 when Trotsky put forward his adventurous permanent revolution "theory," and it continued through the period marked by the onslaught of reaction, in the years of the revolutionary upsurge against the Trotskyite August bloc, as well as in 1915–1916 when Lenin worked out the theory on the possibility of socialism being victorious first in a few countries and even in a single capitalist country, and, finally, on the eve of the armed uprising.

After the victory of the October Socialist Revolution, our party, led by Lenin, had to hold three national discussions. The first one was held in 1918 on the question of the Brest Peace, the second in 1920–1921 on the role of trade unions in building socialism, and the third in 1923–1924 on inner-party issues.

Underlying all these discussions was the question of the possibility of building socialism in our country. Trotsky and the Trotskyites did not believe that it was possible to build socialism in a single country. The CPSU and the international communist movement censured and rejected Trotskyism.

Foreign readers (and *Moscow News* goes to 140 countries) should know about this history of the struggle against Trotskyism. What's more, they should also know that after the victory of fascism in Germany in 1933, Trotsky stepped up the struggle against the Communist Party of the Soviet Union (Bolsheviks) and the Communist International and against the building of socialism, publicly declaring that the approaching war would inevitably spell the defeat of the USSR and collapse of the Soviet system. Technically, economically, and militarily, he said, imperialism was incomparably stronger, adding that if it was not paralyzed by a revolution in the West, it would sweep away the social system born of the October Revolution. Trotsky's stance called for a forcible overthrow of the Soviet government and for taking advantage of the Soviet Union's "inevitable" defeat in the impending war against fascism to further his own ends as "leader." Such was the finale of Trotsky's struggle against Leninism, the CPSU(b) and the Soviet system. Iu. Afanas'ev, who has been studying non-Marxist historiography for twenty years now, could have, without running any "risk" and as befits a scholar, made "comparable evaluations" of the stand taken by Lenin and our party and, on the other hand, by Trotsky and the Mensheviks, on the issues of the revolution and of the construction of socialism. It is not a matter of "labels" (such assessments of the opportunists' activities were made at the Thirteenth Party Conference, the Thirteenth, Fourteenth, and Fifteenth Party congresses, the Fifteenth Party Conference, and the seventh enlarged Plenary Meeting of the Executive Committee of the Communist International); it is rather a question of the essential positions held by the anti-Leninist trends and groups and of the struggle waged against their anti-popular and anti-revolutionary line. Lenin stressed on more than one occasion that the victory of the Great October Socialist Revolution would have been impossible without routing Menshevism. The Trotskyite line was leading to a restoration of capitalism in the USSR. E. H. Carr, an English historian, who has for many years been studying the history of the October Revolution, admits that Western-type bourgeois democracy and capitalism, which the Mensheviks craved, were unsuitable for Russia, so Lenin's policy was the only conceivable one under Russia's specific conditions.

Lenin's works, the CPSU documents, the works by M. Gorbachev and by other party and state leaders, as well as Soviet historians' monographs are all being studied by our students. Today, with the reconstruction under way, they are showing an ever greater interest in the Twenty-seventh CPSU Congress and in the heroic history of the CPSU and the Soviet people who have covered a road comparable to a century.

The energy of historical knowledge should be directed toward a revolutionary restructuring of all aspects of Soviet society's life and history, and toward inculcating among the younger people a sense of historical responsibility for and pride in their homeland, in its heroic history and the present day.

Regrettably, Iu. Afanas'ev's article does not serve these aims and can only disorient foreign readers, especially those who know the history of the CPSU and the USSR.

Doctors of Science (History), Professors:

P. Soboleva, head of the CPSU History Chair, the natural
   sciences faculties, Moscow State University
A. Nosov, head of the CPSU History Chair, Moscow Forest
   Engineering Institute
L. Shirikov, professor, the CPSU History Chair, the Academy
   of Social Sciences under the CPSU Central Committee
S. Murashov, head of the CPSU History Chair, Moscow
   Semashko Medical-Stomatological Institute

Talking about the Past, We Must Keep the Future of Socialism in Mind

Iu. AFANAS'EV

Indeed, it is high time we made the issue absolutely clear by outlining the magnitude of responsibility demanded today from every one of us in the matters of conscience, civic position, and social action.

Two years ago, the April Plenum of the CPSU Central Committee for the first time delineated a historic opening. It was, to a great extent, different from the 1956 opening in that it was more difficult and more promising. It would be absurd to believe that, should we lose the chance now, it would remain open till some other time, as a reserve. Therefore, we will not lose it. We can't afford to. As the millennium draws to a close, world history is pushing ahead and is in no mood to patiently wait another fifteen or twenty years for us to catch up. Our people's revolutionary energy and hope cannot be kept in a freezer. Mikhail Gorbachev is right a thousand times when he insistently and repeatedly hammers this or some such idea home.

Will my opponents be kind enough to accept this idea as the measure of earnestness in our argument?

It is evident that the future of Soviet and world socialism depends, in a great measure, on the timely comprehension of the past and the frankness of our of our self-awareness today. Therefore, I must frankly say that for me the most important point in the group letter by party historians is the definitive statement of their nonacceptance of the very nature of perestroika.

To my mind, the central point in the letter is this: "Restructuring does not mean destruction; it means construction, an ascent to new heights of historical science." This is stated with the well-familiar "monumentality." Yet the formula is grammatical and political nonsense. The prefix "re" in words like "remake, rebuild" does not simply mean building or extending. In Russian, the prefix implies both destruction and construction. The two processes are as indivisible as the two sides of a coin. Perestroika certainly implies construction, but not on a vacant site. It means the restructuring of already occupied space, thick with well-

Moscow News, 1987, no. 19 (May 17–24). English text © 1987 by "Moscow News." The translation has been edited for clarity. Reprinted with permission.

established economic, political, and ideological structures and formations, of which the most valuable, worthwhile, and promising elements ought to be used as the foundation *sine qua non*, while others ought to be discarded as dead weight slowing down the development of socialism's potential. I wonder if my opponents can tell me how the new methods of economic management can be established without destroying the old ones. How can democracy prevail without destroying bureaucracy? How can new thinking be mastered without overcoming the old dogmatic thinking? And more specifically, how can the new historic vision of Soviet society be attained without doing away with the primitive clichés, deliberate silences, and even distortions?

Nevertheless, your formula for restructuring is a position rather than an absurdity. Let's take a closer look at it.

Let's begin with the situation existing in party historiography. It is not according to Afanas'ev that it is "stagnant," as the signatories of the letter allege. I am just one of those scholars who share the opinions voiced at the All-Union Conference of Social Scientists. During the conference, many unflattering comments were made, specifically, about textbooks that can be read only "at gunpoint." At the recent congress of the Young Communist League, Mikhail Gorbachev once again stressed the need for a new, honest, and bold book on the history of our native land and our party, a book that would not pass over dramatic moments or contain blank spots. Don't you think this sounds relevant?

Presuming that the historical sciences have seen no stagnation in the past decades, could you please indicate at least one book published before 1985 which dealt not with "developed socialism's successes," but with, say, the mechanisms of developmental retardation? I would much rather do without this rhetorical question, if the letter of the four had not summed up the situation in "the historiography of the CPSU and the USSR" with such flagrant complacency.

Well, their sincerity is much better than feigned zeal for perestroika. At any rate, it helps evaluate the difficulty of restructuring the psychological stereotypes in the minds of college and university teachers. It is very sad to have to note, in our time, the social passivity and unthinking conformism on the part of many people, living by the principle, "We have been taught so." However, the motto "We have taught so, and we will continue teaching so" is much much worse.

Party history is no rigid code, and the teachers of history must be able to teach themselves better.

My opponents believe that there was no such thing as Stalin's scheme for the victory of the October Revolution and the construction of socialism. What else then underlies the *Short Course* whose significance has not yet been fully exposed in our literature? Let us leave its detailed analysis to historiographic treatises and discussions (but certainly not to the pogroms the four historians have mentioned under the name of "discussions" in connection with the criticism of the "new trend"). I would only like to point out the distinctive features of that scheme, which for all practical purposes reduced party history to the inner- and interparty struggle inside the workers' and democratic movement, treating the clash of opinions, the search for the correct revolutionary approaches, and the differences inside the party leadership as the results of somebody's ill intent and scheming. In retrospect, the groups that came together in the process were labeled "anti-party groupings" motivated by counterrevolutionary purposes. Differences in political views and convictions were dished out as fantastic criminal intentions. It was this version of party history, first formulated in the *Short Course*, that was being subsequently reproduced in publications on the subject.

Lenin's position was fundamentally different. Lenin thought in broad categories. For him, the objective analysis of the masses' position with respect to the revolution and the correlation of classes always came first. He demanded that historical personages be evaluated according to their actual behavior at various stages of the revolutionary struggle, that political wavering not be "blamed on them personally," and that the social roots of dissent be revealed. Lenin knew how to take the political evolution of party workers into consideration, and never allowed their subsequent behavior to overshadow their past, nor relied on his past attitudes in estimating their actions under new and forever changing conditions.

Why shouldn't we note the following generalization by Lenin: "On the eve of the October Revolution in Russia, and immediately after it, a number of very good Communists in Russia committed an error, one which our people are now loath to recall. Why are they loath to recall it? Because, unless there is particular reason for it, it is wrong to recall mistakes which have been completely set right."

The signatories of the letter pointed out that Afanas'ev allegedly referred exclusively to Lenin's "Letters to the Congress" while "passing over in silence the long and fierce struggle waged by Lenin and the party, before and after the October Revolution, against Trotsky and the Trotskyites. . . ." It is not altogether clear what is being insinuated here. Is it an attempt to charge the author with reticence on a controversial issue? Or a hint that he has some ill intent? The time is long overdue that we all realize that the argument of "passing things over in silence" and the like have long lost their value. Nor do they bear on the present scholarly dispute, because there is not a word on either Trotsky or Trotskyism in my statement.

Nobody, myself included, pretends to know the absolute truth. Along with the new textbook on party history now under preparation, other publications of a purely research nature ought to appear, discussions ought to be encouraged. Archive materials and other sources which used to be suppressed or disregarded ought to be introduced into broad use. In many cases, new interpretations and evaluations of certain events, phenomena, and personalities from national history are due to appear. I personally have got more questions than answers. All of us are looking forward to getting these answers through the in-depth analysis of problems pertaining to party history.

What we need is not the "revision of the Soviet people's historic trek," nor a renunciation of revolutionary memories, nor the memories of the Great Patriotic War which are surely dear and sacred to us, but the revision of time-serving lectures and textbooks so as we could work conscientiously and thoughtfully on building the future.

It is noteworthy that the qualities emphasized by Mikhail Gorbachev, namely, honesty and courage, are the most important ethical and political conditions for successful research.

It should be also borne in mind that the past, especially the recent difficult past, doesn't disappear the way scenery passing before the windows of an express train does. Not only do we continue to discuss it; we also carry it in our hearts and in our memories. The forthcoming renovation of socialist society certainly implies a fresh and utterly unprejudiced look at our national history.

Some Questions Regarding the Work of Soviet Historians

S. L. TIKHVINSKII

The state of the social sciences was evaluated in the course of implementing the program of the Twenty-seventh Congress of the CPSU and restructuring all spheres of life in our society, in the important decisions adopted this year by the Central Committee, and in a number of statements by leading party figures. Moreover, tasks were set for further improving the methodological foundations and organizational structure and for raising the ideological, political, and practical role of the social sciences in the life of our society. These fundamental evaluations and tasks were formulated in the resolution of the Central Committee of the CPSU "On the Journal *Kommunist*"; in the speech of General Secretary of the Central Committee of the CPSU, M. S. Gorbachev; at the All-Union Conference of Heads of Social Science Departments; and in the report at the meeting by E. K. Ligachev, member of the Politburo and secretary of the Central Committee of the CPSU, and in his address to the General Assembly of the USSR Academy of Sciences.

Thus, recently the party has given a strong impetus to the development of the social sciences, which form the unshakable intellectual basis of the restructuring now in progress. The party is proceeding from the assumption that

> implementing a course of acceleration, restructuring, and achievement of a qualitatively new condition in Soviet society is inconceivable without increased intellectual and theoretical activity, without a reliable scholarly basis for the practical measures taken to improve social relationships in a society in which socialism is being developed.

What is meant here is the need "to achieve major intellectual advances and to move forward significantly in the realm of theory and the creative inter-

Russian text © 1986 by "Pravda" Publishers. "Nekotorye voprosy raboty sovetskikh istorikov," *Voprosy istorii*, 1986, no. 12, pp. 3–12. Translated by Stephen P. Dunn.

This article is based on a report presented to the General Assembly of the Division of History, Academy of Sciences, USSR, October 21, 1986.

19

pretation of new phenomena and processes of life,''[1] and to enrich the spiritual and moral principle of man and of society.

The renewal taking place in our life, by no means painlessly, as M. S. Gorbachev noted, "places demands of the greatest significance for society on the entire system of the social sciences."[2] Soviet historians must fulfill these social tasks from a principled party position so that the prestige and actual "yield" of historical scholarship will correspond to the requirements of our age and to the tasks of accelerating the development of our society. In other words, at this critical turning point in the history of Soviet society, historians should, after critically evaluating the work they have done, define their place in implementing the party's course in a new way. This place, in turn, is inseparably connected with the role historical scholarship plays in the life of our society in understanding the regularities of social developments, in making important political decisions (taking account of the successes and failures, errors and difficulties of the past, in the name of an optimal, scientifically founded achievement of the goals set), in the inculcation of patriotism and high moral qualities, and in the ideological tempering of the Soviet people.

We need to overcome and abandon obsolete dogmas and stereotypes, and to raise boldly new questions arising from today's needs. Speaking at the General Assembly of the Academy of Sciences on October 16 of this year [1986], E. K. Ligachev noted the great contribution of Soviet scientists in solving major economic problems, but concentrated his remarks on disquieting negative phenomena. In particular, in a number of scientific and scholarly collectives

> there is obviously insufficient openness, insufficient conscious criticism and self-criticism to serve as accelerators of development. We may say that there is an insufficiently principled and mutually demanding attitude, and not enough healthy intolerance of negative phenomena. Some scholars consider themselves infallible and try in every way to escape constructive criticism. For this reason, there exist in some work groups cliquishness and nepotism, an atmosphere of mutual admiration and excessive placidity. There are cases in which personnel are chosen for reasons of personal connections and friendship. Considerations of opportunism and prestige replace the interests of the profession.[3]

The institutions of the Division of History suffer from these phenomena. In critically analyzing these negative manifestations, however, we must not permit all our historical scholarship to be slandered under the guise of restructuring. Its achievements are symbolized by the awarding of the order of the Red Banner of Labor to the Institute of History of the USSR and to the Institute of World History.

A number of organizational questions connected with the restructuring of the work of the Division of History and its institutions were posed in February 1986 before the Presidium of the Academy of Sciences of the USSR, when the division made a ten-year report; in March, at the annual meeting of the division; and finally in June, at the All-Union Coordinating Conference of Directors of Historical Institutions in the country. The meeting of the Executive Bureau of the division in 1986 was conducted in a critical and self-critical spirit. All these features of our life should be taken into account when we summarize the restructuring of scholarship during the time since the Twenty-seventh Party Congress, and when we plan how to deepen this process.

The resolution of the Presidium of the USSR Academy of Sciences on the work of the Division of History notes a number of significant measures for further improving it, formulates the most important directions in the field of historical studies, and lays out important measures such as conducting an All-Union Conference of Historians, reinforcing collaboration between historians and those in the fine arts, founding a society of historians, issuing an annual publication of the scientific councils of the division and a popular-scientific history journal, expanding publishing opportunities through the division's institutes, and a number of others. A more concrete plan for further developing historical scholarship was worked out on the basis of the recommendations of a Coordinating Conference.[4]

In considering the course of restructuring our work, we should not fail to consider such an important event in the division as the introduction of a new payscale for its staff. On the whole this was done in an atmosphere of openness and with a demanding attitude toward scientific contribution and practical and moral qualities, on the basis of clarifying the organizational structures of the institutions and research plans which exclude nontopical themes. As a result of the recommendations made, 112 staff members were let go, including 12 who were judged not to be up to the demands made on them, 28 who were transferred to positions as scholarly consultants and the rest who were changed to emeritus status. At present, the personnel structure of the institutions of the division's institutes is as follows: the total number of scientific associates of all categories (not counting the auxiliary scholarly personnel) is 1,782, of whom 472 are junior associates. There are 414 associates, 570 senior associates, 184 leading associates, 11 chief associates, and 131 sectors and division heads.

At the same time, the review revealed weaknesses and shortcomings. There were manifestations of a leveling tendency in the distribution of pay, and of disagreements between institutes over the criteria for selecting qualified associates. In a number of cases, the proper connection between the work of the examination boards and restructuring in the institutes, and the proper concentration of research forces on urgent and high-priority scientific topics were lacking; due attention was not always paid to young researchers, and also to major scholars of pension age. There is a certain danger that scholarly criteria for evaluating the qualifications of researchers will be replaced by a formal approach, or by subjectivism (for example, by a mere counting of one's published works, without due consideration of their scholarly and practical value). It seems necessary to improve further the procedure of evaluation, including the formation of the boards themselves, in order to give the widest possible openness to the work of evaluation, to prevent subjectivism and other defects.

When the Executive Bureau of the division discussed the recommendations, well-founded fears were expressed over a possible reduction in the training of the leading cadre of staff members of its institutes—those holding the doctorate. Also expressed was the need to increase the pensions of those holding the doctoral degree, and to create favorable conditions for the continuation of work by leading scholars who are forced to leave the institutes because of formal requirements, but who retain their creative potential. The review likewise revealed more fundamental defects and problems.

These are problems whose solutions above all depend on each historian and each research group. They are tied to the need to create "zones of heightened intellectual tension and quest,"[5] and a healthy moral and psychological climate. Progress in this area is slow. If we turn to the sphere of planning, we discover, behind the apparent topicality of the problems chosen for the current five-year plan, significant gaps in the study of such global problems as man and society; the laws of his development; contradictions, including those at various stages in the construction of socialism; the class struggle; the building of a new world; man's striving toward an ideal; spiritual quests and disappointments; the mastery of truth and the heroism of creation through labor; the unmasking of various manifestations of antiscientific, reactionary views on the development of human society; progress in science and technology; the dialectic of productive forces and production relationships in history; and relations between social classes and ethnic and national groups. The study of a number of current problems must be expanded and deepened: national and ethnic structures, transitional periods in the development of the social order, classification of ideological currents by type, the politicization of religion which has taken place before our eyes, the history of the political, ecological, and cultural bonds among peoples of the world, Russian culture, the major turning points in the history of our country, and the like.

Many of these problems are either not dealt with at all or only slightly by Soviet historians. At the same time, these questions are being actively addressed by bourgeois historians who treat them not only on the basis of their own methodological positions, but at times use them for ideological diversions. In the field of Soviet history, this applies to the study of political parties, of the church, of certain tendencies in the development of public thought, etc. It is constantly necessary to seek out urgent problems, evaluating them in a political and scholarly manner, and introducing the proper corrections into plans for research work. The task of increasing the activity on the theoretical front of historical scholarship—working out specific problems of theory and cognition inherent to it, such as, for example, the relationship between the normative and the empirical in the historical process, the content of the category of "socioeconomic order," and the like—is extremely urgent.

The human factor has not as yet been given sufficient attention in our historiography. This defect is to be explained by the neglect of the dialectical character of the relationship between the objective and the subjective. In light of the Twenty-seventh Party Congress, this problem has become one of the most pressing. It is important to be historical in studying the human factor—that is, in studying the general worldview of each epoch, on the basis of which the spiritual foundations of individual personality, the social psychology of classes and social groups, and social priorities and values that in each case determine human behavior are formed. A prospectus for work on this problem is being prepared right now on the order of the division's Executive Bureau.

It is necessary to overcome in the shortest possible time the lag that has been noted in the training of highly qualified cadres of experts in religion. At present this task is especially urgent because of the activity of the Russian Orthodox Church in connection with the one-thousandth anniversary of the introduction of Christianity into Rus' and the sharp increase in foreign Islamic propaganda directed toward the inhabitants of Soviet Central Asia. We must prepare specialists and carry out two kinds of work: both theoretical and practical scholarly work, which would not only further the objective illumination of the role of religion in history, but would also give practical assistance in the struggle against clerical anticommunism and the survival of religion in Soviet society.

In speaking of the further development of historical scholarship, and of the problems that must be solved, we should republish works in the series "The Historical Library" ["Istoricheskaia biblioteka"], which make up this treasure house. They must be accompanied by articles on the roles of their authors in developing Soviet historiography, and by appropriate scholarly commentaries. We must promptly finish the last volume of the *History of the USSR from Ancient Times to the Present* [Istoriia SSSR s drevneishikh vremen do nashikh dnei], and prepare a new popular edition of this work. General, multivolume works—as conceptual expositions of our understanding of major phenomena, processes, and events of the past—are an achievement of Marxist historiography. Their scholarly level and depth of generalization must rest on a solid monographic base. In planning the publication of multivolume works, we must also take account of the difficulties involved in their actual "publication," and the demands of readers.

Serious criticism was directed at Soviet historians from the floor of the All-Union Conference of Heads of Social Science Departments, especially in regard to the depersonalization of many historical events and the periodic rewriting of history. The scholarly level of historical works must be determined by the degree of originality of the factual material introduced, the profundity of analysis from a clear class point of view, and the authors' attachment to philosophical and methodological principles. Only under these conditions will truth and historical truth further the creation of something new, and the achievements of those "intellectual victories" that the party expects from social scientists in the creative interpretation of phenomena and of processes of the past and present. In other words, the truth of history presupposes the interpretation of the past from clear-cut philosophical and patriotic positions, in the full multiplicity of events, phenomena, and processes, by disclosing positive and negative aspects in a conscious, constructive spirit, and in mastering the uninterrupted flow of time, taking account of the progressive traditions of the people that even today nourish our society with vital strength.

We read in the Decree of the Central Committee of the CPSU "On the Journal *Kommunist*":

> An analysis of the past, addressed to the present and the future —this is the necessary element of theory and method, with the aid of which new theoretical conclusions are worked out. Moving in this direction, we must organically combine study of the past with interpretation of the present and penetration into the future, we must address ourselves to the past, as Lenin put it, "from the point of view of what our policy will require tomorrow or the day after," . . . and shift the center of gravity "not so much toward the description of what we have lived through, as toward the lessons of experience that we receive and must receive for our direct practical activity."[6]

The decisions of the Twenty-seventh Congress of the CPSU must be implemented primarily in studies that are new in their themes, conclusions, and scholarly argumentation, and that correspond to the tasks set before the party and the country. To date, unfortunately, no such studies exist. Furthermore, there have recently been cases of another kind: there appeared under the imprint of the USSR Institute of History *Fully Developed Socialism: Questions of Theory and History* [Razvitoi sotsializm: Voprosy teorii i istorii], which repeats conclusions that have been invalidated by life.

Principled criticism and creative discussion of various problems of history must play a major role in restructuring scholarly activity. "The search for truth," M. S. Gorbachev has noted, "must pass through the comparison of various points of view, debates, and discussion, and the breakup of previous stereotypes."[7] We have accumulated quite a few such controversial problems. At the meeting of the division's Executive Bureau in 1984, a list of such problems was recommended to the institute and journals of the division. It is extremely urgent at present to discuss the periodization of Soviet history. This must be done jointly by the Institute of History of the USSR and by historians of the party. There are many controversial questions in the evaluation of individual phases of the Great Patriotic War, and historians have a good deal of work before them here. We have gotten out of the habit of holding scholarly debates and discussions, and frequently divergences of views call forth painful reactions on the part of individual scholars, which turn into "appeals to the authorities" or into labeling. At the same time, we see attempts, under the banner of criticism, to revive old, long-discarded conceptions without making the necessary arguments for them. Some authors still commission reviews of their works, or even write them [themselves], or, in search of false prestige, give them to persons with famous names for signature.

Moreover, many books are not reviewed at all and the output of research institutes evokes no response from the public. The practice of including workers of party and state organs on the editorial boards of many publications leads in a number of cases to their being perceived as "official," and thus above scholarly criticism. An abnormal situation has been created in which the major responsibility for the appearance of a work in print is sometimes borne not by its authors but by editors and publishing houses. This responsibility must lie primarily with the authors and editorial boards, and also the scholarly institutes under whose imprint scholarly studies are published.

The journals of the division are called upon to play an important role in developing debates and establishing a creative climate in historical scholarship. Unfortunately, a spirit of "wait and see" and "play it safe" is still strong in their editorial boards and offices, and researchers complain of this. It is still rare that profound analytical surveys of the state of the art of particular problems appear in journals. At the same time, the editorial boards of journals are making just demands on historians who have gotten out of the habit of writing critical articles and reviews on particular themes, and, what is still worse, claim a monopoly on the treatment of individual questions and resort to accusations against those who hold different points of view. The further successful development of historical scholarship will be impossible without well-argued scholarly debate on its troubles.

In September, the Executive Bureau of the division considered restructuring in the work of journals in light of the decisions of the Twenty-seventh Party Congress. The resolution adopted noted that despite the work done in this regard, the activity of the journals does not correspond to the tasks now facing them. It was recommended that the journals, in particular, deal more broadly with restructuring in the division's institutes, including the publication of materials dealing with the results of the recertification of research associates, and to prepare, together with academic councils, analytical articles on the state of study of particular problems, and to seek new forms of communication with readers and authors.

At present, there is a perceived need for comprehensive and objective reconsideration of the existing system of organizing historical research, and also of its future. Its basic features developed several decades ago and now lag behind reality. The division's institutes that cut across disciplines, such as the Institute of Oriental Studies and the Institute of Slavic and Balkan Studies, have a tendency toward isolation from the historical problems studied by other institutes in the division. Moreover, the work of historians has been negatively affected by the fact that a number of historical institutes (the Institute of the History of Natural Science and Technology, the Institute of the Far East, the Institute of the International Workers' Movement) are located in other divisions of the USSR Academy of Sciences. A more precise definition of the makeup of the social science divisions could obviously increase the effectiveness and raise the quality of their work. An important issue in improving organization is that of transforming the

Leningrad divisions of the institutes into branches. The time has also come to consider uniting the Laboratory of the Conservation and Restoration of Documents (LKRD) with the Leningrad Division of Archives of the USSR Academy of Sciences.

As emphasized at the General Assembly of the Academy of Sciences,

> The chief link in academic scholarship is the research institute. This is precisely where the growth of new scientific knowledge takes place and where the foundation is laid for accelerating progress in science and technology. The most highly qualified scholars are concentrated here. However, in a number of cases, the staffs of institutes are underproductive. The Presidium of the Academy should look into this, and ensure that each scholar works to full potential. It is very important for this purpose to strengthen the leadership of some institutes in the Academy, to pour into them fresh creative forces, and to raise their level of responsibility for the results of scholarship. It is necessary to clear away all obstructions in the form of outdated instructions and directives, to remove everything that hampers research, and to expand the rights of institutes, divisions, and laboratories. At the same time it is necessary for leaders and research groups to make active use of the rights they already have and of those newly granted to them. [8]

The present state of knowledge in the social sciences requires a more precise definition both of the boundaries of historical science proper and of its internal classification, which must be reflected in the formal classification of the All-Union Certification Commission. Regrettably, according to this classification, history does not fall into the category of social sciences, while the history of the CPSU does. As a result, department heads responsible for world history and the history of the USSR were not invited to the All-Union Conference of the Heads of Social Science Departments. Within the science of history proper, classifications are also obsolete and do not reflect the newest tendencies or stimulate the development of a number of applied branches of knowledge. Such fields as "local historical studies," "museum work," and perhaps others as well should be included in this classification, and hence recognized as scholarly specialties.

A reorientation is also needed in the training of historians in the postsecondary schools. The current orientation toward schoolteachers or scientific workers (graduate school) must be supplemented by specialization and training of historians for work in other practical spheres (historical museums, societies for the preservation of historical and cultural monuments, and editorial and publishing work).

The same applies to the internal structure of the division's institutes. They do not yet provide the flexibility and latitude for training scientific personnel, and in particular, for the creation of temporary groups with the freedom to prepare necessary works.

At the moment, historians are busy looking for opportunities to work more effectively. However, loquaciousness often casts a shadow over one of the important sources for such increased efficiency: clear executive discipline and the responsible fulfillment by everyone—whether an academician, the academic secretary of an institute, or a scientific associate—of the decisions adopted by the directing bodies of the institutes, the Executive Bureau of the division, and the Presidium of the Academy of Sciences of the USSR. It stands to reason that methods of administration by injunction are not acceptable in the scholarly world. But what is at issue in this case is fulfillment of the decisions of collective organs, whose function it is to direct research. Problems of coordination and planning of research advance collectives today into the foreground of organizing historical science.

The situation that has evolved in the Academy with regard to long-range planning and the development of comprehensive long-range programs, and inclusion of all interested organizations regardless of interagency barriers, was criticized at the General Assembly of the USSR Academy of Sciences. Almost three years of experience in developing six comprehensive programs by the division shows what a complex matter it was to prepare them, not to speak of actually implementing them even within the division's institutes. It is true that some progress has been made recently: five programs have been confirmed by the Executive Bureau and recommended for publication in the journals put out by the division. We must speed up publication and discussion of these programs so as to draw the division's institutes, and also the postsecondary schools and publishing houses, into the process of implementing them. The institutes must make the necessary corrections in their scientific plans for 1987 by including in them the themes from the comprehensive programs of the division.

The Executive Bureau of the division and its staff is to some degree responsible for the fact that restructuring in the field of administrative discipline is hardly noticeable yet, since they do not fully perform their supervisory functions. Comprehensive monitoring of the work of the institutes, as a form of supervision, is not very efficient. The schedule for such monitoring (which should take place once every three years) has not been maintained. The Executive Bureau of the division assesses results only in a formal way and lacks careful analysis of the defects and difficulties in the work of the institutes.

Historians also have a number of problems relating to interagency barriers, two of which are especially urgent at this time. The first is connected with the supply of primary and secondary sources for historical works. Here, despite appeals, improvement is slow. In Moscow, working conditions for researchers in libraries have deteriorated sharply. As for documents in the archives and statistical material, there is hope that the appropriate agencies will deal with the question of access by scholars and will find reasonable solutions in the spirit of the recommendations expressed at the All-Union Conference of Heads of Social Science Departments. We have to assume that ways will also be found to strengthen the creative ties between historians and archivists. Finally, it is necessary to develop a program for the creation, on the national level, of contemporary data bases necessary for historical investigation. The work of historians would become incomparably more productive if, for example, the Institute of History of the USSR were able to use computers whose memory would include the text of all the chronicles, and the Institute of World History could use a statistical data base including data from foreign censuses, the labor movement, and the like.

The second problem, no less severe, relates to scholarly publication by historians. Researchers are not satisfied with the practice whereby manuscripts pass through Nauka Publishers with the play-it-safe attitude of some editors or with their at times excessive, downright unprofessional interference with the text of manuscripts; and with the lack of due efficiency in publishing books, their small editions, and their poor format. Historians justifiably express displeasure with the narrow publication quotas and the limits on the size of team-written works and individual monographs. At the same time, Nauka can justifiably reproach the scholarly and literary quality of the works of historians, and justly call for improving the quality of the refereeing process and of discussion in recommending works for publication. There are serious reproaches relating to the lack of originality in a number of works and the repetition by their authors of long-familiar facts and opinions. The basic criteria for recommending historical works for publication must be the creative approach to the problem, the use of a broad range of sources, and new conclusions.

We may note at least two other problems whose solution depends both on historians and on representatives of other agencies. The first of these is that of personnel. In recent years an increase in the average age of the main body of researchers has become clearly noticeable. At the same time, the level of professional training of young scholars is causing some concern. According to data for the beginning of July of this year [1986], of the 388 holders of the degree of doctor of historical sciences working in the division's institutes, only 29 were under 50 years old, 166 were between 50 and 60, and 193 were 60 and older, while of the more than 1,000 holders of the candidate's degree, almost half were over 50. The situation is the same with respect to members of the division. The average age of academicians is 75 years, and that of corresponding members of the Academy of Sciences, 63 years. The situation in regard to "rare specialties" is deteriorating. We have a shortage of competent historians of Asia and Africa, and there is an acute need for qualified specialists in economic history, historical demography, the history of culture, the history of religions, and other special disciplines. In the 68 universities of the country (excluding Moscow), there are only six doctors of historical sciences specializing in ancient history. There are only a few more medievalists at these institutes. It is also necessary to give serious attention to training specialists in the history of the republics and regions. We must improve the training of historians in the field of auxiliary disciplines and foreign languages.

The training of historical personnel may be unfavorably affected by the practice of unfounded curtailment of the teaching of history in the secondary and postsecondary schools, by the reform in the certification of highly qualified personnel projected by the All-Union Certification Commission, and by the rearrangement of the network of specialized academic councils for the defense of dissertations in history, carried through without consideration of the wishes of the Division of History. We are disturbed by the possible influence of the salary reform for scientific associates on the training of holders of the doctorate: will holders of the candidate's degree continue their professional training and work on doctoral dissertations or will they confine themselves to themes that are stimulated by the corresponding bonuses envisaged by the new system of payment? We should also discuss, in the commissions of the Division of History on the problems of youth and on liaison with the secondary and postsecondary schools, the proposal for the revival of doctoral study in the system of the USSR Academy of Sciences—the more so since it is envisaged by the reform of the postsecondary schools.

The second problem, whose solution depends both on historians and on the agencies, is the dissemination of historical knowledge. Recently, considerable efforts have been made in this direction. A trial issue of a popular historical journal was published in 1985; a historical video was twice televised; an editorial office for the publication of scholarly-popular literature on history has been revived within Nauka Publishers. An important occasion and form for the dissemination of historical knowledge is the participation of scholars in activities connected with anniversaries and important events. In this respect we have accumulated quite a bit of experience: suffice it to note the eight-hundredth anniversary of *The Lay of the Host of Igor* [Slovo o polku Igoreve], and the fortieth anniversary of the victory of the Soviet people in the Great Patriotic War. Other important dates are approaching, among which we should note first of all the seventieth anniversary of the Great October Socialist Revolution and the fiftieth anniversary of the beginning of World War II. Our most important task is to make use of these anniversary dates for the wide dissemination of the conclusions of Soviet historiography both within the country and abroad.

Overcoming the bureaucratic barrier between historians and members of artistic bodies is directly related to the problem of disseminating historical knowledge. We need a creative alliance and business-like contacts, without mutual accusations and lecturing, between historians and writers, journalists, and the motion picture industry. Once this is achieved, there will no longer be such cases as occurred in the past year, when the writer A. Nikitin published in the journal *Novyi Mir* [New World] an article asserting that *The Lay of the Host of Igor* was of Bulgarian origin. Specialists (historians and literary scholars) demonstrated the antihistorical character of such speculative arguments, but the harm done will be long lasting, considering the wide popularity of the journal.

The expanded ideological and educational role of history demands from historians the ability to write and speak of the past in a serious, balanced, and vivid way, holding strictly to the scientific data and to the Marxist-Leninist methodology for analyzing them.

The increased role of the science of history in our society and the authority of Soviet historians abroad depend on the pace and results of restructuring in the historical field. At the Sixteenth World Congress of Historical Sciences, a special "roundtable" on the theme "The Historian's Responsibility in the Nuclear Age" was held on the initiative of Soviet historians, and a corresponding appeal to the historians of the entire world was adopted. The programs of many colloquia organized by the National Committee of Historians of the Soviet Union include themes connected with international political problems. At present, at a new stage in the struggle of the USSR and all peace-loving forces for averting nuclear war, it is necessary to increase significantly this form of activity by historians, which is most important both in a political and a scientific sense.

The Executive Bureau of the International Congress of Historical Sciences, which met in September of this year [1986] in Dresden (German Democratic Republic), adopted on our initiative an appeal to historians to increase their contribution to solving problems of war and peace and to mobilizing the scientific and humanistic potential and the multifarious experience of history in the struggle to prevent war. Historians could create their own peace movement, as was done previously by physicians and ecologists. As a first step, the National Committee of Historians of the Soviet Union sent a letter to a group of prominent scholars in socialist and capitalist countries proposing a conference on the question of the historian's responsibility for the preservation of peace in the nuclear age. The last meeting of the Executive Bureau of the division approved a plan for disseminating knowledge concerning Soviet peace initiatives. The National Committee must maintain constant control over supervision of the implementation of this plan.

We have considered above only some of the problems connected with restructuring the work of historical institutes in the light of the decisions of the Twenty-seventh Congress of the CPSU. What is at issue, taking account of the new demands, is the solution of two of these problems: the attitude of each individual historian to the demands of society, and the establishment of strong ties between historians and the public. An analysis of the impact of restructuring on the division's institutes shows that historians are still at the stage of critical interpretation of what has been done in the peculiar triangle of "history-historian-society," and of uncovering defects and omissions and of working out constructive measures for radically improving their work. In the resolution of the General Assembly of the USSR Academy of Sciences on the Academy's implementation of the decisions of the Twenty-seventh Party Congress, attention is drawn to the need to increase work on all fronts in developing scholarship, to establish shorter deadlines for completing planned assignments, to improve placement of leading personnel and to lower the average age of the staffs of Academy institutes, and to rejuvenate the makeup of academic councils and editorial boards of journals. Solving these tasks requires decisive mobilization of all forces and serious work by all research groups in the Division of History on the fundamental restructuring of the entire scientific and organizational activity of Soviet historians.

Notes

1. *Kommunist*, 1986, no. 15, p. 3.
2. Ibid., p. 4.
3. *Pravda*, October 17, 1986.
4. See *Voprosy istorii*, 1986, no. 12, p. 111.
5. *Kommunist*, 1986, no. 15, p. 15.
6. Ibid., no. 12, p. 9.
7. Ibid., p. 4.
8. *Pravda*, October 17, 1986.

The Historian and Perestroika

V. A. KOZLOV

Soviet society is restructuring. We have already crossed the boundary beyond which a simplified understanding of our past, ready maxims and prescriptions, attempts to act "in a carbon-copy manner," using as a pattern a "model" of socialism "ossified" at the 1930–40 level, have shown themselves to be unsound. Processes are gaining momentum that are carrying us ever farther into new terrain. The place their discipline will occupy in resolving the pressing social tasks advanced by the April (1985) Plenum of the Central Committee of the Twenty-seventh Congress of the CPSU today depends on historians themselves: will this discipline only record events or will it significantly enrich social practice by rethinking historical experience in a topical way? Will it satisfy modern man's need for knowledge of the past and present or will he turn for historical knowledge and explanations to *belles-lettres* and public-affairs writing? Will the historian succeed in bringing to the general reader a sense of the concrete historical laws of social development or will the historian remain only a purveyor of clearly illustrated factual material?

For the time being, historians of the party and of Soviet society are in a difficult position. Academic councils and publishing houses are now returning, albeit timidly, books that even yesterday would have seemed quite "passable." Historical journals have begun to show a taste for polemical and critical materials. The mass media is constantly publishing letters by readers asking stinging, "hot" questions, to which there are not always answers, even in special historical studies, not to speak of textbooks; the question of criteria for the timeliness and effectiveness of historical research has become sharper. At the same time, books and articles continue to appear about which you can tell only by the date of publication and the use of current terminology that they are supposed to belong to our own time. One feels a certain anxiety among historians. Some of them have found themselves in the position of the "emperor without his clothes," and, like their counterpart in the fairy tale, they often do not notice this.

Serious difficulties are being encountered not only by aficionados of the

Russian text © 1987 by "Pravda" Publishers. "Istorik i perestroika," *Voprosy istorii KPSS,* 1987, no. 5, pp. 110–22. Translated by Stephen P. Dunn.

The author is a candidate of historical sciences.

"methodology of quotation," commentary, and platitudes sprinkled with archival references, but also by those investigators who really do want to make serious changes in understanding the past. Now that they can speak directly and openly on burning historical issues, they feel a heavy burden of *personal* responsibility for what they wanted to say yesterday but didn't, and for what they can and must say today. After all, it is no longer possible to avoid mastering, analyzing, and explaining material with the saving reference to the "sagacious catfish"* to the effect that allegedly "they won't let you talk about that anyway." Moreover, heated discussion of the problems of our distant and recent past is now going on. Writers and journalists, communists and nonparty people, historians and nonhistorians, people of different generations and life experience, are hastening to have their say on questions that the discipline of history has kept quiet about for a long time. Historians themselves are living through a unique period of manifestoes and declarations, which has spilled out of the academic auditoriums and meeting rooms of academic councils into the pages of the popular press.[1]

History must be written in a new way; it must be cleansed of distortions, omissions, and unoriginal commentaries—this is the critical message of the appeals being sounded.

An effort that is necessary and useful to our field is under way. After the January (1987) Plenum of the CPSU Central Committee, the country entered a new phase of *perestroika*: the analysis of the situation has been refined and deepened, a program for further action has been worked out, and it is now necessary to put it into practice by painstaking, everyday labor. The field of history, and particularly of party history, still lags behind the general pace of change. It seems that a critical analysis of the situation that has developed in our field of social science is still far from complete. We still frequently wait for instructions and decrees; we want the "boundaries of what is permitted" to be defined for us. The present author is judging, in this instance, not only by his own experience and that of his colleagues. Actual confirmation of this rather complex psychological situation, and of the difficulties that historians, and primarily teachers, have encountered, may be seen, in particular, in the letter of Docent** A. N. Davydov, which was shown to me by the editors of the journal *Voprosy istorii KPSS*. The letter states:

> We know that lately a series of articles concerning problems of studying the history of the CPSU has appeared in the newspaper *Moskovskie novosti* [Moscow News] (see nos. 2, 3, and 6). An article by Professor Iu. Afanas'ev, "The Power of Historical Knowledge" [Energiia istoricheskogo znaniia][2] appeared

---

*The sagacious catfish [*premudryi peskar'*] is the name of a satirical story by M. E. Saltykov-Shchedrin, published in 1883. The expression refers to cowardly souls who try to avoid getting involved out of fear but who nonetheless suffer a major setback.—D.J.R.

**A Soviet academic rank roughly equivalent to assistant professor.—D.J.R.

in the no. 2 issue for this year. In issue no. 6, an article by Egor Iakovlev says that Professor Afanas'ev is not by any means the final arbiter of truth. A battle of opinions is in progress, it is said. But Professor Afanas'ev's article raises a number of questions about which I would like to hear your opinion as an organ of the Institute of Marxism-Leninism under the CPSU Central Committee. After all, we have to work with students.

1. Comrade Afanas'ev's article says that textbooks sometimes present a Stalinist model of the victory of the October Revolution and the building of socialism in the USSR—a model that is far from the truth.

2. The article says that a wave of Stalinist definitions—"a variety of Menshevism," "a Menshevik deviation," "an antirevolutionary group," "kulak agents," and so forth—crashes down on the unfortunate student, who is compelled to spend his or her mental energy on learning these labels. At the same time, he or she is deprived of the possibility of understanding the substantive theoretical arguments and conceptions of socialism, and of comparing the path of the building of socialism in the USSR with the path taken in building socialism in other countries, and so forth.

The question arises as to whether the model for the victory of the October Revolution and the building of socialism that is given in our party literature can be called merely Stalinist.

Can the definitions of some (above-mentioned) deviations and opportunistic groups that have occurred or existed in the ranks of our party be called merely Stalinist definitions? After all, these definitions are given in the records of plenums of the Central Committee and congresses of the party. For example. . . .

Quotations from party documents follow here.

I quite understand the difficulties encountered by A. N. Davydov and other teachers of party history. Before numerous audiences questions are being asked— publicly and boldly—which, until very recently, students asked only face to face, in private conversations, and only of those teachers in whom they had complete confidence. It is possible that some students make reference to Iu. Afanas'ev in this connection. But can it be that such questions haven't been asked before of other historians? After all, these questions are in essence the result of conspiracies of silence, oversimplifications, and schematism in setting forth party history.

Iu. Afanas'ev's piece, and A. N. Davydov's letter, are polemically opposed to each other. However, we should treat both points of view with respect, being guided by the wise maxim: "It is said that the truth lies in the middle, between two opposing opinions. By no means! Between them lies a problem. . . ."[3] What is this particular problem?

Certainly the problem is not in who is responsible, personally, for the evaluative formulas about which A. N. Davydov is asking (even though some of them, in my view, reveal the personal intolerance of I. V. Stalin, about which Lenin wrote a long time ago[4]). Nor, *a fortiori*, does the problem consist of agreement with the mistaken views of specific leaders of oppositionist groups and deviations. The problem, in my view, is not that of "whether the model for the victory of the October Revolution and the building of socialism that is given in our party literature can be called merely Stalinist." Any "model," although perhaps convenient for didactic purposes and for being learned by heart, will fail at this point to satisfy society's intellectual demands. What is needed now is another level of conclusiveness and persuasiveness, and the overcoming of the old faults of our textbooks, and particularly of historical research—schematism and oversimplification in dealing with the most acute problems in the history of the party and of Soviet society.

The demand for depth and three-dimensionality of historical perception is felt everywhere today. "Half-truth," as G. Kapralov justly wrote in a review of the television miniseries, "Strokes for a Portrait of V. I. Lenin," "which is always the next thing to a lie—the habit of depicting those who entered into polemics with Lenin, who took other positions, and who went over into the enemy camp, as some kind of stupid 'boys to be beaten'—has cost our art considerable intellectual and artistic losses. Can one seriously learn the mastery and courage of revolutionary struggle, and inculcate true Leninist conviction from such 'examples'?"[5]

The party has already given a general assessment of the state of affairs in the study and teaching of the social sciences. As M. S. Gorbachev emphasized at the All-Union Meeting of Heads of Social Science Departments:

> The formulation, forms, and teaching methods in the social sciences that still exist today, promote in no small degree what we call dogmatism and scholasticism. The tendency to seek in "copybook truths," prescriptions suitable for all situations that come up in life, arises out of pedantry, out of reliance not on creative thought, but on the mindless rote learning of banal propositions.
>
> *Lenin, as we know, drew a contrast between rote learning and the process of thinking something through.* And it is precisely the latter that is often in short supply in the teaching of the social sciences.[6]

It is, therefore, a matter of independent *thinking-through*. No one will solve our professional problems for us historians. And mutual accusations, raised voices, appeals for "explanations" to higher authorities, not to speak of attempts to convert polemical excesses into political errors, will hardly be of any help. All of us, after all, are in agreement that history has to be written and taught in a new way. For the time being, no one has any blueprints as to how this ought to be done. But it would be a profound misapprehension to reduce our new tasks to a simple arithmetical operation—the elementary substitution of minuses for pluses (or *vice versa*) in evaluating the past.

When we ask ourselves why "the winds of chance" (the phrase is Konstantin

Simonov's[7]) blew with such ease through historiography, and why, after the "deepening" that began in the late 1950s and early 1960s, we have so easily, in the recent past, fallen victim to the unoriginal commentary method, conspiracies of silence, and oversimplifications, we see the causes primarily in events outside the field of history itself. To a certain degree this can be justified. In analyzing the experience of the past, historians were urged to show "the useful and the good," and furthermore, in such a way as not to touch upon questions involving the transformation of "the good" of yesterday into "the bad" of today. Such an attitude narrowed the historian's field of vision for many years, orienting him toward a "balanced" account of "the good" (primarily) and "the bad" (as an afterthought). This was a result of a "lack of self-criticism," which, as the Soviet philosopher E. V. Il'enkov wrote some time ago,

> is expressed in the fact that the present is represented without the contradictions that are the mainsprings of future development. Under this kind of abstract, self-satisfied "self-consciousness," all preceding development begins, in fact, to be depicted as a process of approximation to some extreme ideal state, which the present imagines. As a result, any figure of the past is depicted only in those abstract features that can be represented as "hints" or "rudiments" of the present state of affairs. Everything else begins to seem "nonessential," and it is precisely those concrete historical contradictions, both created and destroyed by that past stage, which fall into the category of the "nonessential."[8]

This approach is in poor accord with the revolutionary spirit of Marxism-Leninism. It has left an unfavorable imprint on the entire historiography of Soviet society, which has been directly subject to the consequences of the "noncontradictory" conception of the development of socialism. If today we see not "individual shortcomings," joined for decency's sake to our indubitable achievements, but a sea of problems that both explain and give rise to our achievements and shortcomings, it would be strange not to see the same thing in the past. Thus, the general course of *perestroika* and the sharply critical spirit of our transitional epoch create possibilities for critically interpreting our "yesterday."

This does not mean that methodological reefs and theoretical shoals do not await us on our new course. History takes an active part in the discussions and debates of our day. Here a tendency sometimes arises to transfer the conceptions of today mechanically into the past,[9] or there may be attempts to evaluate it as an "inferior present." This relates, in particular, to the effort of some publicists to transfer to an evaluation of the decisions and practices of the transitional period [of the New Economic Policy, 1921–1929—D.J.R.] our present-day conception and understanding of self-financing, our attitude toward heavy-handed administrative methods, and the like. Whether we wish it or not, past events are evaluated not from the point of view of their real contradictions, problems, and possibilities, but according to whether they correspond or not to our present-day knowledge, preferences, and priorities, or even simply to the personal point of view of a specific public-affairs writer.

An example of this pragmatic attitude toward history can be seen to some degree in L. Voskresenskii's article "On the Road to the Socialist Market" [Na puti k sotsialisticheskomu rynku], which was intended to explain to the reader today's interest in Lenin's conception of the New Economic Policy [NEP]. Undoubtedly, the article appeared in response to a pressing need, but it nevertheless cannot help but raise objections. Voskresenskii evaluates "War Communism" quite negatively. In his opinion, the destruction of the country's productive forces in the early 1920s was due not only to a protracted war but also "to no less a degree to the incompetent and voluntarist exercises of 'left' extremists, who tried to 'make state property' of everything down to the last needle and thread." The practice of NEP is viewed in the same way—but this time through rose-colored glasses. In order to validate his viewpoint, the author resorts (along with absolutely accurate reflections on the saving role played by the NEP in restoring the ruined economy of the country) to a prose paraphrase of V. Mayakovsky's poem "Good!" [*Khorosho!*]:

> Spring, 1927:
> —Shops stand with their windows wide open. In the windows are products: wines, fruits. The cheeses are not moldy (!). Lamps glow. "Prices reduced."
> The factories are puffing. There will be more cloth. The cooperative movement has begun to take wing.
> —To the peasant, "work is dear" from early in the morning: "he plows the earth, he writes poems."[10]

Against the background of such a noncontradictory picture of the NEP, which leaves no room either for the class struggle or for an analysis of the serious disequilibrium in the economy, or for a study of administrative support of the economic levers, the change in economic policy at the beginning of the First Five-Year Plan looked unambiguously negative: it is represented as the result of arbitrary bureaucratic behavior, and Voskresenskii sees no objective causes, no categorical imperative for shifting the center of gravity to administrative methods.

While holding various views on the economic mechanism characteristic of the NEP, historians—unanimously, I think—are unable to accept the "images" of "War Communism" and the NEP proposed by Voskresenskii. This is not because the conception he advances is paradoxical and novel, but because it is obviously inconsistent with the generally known facts.

In a publication intended for historians, there is hardly a need to speak of this in any great detail, although we emphasize that these questions are by no means among those that are "finally settled" in historical science.* Nevertheless,

---

*See, for example, the recent debate between E. G. Gimpel'son and I. B. Berkhin [*Voprosy istorii KPSS*, 1986, nos. 6 and 10].

for the evaluation of Voskresenskii's concept about "War Communism," it's worthwhile to cite someone who was not sympathetic either to "War Communism" or to communism in general:

> Confronted with a shortage of nearly every commodity, a shortage caused partly by the war strain—for Russia has been at war continuously now for six years—partly by the general collapse of social organisation, and partly by the blockade, and with the currency in complete disorder, the only possible way to save the towns a chaos of cornering, profiteering, starvation, and at last a mere savage fight for the remnants of food and common necessities, was some sort of collective control and rationing.
>
> The Soviet government rations on principle, but any government in Russia now would have to ration. If the war in the West had lasted up to the present time London would be rationing too—food, clothing, and housing.[11]

These are the words of H. G. Wells, who visited Soviet Russia at the height of "War Communism" in the fall of 1920.

Necessitated by the extraordinary circumstances of the Civil War, "War Communism" did in fact give rise—both in our party and elsewhere—to a number of illusions and utopian conceptions, and called forth false hopes to the effect that it would be possible to build socialism on a wave of revolutionary enthusiasm. However, references to voluntarist exercises of "left" extremists, who tried to "make state property" of everything down to the last needle and thread, can hardly bring clarity to our understanding of such a complex socioeconomic, political, and psychological phenomenon as "War Communism." Had the communists not done what they did, by concentrating the resources of the country (and the need for this was understood not only by the working class but by the peasantry), there would have been no victory in the Civil War and consequently no New Economic Policy either.

Here is another piece of testimony from a contemporary: "We were suddenly overtaken by an unforeseen event. The endless provocations against Soviet representatives abroad, and the mass-scale talk about a possible war by a bloc of capitalist countries against the USSR, provoked panic among some citizens. Hoarding of flour and sugar began, the kulaks and some of the middle peasants began to hold on to excess grain and not to market it."[12] What period does this testimony describe? That same year, 1927. The events developed some time after the spring idyll described by Voskresenskii. And in December 1927, at the Fifteenth Congress of the RKP(b), a frank admission was heard that the country was experiencing "*the economic difficulties of the beginning of a war, without having a war.*"[13]

In conditions of incipient industrialization and of a deteriorating international situation, the economic mechanism of NEP began to show its shortcomings. The situation that preceded the policy shift of 1929 created the need to force the pace of industrialization, concentrating on a few priority tasks,[14] and to do in ten years what other countries achieved in a century. The situation required violations of the "normal" proportions of economic development and consequently the transfer of the center of gravity from economic levers to administrative ones. It was impossible to carry out such an unprecedented reallocation of resources to heavy industry by any other means.

The threat of war, which made it necessary to do this, while violating the normal order of "movement," was perceived by the people of that time as entirely real and imminent. It was not only a matter of conflict on the Chinese and Eastern Railroad, which revealed serious problems in terms of the country's military preparedness. In 1929, A. Gaidar wrote in the Arkhangel'sk newspaper Volna [The Wave]: "The year and day when the tense silence along the thousand-verst western border will be broken by the first salvos of enemy batteries, . . . that year and day and hour is not yet marked by a black border on any calendar in the world. But that year will come, that day will dawn, and that hour will arrive."[15]

The increasingly explosive situation (for that was how many contemporaries viewed it) dictated the need to abandon a number of already worked-out methods, which while inherently good did not suit the new conditions. Incidentally, that possibility had previously been foreseen by Lenin and the party. The resolutions of the Tenth Congress of the RKP(b) announcing the transition to the NEP stated clearly that "the party must be flexible enough to pass over quickly, if need be, to a system of militarization."[16] The same attitude toward a "system of militarization" is expressed in Lenin's letter to the Politburo of the Central Committee on the theses of E. A. Preobrazhenskii (March 16, 1922): "9. The second sentence of Section 2 (against 'methods characteristic of the committees of the poor'*) is harmful and inaccurate, since war, for example, may compel the adoption of these methods."[17] Thus, Lenin made the question of the selection of methods conditional upon the specific situation. In fact, any serious change in the domestic and foreign political situation had to change the proportion and relationship of methods—administrative and economic, compulsory and persuasive, those based on enthusiasm and those based on personal interest.

What bothers me most about all of this is not the inaccuracies Voskresenskii committed, but the fact that this was done with good intentions in order to substantiate some ideas that deserve extremely serious treatment. This places me in a psychologically awkward position. What compels me to enter into a polemic is primarily the pragmatic attitude toward the past—the straight-out attempt to fit it to the demands of the day. Our publicists know as well as I do how lamentable

---

*The committees of the poor [kombedy] were founded on June 11, 1918, to intensify class divisions in the villages, to control food reserves in the countryside, and to extend support for the Bolsheviks to the rural proletariat. The experiment failed.—D.J.R.

the consequences are of taking this road. The past can't be commanded; it recognizes only one form of relations—it has to be taken into account and correctly understood, regardless of whether we like it.

A serious historical analysis of the economic mechanism of the 1920s has the potential to yield considerably more for present-day practice than merely a reminder of the indisputable fact that self-financing is a good thing. The point is that historical experience shows the limitations of self-financing *by a trust*: this form of self-financing was shallow, and did not reach down even to the enterprise, whose profit was dissolved in the unified balance of the trust[18]—let alone to the individual work-station. It also shows the weaknesses of the system of material incentives for workers that was operative at that time in state industries. In a word, objective historical analysis has the capacity to show the possible "hidden pitfalls" involved in self-financing, and the means of avoiding them. But Voskresenskii, in his enthusiasm for the idea of the socialist market, does not even mention what precise kind of market state industry was dealing with. After all, this was the environment dominated by petty-commodity production, which gives rise to capitalism every day. It was by no means the kind of market whose experience may be of fundamental importance for us today.

Idealized conceptions of the NEP certainly have the potential for serving as an emotional argument in a debate but they cannot lead to a true evaluation of the real state of affairs. Let me explain. Lenin's ideas about self-financing and personal incentive were considerably broader than the actual practice of NEP, which is why they have taken on such importance in our day. The NEP was a specific historical form of the realization of Lenin's ideas, intended to serve as a *transitional period*, and to create the preconditions and "bridges" for a transition to socialism. Under today's conditions, however, what is at issue is a form, fundamentally different from the NEP, for the concrete historical realization of the conception of self-financing and personal incentive (the NEP form, as we know, was intended for an economy that combined the features of different social orders)—a qualitatively new approach, a new conception of movement, differing both from the practice of NEP and from the experience of the forced building of socialism during the first five-year plans.

Returning to the question that has unexpectedly led us into discussions of the NEP, concerning the policy turn of 1929—or, more precisely, concerning the need to observe the principle of historicism in the evaluation of the past—I would like to emphasize that it was not only "external conditions," but an inadequate level of professional (including methodological) competence on the part of some scholars that permitted us in the recent past to change value judgments with such ease. That is to say, these judgments did not arise out of a profound interpretation of historical facts on the basis of the Marxist-Leninist dialectic, but merely facilitated and cemented the montage of these facts by subordinating them to a concept of socialism frozen at the level of the 1930s and 1940s, which penetrated historical studies, textbooks, and popular works, and became established in people's consciousness. A whole generation of historians, including the present author, grew up in this "school." Some of us to this very day see the truth as a golden mean between captious criticism and varnishing of the facts. But the truth in fact lies in another dimension of thought altogether, and the position of the historian as a party member and a good citizen does not by any means consist in the ability to serve up in a balanced way deficiencies and successes, difficulties and achievements.

The problem is not simply that the study of the past is impossible without analysis of its errors and miscalculations. This much would seem to be axiomatic for any sensible person. However, it is naive to think that such an analysis is, in general, a simple matter, that its effectiveness is determined only by the good will of the historian, and only by the categorical imperative of telling the truth. Truth in history presupposes the solution of an extremely serious professional question, and is not reducible to pointing out guilty parties, and to emotional philippics. The historian has no right to substitute preaching for explanation and emotion for knowledge. All of these things are obvious. But it suffices to reflect seriously on the problem of what, strictly speaking, is in "error" in relation to the past, in order to understand the nontrivial nature of the problem. Is an error that which is recognized as such by our contemporaries (or could in principle have been recognized as such)? Is it something whose fallacy has been made clear to us today? And in this latter case, wouldn't our movement along the path of knowledge be accompanied by the endless discovery of ever new past mistakes? Applying our current knowledge and understanding to evaluating the decisions and actions of our historical predecessors, we are sometimes inclined to treat these decisions as mistaken. But the criterion here must be different: to what degree was the political leadership, within the limits of the concepts and ideas of its own time, the level of public consciousness, and its opportunities and resources, able to find the best solution? To what extent were errors and miscalculations—and also what we today perceive as such—a result and a reflection of the time, and to what extent were they justified (or not justified) by the real possibilities open at the time in question?

From this point of view, we are confronted not only with the need for new evaluations, but primarily with a transition to a qualitatively new level of historical thought in the profession and among the masses, not only sheltered from the "winds of circumstance" by favorable external conditions for the field's development, but methodologically protected against them.

What situation has now developed in the historiography of the CPSU and Soviet society, if we are to evaluate it in a more general way? The culmination of that stage in the development of historical science that began in the late 1950s and early 1960s with the formulation of a whole series of new problems, continued during the heated discussions of the 1960s (during a general decline in creative thought, and growing ostentation and glorification), and ended with the preparation of a whole series of works of synthesis—this culmination is now at hand.

Some of these works have already been published, others are being prepared for press, and work on a third group is now at its peak. At one time, it was precisely the prospect of the appearance of these fundamental generalizing works that provided the program and the subject matter for numerous local studies. These works themselves with all their achievements and deficiencies, of course, determined the level of subsequent generalizations.

It is hard to imagine that during the coming decades, Soviet historical science will be concerned only with filling in the factual lacunae that have turned up in the course of developing these works of synthesis. As applied to our field, this would be a truly extensive path of development—perhaps tranquil, but not very efficient. It's also hard to imagine something else—that after twenty or thirty years, works of generalization on the history of the party and of Soviet society as a whole, the working class, the peasantry, and culture, will simply repeat the model and approaches developed for today's multivolume works, and that, to use philosophers' terms, we will reach a methodological ceiling in the "holistic perception" of the development of society.

Thus, the new stage in society's development objectively corresponds to a new stage in studying its history. It seems to me that the greatest successes in this new period will be connected with strengthening individual work in the field of history. Team-written works with their inevitable accompaniment—the depersonalization of research, the gathering of sometimes dozens of scholars under one roof—are useful for summing up, and for reporting on what has been achieved. But when there is a demand for renewing the cognitive structures of historical knowledge, success calls for small working groups made up of like-minded people, and for single creative individuals. The monograph becomes the prevailing form of research.

In the historiography of the CPSU and the USSR, we are faced today with what is called in the philosophy of science "a problematic situation": the well-plowed field of traditional themes and problems is being depleted, and our gaze is increasingly turning to historiographic virgin land; old approaches are being exhausted, and new ones are created with great difficulty. Researchers inevitably are faced with the acute questions that arise in such situations: what needs to be done and how should it be done? Are we to continue, so to speak, the extensive accumulation of factual data to illustrate conclusions already known, or are we—continuing the analogy—to take the intensive route and ask ourselves questions that don't yet have clear and final answers?

Traditional historical generalizations were often constructed according to the following model: the investigator set forth (or sometimes merely paraphrased) the content of some important political decisions, and then showed, on the basis of documentary evidence, what the CPSU and Soviet state had done to put them into practice (at the beginning of the period the prerequisites were developed and the tasks set; and at the end of the period the tasks were essentially solved). Under this approach, which until recently satisfied many historians, the development of

Soviet society took on the appearance of progress toward some "noncontradictory essence." The contradiction in the development of socialist society is that the "mainspring," the source of "self-propulsion," manifested itself, as it were, in the "interstices" between periods. The question as to how the tasks themselves are formulated as a result of debates and sharp differences of opinion, a question that reflected real contradictions, and of how they are solved, giving rise not only to "forward movement," but to new contradictions—all this, if it did not fall outside the limits of historical research, was at least simplified. What could this kind of history teach us? Primarily, efficiency—the fact that if tasks were posed, they certainly had to be solved. But the art of thinking independently, the dialectic, the understanding of the laws of society's historical movement and one's own place in this movement—these things cannot be learned this way.

Methodological miscalculations in treating the history of the party and Soviet society (and these are specially noticeable in the instructional literature) have led to serious educational losses. This is most plainly visible in the mosaic picture the 1930s represent in the consciousness of the contemporary person: the striking enthusiasm of the first five-year plans, and the crude violations of Soviet legality; the growth of a feeling of personal dignity in millions of people, and the personality cult; the fierce resistance to an actual, active class enemy, and the "enemies of the people," whose ranks included many honest and devoted communists and nonparty people. All of this did in fact happen. All of it must be known and remembered. But equally far from the truth are attempts to judge the 1930s by current laws, abstracting from the sharpness of the class struggle in the transitional period and from the peculiarities of the building of socialism in one country, as well as the complete justification of all errors, distortions, and violations of legality by the "severity of the time."

Errors do not eradicate successes, but neither do successes justify errors—this truth is obvious enough. However, there is a paradox in that the "white" and "black" parts of the general picture of the 1930s seem to exist independently of each other, and that one part of this picture is formed under the influence of scholarly and popular historical research, and the other is based on information taken from other sources, not "digested" by professional history. As a result, in ordinary, everyday debates about the distant and difficult times before the war, an oversimplified, metaphysical logic often prevails—the wholesale justification or condemnation of the past. In the everyday, "working" model of the 1930s, which the present-day person uses, the "positive" or "negative" prevails, but the dialectic is usually absent. As a result, the perception of the epoch as a whole is destroyed.

This phenomenon is very complicated to explain. Let me state only one preliminary consideration. In the late 1950s and early 1960s, during an open and public discussion of the problem, references to "the personality cult" frequently figured in historical scholarship as a universal explanation for all the problems and difficulties of the prewar period. In this process, the concept itself was treated very broadly. The beginning of a "deeper approach" to the problem was scaled back to practically nothing at the end of the 1960s. The theme of the personality cult was essentially removed from analysis of the prewar five-year plans into a kind of "reservation"—one or two pages in textbooks and works of synthesis, devoted to a paraphrase of the well-known resolution of the CPSU Central Committee. This was frequently justified by the claim that enough had already been said about this question. The vacuum thus formed began to be quickly filled by an "oral tradition," and by everyday and far from scholarly explanations. In the study and description of the dramatic prewar period of Soviet history, our discipline must "restore its reputation," and must do so on a modern methodological level, avoiding one-sided evaluations and judgments.

Unfortunately, I can't find in contemporary historiography any convincing examples that treat the theme. However, it seems to me that we have an instructive example in *belles lettres*: Aleksandr Bek's novel, *A New Assignment* [Novoe naznachenie],* gives an objective image of a communist executive of the late 1930s and 1940s—a "soldier of the party," a "fighter for the fulfillment of directives." As the writer correctly maintains, there had not yet been in history people like Aleksandr Leont'evich Onisimov: "The epoch had given them its stamp, and grafted onto them the primary valor of the soldier: to execute orders! The rule of the rank-and-file warrior—it's an order: no ifs, ands, or buts—became their motto, their 'credo.' "[19] Onisimov hates the flourishes of the feudal lord; he can't stand relaxing at home in the evenings; he knows only one thing—work. On the other hand, he is accustomed to "keeping the staff on its toes," being guided by the authoritarian rule of "to trust is to perish." He is intolerant of opinion "from below" and of "independent action" by subordinates. Onisimov, in Bek's words, "didn't think about the epoch's paradoxes and contradictions. As a communist he simply avoided questions that might have disturbed him, his reason and his conscience: it isn't my business, it has nothing to do with me, it isn't for me to judge. His beloved brother died in prison, and in his heart he mourned Vania, but even then he was firm in his 'Don't judge!' "[20]

These people are "inscribed" into their time; they reflect in their spiritual world its contradictions, difficulties, and mistakes. It is very simple to pass verdicts of conviction or acquittal on them. After all, it was given to Onisimov and his comrades and colleagues to live in their severe, difficult, and heroic time, while we are given only the safe and speculative knowledge of it. Executives of Onisimov's type were rigidly "attached" to their epoch: their style of work was intended for solving a narrow range of tasks under the extreme conditions of building socialism in one country. Beyond these narrow limits their leadership methods were corrupted into bureaucratism, high-handed administration, and the suppression of initiative from below.

Historians, in my view, have yet to do what Bek did through fiction. It is true

---

*Published in 1987 by Knizhnaia palata in Moscow.—D.J.R.

that at one time historians had almost done this—for example, in preparing Volume 9 of the *History of the USSR from Ancient Times to Our Day* [Istoriia SSSR s drevneishikh vremen do nashikh dnei] (the publication's original manuscript has survived). And right now one can hear talk among historians about the need for special studies on the history of the personality cult. This point of view certainly has a right to exist. But still, in my view, the perspective on prewar and postwar history proposed by some historians is fraught with the danger of serious distortions. Under this approach, we take the risk of transforming the epoch of the building of socialism, and of the heroism, achievements, and struggle of the Soviet people into "the epoch of the personality cult." This would be both unjust and historically illiterate. On the other hand, there is today a need in society to create genuinely scholarly political biographies of I. V. Stalin and other leaders, particularly of N. S. Khrushchev.

The drawbacks in treating controversial problems in party history are directly connected with the fact that the concrete historical contradictions of socialist society have to a considerable degree dropped out of the sphere of historical analysis. As a result, historical thought has frequently focused primarily on the "visible" changes that took place, and has frequently fallen into description and unoriginal commentary, getting stuck on the showing of the "external aspect" of the process, and, as it were, abstracting from its deeper foundations. The latter, in this case, become the prerogative of philosophers and sociologists, who, according to a widespread opinion, are supposed to "generalize" the facts piled up by historical science. The unified process of rising from the abstract to the concrete has been divided, as it were, by departmental barriers, and the place of theoretical concreteness has unjustifiably been taken by empirical concreteness. This, I think, is the main internal cause of the surprising openness of historical science to the "arbitrariness of circumstance," for which we are so often and justly reproached of late.

The inadequate historical underpinning of the theoretical concepts regarding the complex dialectics of the development of Soviet society is due in no small degree to the establishment in the public consciousness of a frozen "model" of socialism, and to the spread of harmful illusions: it is supposedly sufficient to make a "good decision" in order to solve all problems once and for all. In essence, these illusions are an obligatory attribute of an obsolete type of thought on which quite a few just and sharp words have been said in party decisions recently. This old type of thought was evident, in particular, as an effort to search for "immediate curative decisions," and confidence in their high efficacy. With the end of the transitional period, however, the practice of "one-time" actions, directed toward solving the problem of "who will dominate" [*kto kogo*] and toward liquidating one of the contending extremes, yielded to decisions of a fundamentally different type. The nonantagonistic contradictions of socialist society presuppose, not the destruction of one of the extremes, but their conscious unification.[21] The need to foresee only the immediate, "final" result of one's actions retreats in the face of the need to foresee a new form of contradiction, and, on this basis, to "unite" the opposites—that is, to use them for further development.

The main problem, of course, is not to declare this rather obvious principle, but to translate the general theoretical statements into the language of concrete history. Historians are called upon, in this connection, not to supply new facts in and of themselves, but to supply thoughts and ideas—not paraphrases, but thinking. Factual material is the foundation of any historical research, but only the foundation, the groundwork, on which the building of historical generalizations is constructed. Too often we knew in advance the ultimate result of our research (research, and not popularizing work), and had only to choose the facts to fit this conclusion. Perhaps we confirmed in this way truths already known, but we could not discover new ones.

The direction in historical science that can conditionally be called the analysis of alternative situations opens up, it would seem, great opportunities and prospects for significantly deepening historical analysis.[22] The question is too serious to be touched upon in passing here. Let me say only that in my view, historical research conducted along these lines is capable of taking on qualitatively new features and changing its traditional forms fundamentally, which are to a large degree already falling behind the demands of our contemporaries. The concentration of exposition around the critical points of development of society, the consideration of history from the standpoint of the dialectics of what was possible and what actually happened, the theoretical and concrete historical validations of the invariance of the historical process, opening up the potential possibilities of past reality, and, in the final analysis, the possibilities of the present day: all this is capable of bringing historical knowledge to a new level of argumentation and persuasiveness, of increasing the contributions of historians to working out the methodological foundations and practices of scientific management of society. What we are talking about in this instance is not the fantasy of the "what if" principle, which is so characteristic at times of ordinary speculations, but the uncovering, on the basis of concrete history, of the actual dialectics of objective conditions and the subjective factor at the turning points in society's development.

The search for approaches to "alternative situations" is not the only methodological prospect. In the latest monograph by I. I. Mints, *The Year 1918* [God 1918-i], we are dealing with a promising set of methodological developments, directed not only to validating a model of consecutive exposition of events, but to working out means of subordinating this exposition to one or more basic contradictions of the period under study, "controversies of the moment" [gvozdy momenta], and giving, on this basis, a unified picture of it rather than a mosaic. Generally speaking, the main direction of these methodological developments, it seems to me, is being displaced today toward these same "interstices" between periods, where, according to the traditional formula used in generalizing works on the history of Soviet society, the contradictions were "hidden," to use a metaphor. At the same time there is a sharp increase in the importance of psychohistorical research and the analysis of history's "human dimension," and of the historical regularities of coordinating purposeful human activity under conditions of building and perfecting socialism.

On this basis not only historical research but also the teaching of history is capable of being transformed into a fascinating search for truth. I imagine "methodological games" before student audiences, in which the study, for example, of the position of the right deviation or the "left communists" in the period of the Brest-Litovsk Peace will involve not learning ready-made formulas and evaluations, but critical analysis of a proposed alternative route. I am convinced that such a study of the history of the party and Soviet society will give a young person such striking political lessons, and will teach up-to-date and independent thinking in such a way that this study will become one of the most popular school subjects. This will be truly living history, capable of persuading and not merely instructing, and inculcating one of the chief qualities needed by our contemporaries—the ability not to take a word on faith, or to speak a word against the truth.

Measuring the future by himself, and reflecting on the present, modern man is looking ever more frequently into the mirror of the past. The historian's task is not to polish this mirror until it shines, or to blow past "layers of dirt" from it: the main thing is to make certain that the mirror is not clouded or crooked.

Notes

1. Iu. Afanas'ev, "Energiia istoricheskogo znaniia," *Moskovskie novosti*, January 11, 1987, pp. 8–9; idem, "S pozitsii pravdy i realizma," *Sovetskaia kul'tura*, March 21, 1987; I. Mints, "Oruzhie ne menee ostroe," *Ogonek*, 1987, no. 1; A. Samsonov, "Znat' i pomnit'," *Argumenty i fakty*, 1987, no. 10, pp. 1–2; and others.

2. The author of the letter is referring to the text of a paper given by Professor Iu. N. Afanas'ev at the Moscow State Institute of Historian-Archivists.—Editors, *Voprosy istorii KPSS*.

3. I. W. Gete [J. W. Goethe], *Izbrannye sochineniia po estestvoznaniiu* (Moscow, 1957), p. 393.

4. See V. I. Lenin, *Polnoe sobranie sochinenii* [*PSS*], vol. 45, p. 346.

5. *Pravda*, January 26, 1987.

6. *Kommunist*, 1986, no. 15, p. 5.

7. See *Chetvertyi s"ezd pisatelei SSSR, 22–27 maia 1967 goda: Stenograficheskii otchet* (Moscow, 1968), p. 160.

8. E. V. Il'enkov, *Dialekticheskaia logika: Ocherki istorii i teorii*. 2nd expanded ed. (Moscow, 1984), pp. 256–57.

9. There is, it is true, another diametrically opposed but equally mistaken tendency which was pointed out by I. P. Prusanov. See *Voprosy istorii KPSS*, 1987, no. 2, p. 78.

10. L. Voskresenskii, "Na puti k sotsialisticheskomu rynku," *Moskovskie novosti*, November 30, 1986, p. 12.

11. H. G. Wells, *Russia in the Shadows* (London, n.d.), pp. 18–19.

12. A. G. Zverev, *Zapiski ministra* (Moscow, 1973), p. 95.

13. *Piatnadtsatyi s"ezd VKP(b). Dekabr' 1927 goda: Stenograficheskii otchet*. In 2

vols. (Moscow, 1962), vol. 2, p. 1094.

14. A. S. Tsipko, *Nekotorye filosofskie aspekty teorii sotsializma* (Moscow, 1983), pp. 200–201.

15. Cited in T. Gaidar, "Golikov Arkadii iz Arzamasa," *Novyi mir*, 1986, no. 7, p. 151.

16. *KPSS v rezoliutsiiakh i resheniiakh s"ezdov, konferentsii i plenumov TsK*. 9th ed. revised and expanded (Moscow, 1983), vol. 2, p. 327.

17. Lenin, *PSS*, vol. 45, p. 44.

18. See Z. K. Zvezdin and S. V. Kul'chitskii, "Problema industrializatsii v sisteme ekonomicheskoi politiki perekhodnogo perioda," in *Ekonomicheskaia politika Sovetskogo gosudarstva v perekhodnyi period ot kapitalizma k sotsializmu* (Moscow, 1986), p. 88.

19. *Znamia*, 1986, no. 10, p. 42.

20. Ibid., p. 29.

21. See Lenin, *PSS*, vol. 42, p. 211.

22. See, for example, P. V. Volobuev, "O probleme vybora putei obshchestvennogo razvitiia," *Voprosy filosofii*, 1984, nos. 1, 2; I. D. Koval'chenko, "Vozmozhnoe i deistvitel'noe i problemy al'ternativnosti v istoricheskom razvitii," *Istoriia SSSR*, 1986, no. 4.

Part Two

THE DEVELOPMENT OF
SOVIET SOCIETY, PARTY HISTORY,
AND THE SOVIET MEMORY HOLE

Ever since the 1930s, official histories of Soviet society presented grossly distorted views of reality. Chronicling one dubious success after another, in dull,
lifeless, formulaic language, these monochromatic accounts falsified party history, vilified so-called enemies of the people, and silently passed over any assessment of the roles of many major figures. By 1986, however, public affairs writers
as well as maverick historians such as Afanas'ev had blown the whistle on this
situation. Things began to change not only because tremendous unrest and dissatisfaction had accumulated within the profession itself, but also because the party
leadership had called for a prompt turnabout.

In the wake of a reassuring message by Gorbachev to the June 1987 Plenum of
the Central Committee that ''each generation has made its contribution to the . . .
conquests of [the] October [Revolution],'' the official party journal, *Kommunist*
(The Communist), sponsored a roundtable on ''Basic Changes in the Development of Soviet Society,'' which was published at the very end of 1987. Although
historians differed in their sense of how to introduce correctives into the discipline, as many influential historians had been compromised during the preceding
era, by 1987 they were beginning to respond seriously to the controversial themes
being raised in the periodical press and by publicists. The editors of *Kommunist*
brought together an impressive group of influential historians of Soviet society:
M. P. Kim, a senior member of the profession; A. M. Samsonov, who earlier in
the year had published a spirited attack on Stalin; Iu. A. Poliakov, chair of the
Academy of Science's Council for Historical Ethnography and Geography; V. Z.
Drobizhev, a well-respected historian from Afanas'ev's institute; and V. A. Kozlov, the party historian whose thoughtful essay on the historian and perestroika
appears in Part One of this anthology. It is not surprising that one of the first
questions the roundtable addresses concerns the periodization of Soviet history.
This issue divided the participants, with Kozlov in particular raising the most
searching and intelligent objections to traditional approaches to the matter.

The fact that the exchange was published in the official party journal did not go unnoticed by Soviet readers, and must be viewed as a positive development. The reassessment of the periodization of Soviet history opened up questions regarding the Stalinist 1930s, and led to attacks against "dogmatism," a catchall for the deplorable practices of the past. In reading the discussion, it is clear that the reform-minded speakers were as concerned with improving the moral climate by removing obstacles to the honest writing of history as they were with reassessing the past. All in all, publication of this roundtable encouraged the reformers. As Iu. A. Poliakov appropriately predicted, "On the whole, the major debates in the historical discipline are still to come. . . ."

It is equally noteworthy that the heretofore tedious and soporific publication of the Institute of Marxism-Leninism, the journal *Voprosy istorii KPSS* (Problems of the History of the CPSU), had been transformed by the summer of 1987 into a forum for *perestroika*. In the fall, the Academic Council of the Institute of Marxism-Leninism convened to review the publication's future. The summary of this meeting is published here ("The Role of the Journal *Voprosy istorii KPSS* in Restructuring Party History").

"Perhaps not since Lenin's time have there been such favorable conditions for the objective treatment of the history and current policy of the CPSU and for genuine scholarly creativity. . . ." With this introduction the discussion turns to the obvious: true restructuring of the historical discipline cannot come about unless the history of the party is rewritten objectively. Addressing issues that had been raised elsewhere by the profession, the discussion appeals for an end to dogmatism; for creating a respectful attitude toward debate (and more of it); for opening up archives long closed to investigators; for meeting the people's demand for unadorned, objective examinations of the past; for further democratization; and for an ambitious publication program that would put documents heretofore considered sensitive into circulation.

The final selection in this section is a summary of the proceedings of a meeting of research associates from institutes of higher learning affiliated with the party. The role of the individual in history is the question under investigation, both the outrageous disappearance of some individuals into the Soviet memory hole, and the gross exaggeration of the role of the Soviet Union's various leaders. Here the linchpin is the history profession's assessments of Stalin and his legacy in transmogrifying the historical discipline into a branch of the official propaganda organs. The participants admit that sterile and falsified official histories have alienated the population, particularly young people, have prevented the development of historical consciousness, and have hindered people's ability to think historically. All in all, such reasoning by the most politicized element of the Soviet historical profession augured a better future for the discipline in general.

Basic Stages of the Development of Soviet Society

A Roundtable of the Journal "Kommunist"

As we approach the seventieth anniversary of our socialist history, we look more and more frequently and persistently back over the path that our country has traversed, striving to penetrate the essence of events that no longer reverberate, and to evaluate accurately and truthfully both our achievements and our mistakes. "Each generation has made its contribution to the development, strengthening, and defense of the conquests of October," M. S. Gorbachev noted at the June (1987) Plenum of the Central Committee of the CPSU. "We are justly proud of our history, and look with confidence to the future."

The history of the socialist fatherland is an inexhaustible "problem area" for research. A great deal has been accomplished here. However, quite a few questions have accumulated concerning our historiography, and there are still "blank spots" and undeservedly forgotten events and names. Historical science is gradually abandoning dispassionate "descriptivism" and the repetition of old models and stereotypes. An urgent need has arisen to interpret historical experience more profoundly, and to enrich with it our current social practice. There is much talk about this right now, and scholars—by no means historians alone— are debating and advancing the most varied judgments. It is precisely these circumstances that prompted the editorial board to invite scholars specializing in Soviet history to exchange opinions at a "roundtable" and to answer specific questions. The participants in the discussion are I. I. Mints, M. P. Kim, and A. M. Samsonov, full members of the USSR Academy of Sciences; Iu. A. Poliakov, corresponding member of the USSR Academy of Sciences; Doctor of Historical Sciences V. Z. Drobizhev; and Candidate of Historical Sciences V. A. Kozlov.

S. Kolesnikov and S. Khizhniakov of the editorial staff of Kommunist *prepared the materials of the roundtable.*

Russian text © 1987 by "Pravda" Publishers. "Osnovnye etapy razvitiia sovetskogo obshchestva. 'Kruglyi stol' zhurnala 'Kommunist,'" *Kommunist*, 1987, no. 12, pp. 66– 79. Translated by Stephen P. Dunn.

The October Revolution and restructuring

We speak today of the close relationship between the October Revolution of 1917 and the present—a time of restructuring and revolutionary renewal. What are the similarities between these periods and historical situations, and what are their differences and peculiarities? In emphasizing the revolutionary changes taking place in society, we must consider the processes from the point of view of historicism and the correct interpretation of historical experience. V. I. Lenin felt it necessary to distinguish, in the lessons of the past, "two heritages"—what we take with us into tomorrow, and what we reject. How is this problem solved with reference to the last few decades of our socialist history?

I. I. Mints: When I read the appeal of the CPSU Central Committee to the Soviet people, I was involuntarily reminded of Lenin's appeal "To the citizens of Russia!" on October 25, 1917. Seventy years have passed, so what's the connection? I think it's extremely close. Vladimir Il'ich was then announcing the transition to the building of socialism, and naming approximate stages of development. The current appeal by the Central Committee clearly relates to restoring and perfecting socialism precisely as Lenin saw it, and Leninist principles for its development. I see here similarity by way of continuity. We are continuing—and this also is clearly stated in the appeal of the Central Committee—the October Revolution in what we do today.

Of course, there is also a serious difference in the situation, since seventy years have passed. The difference is mainly that in October 1917 we took power—that is, power passed into the hands of a new class—and this is the major sign of revolution. In our time it is not a matter of power, but of the methods, the form, the approaches to solving the many tasks before society in as revolutionary a manner.

The Central Committee appeal states with pride that we are not renouncing what has been achieved in seven decades. This remains inviolable. We are not destroying, but restructuring. For that reason we draw from the past everything that improves and accelerates our work and moves us forward. We renounce the negative features that have accumulated, the incorrect ideas that have developed, the subjective evaluations, defects, and errors—in short, everything that hinders the strengthening of socialist society. And we retain the basic element in the construction and development of socialism—namely, our progressive movement.

Iu. A. Poliakov: In comparing 1917 with 1987, we must not make formal analogies. These are always relative. After all, we have other tasks, the epoch is completely different, and the forms and methods of mass action are also different. The continuity is really the main thing—the continuation of the conquests of the revolution, and the implementation of the revolutionary goals of October. I would say this: in 1917, we had to embark upon socialist transformations through armed struggle. We continued further along an untried path. The difficulties are obvious. We lived through a great deal, but the pace slowed, and very serious interruptions took place. Now we have again moved forward and are gaining momentum. One can look at 1917 and 1987 and compare the scale of the goals and the problems. The most important consideration here is the activity of the masses. The victory of October would have been impossible without drastic, unselfish action by workers, soldiers, and peasants. The success of the restructuring is impossible without the most active participation of the workers, the intelligentsia, and the peasantry. In the October Revolution, the basic task was, as Lenin emphasized, that of raising "the lowest depths of the people to historical creativity." And now the main issue is to activate the human factor.

V. A. Kozlov: The present requires a somewhat different view even toward the October Revolution, which seems like ancient history. What do I mean? A revolutionary leap always has its own unique and fundamental features. It has its psychological side. During revolutionary change utopian thought, an orientation toward direct action, and so forth, become more active. This was the case after the October Revolution and we see this to some degree in mass consciousness today. How does this happen and why? Can historians answer this question? No, we can only ask it.

Lenin spoke of the difficulties of the transition from the period of "mass rallies" to normal everyday work. Why is this always so difficult? Why was restructuring on the psychological level after the April Plenum successful, so that in general we achieved a moral and psychological upturn? And why is it now proceeding with such difficulty in practice? This could also be shown in sociological terms from the example of the October Revolution. But has it? No!

Further, the most acute problem is the psychological exaggeration that frequently accompanies revolutionary action. Do we know anything about this kind of psychology, other than in a most general way, other than quotations from the works of Lenin, who warned about this danger? We don't know the sociopsychological and sociological laws involved in such phenomena.

We know Engels's position: a revolution is the most authoritarian thing on earth. What does this mean when applied to our own revolution, our own restructuring? Where does the problem of authority end, and the problem of, let us say, "leadership" [vozhdizm] in the transitional period begin? What does the problem of authority mean in regard to today's restructuring? This question, I think, concerns leaders of collectives on all levels.

I'd like to say something about another problem in connection with the experience of the revolution and its significance for our own day. As early as the first years after the October Revolution, there were a whole series of interesting organizational and economic discoveries, whose significance we underestimate to this day. Take, for example, [Iurii] Larin's well-known plan for supplying workers through the collective, introduced experimentally in 1921. Afterward, all this was stopped for some reason, although it seemed to work. If the plan for supplying workers through the collective were transferred to a monetary form of payment (the payments at that time were in kind) it would essentially be the first form of collective contract for work, with rations given not in accord with the number of workers, but with the final result, with the fulfilling of production norms. The idea began to be implemented simultaneously with the introduction of NEP, and . . . didn't go any further. The question is: why didn't it?

There is an opinion that during the first years of Soviet power, full cost-accounting [*khozraschet*] prevailed in state industry. Speaking honestly, we haven't studied this problem very much. Based on my personal assessment of the literature, I would argue there was what we might call "trust cost-accounting," and this meant that it didn't apply to each specific enterprise, let alone to each workplace.

In evaluating NEP, we take only part of what Lenin said about the fact that it was built not directly out of enthusiasm, but on economic calculation and personal interest. What does enthusiasm mean as an element in the management of the economy under NEP? Neither historians nor economists know the answer to this question.

M. P. Kim: The direct link between October and the present is not that the current situation is analogous to the one that existed during the October Revolution: there can't be any comparison of the situation or the reality. What is at issue is the spirit of the October Revolution—Lenin's understanding of the tasks and ideas of October, and the spirit of creativity—which finds an echo in our approach to today's problems, the problems of radical restructuring. In spirit, this is a revolutionary and creative restructuring. Here we have a direct continuation of what went on during the October Revolution, and in the period just after it, when Lenin was participating directly in the life of our party. That stage was the most fruitful, the most creative. After Lenin, the creative development of Marxism-Leninism and of our party actually experienced a decline. This took place because Leninism was understood in a rather peculiar way and much of what Lenin suggested or established was forgotten and somehow buried in oblivion, distorted, violated, or retreated from. This is why today we need to restore Lenin's creative spirit in full measure in our thought and historical research.

If we are to speak of what must be abandoned and what must be continued, then certainly we must continue everything that has been achieved by the creativity of the popular masses under party leadership, and free ourselves from negative phenomena in our life.

I think reinterpretation of the past is an entirely natural phenomenon for historical science, since it cannot help returning to the evaluation of past facts in the course of time. This is true, in the first place, because life itself reveals new consequences of what has been, and in the second place, because our knowledge of society, regrettably, is in many respects axiomatic. In my view, our discussion on this level as historians is significant insofar as we must today develop more actively, and say something new in our field.

Let me emphasize once again that we must free ourselves from all later developments that distorted Leninism, and continue further discussion of what is characteristic of Leninism as a living and creative doctrine.

Question: And what specifically would you consider as distortions?

M. P. Kim: In general, there are quite a few things to be included here. Lenin thought that history must be studied objectively, and must take into account the fact that our country was the first to establish socialism. Take, for example, the problem of the relationship between that which is common to mankind and that which is peculiar to a class, or the problem of contrasting capitalism with socialism. Up to now we have understood this question in an oversimplified way. Lenin, after all, emphasized the common bond between that which is common to all humanity and that which is peculiar to socialism: socialism must adopt and continue what is common to all humanity after freeing it from everything conditioned by class exploitation and class antagonisms. The somewhat abstract contrasting of socialism with that which is common to all humanity, however, has led to our weakening the position of socialism in the competition for world civilization and in relation to what was valuable in all of human development.

When we turned to revolution we rejected capitalism: our task was one of destruction. And when we won, it was necessary to decide what weapons we would take from capitalism, and how what was of value in it for human civilization was to be determined, adopted, and expanded. Lenin, for example, said that the Taylor system should be utilized for developing the productive forces in our society. But we had an obvious contempt for bourgeois technology and science! Precisely this kind of abstract contrasting of socialism with capitalism weakened our position and led us to underestimate the historical potential that the working class and socialism could have had, given a correct, critical adoption of all those valuable elements that capitalism had and still has.

Lenin taught that history should be studied objectively—without making it either better or worse than it was. And we repeated this, as everyone knows. But it is one thing to repeat, and quite another to act. In reality, we retreated from Leninist norms in history, and took a selective approach to events and facts. That is, there were facts that were necessary to study, set forth, and praise, and facts that didn't reflect the triumphal march of success, which were forgotten and avoided. The selective approach to research is one of the most serious defects in our historical studies. This is why some problems remain entirely neglected and incorrectly evaluated.

Take the problem of the noncapitalist path of development of various peoples of our country! We depicted this process in a kind of romantic light, only as a great achievement of revolution, as a "plus" in the revolutionary process. This was a complex question, however, which complicated our development in some ways, and sometimes bred serious confrontations and contradictions in our social relations, primarily in relations among nationalities. It's now often said that in Central Asia and in certain other republics our policies are eradicating the consequences of tribalism such as the practice whereby personnel are promoted according to tribal relations, or of nepotism, where this happens according to family, geographic, or other ties. Did tribalism develop among us only in the 1970s? Didn't tribal and kinship relations influence the placement and promotion of personnel, and their use, long before then? We avoided these questions, didn't speak of them, and thought that this was connected with certain peculiarities of national cultures and ways of life and were inclined to think that these were problems of the bourgeois-democratic revolution and not the socialist one. The character of a revolution, however, is determined not by what is rejected but by what society is transformed into. And if prebourgeois relations are transformed by us into socialist relations, then this is part of the problem of the socialist, and not of the bourgeois-democratic revolution. Inattention to this led to serious omissions in our historical research.

In general, we've depicted history in a somewhat schematic and oversimplified way, and therefore the consequences are rather serious. The history of collectivization is an example of this. That an accelerated timetable was required for collectivization can still be explained by external danger, the danger of approaching war. But within the limits of this general accelerated timetable, collectivization could have been conducted less painfully with full observance of Leninist norms and principles for uniting peasants into large collective farms— with observance of the principle of voluntarism, and with due organizational preparation. There were very few people like Sholokhov's Davydov,* and we didn't train people who could have led large collective farms right away. The necessary material and technical base was also not created. And psychologically we didn't prepare the peasants adequately for this. Thus, the history of collectivization must likewise be seriously studied.

V. Z. Drobizhev: What heritage are we renouncing? A lot of things have already been discussed under this heading. I think that we must also renounce such an unpleasant heritage as the "figure of silence." We are accustomed to keeping silent on what took place in the past. It seems to me that the "figure of silence" is characteristic of us even today. This position developed during the repression under the personality cult: it crossed someone out from the register of the living, and also from active history. But what are our practices today? We are living as though N. S. Khrushchev and L. I. Brezhnev had not headed the Central Committee of the party for a number of years. We must not take this attitude

---

*Davydov is the hero of Mikhail Sholokhov's novel of collectivization, *Virgin Soil Upturned*, who is said to be based on an activist in Rostov. See Lynne Viola, *The Best Sons of the Fatherland* (New York: Oxford University Press, 1987), p. 4.—William B. Husband.

toward our own past. We must not transform our history into an uninterrupted chain of errors and crimes. If one reads certain journalistic works, one will involuntarily ask how the country could have been transformed from a backward one into an advanced one. After all, this is the seventieth year of the heroic history of our people.

I think that the activity of, let us say, N. S. Khrushchev must not be approached only with negative evaluations. We have become accustomed to painting everything either black or white. Life is more textured and colorful. Take the reforms of the 1960s. We know of the discussions that began in *Pravda* in 1961. What was thought up was very interesting. Why didn't it amount to anything? If one judges and paints only with black, then, in my opinion, we will never restore history and raise its prestige.

It seems to me that the main condition for developing our field is in abandoning the ''figure of silence,'' and in progressing to a comprehensive analysis of the facts instead of vacillating back and forth.

On the stages of socialist history

Looking at the seventy-year path traversed by the country of the Soviets and separating oneself from the starting point of its history in October 1917, one sees more clearly and in bolder relief the stages by which society ascended the path of social progress and the coming into being of a communist social order. Our knowledge of this process is constantly growing more precise. How precisely is the generally accepted model of the basic stages of development of socialism in the USSR correlated with the reality of historical facts, the interpretation of which is now emerging onto a new and higher level? The party is calling on us to remove from the post-October history of the country and the history of the party the "blank spots" and the unjustified silences. What is the opinion of historians on the "lacunae" in our historiography and on the problems that have been neglected or only partially studied?

M. P. Kim: In this connection I would like to say that we have to create a scholarly periodization of Soviet history. This is certainly not the most important question facing the science of history, but there is no scientific history without a scientific periodization. The periodization that has existed up until now is completely unscientific. Unfortunately, it was widespread, since it was given in the textbook on party history, which at first played a positive role but recently, particularly in the chapters dealing with contemporary history, ceased to correspond to the facts. Take the periodization offered in the 1985 edition of it. You will see that the transitional period ends—and the phase of completing the building of socialist society and the gradual transition to communism begins. But if you will forgive me, that phase even today lies in the future. The textbook is based on resolutions of the Eighteenth Party Congress. But, after all, this is in glaring contradiction with reality, with life, and on this basis we have already rejected the idea that the stage of building communism in fully developed form has begun, as the periodization of history from the end of the 1950s until the mid–1960s defined it. After this, according to the periodization accepted at that time, the history of fully developed socialism would begin at the start of the 1960s. This was also a case of running ahead of history.

I think that we must now formulate a new periodization. We have to begin by isolating the major turning points of the past seventy years. This is a rather long period for the history of our country—a history with a rich content, a rapid tempo, and eventful in terms of what we have experienced and have done. Then later, within these larger periods or epochs, we have to note individual phases.

I think that we should distinguish three major turning points in the seventy-year history of Soviet society in which socialism came into being and developed. In the first place, there was the transitional period between capitalism and socialism, in the course of which socialism came into being (or the creation of the foundations of socialism, or of building socialism in its fundamental features). Then comes the period of completing the building of socialism with the stage of its full and final victory emphasized. I begin this period with the Great Patriotic War and end it in 1985, because the new, third turning point is, beyond question, the present, the restructuring that lays the foundation for a major new epoch in the history of the further development of socialism and the gradual transition to communism.

Some people may object, asking why I extend the transitional period back to the beginning of the war. If we recognize the war as a turning point, the second point from which to calculate after the October Revolution, then everything that existed before the war must be classified as part of the preceding period of transition. We are convinced that the war is a second major turning point with which a new major period begins by the following: If the October Revolution was a struggle, a civil war of the working class and the peasantry against the landlords and the capitalists within the country for socialism, then here [during the Great Patriotic War] socialism that had already been built in reality entered into a struggle with imperialism, with its striking power. I think that to defend socialism when it was already built is just as important as to build socialism.

There is one more important external consideration: the second period of the periodization must be connected with the formation of a world system of socialism. For this reason, on the international level, and on the level of the history of the fate of world socialism and the development of our country, the war is certainly the beginning of a new phase (1945–65) [sic] which I would call the phase of the full and final victory of socialism.

As for the contemporary period, I think it is still difficult for us to evaluate its significance comprehensively. But life is already showing us what an important turning point in the history of our society we're dealing with.

Within the limits of these three major periods we can isolate a number of subperiods. These are the October Revolution itself and the Civil War, and in connection with the fact that in these years, a special economic policy—war communism—was implemented; this also has to be considered separately. Beyond this I distinguish the first, or beginning, stage of NEP (1921–27). I will encounter the objection that if we speak of a beginning phase, we also have to speak of subsequent ones. But the point is that NEP, as I am convinced, functioned in the spirit in which Lenin understood it only up to 1927. On the basis of economic relations, the interaction between the working class and the peasantry served as the basis for this policy, with capitalism and state capitalism being permitted, and then from 1928 on, when we embarked on the reconstruction of the economy and began the full-scale building of socialism and began an attack on the entire front, NEP was severely deformed. It ceased to exist in the framework and within the limits that Lenin had in mind. The method of economic interaction between the peasantry and the working class was replaced by a directive-administrative method, abolishing the economic levers that regulated this union. I distinguish 1928–41 as the state of full-scale construction of socialism, which completed the building of socialism in our country.

Question: You have defined the period 1921–27 as the first phase of NEP. The boundary between 1927 and 1928 itself seems precise enough. But, on the other hand, you have named as the basis for this the transition to the full-scale building of socialism—that is, an entirely objective process, the conditions for which were fully present. But can we, all the same, reduce the causes of a change in economic policy, which actually took place and began in 1928, solely to objectively conditioned causes, or was there some kind of subjectivist deviation here?

M. P. Kim: We have to bear in mind here not only the interrelationship between the peasantry and the working class, although this is the main question, but also other issues—the question of industrialization, and that of workers' wages. We have begun to speak of the fact that after 1928, in place of stimulation of the economy and the economic factor generally, extraeconomic factors were active, such as a virtual restoration of the food-requisitioning program of the period of war communism, and of exchanges in kind. However, there was no transfer of the basis in industry to an in-kind basis: the wage system was not abolished, and war communism, the food requisitioning program, and the transfer of pay to an in-kind basis, let us say, in connection with obligatory deliveries to the state by collective farms—are quite different things. Therefore, I think we shouldn't speak of a full return to the period of food requisitioning and war communism. NEP was played out, I believe, at the beginning of the '30s—in 1932–33, if we bear in mind Lenin's position to the effect that the function of NEP was the socialist transformation of the peasantry, and building of the foundation for a socialist economy.

I. I. Mints: How precisely does the generally accepted logical scheme correspond to the facts? I would answer this question from a different perspective. Namely, we have achieved enormous successes, we have no exploitation of man by man, no exploitation of one people by another, no unemployment, etc. We're offering the whole world an alternative, a way out of the impasse into which imperialism leads mankind. It seems to me this point of view should guide us in preparing new textbooks on history. At the Institute of the History of the USSR, we've begun such a discussion, but I'd like to emphasize that we first need to question our own reality, our own accomplishments. I would divide Soviet history into three major periods: the first, the victory of socialism in the USSR; the second, the transformation of socialism into a world system (the Great Patriotic War comes in here); and the third period in which we are living, as a continuation of the work begun by the October Revolution.

Now about "blank spots" in the history of our country: there are certainly a lot of them. We have to distinguish "blank spots" that have been formed due to the absence of data or interest in them, from "blank spots" formed when certain problems were consciously crossed out or omitted. The first, of course, can't be eradicated "at one sitting." Here we can think a bit about what we haven't yet dealt with, what we haven't talked about; this is a lengthy process. The second— those that were the result of a conscious effort by virtue of political events in our country, also have to be reviewed, but with extreme care. I would ask, for example, this question: our adversaries are now writing mainly about the history of the Soviet regime at the end of the 1930s, carefully avoiding the previous years. Exclusively about this! We must answer them, and show that the history of the Soviet regime doesn't begin in the 1930s, but in 1917. Then there's the question of names: it's true that we must restore names, but the mere mention of names doesn't mean that we're acquitting everyone. We are acquitting only those who are falsely accused. Can we ignore the harm that Trotsky did, and not only in the days of Brest, but afterward?

Iu. A. Poliakov: The question of eradicating "blank spots" is very complex. We have to be specific: "blank spots," as has been noted here, are of different kinds. There are closed areas, which are beyond study. That's one thing. The documents haven't been given to researchers. Take, let us say, the struggle with bureaucratism—this seems quite simple. But this is practically a closed subject, despite the great danger of bureaucratic distortions for the normal activity of the party and society. There are problems—and they can also be considered "blank spots"—which have been studied superficially and one-sidedly, and because of this have been transformed into "blank spots" and "lacunae" in science. And finally, there are problems that were considered axiomatic, but in fact call for review. They can be listed among the "blank spots."

V. Z. Drobizhev: I think that we have an unusual number of "blank spots." I could name several of them. First, the 1930s, which we practically don't study at all. Yet this was a phase in our country's history when not only the foundations of our achievements were laid, but also those of many subsequent negative tendencies and of what put out shoots later on. The 1930s have remained closed to our research. We are so accustomed to "storming" and "gales"; the second five-year plan had neither gale nor storm, and in the prewar years other problems arose. We have simply left the thirties out of our field of vision.

The second problem is that of the history of the theoretical thought of our party. In this connection, we have said that theory and its development were curtailed. I agree this is true. Nevertheless, there is a great deal that is interesting. But we have crossed V. M. Molotov and N. S. Khrushchev out of history; we didn't cross out S. M. Kirov, F. E. Dzerzhinskii, and N. A. Voznesenskii, but neither did we study them the way we should have, viewing their theoretical writings as if they were but a few statements. Who specifically took part in working out particular questions? How did the accumulation of theoretical knowledge take place? What was the mechanism for processing party decisions? All this is outside the framework of our historical research.

One of the very significant questions, it seems to me, is that of the social dynamics of Soviet society. We have thousands of works on the working class and on the peasantry, and a few on the intelligentsia; however, of the studies on the working class I cannot name even one that had a mass appeal. Unfortunately, the multivolume history of the Soviet working class that is being prepared by the Institute of History of the USSR is being published in a pitifully small edition and it isn't clear whom it's intended for. That is, it is neither a detailed monograph nor a generalized study that would have sociopolitical significance. But a huge sea of questions has accumulated. There's the question of who belongs to the working class. As previously, we understand the working class to be only the industrial workers—which isn't at all the way things are in the contemporary world. The question of the relationship between the working class and the peasantry is reduced in our studies to the problem of workers' patronage over the countryside. In comparison with this, perhaps, only the histories of the trade unions may be more boring. These books are painfully dull. This is an unusually acute problem that has today taken on new resonance. The working class's makeup has changed, and has absorbed millions of people from the countryside. Who has come out of the countryside? How has the countryside influenced the city? Shouldn't we look for the roots of the cult of personality in the petit-bourgeois element that swamped the city? After all, those who came to the city included not only working peasants but also peasants who were embittered by the mistakes that had been made during collectivization.

There is one other question I would like to raise: that of democracy and bureaucratisim. How has bureaucratism formed on the soil of Soviet democracy? An exceptionally interesting question. We are now studying the makeup of the soviets and of the deputies to congresses of local soviets. You know, there are some curious observations. In the 1920s, the turnover in the soviets was minimal.

In the 1930s it rises sharply. Outwardly, it's all very democratic: a third of the members of the congresses are replaced. At whose expense? At the expense of workers and peasants. The worker from the factory bench, the peasant from the plow. But the leaders of the congresses of soviets—the members of the Central Executive Committee, the people's commissars, the members of the governing boards of the people's commissariats—never change. Thus, a mechanism of separation of power and management is coming into being. This is a curious process.

A. M. Samsonov: I would like to draw attention to the general theme of our meeting: the basic stages in the development of Soviet society. My opinion is that questions of periodization play a subordinate role in the study of the historical process. They are very important questions, but in the final analysis they aren't the ones that determine the success or failure of research. Various versions of the periodization of the history from 1917 up to our own day have already been offered. I personally think that the periodization can be developed in three main periods. The first is the October Revolution and the Civil War, then the period of the building of socialism, and finally the Great Patriotic War and the postwar period. Each of them respectively can be divided into stages. There can be other variants. The problem is in how the history of the past is set forth in Soviet historiography, what defects and drawbacks there may be, and what prevents the successful development of the historical discipline.

We must also not forget about self-criticism. It hasn't yet been said here that our historical discipline, like, incidentally, the other social sciences, has been subjected to severe and quite justified criticism. History lags behind those problems that face society, and we feel this in our immediate work. We must speak of the defects. This is why right now, when restructuring—the revolutionary restructuring of society—is under way, I see the similarity of our own days with those of the October Revolution precisely in the revolutionary approach to solving the tasks that are placed before the people, for workers in both the sciences and the humanities. In particular, it is necessary to be bold and tell the truth, without being stopped by frozen forms and stereotypes.

The question arises here: what causes such a phenomenon as, for example, the ''Pamiat''''* society? Naturally, people, especially the young, have an immense need to understand what is happening now and also what has happened. It is only when a good cause falls into the hands of political extremists that we have trouble. We must satisfy the healthy demand of people to know and remember their history. We must speak at full volume and speak honestly, without being afraid of what people abroad, for example, may think of us, or that they may use something we say to criticize us. I therefore think that the most important problem

---

*''Memory,'' a conservative, anti-Semitic group that has seized glasnost' as an opportunity to publicize its views.—William B. Husband

facing us during restructuring is the problem of historical truth.

V. A. Kozlov: We must define some principles of periodization, within whose limits the further movement of the discipline can be carried out. All this is clear. There is another mood that is rather widespread among historians, however, which proposes that we create a commission to work out a periodization, and then set forth definite recommendations. This would make it easier for dogmatically minded historians to write such history. But what shall we do with those who want to write it creatively? Here's an example. A book has now been prepared on advisable activity for people under conditions of restructuring. In the process of working on it, certain critical periods of Soviet history were discovered that don't fit into any periodization and are not laid down in it in any way. And I'm afraid that among the historians some Procrustes who act in the manner natural to such people—namely, surgically—will say "It doesn't fit into the periodization" ["so let's cut if off."—Trans.]

For some reason, we've decided that all our problems boil down to coming up with new evaluations. We haven't once asked about the bases or the approaches on which these evaluation will be made. The traditional model of historical generalization—from the multivolume publication of the Academy down to the school textbook—has become catastrophically obsolete, and the cosmetic means of curing this doesn't lead anywhere. This model developed in the 1930s, when we had definite priorities for developing society (with industrialization in first place and the like). This determined the very organization of the material. Now we say that we must look for some new approach. In the pages of *Kommunist* people have justifiably written that these approaches must be centered on the human being. This means a search for some other way of organizing and setting forth the materials. Speaking figuratively, we've had the natural-science approach, and now we need an activity-oriented approach: that is, we need to show history through the purposeful activity of human beings and then, I'm deeply convinced, there'll be editions of our books amounting not to 2,000, but to 200,000, since there is nothing more interesting to a human being than another human being. And if a living human being appears in history with a personality, interests, hopes and concerns, prejudices and confusions, that history will be quite different. Our model, however, doesn't take account of any of this.

In particular, we are afraid to attack the problem of the transition to all-out collectivization because we don't know how to analyze the alternative situations and processes for working out political decisions. We historians take the political decision as some kind of given, and then speak, in a purely provincial spirit of how this was implemented. But the source of the decision is included in the working out of the decision, when the change is made. Thus, we lose that source of movement, it falls through the "cracks" between the periods, and in general the dialectic "doesn't work."

M. P. Kim: I want to answer V. A. Kozlov. I sensed in his remarks a certain nihilistic attitude toward periodization as such. It's as if he were saying that we should look at history as the activity of people without any special stages or periods whatever, since these will pin down the objective historical study of events. Here we may have a divergence between the general periodization of the entire history of society and the periodization of history in individual spheres. Each sphere, each direction, may have its own tempo, its own units of time. But this doesn't deny the fact that in general periodization still has to be given, bearing in mind the main and pivotal element in the process—the mode of production, the relationships among classes, etc. And there can certainly be deviations in individual spheres without affecting the main point.

V. A. Kozlov: Periodization is needed, but it must be the result of new research and not some kind of framework within which we place ourselves. There is a definite historical background on which the discussion of periodization lies— a background that can deform the ideas you have correctly presented. I fear this.

M. P. Kim: The various opinions on periodization are often explained by the fact that there is a tendency to make 1956 a turning point and the end of the transitional period, connecting this with the exposure of the cult of personality and the well-known resolution of the Central Committee. Of course, to a certain degree, this is permissible when we handle questions, let us say, about the role of the individual, violations of the Leninist norms of life, or their restoration. But in the history of Soviet society as a whole, I think there is no scientific basis for making the year 1956 a turning point and the end of the transitional period. Therefore, despite the fact that in certain sectors or spheres of life there are individual stages of periodization, we still need a general periodization in the history of society, which must be based on changes in the mode of production, on the class structure of society, on politics, etc.

Iu. A. Poliakov: We must today solve general problems, not concentrate on certain narrow questions.

A. M. Samsonov: Is the repression of the 1930s a narrow question?

V. Z. Drobizhev: I support Maksim Pavlovich in his persistence in discussing periodization. For us, periodization is not simply the result of research, but also an instrument for it. If there is no periodization, this in itself makes research more difficult. Besides this, while the staff members of an institution in the Academy can put the question of periodization on the back burner, we as teachers can't do this: we have to prepare in the next year for a new teaching program. This is why this question is very important from a scientific and pedagogical point of view.

I would like to express a few thoughts on periodization. I would retain the transitional period as we have had it up to now—until the mid-1930s—because the decisions of the party and all the factual material, the analysis of the economy and the social structure of society, show that socialism was basically constructed by the mid-1930s, and, to all appearances, this is the end of the transitional period. I support those comrades who propose that the mid-1950s be considered a turning point. At that time, both on the economic level and that of the social structure of the population, great changes had taken place in the country and in the intelligentsia; on the political level as well, this is a very significant turning point. From the mid-1950s onward, I would speak of a third period, which continued up to 1985. From 1986 a really new stage begins—the stage of the struggle for the renewal of socialism.

There's something to be said about subperiodization, but that is a special topic. On the whole, it seems to me, the problem of periodization right now requires a comprehensive discussion, but not the way this was done in developing the program on the history of the party, when everything was decided in secret, the programs were published, and then the teaching process was constructed in accordance with the periodization ratified by the Ministry of Higher Education.

History and historians

Historical science is right now going through a difficult and important period in its development. What must be done to raise historical research to a qualitatively new level?

Iu. A. Poliakov: On the whole, the major debates in the historical discipline are still to come, and we will have to return again to the question of the complete and final victory of socialism, and to much else, I think. But we must do today's work today. The main thing is to write and work, but this takes a long time; we can't produce new studies all at once. It's time to stop holding meetings and to begin working. My namesake, the prose writer Iurii Poliakov, correctly said at the Twentieth Congress of the Komsomol that we have to demonstrate our devotion to restructuring not by "raising our hands," but by working at our desks. What has to be done right now in order to raise the level of the historical discipline as high as possible?

It is already axiomatic that we have to write the truth, and not avoid painful questions. This has been repeated over and over again. But it has to be made more specific. I would formulate it this way: Clio has to be taken out of the swaddling clothes of opportunism. The question of the relationship between scholarship and politics has been raised here: we'll probably have to return to this more than once, and this is a subject of enormous complexity. We somehow have to overcome opportunism, to overcome the oscillation between unbridled praise and quotation and complete silence.

We have to populate our history with real people. The "figure of silence" has become too widespread, however, and even to this day many important figures of the past are invisible. We have not only to list historical figures, but to also show living people, figures in the party and in the state, scientists and artists, with all their doubts and mistakes, with their frustrations and agitations, their achievements, victories, and failures—that is, we have to give three-dimensional, and not wooden, descriptions of them. We also have to show ordinary people with their thoughts and views, and reveal their intellectual and artistic world and way of life more fully. We have to know—although this may perhaps be primarily an ethnographic enterprise—how they looked, how they dressed, in order to see them not only at work but in their everyday lives.

Our Marxist methodology is correct, and we shouldn't permit it to be dismissed, or let it be said that it isn't able to reveal the truth. It has permitted us to overcome many difficulties in the development of the science, and in a number of cases to look into the historical process in depth. The spirit of our methodology requires a creative approach, but we have begun to use it like a catechism. We must once again see our methodology as a compass that helps us find the right road, and not as a map on which the route to the final goal has been drawn beforehand.

We must achieve a high professional level. We don't often pay attention to this, and many think it's easy to study history, anyone can do it. For this reason, our personnel, among other things, are often recruited from extremely varied backgrounds, and many people come to the historical discipline without adequate professional training. We have to know how to write, and we have to pay particular attention to this. How we write, how we argue, how we prove things—not by quotations, but in such a way that the living thought should jump off the page: this is what we have to achieve.

And, finally, we must achieve a high literary level in order to put an end to the clichés that torment us, to the primping, countless stock phrases, stereotypes, and bureaucratic expressions. There should be individuality and personal style. The question of editing by publishers is also important because often it's the editors who smooth everything over.

If, in our practical work, we achieve even part of what I refer to, the qualitative level of historical research will certainly rise.

V. A. Kozlov: We have some problems on which the masses more and more often look to historians for advice. These include the problem of the cult of personality, the problem of party factionalism, and the problem of collectivization. It must be recognized that we are not now in a position to answer any of them. We have no ready answers and to expect them right now, when historians have finally gathered together but are getting ready to go home, is probably naive. If we, in our discussions, limit ourselves to stating that the cult of personality has to be studied, that the problem of party factionalism has to be studied, and to repeating once again that there should be no "blank spots" in history, our readers probably will not understand us.

In examining the 1930s, it is not a matter of access to archives. We have not come up against a shortage of archival materials, but against the obvious inadequacy of general sociological ideas and approaches that would take us out of our impasse here. It seems to me that before going into the archives we must have a clear research program that would not be limited to the conviction that the cult of personality was bad. On this question there is no disagreement among us. So let's now look, from the point of view of such a research program, at what is now happening in the realm of social and political journalism. In my view, a kind of bias has become noticeable at one level—the level of the approach outlined in Lenin's "Letter to the Congress" [Pis'mo k s"ezdu], which is limited to [a consideration of] Stalin's personal traits. Lenin had a very profound prognosis and warning, formulated in his letter to Molotov in March 1922 about the ranks of the party. This letter says that the proletarian element of the party at that time consisted of an "extremely thin stratum" of revolutionaries, who may be called the old guard of the party. Any split in this "extremely thin stratum" may lead to the loss of its prestige, and as a result future decisions may no longer depend on it.

Subsequent events unfortunately developed in accordance with this prognosis: there was a split, there was an intraparty struggle, and the result was that decision making no longer depended on the old guard of the party. This is the kind of approach, I think, that we have to look for—a sociological approach because in fact there was pressure on the party from the petit-bourgeois elements—the bearers of the psychology of "leadership." The party was not able to bring to bear against all this the unity of the old party guard, which might have freed it from the problems that arose. In my view, research should be conducted in this area, and not on the peculiarities of Stalin's personality, although that certainly can't be neglected. We have here a case of distortion: instead of explaining and correcting, we often break out into lamentations and philippics on this score, which, in my opinion, is impermissible for historians.

The right to pass moral judgments on the past is certainly a problem of historical knowledge. However, we haven't learned even to ask moral questions in the language of historical science: what are good and evil in relation to the past? Everyday concepts must not be transferred to the evaluation of historical processes. We haven't raised this issue, and it must be raised. One more thing: we've committed a strange error in evaluating the repressions of the 1930s; the old guard of the party appears before us chiefly as a victim. But it became a victim because these people were primarily opponents of Stalin's personality cult that was becoming established. This was real, and comes to the surface even in the sources we have at our disposal. Until now this problem has not been studied, even though it is a matter of preserving the Leninist tradition in the party—the tradition that led to the Twentieth Party Congress, and at the same time it explains the inconsistent process of democratization after the Twentieth Party Congress. In the end, the struggle of the old guard of the party for Leninist norms and its attempts to resist a regime of personal power is what has led us to an understanding of the restructuring that's going on today. It is precisely this angle of vision on the problems connected with the cult of personality, I think, that will be most fruitful.

One more thing: after 1956 something strange happened to us in connection with the use of this concept itself. We colored the problems of the prewar period with the term "cult of personality" and this, as it were, freed us from the need to analyze it. In fact, once something was "under the conditions of the cult of personality," what good could there be in it? And on the whole, we didn't deepen our knowledge. Although I may be wrong, I think that a return to the level of work of the late 1950s and early 1960s is now taking place. We can begin with this level. Let's take off from it and move toward an understanding of the phenomenon itself. It's even hard to study this psychologically: the "emotional" background depresses one. But it is necessary.

We have to "examine" each historical study from the point of view of whether the dialectical method works, whether Marxism is present in it only in the form of ritual phrases or whether it "works" as a means of understanding historical processes. This kind of evaluation of work already done does not exist, and without it we can't estimate with adequate clarity where we've gotten to, and how to get out of this position.

Here's one example: I offered a little book to a publisher devoted to the period from the 1960s to the 1980s. I wasn't explicitly turned down but I was given to understand that it was better "not to dig into this," because "the evaluations haven't been firmed up yet." But after all, who is supposed to work out these evaluations? There are general evaluations, but there are also some specific historical problems that we must solve.

A. M. Samsonov: I'd like to talk about those inhibitory mechanisms that actually prevent a real restructuring in the sphere of history, beginning right in the academic collectives.

The opinion has become established that in scholarship there should be only one point of view. I'm not going to give examples: we all know them. A study has been prepared, and all of a sudden it turns out that the author disagrees with the point of view of other historians. That's the end of it: the work isn't accepted by the publisher. Why? On the one hand, we say that we need debates, and on the other hand, we consider any debatable points impermissible in our research. Debates should be held not only on the pages of journals—where, incidentally, they are very rare. They should also be present in books.

Completely unjustified criteria have developed in our research institutes for evaluating the work of a historian. How is the research process organized? Certain subject matter is laid down in the plan, the titles, size, and deadlines for completion of studies are specified, after which the public and the administration of the institutes see to it that the deadlines, and also the specified sizes, are kept to. The work is completed and accepted for publication—and that's the end of it. But, after all, it would seem that we should only begin here to study the life of a book. What kind of a study is it? What is it based on? What kind of interest did it provoke? Or, perhaps, the reverse: did it arouse no interest at all? We never ask ourselves whether a historian's book is in demand at the library, and how often, or how the small editions that enter the trade network are distributed. The impact of the book doesn't concern us. I therefore think that the time has come to review the criteria for evaluating the work of historians and for being guided not by the quantity or by "gross output" in the field of historical science but by the effectiveness of our research.

We have spoken here of the difficulties that arise when our manuscripts arrive at publishing houses. The approach there is undifferentiated, and the traditional question that the editor asks of the author is "where has it been printed or said already?" And what kind of a study is this, if the same subject has been studied before, or written or spoken about before? The author has to say or create something new. For this reason, in the restructuring plan we have to reread the pages of the past, which retain the imprint of subjectivism, varnishing of the truth, and one-sidedness. And we have to interpret the events, particularly of the 1930s and of the Great Patriotic War and the history of the 1960s and 1970s, objectively on the basis of previously unavailable documents (and it's important to make them available).

When the investigator tries to study the past outside of the previously accepted formulae and stereotypes, he immediately encounters difficulties. We have already mentioned names here. We certainly need different colors to portray the character of a historical figure. But we must see that the portrait corresponds to historical reality. If we consider that history is a creative discipline (and one sometimes has one's doubts about this), then it shouldn't have any forbidden zones. Nonetheless, they do exist. It may be that the time hasn't yet come when a historian can write, say, a monograph about Stalin, but that time must come. This is already done in literary journals and other publications. I receive a lot of letters in response to my writings; they are varied, which is also very interesting. There are some that are just plain hard to read because the writers react to what I say with such fury. But I must say that the majority of letters support my criticism of Stalin's personality cult, in particular based on specific historical material. The time really has come for this.

Sometimes people ask whether there was a cult of Khrushchev or Brezhnev. For example, this question was asked on television of a certain philosopher who said no, there were no such cults. I think his answer was correct; however, we shouldn't put a full stop after this, but admit that the activity of both Khrushchev and Brezhnev at particular stages revealed an element of voluntarism, a weakening of the collegial style of leadership, and a replacement of genuine democratism by window dressing. We know what this led to. For this reason, I would like to emphasize that, in analyzing the positive and negative experience of the Soviet state at various stages of its development, it is important to show how the defects were overcome, and how tasks of enormous historical significance were successfully carried out. The main line of our research must be our positive beginning [in 1917]. Let us remember how backward our country was in the beginning, and that it is now a great power. This does not mean that we must close our eyes to all the negative things that existed along our road. It seems to me that it is vitally necessary for us to concern ourselves with restructuring, and to begin first with ourselves.

What enormous interest has now arisen in our periodicals and in our daily press! People are attracted not only by the controversial nature of what is published, but also by the fact that it is the truth. What is published in the press is often just as frank as it can be—extremely frank. But this principle—to tell the truth, the whole truth, and nothing but the truth—hasn't touched the historical profession. Writers speak and facts confirm that they had at least some materials on hand. How many years have passed since Anatolii Rybakov began to write *Children of the Arbat* [Deti Arbata], or Daniel Granin *The Diehards* [Zubra] or Vladimir Dudintsev *White Clothes* [Belye odezhdy]? But they at least wrote, even though they knew that their work wouldn't be printed, and many of them, incidentally, never expected that such a time would come. Do historians have any such manuscripts? This is what is alarming. We must see that historians make an effort and understand that they have to write history as it really happened, and make sure that it reaches the reader.

Question: This is precisely what our readers write in letters to the editor. Let us quote a passage from one such letter:

> Historians avoid discussing moral consequences of the cult of personality, the class nature of the cult in our conditions and its petit-bourgeois nature. When will historians begin to do what belletristic writers are doing with a certain emotional pressure? They are doing it, after, all, and are working.

Is literature in fact ahead of the historical discipline?

A. M. Samsonov: We must master what restructuring requires of us. In the Division of History of the USSR Academy of Sciences, multidisciplinary problems are being worked on. This is very necessary. Then programs for the future are being developed. Also very necessary. People now speak persuasively of the importance of the periodization of our history. There is no question about this. But we were doing all of this ten and even twenty years ago, including discussing periodization. All the same, this is not the main task, and this is not what is expected of us. Who is more important: the writer or the historian? Whose prestige is higher? This isn't the problem. How have each of us done his duty—particularly we historians? I think that we have greatly lagged behind.

Is history really a less entertaining field than *belles-lettres*? We must admit, by way of self-criticism, that we lag behind in a professional sense, and in the civil sense: the interest in historical books is at a low level and this has to be taken into account; we have to overcome everything that hinders us.

I, for example, have long been trying to get order no. 227 of July 28, 1942, which was read to all troops at the front, published in full. I sent the letter to the highest military authorities, but there's been no answer. This is only one example. At one time I studied in detail the materials of the Supreme Military Headquarters—the conversations with the fronts. Extremely interesting material! But all this is closed. Some things are now being declassified, but, on the whole, these seem to be half measures.

What we need is access to documents—that's the first thing. To solve the problem of who answers scholarly questions—the editor for the publishing house, or the scholar and the academic collective—that's the second. So far, the editor has the say and the whole system of work is set up so that he gets a prize if no "difficult" situations come up. Therefore the scholars' hands are tied. We must not take a wait-and-see position but must in some way fight so that we can write interestingly and in a way that will satisfy the reader.

I. I. Mints: A few words in regard to the letter, an excerpt from which was just read here. Yes, *belles-lettres* has sometimes gone further than history. But the trouble is that in novels, let us say, the debauchery of Catherine II is declared to be "activity on behalf of the state," or someone all of a sudden presents the Masons as a moving force of the revolution. And there aren't any real facts to back this up. It seems to me that the struggle against such legends might be more effective if historians set to work more actively.

Everything that is said about restructuring relates to us directly and immediately—everything, beginning with the struggle for discipline, for the observance and establishment of our norms. Access to information, criticism, and self-criticism concern us to an equal degree. In the field of history, the distinctive feature of restructuring, in my view, can be reduced to the problem that we study; what questions are we concerned with today? Do we have to throw out everything that is old, or should we pose new problems? I wouldn't throw out the old, because all of this retains its value, even though new topics are appearing. For example, right now in the West, our program for building socialism is being rigorously criticized, and it's being said that there was an alternative to the October Revolution. There was no alternative to the revolution; Russia could be saved at that time by only one course—the establishment of a new regime, the regime of workers and peasants. The people turned away from all parties, including those of the compromisers, and supported the Bolsheviks.

Or take the question of the Civil War and the intervention. It would seem that this was a bygone page of history. But when you hear that in the United States a film about the "conquest" of that country by Bolsheviks has appeared, and when you hear the threat of an anticommunist "crusade" from the president himself, and appeals to "throw socialism into the dustbin of history,"* you begin to realize that it is now necessary to concern oneself again with the subject of the intervention—perhaps from another point of view. Up to now, we've spoken of it chiefly from the point of view of diplomatic history and the like. This is now inadequate. We have to show what this or that capitalist country was actually doing during the intervention.

V. Z. Drobizhev: What is hindering us today? It seems to me that we are chiefly hindered not by the censorship of the publishing houses, but by the censor in our own heads. We have been so indoctrinated over the course of many years that it is difficult for us to abandon the clichés that have become rooted in us. I recently began to write an article about workers' self-management, and caught myself thinking that I would comment on recent legislation in this regard, although the history of workers' self-management is by no means synonymous or similar. Or take this question: we are now beginning to talk about returning to a tax-in-kind. We have not returned to the tax-in-kind mechanically, but in practical terms are discovering or working out the public economy of socialism all over again. Today there are entirely different historical conditions; it's a different epoch. Lenin, in developing the system of NEP, had in mind a transitional period and not one of fully developed socialism.

The second condition, it seems to me, of our own restructuring, is in raising the professional level. After all, it's no secret that quite a few talented people have left the field of Soviet history and party history to go into other fields of the historical discipline, and that the influx of young people has almost stopped.

I remember a case in which I was given a book from Mysl' Publishing House to review. I wrote that the book was unprofessional. The author came to thank me: "It's a good thing that you didn't accuse me of political errors. This I can quickly correct: just tell me where to make the corrections—on which pages." Lack of professionalism is revealed in the fact that we are not able to analyze all the assembled facts that have come down to us. One small individual fact is chosen, and then fitted into a certain model.

The third condition is improving publishing. We've stopped publishing documents. Unfortunately, that's the way it turned out. We celebrated the fortieth anniversary of the October Revolution with an impressive series of documentary publications—extremely valuable documents, extremely interesting ones. We marked the fiftieth anniversary of the October Revolution with only a few sub-

---

*Mints apparently refers to President Reagan's November 18, 1986 speech at the Tenth Anniversary Dinner of the Ethics and Policy Center, Washington, D.C. If so, his paraphrase is misleading. Georgii Arbatov reported the speech in *Pravda* (November 21, 1986, p. 5) as an announcement of a "crusade." Although anticommunist in tone, the speech refers only to "our bipartisan crusade to make America stronger." On this occasion, Reagan did not employ the "dustbin of history" metaphor.—William B. Husband

stantial publications, and for the seventieth we prepared very few. For example, we don't publish the protocols of the congresses of soviets (stenographic reports). The documents of certain congresses of soviets are kept in the rare book department of Lenin Library. They were published in miserably small editions, are worn out, and have become bibliographical rarities. And yet this is an invaluable historical source! We have fallen far behind in our publishing activity.

M. P. Kim: Why do we concern ourselves with commentaries? Because we have developed this tradition. The Twenty-second Congress declared that we had entered the period of all-out building of communism. I once tried to object, in connection with the proposed slogan: "Let's transform Moscow into a model communist city!" I said: what communism? Let's first transform the capital into a model socialist city, and then into a communist one. What do you mean: is Moscow going to enter communism while the rest of the country isn't yet socialist? I also objected to the idea of saying that from 1961 onward our society was a fully developed socialist society. However, I had to propose a different version: fully developed socialism wasn't yet here, but the building of it, the process of entering into this stage, has been long-drawn-out (it extended for eighteen years). If I'd objected openly, what I said simply wouldn't have been printed. For this reason, we must now give scholars the opportunity—in ways we certainly can search for—to express their opinion not only on the mistakes of the past, but also on certain statements that are made today, if they don't agree with them. Otherwise, history will repeat itself yet again: after ten years, people will say, "What's this? There were mistakes, and you kept quiet, agreed, or merely commented?" Right now, let's not only comment but criticize, suggest, and help to find the best solution.

In order to raise historical research to a new qualitative level, it is necessary to do what the new thought invited us to do—take a creative approach to all questions. This means to liberate our thought from dogmatic features and from a primitive understanding of our function as limited to merely commenting on authoritative statements, evaluations, and documents—and to pursue independent creative thought. In the field of historical science this can't be done in as much of a hurry as, let us say, in *belles-lettres*.

The historian can't choose individual pieces from the biography of an individual or from a small historical stage, as an artist does in such cases, or embody in images what he understands. The historian has to look at history comprehensively, in strict chronological sequence of the individual stages, and therefore the task is that much more complicated. In saying this, I don't by any means intend to make excuses for historians: our restructuring is proceeding slowly, but an especially thoughtful attitude toward the problems at hand is required here to a greater degree than among artists or literary people. Right now, in my opinion, the following formula of thought prevails among certain belletristic and public-affairs writers: what used to be bad is now good, and what used to be good is now bad. This is a very scathing formula, since it attracts those who evaluate things emotionally. It seems to me that we need more serious research, which must reconstruct historical truth, the process of coming into being and development of real socialism in our country. And for this reason, the position of the party and its leaders that our history has to be reproduced and illuminate both the negative features and the positive ones is quite correct. Not one-sidedly, but comprehensively.

From the editorial staff

The changing times, the huge work of restructuring, the stern lessons of truth taught by the Twenty-seventh Party Congress, and the increased interest in our past—all these insistently demand from historians an innovative, bold analysis of the decades that have just passed, an analysis free from recurrences of the chronic infirmities of historical research—pedantry, formalism, dogmatism, suppression, and epidemics of opportunism.

Questions of the scientific periodization of the history of Soviet society, widely touched upon by the participants in the "roundtable," are, beyond question, highly significant. Periodization is helpful in the deep study of the content of the historical process, and in making the historical limits of individual stages of development more precise, and serves as a methodological instrument of cognition. However, one must not, of course, consider this problem central and self-sufficient in the realm of scholarly interests of historians. And naturally the discussion could not undertake to work out some final period of periodization: this will be done by scientific collectives in the course of the discussion that has now begun.

It is especially important to base ourselves, in our research, on the fundamental historical approach, on the dialectical principle of history. V. I. Lenin often called upon us to do this, demanding that, in analyzing processes taking place in society,

> the basic historical connection not be forgotten, and that each question be looked at from the point of view of how the given phenomenon arose in history, what major stages it passed through in the course of its development, and that we look, from the point of view of its development, at what the thing has now become [*Poln. sobr. soch.*, vol. 39, p. 67].

This methodological principle of Lenin's is enormously significant for the study of the history of Soviet society and of developing socialism. This is precisely the position from which it is necessary to uncover and interpret the events of the October Revolution, the transition to the New Economic Policy, the subjective and objective conditions for the processes of industrialization of the country and collectivization of agriculture, the dialectics of the origin of socialist culture, and the development of national and political relations. Such an objective, sober study of the past will help us to decide the question of what to reject out of the accumulated experience, and how; of what to take from it, and how; of what should be done, or not done, and how, in order to avoid repeating mistakes. After all, the dialectic of continuity and innovation in relation to historical and social experience consists precisely in the fact that it is necessary in each individual case to look extremely concretely at the present in the context of history, in connection with the general direction of movement of society toward the higher forms of its organization.

A number of problems arise here. The historical process is indivisible and uninterrupted; "what is happening with greater and greater speed before our eyes is also history" [ibid., vol. 3, p. 632]. In the science of history it is important not to lag behind this accelerated movement, and to write a genuine history of the present, which, of course, cannot be reduced to a mere commentary on documents, but will permit "following through" of the tendencies of the development of society, and the help in looking ahead and foreseeing the future. This ability, which is fundamentally and methodologically validated in the classic historical works of the founders of Marxism-Leninism, is still clearly in short supply among us.

Another problem relates to the approach to "blank spots" in our recent history. These historiographic "lacunae" are connected, as a rule, not merely with the "figure of silence" but also with deformations in the treatment of specific historical events. Here it is appropriate to recall the Marxist position that "incorrect ideas . . . are in the final analysis incorrect ideas about correct facts. The facts remain, even if the ideas about them prove to be false" [K. Marx and F. Engels, *Soch.*, vol. 20, p. 476]. The matter at issue is that of establishing the actual content of events on the basis of a broad range of sources, and of creating the fullest possible picture and revealing the historical truth. This should be furthered by easing access to archival holdings, expanding the publication of documents, and lifting unjustified restrictions on research.

There is one more aspect of some importance connected with evaluations of past events. In these evaluations, emotions often prevail over reason, and scientific analysis is replaced by sheer moralizing. Particular individuals and whole periods of history are painted in uniform colors—either bright or dark. History is multilayered and multicolored, and moral evaluations must be firmly based on historicism. Rashness, sensationalism, an effort to "run ahead of progress," which almost, if not quite, show themselves in some of the published material, are damaging to the cause of knowledge of historical truth. It is important to study the past from consistent Marxist-Leninist, class positions, arranging everything, as the saying goes, by order of priorities. One must not give in to any one-sided conceptions or moods. We cannot base our attitude toward everything that happened after the October Revolution on these.

Speaking at the Twentieth Congress of the Komsomol, M. S. Gorbachev recalled the significance that Lenin attributed to the formation of historical consciousness. It is necessary that the history of our socialist Fatherland should generously feed the feelings of civic duty of each Soviet person: it is necessary that this should be an honest, courageous, absorbing history, which does not avoid the dramatic aspects of events and human fates, and that it describes to the full the heroic path of the country and the party—the path of the October Revolution, the path of the pioneers.

The Role of the Journal "Voprosy istorii KPSS" in Restructuring Party History

F. N. SMYKOV

This question was considered at a meeting of the Academic Council of the Institute of Marxism-Leninism under the CPSU Central Committee held on October 26, 1987. The concrete, business-like discussion was beneficial not only to the journal's staff, but also to those participants in the meeting who are interested in the development of the discipline of party history.

Recently, well-prepared discussion has taken place in the Institute of Marxism-Leninism of the CPSU Central Committee on the cardinal questions involved in strengthening the contribution of scholars of this institute to the social sciences. The meeting on October 26 was likewise well-prepared. A commission set up to study anew the journal's activity and its role in restructuring party history carried on this work for more than two months. The commission's conclusions and proposals were constructive.

The position of the journal

Professor V. I. Kas'ianenko, doctor of historical sciences and the journal's editor-in-chief, presented a paper, "The Role of the Journal *Voprosy istorii KPSS* in Restructuring Party History." The deepening and expanding restructuring in the country, the moral and political atmosphere in our society to which it has given rise, and the increased interest of the Soviet people in its history, he said, have created favorable conditions for developing party history, for expanding research activity, and for elevating the journal's role in achieving a qualitatively new condition in our field.

Perhaps not since Lenin's time have there been such favorable conditions for the objective treatment of the history and current policy of the CPSU and for

Russian text © 1988 by "Pravda" Publishers. "Rol' zhurnala 'Voprosy istorii KPSS' v perestroike istoriko-partiinoi nauki," *Voprosy istorii KPSS*, 1988, no. 1, pp. 135–50. Translated by Stephen P. Dunn.

genuine scholarly creativity as that which developed after the April (1985) Plenum of the CPSU Central Committee. Scholars have been given a unique opportunity to bring the discipline of party history to a qualitatively new theoretical level, and to increase significantly the effectiveness of its social role. The editorial board, staff, and contributors look upon the fulfillment of these tasks as their party and civil obligation, and as their contribution to the theory and practice of restructuring and acceleration.

The speaker then expressed some conceptual ideas for renewing party history and the journal, which are conditioned by the general conception of the revolutionary restructuring of all spheres of our society worked out by the party. This envisages a rational, methodologically and politically tested renewal and illumination of all periods and problems in the history of the party, especially those in the years since Lenin's time, and in particular those pages in it that were distorted by the Stalin cult, subjectivism, dogmatism, stagnation, and the braking mechanism from the 1960s through the first half of the 1980s. Revolutionary restructuring also envisages the revelation of the historical and epistemological roots and objective and subjective causes of the problems mentioned above.

Historians, together with philosophers, face the task of reinterpreting much of our understanding and revelation of the objective laws of social development, and their concrete manifestation in the dialectic of the historical process and in contemporary restructuring. They also need to show the unity of innovation, continuity, and prospects for developing our society up to the year 2000, arming the present generation of investigators with the lessons of history and historical truth, while correctly applying the principles of historicism and class in analyzing the current problems of the transitional period and the turning points in our history, and also in making judgments about alternative programs, policies, and methods of transformation, and the regularities, logic, and costs of the class struggle. We are obliged to fill as soon as possible the blank pages in our history and to explain the distorted treatment of events, and also the ''convenient facts'' against which M. S. Gorbachev warned us.

We must, V. I. Kas'ianenko continued, study the dialectic of contradictions in social development and the role of the CPSU in resolving them, in relation to all periods and major events, and not, of course, only to those with positive final results. We must restore Leninist methods and Bolshevik traditions in research on party history, making use of the experience of historians and of the 1920s practice of conducting debates among social scientists. We must overcome as soon as possible dogmatism, the practice of limiting ourselves to description, and pedantry. It is also important that in the heat of the justified criticism of the discipline of party history for depersonalizing history and for dealing in banal official portraits, damage not be done to its theoretical and philosophical bases and functions. In the course of renewal, we cannot permit the devaluation of genuinely scientific knowledge in the field of history of the CPSU and USSR. Over the past twenty to twenty-five years, historians of the CPSU have forgotten how to conduct objective and fruitful debates, and to create historiographic and critical works (surveys and book reviews) that effectively influence the quality of research, publications, and lectures in college-level courses on the history of the CPSU. The practice, purposes, and strict differentiation of our counterpropagandistic efforts need serious reorganization.

In the interest of renewing science and promoting restructuring, acceleration, and the deepening not only of economic, but also of ideological collaboration among fraternal countries and parties, we must significantly intensify the collaboration of our journal with the historical journals of the socialist countries, since at present this work continues largely in the old way, with an inadequate level of professionalism and performance.

The editorial board and staff of the journal, together with the Division of Party History of the Institute of Marxism-Leninism, are studying all these conceptual directions, taking account of the demands of perestroika and renewal. Analysis of the contents of the twenty issues of the journal that appeared after the [Twenty-seventh—D.J.R.] congress and especially after the January (1987) Plenum of the CPSU Central Committee, shows that new tendencies and publications in the journal in the spirit of restructuring are expanding, but not as fast as they should, and not on the necessary professional level. Thus, for the first time in its history, the journal contains debates on four current problems and topics: the historical experience of the CPSU and the present; periodization; a new textbook on party history; and the experience of the CPSU and the fraternal parties in improving life. A discussion is likewise beginning on the current problems and "lacunae" in the history of the CPSU in the 1960s and '70s.

The journal has published original articles and materials such as "Continuity and Innovation in the Activity of the CPSU" [Preemstvennost' i novatorstvo v deiatel'nosti KPSS] (no. 6, 1986); "The First Lessons and Urgent Tasks of Restructuring" [Pervye uroki i neotlozhnye zadachi perestroiki] (no. 10, 1986); "The Party's Personnel Policy during Restructuring" [Kadrovaia politika partii v usloviiakh perestroiki] (no. 2, 1987); "Historical-Party Considerations of the Concept of Acceleration: Research Problems" [Istoriko-partiinye aspekty kontseptsii uskoreniia: Problemy issledovaniia] and "An Allergy to Historical Truth" [Allergiia k istoricheskoi istine] (no. 4, 1987); "The Historian and Perestroika" [Istorik i perestroika] (no. 5, 1987); "Aren't We Departing from Historical Truth?" [Ne ukhodim li ot istoricheskoi pravdy?] (no. 6, 1987); "On the Personality Factor in the History of the CPSU" [O lichnostnom faktore v istorii KPSS] and "The Truth of History and Stereotypes of Dogmatism" [Pravda istorii i stereotipy dogmatizma] (no. 9, 1987); "The Main Guideline Is Historical Truth" [Glavnyi orientir—istoricheskaia pravda], "Against Stagnation and Imitating the Truth" [Protiv zastoia i imitatsii pravdy], and "On the Question of the United-Front Tactics in 1921–24" [K voprosu o taktike edinogo fronta v 1921–24 gg.] (no. 10, 1987); "On Some International Aspects of Restructuring" [O nekotorykh mezhdunarodnykh aspektakh perestroiki], "Overcome the Braking

Mechanism, Strengthen the Connection between Research and Real Life'' [Preo-dolet' mekhanizm tormozheniia, ukrepliat' sviaz' issledovanii s zhizn'iu], and "Restructuring and the Strengthening of Relations among Social Scientists'' [Perestroika i usilenie vzaimosviazi obshchestvovedov] (no. 11, 1987); and others.

The following new sections have appeared in the journal's pages: "The Historian and Restructuring," "The History of the CPSU in the System of the Social Sciences," "The Comintern Reconsidered," "Polemical Notes," "Our Questionnaire," "Our Readers Ponder, Debate, Suggest," "Restructuring: Practice, Tendencies, Problems," "The Tribune of the Scholar-Public-affairs Writer," and so on.

The editorial board and staff of the journal are well aware that this is only a modest beginning. Many items of mediocre quality are being published, and conceptual, historiographic, source-research, historical, and other articles that would restore truth to the history of the 1920s–40s and the 1960s–70s and rehabilitate some party figures and scholars, including historians—that is, which would help in writing history, with all its pluses, minuses, contradictions, ideo-logical and political confrontations, and personal tragedies—are not being pub-lished enough. We should be publishing history with its heroism, drama, and human tragedies, "in which," as M. S. Gorbachev emphasized at the Twentieth Congress of the Komsomol, "there would be no blank pages, subjectivist prefer-ences, and antipathies, history whose value would not depend on epidemics of opportunism."[1]

Recently, various points of view have been expressed in the pages of a number of newspapers and journals on specific questions of party history. Despite a certain lack of competence and some methodological flaws, emotionalism, and immaturity, the publications on historical problems sharpen our attitude toward the renewal of party history, call our attention to individual blank pages, delve into previously taboo themes, and contain quite a few useful judgments and evaluations.

Comprehending the truth, vital justice, and the true lessons of history is a complex process requiring strict observance of methodological principles and a feel for politics. Such problems as the Stalin cult and its negative consequences, struggles within the party under Lenin and Stalin, the repressions of the 1930s and '40s, departures from Lenin's legacy in the practical implementation of economic, cultural, nationality, legal, and social policy require especially careful research and sustained attention. Here there is need for analysis based on docu-ments, the reconsideration of many evaluations and conclusions that have become entrenched in the literature and in historians' consciousness, and a sober party approach, devoid of the slightest distortion of the truth. On these questions, we still have debates ahead of us—both with dogmatists and with adherents of subjective group interests, unscientific conceptions and surmises. The editorial board will in the future continue to mobilize the efforts of authors to rid us as soon as possible of flareups of the old diseases—ignoring the principles of historicism, keeping silent about certain phenomena, events, and persons; soulless commentary; opportunism; hasty conclusions; and sensationalism. In this process, Marxist-Leninist methodology, truth, and the interests of genuine restructuring will be our only guides.

Renewal and restructuring in the discipline of party history are unthinkable without preliminary critical analysis of it by means of historiographic work and work with sources, and without bringing unpublished documents into circulation. Unfortunately, the speaker noted, for a number of objective and subjective reasons, our efforts with regard to this direction of restructuring remain unsatisfactory. With rare exceptions, historiographers, source specialists, critics and reviewers, and archivists are adopting a wait-and-see attitude. Historians require new documents, and they do not yet have access to the necessary central and local archives.

Despite these and other difficulties, among which the most sensitive for the reorganization of the journal are inertia, the changing of generations of scholars and postsecondary teachers, the absence of new documentary materials, and the slow turnover in the body of contributors, the journal is renewing the concept and treatment of historical events, reconsidering analytical and theoretical conclusions and evaluations, and more decisively transforming the mode of thought, style, and approach to the study of specific critical issues in all periods of the history of the CPSU. Without going to extremes, and avoiding one-sidedness, the editorial board and contributors are now concentrating on working out complex conceptual and methodological problems and on strengthening self-analysis of the field.

Along with philosophers, historians of the party must return to the problem of the relationship between the past, the present, and the future in the historical process and the practice of using Lenin's methodological principles for learning about history and the present, and to the problem of the role of the masses and of the individual in history. For it is precisely these methodological principles that concentrate in themselves that which is connected with social experience, the lessons of truth with the aim of restructuring and defining the prospects of improving socialism. The principles of class analysis and historicism are inseparable from the recognition of the objective character of progress, the regularities of the creation of socialism, the logic of class and intraparty struggle, and the role of individuals in history.

In connection with the reform of postsecondary education and the resolution of the CPSU Central Committee on restructuring the system of political and economic schooling for working people, V. I. Kas'ianenko said, the staff and editorial board of the journal, the Ministry of Higher Education of the USSR, and the All-Union House of Political Education [*Vsesoiuznyi dom politicheskogo prosveshcheniia*] under the CPSU Central Committee organized a discussion on the historical experience of the CPSU, on periodization, and on the draft curriculum for students in evening courses on Marxism-Leninism. The staffs of nearly all departments of party history in postsecondary institutions and higher party schools are discussing the articles by N. A. Barsukov and N. N. Maslov, which opened the discussion, and also the draft curriculum. The editorial board publishes the results of these discussions regularly.

Emphasizing that the journal *Voprosy istorii KPSS* is an organ of the Institute of Marxism-Leninism, and therefore considers its primary obligation to be the reflection, in what it publishes, of all scholarly tendencies in that institute—and to a certain extent the journal does do this—the speaker noted that so far this is done unsystematically, primarily on the basis of personal relationships. As a result, the collaboration of the research staff of the institute with the journal remains on the same level as before the Party Congress, and before perestroika. The research staffs of the various departments and sectors make no effort to inform the scholarly public of the results of their research: plans for publishing documents contained in the Central Party Archives are lacking; the branches of the institute in the union republics, in Moscow, and in Leningrad have not yet become centers of restructuring or initiators of renewing party history or of innovative publications. Many historians are waiting for something and relying on others, including the journal, while forgetting that it is after all not a research institute. The analysis of material published in the journal after the Twenty-seventh Congress of the CPSU indicates that the basic cadre of authors does not consist of staff members of the Institute of Marxism-Leninism. Their share in the articles published amounts to only twenty-three percent.

Only with the help of staff members from the institute's sub-branches and of coordination of the Institute of Marxism-Leninism have the institute's leading personnel on party history under the central committees of the communist parties of the union republics begun to be published in the journal. A similar situation with regard to using the journal in the interests of restructuring the subdivisions of the Institute of Marxism-Leninism and its branches is quite abnormal.

The poor participation of the institute's young scholars in the journal is especially disturbing. Only a few young scholars (S. E. Grechikho, N. E. Tikhonova, A. Iu. Chepurenko, O. V. Naumov, V. N. Shepilev, and A. D. Plotnikov) try to publish the results of their research in its pages. The majority of them, however, are passive.

Against this generally unfavorable background, the editorial board is especially grateful to those staff members of the Institute of Marxism-Leninism who consider the journal their own. It sincerely thanks G. M. Adibekov, V. Ia. Bondar', V. V. Gorbunov, V. I. Desiaterik, V. V. Zhuravlev, A. G. Zdravomyslov, M. V. Iskrov, Iu. K. Malov, L. M. Minaev, M. P. Mchedlov, A. A. Pavlenko, R. M. Savitskaia, A. M. Sovokin, R. V. Filippov, F. I. Firsov and others, who actively publish material about current topics in the journal.

Recalling the words of M. S. Gorbachev to the effect that perestroika presents each person in each working group with new criteria and evaluations for work,

V. I. Kas'ianenko emphasized, in conclusion, that in order to restructure, the editorial staff of the journal would have to raise significantly its professional standards and criticize more aggressively everything that slows down and hinders the renewal of party history, and overcome the wait-and-see psychology and inertia of many historians. The editorial staff and the staff of the Division of the History of the CPSU at the Institute of Marxism-Leninism are trying to focus their attention on such questions as the working out of fundamental problems of party history, the comprehensive treatment of the path through which the party has passed, the illumination of its leading role, especially at turning points, the dialectic of continuity and innovation in party politics, the status and prospects of developing party history, and improving the quality of research and teaching of the history of the CPSU.

The commission's opinion

In order to give the commission a genuinely democratic character in preparing the question of the journal's role in restructuring party history, its chairman, G. M. Adibekov, senior research associate of the institute and doctor of historical sciences, said it did not confine itself to study of the journal's content and conversations with staff members, but tried to take maximum account of the opinions of institute staff members. This helped in reaching objective conclusions about the status and prospects of the editorial board's work.

The content of *Voprosy istorii KPSS*, the speaker noted, certainly depends to a great extent on the scholarly level of its contributors. At the same time, the positions of the author and the journal do not necessarily have to coincide. Only in a scholarly polemic, distinguished by convincing argument and honesty, and the high professional level and conscientiousness of the opponents, can the truth be born. And the full truth is the goal, without which there is no perestroika.

Pausing to describe the journal staff, G. M. Adibekov reported that at the end of 1986 a recertification of its members was conducted. He had occasion to take part in the work of this commission as secretary of the local organization of the Union of Journalists of the USSR. On the whole, the editorial staff is adequately qualified. Experienced and well-qualified journalists and editors take part in this work. But there are obviously poor ones of whom it is difficult to expect anything in the future.

The journal's editors must give this problem special attention. It is, after all, no secret that some members of the editorial staff lack initiative precisely because of poor knowledge of the problems dealt with by their sections. In order for the journal to become a real organizer of perestroika in party history, we must first of all raise the level of professional and theoretical training of its staff members— that is, begin restructuring with ourselves. There are still quite a few problems here. We must free ourselves from the baggage of the past, from obsolete ideas and stereotypes, and we must restructure our thinking. Without this there can be no movement forward. The farther we go, the harder it will be to explain the lag of a scholarly journal behind other journals in the social sciences and politics in formulating urgent problems.

The members of the editorial board must overcome their own considerable obsolescence, G. M. Adibekov continued. This is evident in meetings that consider what to publish, and also in the content of the latest journal issues, in which the spirit of restructuring is especially noticeable. But we still face a huge amount of work in order to finally overcome timidity in formulating questions, and in order for the journal to become a genuine generator of ideas, an initiator of new and bold approaches. Finally, it is time to stop being afraid of the nonstandard, nontrivial solutions proposed by authors and corresponding to the historical truth; it is time to provide for a genuine, revolutionary renewal of such social sciences as Marxology, Lenin studies, history of the CPSU, party construction, scientific communism, and the history of the international communist movement. And the sooner this happens, the better, because people judge how the scholarly activity of the institute is being restructured by the journal. This raises significantly the editorial board's responsibility, and dictates for it a greater role in shaping the journal's content, and for the renewal of all directions of its work.

Today we are witnessing an unprecedented interest in the history of the CPSU. The journal, which is the main one in this field, must satisfy this interest. But only in this field? Certainly not. We must promote perestroika in the remaining social sciences represented in the journal as well. Incidentally, many staff members of the institute with whom I have had occasion to speak have said this. They consider it wrong that some publishing house employees or members of the editorial board insist that all materials from a variety of disciplines have the character of party history. One cannot help seeing the contradiction between the title of the journal and the broader character of what it publishes. It is clear that this contradiction should be resolved.

G. M. Adibekov emphasized that the reader deserves more attention. Meetings between members of the editorial staff and readers should be organized more frequently and in a greater variety of forms. Various methods of presenting material in the pages of the journal should be employed more boldly: more interviews should be published, not only with one but with several scholars who, in addition, hold various views on this or that problem. Essays on historical themes, and surveys of letters by readers, replies to letters, and the like, should be published, and each issue of the journal should include differing points of view. More replies (both positive and critical) to the editors about material published in the journal should be given, etc. Increased reader interest will raise the journal's circulation.

The question of improving the journal's ties with the divisions and sectors of the Institute of Marxism-Leninism and its branches is of current interest. Staff members of the institute rarely publish in the journal. Why is this? Apparently, we see here a manifestation of the civic passivity and indifference to scholarship prevalent for many years, which has not yet been overcome. This is due to indifference to the affairs of the institute, including the journal, as well as to the absence of new approaches, and to the inability or lack of desire to reinterpret critically the results of one's work. It is clear that the managing board, the party and trade-union committees, the Komsomol committee, the Academic Council, and the entire collective of the institute, must draw serious conclusions from all this, and work out a system of measures to involve the entire scholarly staff in the creative process, and to stimulate those who are working conscientiously. The work plans of divisions, sectors, and individual staff members should include publication in the journal, which is the organ of the institute. In summing up the results for the year, account should be taken of the publication of such material in the journal.

At the same time, we should see that the editorial board constructs its long-term plans (and the commission proposes that it have two- and three-year plans in addition to the yearly ones) on the basis of the five-year plan of the institute and its branches, and takes account of the plans of a number of academic councils of the USSR Academy of Sciences. It should be a rule for the staff members of any scholarly subdivision of the Institute of Marxism-Leninism to publish everything new in their own journal.

The commission thinks that only by joint efforts will it be possible to further raise the journal's theoretical and scholarly level. We should not wait for the publication, say, of the multivolume series on problems of the history of the CPSU or of the works being prepared in other branches of the Institute of Marxism-Leninism. The main thing while preparing these works, and before their publication, is to acquaint our readers with the creative work of the institute's collective. This relates to individual as well as team-written works.

Adibekov then emphasized that a sophisticated study of current problems of Marxology and Lenin studies, of the intraparty struggle during the transition period [that of the New Economic Policy—D.J.R.], of the processes of democratization in Soviet society, of the experience of the ruling parties in the socialist countries, of the activation of the human factor, and of the history of the international activity of the CPSU, depends to a considerable degree on the publication of new documents. The ideal thing would be for the documents of the CPSU and the international communist movement to be systematically published. Our hopes here rest on the institute's managing board.

The commission concluded that the editorial collective of the journal *Voprosy istorii KPSS* has embarked on restructuring, that today's discussion at the meeting of the Academic Council will permit it to identify the path for accelerating restructuring, and to make a large contribution to the renewal of party history, responding to the requirements of the times and the demands of the party.

Toward renewal through common efforts

The following questions were at the center of attention at the meeting of the Academic Council: how the journal should be reorganized; what aspects of it are working well and which ones still are not; whether it is in the forefront of the renewal of party history; what its relationships are with the scholars and subdivisions of the Institute of Marxism-Leninism; and how it is to function in the future. Many participants in the meeting noted that the journal has embarked on the path of restructuring, and named articles and new departments in the spirit of renewal, which they liked. But as the saying goes, things are more obvious from the outside. The members of the editorial staff are not resting on their laurels: they regard the positive statements made to them as advance praise, which must be earned by further work. Therefore, the critical comments and constructive suggestions for improving the journal and restructuring party history are especially valuable for them.

In his address, the head of the Division of Party Construction of the Institute of Marxism-Leninism, Professor V. Ia. Bondar' (D. Hist. Sc.) said that the journal was to some degree a mirror reflecting our own mistakes and deficiencies. We have common shortcomings, including that of lagging behind life. At times, acute questions arise to which we cannot give answers. Take the problem of personnel. The party is now demanding that we draw conclusions from the experience of work with personnel at different stages of our history. The journal is not yet able to throw light on these questions, since we, as scholarly workers, are not yet prepared to provide these materials.

In this connection I would like to remind you that the Division of Party Construction at one time asked for and received permission to prepare a history of party construction in three volumes. Nothing came of this. But, after all, we frequently have to turn in regard to various questions to the party's historical experience in the field of party construction, which has to be taken into account to restructure party work under current conditions. And each time we essentially begin over again, wasting our forces in studying the experience of party organization work in various historical periods.

Or take the scholarly development of the democratization of intraparty life and of our life in general. Here as well we are lagging behind the demands of practice.

Thus, to be closer to real life is one of the tasks both of our journal and of all the staff members of the Institute of Marxism-Leninism.

Doctor of Historical Sciences M. V. Iskrov, head of the Division of Branches and Research Coordination of the Institute of Marxism-Leninism, also spoke of the need for further strengthening the journal's connection with real life. He emphasized that materials published in the journal by the secretaries of party committees and other leading workers do not solve this problem—particularly when they take the form of "personal reports" [monostat'i]. We must get away from heavy, clumsy items.

It seems that the basic connection of the journal and of our institute as a whole with real life should strengthen our contact with party workers. Last year, for example, our division, together with the Division of Party Construction, held a roundtable discussion on problems of party leadership in scientific and technological progress. Social scientists, workers in the party, government, and the economy, including secretaries of [urban] raion party committees of Moscow and other cities took part in it. The meeting was useful, both for the scholars and for the practical workers. The journal also provided good, readable information about this roundtable at the time.

Right now our division, the Division of Party History, and six Moscow party secretaries are preparing a meeting to exchange experience in restructuring and in improving the style of party work. The journal should be the first to publish reports of discussions of this kind, since this is the main place where its link with real life appears.

Giving a positive evaluation of the journal's work on restructuring, and citing many examples in support of his opinion, the speaker singled out the tenth issue. He said that all the articles in this issue contributed to an understanding of our field's present development.

Pausing to consider questions of historiography, M. V. Iskrov said that party history could not move forward without development in this area. The journal has made a start on this work, but it needs help. Regional meetings are being planned on historiography in Central Asia, the Transcaucasus, and in the Baltic. It seems that if we keep track of what has been done and what remains undone in working out the history of the party and party construction, we will really begin to manage our field.

Holding such meetings will make it easier for us to discover talented historians on whom we can readily rely, and will thus help the journal to put together a group of creative contributors—authors of living historical thought.

Doctor of Historical Sciences A. M. Sovokin, head of the Sector of the Works of V. I. Lenin at the Institute of Marxism-Leninism, said in his address that in the past few years, especially after the April (1985) Plenum of the CPSU Central Committee and the Twenty-seventh Congress of the CPSU, the journal began to call the attention of scholars to the study of the historical experience of the CPSU and its significance under conditions of restructuring in the political, economic, social, and intellectual spheres of Soviet society. Useful articles on the urgent tasks of restructuring, on the concept of acceleration and its connection with historical experience, on the establishment of the moral principles of socialism, were published in its pages, and there were also a number of items of debate on the periodization of party history and on the history textbook of the CPSU. Unfortunately, historians are not very active in the debates or in preparing materials for their journal. Even the staff members of the institute's Division of History of the CPSU rarely publish in its pages, and when they do it is usually not with articles that define that aspect of the journal.

Certainly, the journal bears some responsibility for the state of affairs in the discipline of party history. It does not fully expose deficiencies in the works of party historians. It has not succeeded in directing their creative energies to the study of many difficult and inadequately handled problems.

We know that V. I. Lenin considered the search for facts and documents on party history the only means of finding the truth.[2] It is precisely along this path that historians can rise to the level of today's high demands and begin serious source research and publication of documents on the history of the party, which will attract the attention not only of investigators but also of all those who are interested in these problems.

Precise and indisputable facts are especially necessary when there is a serious desire to make sense of the complex and difficult questions of history or of public life. Facts are the nuts and bolts of historical science, and if you take them as a whole and in their interconnections, they are a truly convincing thing—so thought Lenin, who concluded that it was necessary to create "a foundation of precise and indisputable facts, which could be relied on, and with which one could compare any of those 'general' and 'approximate' judgments which are so boundlessly abused. . . . In order that this be truly a foundation, one must take not individual facts, but the entire totality of facts relating to the question under consideration, *without a single* exception."[3] All historians know these words of Lenin practically by heart, but in practice it has not yet been determined conclusively what the totality of facts is when it comes to the social sciences.

I believe that the main task is to restructure the discipline of party history and to resurrect the revolutionary spirit of Leninism in working out all problems of party history and in writing a vivid, accurate history of the CPSU.

In speaking of the need to increase the number of publications in the journal on questions of intraparty democracy, the deputy director of the Institute of Marxism-Leninism, Professor M. P. Mchedlov, doctor of philosophical sciences, suggested the development of the following themes: the interrelationships between the secretary and the bureau of the party, the party committee, and the staff of the party committee—that is, from the bottom upward. He said the secretary of a party committee bureau should be offered the floor; then the secretaries of the raion committee, the city committee, the oblast CPSU committee, and the secretary of the central committee of the Communist party of a union republic. These speeches would show the development of relations of the secretary of the bureau of a party committee with the bureaus and committees in which he works. One of the secretaries of the CPSU Central Committee should be asked to speak on how actual collegiality of party leadership is obtained. If we succeed in shedding light on this problem, both on the horizontal and on the vertical plane, I think this would be what we need. Thus, we must find new aspects in party subject matter, particularly in that of party construction, and shed light on them on a scientific basis, Mchedlov emphasized.

Doctor of Historical Sciences L. F. Morozov, senior research associate of the institute, in noting the pluses and minuses in the journal's work, said that it inadequately handled the problems of the transitional period. In addition, there were issues of the journal in which not a single item on this period was published. What, in his opinion, should be dealt with? First of all, such a topic as V. I. Lenin and commodity-money relationships, which must be broadly used both in the transitional period and in the epoch of socialism. We should also discuss problems of economic strategy and tactics in the transitional period and the question of alternatives in building socialism.

The speaker suggested that the members of the editorial staff tap the experience of the journal *Proletarskaia revoliutsiia*,* which published interesting reminiscences. One can only welcome, Morozov said, the fact that the journal has begun to publish memoirs by participants in the Great October Revolution. He would like to see reminiscences of the building of socialism as well.

Improving the content of the section "People, Events, Facts" would promote readers' interest in the journal. About twenty years ago, interesting articles on party figures appeared in this section, not only on anniversary dates, and not only on the most prominent figures. It would be worthwhile to revive this tradition.

At the present time, said Candidate of Philosophical Sciences N. E. Tikhonova, junior research associate of the Institute of Marxism-Leninism, the journal is trying to respond to serious questions that arise in party history, and is carrying more varied material. Turnover among the journal's contributors is also noticeable. She stated that readers certainly expect a good deal from our journal. It's clear that by itself, the journal can't justify these hopes if scholars aren't actively involved in perestroika. If they submit interesting articles, then the journal itself will be interesting.

However, something—and something quite important at that—also depends on the journal's staff. This relates, above all, to organization. Present work arrangements in the editorial office are quite complex. One can't expect items that have been in preparation for publication for a year and a half to be timely. The members of the editorial staff have also not overcome their timidity.

She then noted that we know that quite a few stereotypes, clichés, and even prejudices form in scholarship. The mass media have taken it upon themselves to "stir up" these stereotypes and clichés, focusing readers' attention on the most painful problems—for example, the personality cult, the repressions of the 1930s and '40s, and the like. Certainly discussion of these questions is important and necessary. Surely, however, a scholarly journal should not concentrate attention only on such problems. Other questions, in a scholarly sense no less important, must also be posed. For example, I haven't encountered any stimulating articles on the second half of the 1940s. This is not normal. After all, after the war, when the economy returned to peacetime production, the foundations for those serious

---

*The principal journal of *Istpart* [the Commission for the Study of Party History and the History of the October Revolution] between 1921 and 1928, and afterward taken over by the Lenin Institute.—D.J.R.

problems we encounter today were surely laid. It's apparent that this period demands concentrated attention and study.

In conclusion, I would like to make one more point. Venerable scholars are now taking part in scientific debates. For them, the periods of which they speak were the times in which they lived. Even before now, they knew what was bad and what was good at that time, but whereas previously they wrote only about the positive in those distant years, they now are speaking essentially about negative phenomena and uncovering "lacunae."

And what impact does this have on today's younger generation? We studied out of textbooks in which the history of our society was offered up primarily in triumphal tones. Now it suddenly turns out that there was apparently nothing good at that time, and that all of this was a whitewashing of the truth. Therefore, we have to reconsider all the ideas we have had up to now about the history of our country and the party. In truth, this pedagogical, philosophical aspect must not be lost sight of in the course of discussions now in progress. Whatever critical articles we publish, they must reflect life as it was. We must not depict everything only in black.

Professor R. V. Filippov, doctor of historical sciences and senior research associate of the Institute of Marxism-Leninism, said in his speech that the tasks of *Voprosy istorii KPSS* at the contemporary stage are defined by many party documents, but especially by the Resolution of the CPSU Central Committee "On the Journal *Kommunist*" [O zhurnale *Kommunist*]. As for its role in restructuring party history, he continued, it was reducible, in his view, to restoring the prestige of our field. This means returning party history to the status of a genuine branch of scholarship, which can in fact fulfill the social and political functions appropriate to it. Only in this case can it carry out the social assignments given to it by further restructuring.

The unenviable position in which historical science found itself during the years of stagnation was to a large extent connected to the fact that scholars for too long have brushed aside "base truths," in favor of "the uplifting deception."[4] Now there is a return to "base truths," and this is a good indication of perestroika. In point of fact, it wasn't so long ago (for example, during discussions on the situation in the discipline of party history with regard to the specific problems of the Great October Revolution and the transitional period, which were held at the Institute of Marxism-Leninism in April 1987) that the mere mention of negative developments in the history of the party prompted indignation on the part of the dogmatists, an essential element in whose position was reducing the historians' role to that of commenting on party documents, and denying the significance of the negative experience in historical thought.

The fact that staff members of the journal no longer accept this position is a significant sign of perestroika. However, their position is difficult. Pressure from official authorities—pressure that, incidentally, is by no means always competent—has not yet been overcome. At the same time, the development of democracy gives rise to an assault against incompetence from below. It is by no means easy in this situation to be firm, and to resist all incompetence, wherever it comes from. In connection with this, it would be well to develop seriously the theme "The Braking Mechanism in the Discipline of Party History."

In regard to stereotypes, the speaker continued, they exist both in our field and in the journal, and they must be gotten rid of. For example, what was the situation in the journal until recently? In the first place, everything in it had to be correct (from the point of view of the editorial staff, of course); second, there had to be a uniform style and language; and third, there could be no hypotheses, and no emotion (as though you could solve anything without emotion!). In fairness, it should be noted that the journal has now begun to overcome these stereotypes.

The journal must give authors the opportunity to set forth their positions. Furthermore, it is not making adequate use of its right to express its view toward what is published. Read the old journals—for example, *Proletarskaia revoliutsiia*—and you will see that, whenever an article by an author whose position the journal does not share is published, there are two or three pages in the same issue that give a closely argued critique of this position, and readers are invited to participate in the debate. In a word, a respectful attitude toward "dissidence," and toward public debates, out of which the truth is born, is needed. After all, it's justly said that the right and obligation of the historian is to bear witness before history according to his conscience, regardless whether anyone likes it or not.

The discipline of party history, R. V. Filippov went on to say, cannot exist without historiography. M. V. Iskrov correctly emphasized this in his speech. But up to now, historiography has been assigned a subsidiary, secondary role. Its neglect has given rise among us to, among many other things, an excessive contempt for our predecessors' experience. As a result, the Americas are rediscovered, and wheels reinvented at each step. Articles are published everywhere from which you won't find out who posed this problem before, how it was solved, and so on and so forth.

The journal is making an attempt to restore historiography and is publishing serious historiographical articles on individual problems. But these are only the first steps, and there's a tremendous amount to do here. On the one hand, many scholars underestimate historiography as a field, and on the other, certain methodological problems of party historiography are obviously inadequately treated. The historiographic process must be shown in all its complexity and dramatic force, for here we have a source for the enormous experience of the CPSU in its various stages, and a reliable means of stopping the flood of writing that discovers again what has already been discovered and studied.

Filippov concluded that it is good that the journal publishes under the heading "At the Sources of Our Field" articles about major historians of the party. However, he would like them to have less of the polish of something written for an anthology or for an anniversary, and more serious analysis of creative searches of the pioneers in our field, so that they would show not only their achievements but also their failures.

Doctor of Historical Sciences K. K. Shirinia, consultant of the Institute of Marxism-Leninism, noted that the orientation of the journal toward a wider readership, and not only to historians of the CPSU, is legitimate. When the question is posed in this way, the demand spoken of here may become more understandable: to adopt many forms of presenting material, and to speak more effectively on the urgent topics of the day. It's clear from the materials published that the journal itself is now attracted to scholarly public-affairs articles because this genre gives an opportunity to promote more rapidly what has already become the order of the day, but can't yet be shown with a large scholarly apparatus. Other demands made on the journal, with regard to the need to increase its attention to historiography, the publication of documents and reminiscences, and the like, are also legitimate.

There are questions that the journal can solve, however, only with the help of the managing board of the Institute of Marxism-Leninism. The journal was criticized here—and to a certain degree legitimately—because items on the international activity of the CPSU are published basically to coincide with anniversaries. In fact, there is no settled policy with regard to the handling of this subject matter in the journal. The task now is to fill in this gap. And for this it is necessary to open up access for researchers to the appropriate archival documents.

Filling in the gaps in the party's prehistory and at various stages of party history, and the removal of deformations and distortions of various kinds in this discipline should become the focus of restructuring the journal, Docent D. I. Poliakova, candidate of historical sciences and senior research associate of the Institute of Marxism-Leninism, emphasized in her speech. We need systematic work in this direction, well thought out in its details, by all the divisions of the editorial staff and we should accordingly commission articles from authors or groups of authors who have been working fruitfully on these problems for a long time.

It has already been noted that the journal's ties to the social science departments of postsecondary educational institutions and research institutions, including branches of the Institute of Marxism-Leninism, are shallow and weak, and that therefore the "geography" of the authors represented in the pages of *Voprosy istorii KPSS* is still rather narrow. Nonetheless, we should not fail to note the real effort of the editorial board to enlarge the number of contributors and to recruit, in particular, specialists in nonparty history. I think there is no contradiction between the journal's title and the broadening of its subject matter by way of studies in related social science disciplines. The publication of works by nonparty historians, philosophers, and sociologists has enriched the creative potential and deepened those aspects of the journal's activity that relate to its content.

There is a long tradition of holding debates in the pages of *Voprosy istorii*

KPSS. This is a kind of laboratory for honing the edge of research and collective endeavors. Usually a debate is topped off by a generalizing editorial that comments on the material presented. It seems to me that this is insufficient. I would like to see thoughts expressed in journal debates receive wider distribution. I propose the publication of a book based on the last three debates—on the historical experience of the CPSU, the periodization of party history, and "What Should the Textbooks of the History of the CPSU Be Like?"

The journal should become not only a tribune, but a school for training historians, a place for testing new research approaches and new formulations of problems. It may be expeditious to organize a practical training session for historians of the party under the Division of History of the CPSU and the Council of Young Scholars of the Institute of Marxism-Leninism, which would have access to the pages of the journal in a special department. This would facilitate expansion of the body of contributors to *Voprosy istorii KPSS* and formation of a new generation of scholars.

D. I. Poliakova said in conclusion that the journal will increasingly draw the attention of readers as those qualitative changes that are already taking place in it become deeper. But we also must not forget about improving the form of the material, and about offering a variety of genres. The departments in the journal are still rather static. Furthermore, some of them—for example, "People, Events, Facts"—at times disappear for long periods from its pages, and the items published in it, as a rule, set forth the biography of someone from A to Z. It is possible, it would seem, to choose interesting turning points in a person's life and take off from these in order to present the material in a new way. The department, "Criticism and Bibliography," in my opinion, is also somewhat antiquated and does not represent the new branch of historiography, source research, and scholarly criticism.

Professor V. V. Zhuravlev, doctor of historical sciences, deputy director of the Institute of Marxism-Leninism, and head of the Department of History of the CPSU, said that the steps taken by the journal in restructuring noted here are significant and give rise to optimism. In thinking of the future of the journal, however, we should once again reflect on what type of journal it should be. It is obvious that it must remain a scholarly publication, but in so doing it cannot be oriented only toward specialists. An important element in its reorganization consists in combining a maximum of scholarly character with a good dose of popular appeal, and responding to the demands of the broad mass of readers. The journal is trying to satisfy this interest, but it is not yet entirely succeeding. This is the fault, of course, of the discipline of party history as a whole, including the Division of the History of the Party at our institute.

The speaker further noted that the scale and level of development of a whole series of problems in the journal do not satisfy either the broad reading public or historians of the party. And at the same time, it is not fitting for the journal to seek sensationalism in the history of the party during the transitional period. On the contrary, it is important to offer a carefully weighed, scholarly approach against this sensationalism.

The journal is only just now beginning to solve the task of revealing the dialectic of the history of the CPSU through the dialectic of the fates of major figures in the party, including those whose fates during the revolution and the building of socialism were complex and whose paths were ambiguous.

For all the positive changes in the journal, it lacks sufficient boldness and controversy, on the one hand, and tolerance of nontraditional scholarly points of view on the other. Certainly we have to avoid "convenient facts," but it is offensive when a controversial but legitimate formulation of a particular question is avoided. If some item submitted for publication contains a legitimate scientific hypothesis that constitutes an analysis of the totality of known facts, this should be published, even in those cases where the editorial board does not agree with the hypothesis.

According to Zhuravlev, the central thrust of the journal's activity at present is toward problems of historiography and source research. There is a gap here, but it isn't the journal that is to blame for this but the discipline of party history as a whole. In order to restructure the field, we have to evaluate the historiographic legacy. However, when we try to do this the journal faces a complicated situation. On the one hand, there are few trained historians able to look at the old historiographic baggage from new positions. On the other hand, those historians who do possess the skill of historiographic analysis are frequently guided by the following consideration: "Who am I to criticize my colleagues on this matter?" We must add to this the unparalleled labor-intensiveness of preparing historiographic articles. Here, then, are the subjective and objective reasons why it is so difficult to obtain a serious article on historiography.

Zhuravlev admitted that the institute's Division of Party History plays an inadequate role in reorganizing the journal. The sector heads of the division almost never publish in its pages, and if they do, it is not on important problems. Conditions are now ripe for having the division's research associates plan items for the journal. People agree, the speaker noted, that each research associate of the division shall mark his or her participation in the multivolume history of the CPSU by submitting an article. These items will be included in the plans of the division and the journal.

The journal must try harder to abandon stereotypes. A significant number of the articles by leaders of party organizations—in the form in which they are submitted to the journal—cannot satisfy today's reader. In most cases, they are essentially reports, often saturated with local considerations, which are hardly interesting for the general reader. They should be presented in the form of interviews by specialized historians with the secretary, let us say, of an oblast party committee on the particular problem, so that the secretary would have to answer questions presented by scholarship.

There's one other problem I'd like to talk about. The journal is organizing scholarship. However, we still expect more help from it in the activity of the All-Union Council on the Coordination of Research in the field of party history and party construction. This council has now been turned into a registrar of those spontaneously developing processes in party history that are determined by the interests of writers of dissertations. In order for the journal to become, in fact, a headquarters for historical science, we must first of all develop a prioritized program of research topics in the field of party history and party construction, and discuss it broadly in the pages of the journal. And then, having such a program, the council, along with the journal, will determine what programs in the field of party history should be worked on.

Not only the speeches at the meeting of the Academic Council expressed concern for further enhancing the journal's role and restructuring the discipline of party history. This concern was also raised during direct discussion between members of the editorial staff and staff members of the Institute of Marxism-Leninism, and also in specific written proposals—those, for example, sent to the editorial board by Candidate of Economic Sciences A. A. Pavlenko and Doctor of Historical Sciences Iu. K. Malov, both senior research associates at the institute.

Pavlenko suggested that the journal publish more articles devoted to the theoretical heritage of Marx, Engels, and Lenin, and also to the present. It is necessary to struggle relentlessly for the purity of the Marxist-Leninist theoretical heritage, he noted, and against the suppression, covering up, inaccurate treatment, or outright distortion of the position of Marx, Engels, and Lenin on a given question, and to routinely publish articles against bourgeois ideology and falsification of CPSU history. We should publish in the journal items on the historical experience of our party that are useful both to us during perestroika and to the contemporary communist movement.

Since we are speaking of enhancing the journal's role in working out current problems in party history, and in further developing Marxist-Leninist party doctrine, writes Malov, it is quite obvious that here we cannot avoid the question of the place and role of the CPSU in restructuring, especially in its new, second phase, and of the party's interaction with other political and economic organs under conditions of democratization and economic autonomy. In other words, a sophisticated working out is needed of the contemporary conception of the party's leading role, which is noted in M. S. Gorbachev's speech at the meeting of the CPSU Central Committee discussing the tasks of party work in implementing the main directions of the second stage of restructuring—democratization of the entire life of society and radical economic reform.

In fact, over the last two or three years, our idea of the function of various institutions in society and of the totality of socialist social relations has been significantly enriched, and it is only in the conception of the role of the party that nothing has essentially changed. An impression is being created that the process of qualitative renewal of Soviet society, the radical change not only in the form, style, and methods, but also in the principles of administration and economic leadership, has left only the party untouched. It seems that the journal should address these questions more actively and contribute to perestroika.

The time has indeed come to have on the editorial staff an associate who studies, as a specialty and not simply occasionally, questions of ideological struggle and bourgeois ideology, as is done in many other scholarly journals, instead of assigning this work to all staff members, many of whom are acquainted with its particulars only casually.

What does restructuring of scholars mean?

V. Ia. Bondar' brought up this question in connection with the discussion of the journal's tasks with regard to restructuring party history. He asked: what does it mean to restructure a discipline, a scholar, a scholarly worker? He answered that in the literal sense of the word, the restructuring of a scholar surely means his intellectual reorientation, changing his system of thinking, the reorganization of his consciousness, talent, and scholarly experience. Can this be done? It is almost impossible, because everything a scholar writes represents his ego, which has been shaped by suffering and which is embodied in his books and articles. This would be easy only in the case of someone without an ego, but such a scholar has not become a personality, and this in turn means that he does not have the right to be called a scholar.

Those who yesterday said one thing and today have suddenly "reconstructed themselves," and begun to speak "the truth," are rather common now. In these cases, the feeling arises that frequently "the truth" has begun to be spoken by opportunists. Striving to reach the center of public consciousness, they give birth to false sensations, neglecting in the process the requirements of scientific objectivity. The serious scholar is obligated always to be at one with the truth and to write the truth, to seek the truth, and to defend justice with all his work.

Consequently, Bondar' continued, it is not possible for everyone to reshape this aspect of his ego, nor is there always an opportunity to do so. Nevertheless we must all restructure ourselves. How? We can answer this question only by analyzing the essence of scholarship. I have already touched upon one aspect of this, but there is also another. The true scholar is characterized by a constant critical attitude toward himself or herself, constant searching, constant dissatisfaction. He or she cannot admit the thought that his or her work is beyond the power of the dialectic. In other words, the true scholar, while remaining in essence unchanged, will nevertheless change and grow in the search for truth. And this is what perestroika must be based on.

We must begin the restructuring of historical science with ourselves, by analyzing the experience we have accumulated, in order to more easily see our own deficiencies, and to look more deeply at those scholarly problems that concern us.

According to Bondar', if we look at the journal's work, taking account of these considerations, we can say that its staff members acted correctly, when, in implementing perestroika, they did not hasten to open up their pages to those who were "restructuring themselves" too rapidly, but, on the contrary, recruited a number of scholars for whom restructuring is not on the tip of the tongue, but is the result of a serious critical reevaluation and deepening of their positions.

As an example, Bondar' referred to V. M. Selunskaia's article "The Communist Party in the Struggle for the Collectivization of Agriculture in the USSR" [Kommunisticheskaia partiia v bor'be za kollektivizatsiiu sel'skogo khoziaistva SSSR] (no. 9, 1987). It is written by an author for whom the "traditional" approach to the problem of collectivization is combined with a critically weighted objectivity. Selunskaia did not abandon a single one of her previous positions, but took a step forward in understanding the problem, made a number of corrections, reinterpreted some evaluations and historical facts, and gave them a new interpretation. As a result, knowledge of the problem was augmented considerably. This is perestroika. There is no sensation here, but there is scholarship.

Something similar can be said about such articles as V. A. Kozlov's "The Historian and Perestroika," O. T. Bogomolov's "The Socialist Way of Life: Paths of Renewal" [Sotsialisticheskii obraz zhizni: Puti obnovleniia], N. A. Barsukov's "On the Turning Points, Basic Transitions, and Stages of the History of the CPSU" [O perelomnykh rubezhakh, osnovnykh periodakh i etapakh istorii KPSS], and R. V. Filippov's "Aren't We Departing from Historical Truth?" (no. 6, 1987), and others. There is no falsity in these articles; they are written honestly, and this is restructuring. After all, the essence of perestroika for each of us is to be honest in large and small things.

The journal's task is to continue to support authors like these, and to search out new, young, honest researchers, who speak the truth, analyze questions deeply, and draw well-argued conclusions.

In touching on the question of the restructuring of a scholar, A. M. Sovokin disagreed with some of the things said by the previous speaker. He thought that V. Ia. Bondar' went too far in asserting that the restructuring of a scholar is the restructuring of his or her consciousness, talent, and scholarly experience, and that the reconsideration of his or her works allegedly deprives him or her of the right to be considered a scholar. This position can hardly be shared. In fact, the scholar, in carrying out research, sets one goal—the search for the truth, the search for real facts and indisputable proof, which constitute the basis and the foundation of any research in party history. If in the scholar's work the facts do not correspond to historical reality, the conclusion drawn on the basis of these facts is inaccurate. In that case, the scholar not only may but is obliged to reconsider his or her previous opinion and say openly how he or she was mistaken, and to what conclusion he or she came on the basis of new facts, previously unknown.

In this connection, I would like to emphasize that in life we hardly ever encounter people (including scholars) who do not make mistakes. The problem is not that people are mistaken, but that they often persist in their errors. The intelligent person is not the one who doesn't make mistakes—there simply are no such people—but the one who makes mistakes that aren't very serious, and recognizes and corrects them. Lenin taught us this.

R. V. Filippov also expressed his attitude toward the problem of restructuring individual scholars. He disagreed with Bondar"'s assertion to the effect that the true scholar is always "obligated to be at one with the truth," is originally virtually in the embrace of the truth, and if he or she changes views, cannot then be considered a true scholar. Pointing to well-known scholars who more than once changed their views on particular problems, the speaker noted that a change in views by an historian is not always determined by considerations of opportunism, and often flows naturally out of the very nature of scientific knowledge.

At the same time, the idea expressed by Bondar' for a struggle against opportunists found universal approval among participants in the Academic Council meeting. More than this, M. P. Mchedlov proposed that the journal speak out against opportunists in science who, disregarding objectivity and scientific procedure, try always to be ahead of progress.

G. L. Smirnov, director of the Institute of Marxism-Leninism, focused attention on the need for restructuring social scientists. Noting the importance of posing this problem, he emphasized the degree of vagueness involved in statements about restructuring scholars. "It seems to me," the speaker said, "that we must not refuse anyone the right to restructure. More than this, all of us are obliged to undergo restructuring. M. S. Gorbachev, general secretary of the CPSU Central Committee, is constantly talking about this. In the process of restructuring it will be necessary to abandon in the process of restructuring certain favorite formulas and positions that all of us have at one time or another proclaimed and defended."

Of course, when it is a matter of a certain kind of statements of which V. Ia. Bondar' spoke—statements saturated with an opportunistic spirit—we must be specific in our discussion. As for those who intend to maintain the antiquated positions on which we stood five to seven years ago, they will have a very hard time.

The documentary base—the foundation of historical science

There was not a single speech at the Academic Council meeting that did not touch, to one degree or another, on the question of the documentary base of research in party history. This is natural, since without documentation historical science cannot develop. All the speakers agreed that the journal publishes too few documents. However, opinions differed as to why this is so. One view was expressed by the deputy head of the Central Party Archives of the Institute of Marxism-Leninism, Candidate of Historical Sciences and Docent V. V. Anikeev.

Our journal, he said, is in the most advantageous position relative to other social science journals because the Institute of Marxism-Leninism has a documentary base that no other research institute in the country that has its own journal can match. Few documents, however, appear in its pages.

He named the documents contained in the Central Party Archives of the Institute of Marxism-Leninism which, in his opinion, would permit the journal *Voprosy istorii KPSS* to conduct a systematic and purposeful publishing program, and offer surveys on the type and subject matter of documents. Among them, Anikeev named the following:

—documents of higher party organs—particularly the materials of the fifth and sixth conferences of the RSDRP and of the plenums of the RKP(b) Central Committee from March 1918 through 1922, which, as a rule, were held under the leadership of V. I. Lenin;

—the minutes of the meetings of the Council of People's Commissars for 1917–21;

—documents sent to Lenin from 1917 through 1922 on questions regarding the building of the economy, the state, and the party, the leadership of the Red Army's military operations against the united forces of the domestic and foreign counterrevolution during the Civil War, and on questions of foreign policy and the international communist movement;

—Lenin's correspondence and that of central institutions led by him with the local party organizations in the years of reaction (1907–10);

—documents on the organizational activity of the Central Committee of the party during preparation of the October Revolution; financial documents and also certificates and credentials of the RSDRP(b) Central Committee issued to representatives of the Central Committee who were sent to the localities or who arrived from the provinces to visit the Central Committee; the correspondence of the Secretariat of the RKP(b) Central Committee with local party organizations in the decisive months of the Civil War (July-December 1919), and in the preparatory period and the first stage of NEP;

—the correspondence of the Ul'ianov family through 1917 inclusive;

—the proceedings of individual plenums of the executive committee of the Communist International, connected with the strengthening of the fraternal parties and creation of a united front;

—documents of the regional bureaus of the party Central Committee—in particular, the Caucasian, the Central Asian, the Northwestern and Southeastern, the Urals, the Siberian and the Far Eastern, and of the bureaus of the VKP(b) Central Committee for the Baltic republics, and also of the regional bureaus of the CPSU Central Committee for the 1950s and 1960s.

After listing some additional documents, V. V. Anikeev concluded by expressing doubt that all this could be published in the journal given its present size.

He raised the question of recruiting personnel from all departments and sectors of the Institute of Marxism-Leninism, and also of the Academy of Social Sciences under the CPSU Central Committee and the Moscow Higher Party School, to assist in preparing documents for publication.

A very rosy picture, isn't it? It turns out that everything is up to the journal. It has such wealth at hand, such possibilities, such magnificent prospects. It's even been proposed that the journal be expanded in order to cope with the publication of the documents that are about to flow out of the Central Party Archives.

But what is the actual situation? Here is what V. V. Zhuravlev said on this score at the meeting of the Academic Council.

> V. V. Anikeev has set forth here a program for publishing documents that gives rise to great optimism. But, you see, he is proposing his own rules for the journal: here is this, and this, and this for you from our bounty. . . . But it seems to me that the discussion must be conducted on another level. The journal, together with the the Central Party Archives and the Department of Party History, should choose those documents that are most important and necessary to science, and then it should decide whether or not to publish them.
>
> Previously, all new documents about Lenin were published in the journal immediately after they were found and placed in the Central Party Archives. They quickly became known to the scholarly public and to all Soviet people. But some time ago, this natural way of doing things was changed. The institute's Sector of the Works of V. I. Lenin began to "salt away" new documents for the next Lenin collection, and, as it turned out, to delay their publication for years. If individual documents about Lenin appeared in the press before the next Lenin collection was issued, this didn't happen in our journal.
>
> At one time, information on all new document acquisitions in the Central Party Archives was published in the journal each year. Now this practice has stopped, and this in the present situation is intolerable.

Previously, surveys of the holdings of the the Central Party Archives were published. Now they are not. V. V. Zhuravlev emphasized that this situation needs correcting.

In fact, the existing situation with regard to the documentary base for research calls forth legitimate reproaches from historians of the party. On the one hand, they do not have access to any archival sources, and on the other hand, the journal itself publishes few documents. The journal must, without fail, be helped in preparing documents for publication, in the opinion of M. V. Iskrov. "I think that not a single issue should be published without including documents," he said. A. M. Sovokin fully shared this point of view. He asked the question: can one study a particular problem without documents? The speaker expressed hope that the Academic Council would draw the appropriate conclusions in relation to the subdivisions of the institute and would determine what they should do to create a documentary basis for the history of the CPSU and for the publication of documents.

The need to expand the source base for research and to lift the ban on access to a number of archival holdings has been emphasized here often, said D. I. Poliakova. There is no question that the study of archival documents and a critical reading of them is necessary for a scholarly publication and that it guarantees that articles submitted to the journal will be more convincing.

But even the sources accessible to us—the published stenographic reports and proceedings of party congresses—open up, in their turn, quite a few heuristic opportunities for new approaches in scholarship, for reinterpreting historical themes that have been inaccurately reflected in the literature, for the liquidation of "blank spots" and the depersonalization of history. However, we are still paralyzed by the customary timidity of thought, the inertia of fixed evaluations and established judgments.

R. V. Filippov noted that our tradition of source research inculcates timidity in relation to party documents. The well-known source specialist M. A. Varshavchik holds the view, he continued, that the documents of the higher party organs are subject only to comment and cannot be subjected to critical analysis. This is an antiscientific way of posing the question. I am convinced that a person who is guided by this notion, even if he or she has everything that our archives have at their disposal, will give us the same old rubbish, from which we read nothing new and do not see historical truth.

For a comprehensive and truthful treatment of the international activity of the CPSU, and of its role, for example, in the Communist International, said K. K. Shirinia, we need to rely on a broad range of sources and to put archival materials into scientific circulation, without which scholarly research is held back. This question has to be solved, otherwise we will move ahead only slowly.

The Comintern materials in the Central Party Archives show that CPSU representatives in that organization posed many questions of an international character in a profound and accurate manner, and made interesting proposals. As a rule, even during the period of enthusiasm for a left-wing course in the executive committee of the Communist International, many resolutions and recommendations of the Comintern and the CPSU delegation were distinguished by their high theoretical level, and were restrained in a political sense. Along with these, however, there are documents that show the illegitimate methods by which debates were settled in our party in Stalin's time, when opposition was simplistically evaluated as a hostile class action. Investigators also need these documents so that truth may triumph in their scholarly treatment.

In ending the discussion on the publication of new documents in the journal, it is necessary to emphasize the presence of extreme caution and of a wait-and-see attitude on part of the leadership of the Central Party Archives of the Institute of Marxism-Leninism. This is certainly to some extent the fault of members of the editorial board who obviously do not show the necessary activism and insistence.

V. I. Kas'ianenko mentioned this at the meeting of the Academic Council. It is true that recently the editorial board has begun to print regularly the minutes of the meetings of the Council of People's Commissars of the RSFSR. In issue no. 10 for 1987, there appeared protocol no. 1 from November 15, 1917, and in the November issue, the minutes of the second and third meetings of the Council of People's Commissars. The scholarly public welcomed these publications. But we must say that the journal's possibilities are certainly limited. Here V. V. Anikeev is right. For example, it will take at least ten years to publish all the minutes of the meetings of the Council of People's Commissars for Lenin's period. For this reason, in publishing documents we must rely not only on the journal, but must issue them in collections.

Along with increased publication of documents, we must not forget about another important way of expanding the source base: acquainting scholars with archival materials through surveys of documents. Of course, this work is extremely labor-intensive: one has to survey tens of thousands and even hundreds of thousands of documents in order to choose the most valuable ones. This work cannot be done after hours; it must be done on a planned basis.

The main focus should be on current problems

G. L. Smirnov spoke at the conclusion of the meeting of the Academic Council. The discussion over the journal's work, he said, was diverse, businesslike, and comradely. It will, beyond question, help the editorial staff and the editorial board in solving the problems involved in restructuring the field of party history. For all the problems and deficiencies spoken of here, the journal is somewhat ahead of the Section of Party History. In general, this is as it should be: the journal is obliged to become the pioneer of perestroika. The people who work on it, with the help of the Division of Party History, are trying conscientiously to carry out the tasks entrusted to it.

With a whole series of publications, including the measures carried out by the institute, beginning with the citywide debates on party history in April 1987, and by the Academy of Social Sciences under the CPSU Central Committee, the journal reflects the development of thought in the field of party history. As has already been noted here, the turn toward perestroika in its work is particularly noticeable beginning with issue no. 5 for 1987. This issue shows that the editorial board was finally beginning to feel firm ground beneath its feet, and was finding authors who were able to pose controversial questions in a professional way.

Naming a number of articles that reflect the spirit of perestroika, Smirnov paused to consider the discussion on problems of periodization of CPSU history, which the journal is conducting. This is very necessary, he noted. It must be continued and the very deepest foundations of periodization must be reached. Participants in the discussion correctly felt that the dates of party congresses cannot be taken as the basis for periodization. It is hardly the point to orient ourselves solely on the basis of documents. Here we need objective analysis of the relationship of documents with history: that is, it is necessary to evaluate the activity of both local and central party organs, problems in the development of the political sphere, culture, etc. In a word, reality must be taken as an integral whole.

At the meeting much valuable advice and numerous proposals were given for further improving the work of the editorial board and content of the journal, G. L. Smirnov said. I believe that the staff will take advantage of them. Nevertheless, the main task of the journal is to concentrate on the problems of CPSU history that have not yet been finally clarified. This is a primary task for the institute's Division of Party History. Without a thorough working-through, we cannot speak in any serious way of the restructuring of the field of party history. At the same time, both in the editorial board and in the Division of Party History of the Institute of Marxism-Leninism, these problems have been defined with sufficient clarity. Some of them have already been discussed in the pages of the journal, and others are being made clear now.

Take, for example, the prerevolutionary period. What problems require additional research? Primarily the relationship of Bolshevism with its predecessors, especially the Populists [Narodniki]. It is obviously time to be precise about what the Bolsheviks borrowed from their heritage, and what they discarded. Problems connected with the Sixth (Prague) All-Russian Conference of the RSDRP also require additional research. The Short Course of the History of the VKP(b) [Kratkii kurs istorii VKP(b)], as we know, asserted, contrary to historical truth, that this conference "laid the foundation of a party of a new type," while in reality, the origin of Bolshevism dates from the Second Congress of the RSDRP.

There is no denying that the Great October Socialist Revolution needs to be studied more deeply, and not so much because of our domestic needs as because of international ones. After all, to this day the idea exists and is being spread that during the October Revolution, Trotsky had a "special role." We know that in his article "The Lessons of October" [Uroki Oktiabria], he asserted that in fact the October Revolution was accomplished already on October 9, when the Petrograd Soviet resolved that the revolutionary troops would not be removed from Petrograd, and this allegedly decided the victory.

Then we have the question, the distortion of which has now taken on huge dimensions, of War Communism and NEP. Everything that people want to compromise, they label War Communism. But the policy of War Communism saved the young Soviet republic. The same is true of NEP. Certainly this was not a halcyon period in the history of our country, but a period of searching and of ferocious class struggle.

Questions of ideological and theoretical struggles of the 1920s require the most concentrated attention of researchers. There is a very complex issue here. This is in fact the epicenter of the ideological upheavals and course of our party. If we delve properly into these questions, we will have a better idea of that which later developed on the canvas of history because it was precisely at that time that the sharp struggle with the most important problems of creating the new society began, that conceptions of the country's industrialization and collectivization of agriculture were worked out, and that the various points of view on the ways to transfer the peasantry to a socialist track developed. The discussion between E. A. Preobrazhenskii and N. I. Bukharin on primitive accumulation is an excellent example. Strictly speaking, it constitutes the main issue in a theoretical sense—the key to the problem of industrialization, and to the country's further development, thanks to which we can understand a great deal of the subsequent behavior of various party groups.

There are the problems of industrialization and collectivization, which, of course, cannot be dealt with in two or three articles, and on which we must work thoroughly. It must be borne in mind that the greatest number of abuses of power occurred precisely in this period. Historians know that I. V. Stalin, who had spent about three weeks in Siberia, at first, applied repressive measures during the grain requisition, and that L. M. Kaganovich, who had been sent to the North Caucasus, arrested dozens of secretaries of raikoms of the party.

In this connection, of course, the figure of Stalin arises again. We will, apparently, have to return to him more than once. The interests of developing the field of party history demand this. And, of course, there can be no straightforward evaluation here. It's now known that many lawless acts and repressive measures were carried out not only with Stalin's knowledge, but on his initiative. At the same time, it would be incorrect to reduce Stalin's role to repression alone, because the victory of the policy of industrialization and collectivization, and the saving of our country from Hitler are also connected with him. These are the positions we have supported and will support, and in this respect, in truth, we do not need restructuring.

The list of inadequately studied problems could be extended. But as I have already said, they are known to the journal's editorial staff and the personnel of the Division of Party History. The main thing is that there should be no formalism in the approach to their interpretation. If an article has been published on some question, and it appears to make a definitive statement, it's as if the job were finished. But if necessary (and in most cases, it is), we should turn to that problem not once or twice, but perhaps ten times. It isn't necessary that these articles be thirteen or fifteen pages long. One can also write three pages, but in such a way as to attract attention. We shouldn't be afraid of small formats. Space would be opened up in the journal that could be used for other themes.

Pausing to consider the improvement in the journal staff members' style of work, G. L. Smirnov emphasized that the practice of dressing up authors' articles "in a set style" should stop. It is especially impermissible when an editor "fixes up" an article by toning down an author's formulation of a problem. This is most frequently done with young scholars.

In general, the role of the editor today, especially in a scholarly journal, should be reduced primarily to organizing the material, to showing initiative in posing problems, and to assisting authors in terms of technique. The editor should not cross out commas, and change negative words to positive ones.

Smirnov then made a number of remarks on the journal's plan for 1988. It needs serious correction, he said. In the first place, the formulations in it are so general that one can't see the problems behind them, or their degree of controversy. In the second place, we must pay more attention to the problems of the transitional period. These problems need a sustained, sophisticated, and more precise approach. It is now generally clear that the ban on discussing problems and on mentioning names is lifted. We must open our archival holdings for reading and processing, which means that we must reinterpret many things. In the third place, the number of publications projected on problems of democracy is quite inadequate. Those that are projected are too general.

In dealing with the department "Criticism and Bibliography," Smirnov said that the journal must either abandon book reviews as a form or change them radically. If there's a problem with a book, let's review it. If there is no problem, publish a notice of its appearance, and let it go at that. Otherwise we waste space on compliments. Of course, there are very good books. In those cases we don't need to regret the compliments. But as a rule, they should be avoided.

Pausing in conclusion to consider relations between the Institute of Marxism-Leninism and *Voprosy istorii KPSS*, Smirnov noted that they are now normal and businesslike. We do not impose on the editorial board behavior for every day, we don't bother them with trifles, but at the same time, we do discuss questions of principle, he emphasized. Let's hope that the discussion in the Academic Council will help the journal's staff to participate more positively and skillfully in the process of restructuring the field of party history.

The resolution adopted by the Academic Council emphasized that the focus of materials published by the journal should be the study of inadequately investigated aspects of Lenin's plan for building socialism, the problems of ideological and theoretical struggle in the party during the transitional period, the party's personnel policy, the party's leadership of restructuring, the links between the historical experience of the CPSU and the current world revolutionary process, questions of historiography and source research in the history of the party, and the struggle against bourgeois, social-reformist, and revisionist distortions of the history of the CPSU.

Notes

1. M. S. Gorbachev, *Molodezh'—tvorcheskaia sila revoliutsionnogo obnovleniia: Vystuplenie na XX s"ezde Vsesoiuznogo Leninskogo Kommunisticheskogo Soiuza Molodezhi 16 aprelia 1987 goda* (Moscow, 1987), p. 29.

2. See V. I. Lenin, *Polnoe sobranie sochinenii*, vol. 23, p. 68.

3. Ibid., vol. 30, pp. 350–51.

4. See ibid., p. 351.

On the Personality Factor in the History of the CPSU

V. G. VERIASKIN

This problem was the subject of a methodological seminar held on June 11 in the Department of History of the CPSU, Academy of Social Sciences under the CPSU Central Committee. Other participants in the seminar included research associates of the Central Committee's Institute of Marxism-Leninism, instructors at the Moscow Higher Party School, the V. I. Lenin Military-Political Academy, the Higher Komsomol School of the Komsomol Central Committee, and other scholarly and teaching institutions in the capital.

In opening the session, Professor N. N. Maslov, doctor of historical sciences and head of the Department of History of the CPSU of the Academy of Social Sciences, noted that historians of the party are faced with the important task of raising the theoretical level of scholarly research, and overcoming completely the stagnation that developed in the period when, in the words of M. S. Gorbachev, "living discussion and creative thought departed" from theory and social science, "and authoritarian evaluations and judgments became indisputable truths, subject only to commentary."[1]

Concern about the present state of research in party history, which was expressed at the All-Union Meeting of Heads of Social Science Departments, is quite justified. This concern is connected, in particular, with the depersonalization of many historical events,[2] which in turn lowers the ideological, moral, and instructional value of scholarly works, and the interest of Soviet people in them.

We quite legitimately look upon historical events as the result of the actions of the working masses and the party. At the same time, we frequently fail to show the role of specific individuals in concrete circumstances, their fates, successes, confusion, and errors, thereby depersonalizing history and depriving it of its heroic and dramatic quality. After all, in recognizing the masses as the decisive force in historical progress, Marxism-Leninism does not deny or underestimate the role of individuals in history. "History," Lenin points out, "consists entirely

Russian text © 1987 by "Pravda" Publishers. "O lichnostnom faktore v istorii KPSS," *Voprosy istorii KPSS*, 1987, no. 9, pp. 150–55. Translated by Stephen P. Dunn.

The author is a candidate of historical sciences and a docent.

of the acts of individuals, and the task of the social sciences is to explain these acts. . . .''[3]

Prominent individuals and leaders always played a very important role in the revolutionary struggle of the working people. "We are deeply convinced," Lenin said in his eulogy for Ia. M. Sverdlov, "that the proletarian revolution in Russia and in the whole world will bring forward groups and groups of people, will bring forward numerous strata of proletarians and of the working peasantry, and this will provide that practical knowledge of life, that organizational talent—if not individual, then collective—without which the million-fold armies of the proletariat cannot come to its victory."[4]

The best representatives of the working class, of the peasantry, and of the revolutionary intelligentsia linked their fates to that of the Communist party. Its history is also the history of millions of people, representing generations and different strata of society. These are not cogs in the party and state machinery, but individuals.

In having the seminar consider personality in the history of the CPSU—a problem almost forgotten by historians of the party—we will improve the teaching of CPSU history and serious study of the processes and phenomena of party history.

Iu. V. Derbinov, G. V. Petriakov, and I. E. Gorelov, all professors and doctors of historical sciences, presented papers at the seminar dealing with various aspects of the personality factor. The first of these speakers, critically analyzing the contemporary scholarly and textbook literature on this problem, compared it with the current practice of party life. Iu. V. Derbinov noted that the general sociological law discovered by Marx concerning the decisive role of the masses in history is treated in the literature without considering social practice. The dogmatization of theoretical positions has hindered the interpretation of complex social phenomena. As a result, the history of society and the party has become depersonalized. This has at times not prevented the exaggeration of the role and significance of individual leading figures, however, and the overestimation of their personal contribution in all spheres of life and in all activities of society.

The textbook literature on the history of the CPSU and on party construction was created according to a rigidly simple formula, in which the principles of historicism, the class principle, and the party principle were interpreted in such a way as to emasculate the creative element in the communist party's activity. Participants in historical events always occupied places assigned beforehand, were divided only into two camps, and struggled with each other by methods known beforehand. As a result, only a model entered people's consciousness, for the *dramatis personae* were missing.

Now, when interest in our history and in our past is increasing, and when historical stages and individuals are being reinterpreted, we should not create a distinctive balance at the expense of showing positive and negative heroes. Marxist-Leninist methodology offers a well-tried, multifaceted, systemic analysis of historical reality, which ensures objectivity, not through voluntaristic choice of characters, but through dealing with events and phenomena in all their complexity.

All of us clearly understand the need to take account as much as possible of the rigorous lessons of history. The time has come to reevaluate many established ideas that have previously been considered indisputable. This is apparently connected with glasnost', and not with voting, which is resorted to in those cases when there is an effort to shed one's own responsibility and transfer it to the group. Simple and even secret voting does not always serve as a criterion of democracy. After all, the truth is sometimes proclaimed by a creative and seeking minority, after which time the majority, lagging behind in the process, requires time to reach an understanding of it.

On the basis of specific examples from the life of the party and Soviet society, and from the implementation of the personnel policy of the CPSU under contemporary conditions, Iu. V. Derbinov traced the processes connected with the objectively conditioned increase of the individual's role in actively and consciously participating in restructuring all aspects of socialist society. Derbinov emphasized that these processes permit an even more profound revelation of extremely complex mechanisms of action of the general sociological laws discovered by the founders of communism. These processes also permit us to avoid reducing the above-mentioned laws to a primitive and one-sided scheme, and to learn to take full account of the objective requirements of the CPSU and of all its units, in the name of successfully implementing the strategic course toward accelerating the socioeconomic development of our country and implementing the changes that will open up new possibilities for exploiting the advantages of the socialist system.

Arguing for the theoretical and political urgency of the problem under discussion, G. V. Petriakov noted the inadequate degree to which the personality factor has been considered in Soviet historiography. In particular, the questions connected with the Stalin cult require deep and comprehensive study. Fundamental appraisals on this score were given at the Twentieth Party Congress, in the Resolution of the CPSU Central Committee "On Overcoming the Cult of Personality and Its Consequences" [O preodolenii kul'ta lichnosti i ego posledstvii] of June 30, 1956, and in a number of other documents. However, today these questions can hardly be considered to have been exhausted for party history.

Additional scholarly research and revelation of the objective and subjective causes of the Stalin cult and its concrete manifestations are necessary. We must give a complete and fully argued evaluation of the negative consequences of this phenomenon in various spheres of public and political life. One-sided interpretations of Lenin's "Letter to the Congress" [Pis'mo k s"ezdu], not only in scholarly publications but also in the teaching of the social sciences, raise definite objections. Instead of a deep and comprehensive analysis of this most important document, we still encounter artificial "truncating" of Lenin's judgments, and the "editing" of Lenin's texts to suit particular occasions.

According to Petriakov, the question of Stalin's appointment as general secretary of the Central Committee of the party at the April (1922) Central Committee Plenum, at which this office was established for the first time, should be fully and comprehensively studied on the basis of documents. As early as December 1922, Lenin posed the question of whether it was advisable to replace Stalin with another person in this post.

The question of the time in which the cult of personality appeared also needs further study. Until recently, the emphasis was placed in this regard on the last years of Stalin's life, which, in Petriakov's opinion, is hardly justified. The conference of Marxist agricultural experts (in December 1929), at which Stalin delivered a speech, "On Questions of Agrarian Policy in the USSR" [K voprosam agrarnoi politiki v SSSR], can be considered a kind of landmark in the development of this phenomenon. Afterward his lamentably famous letter to the editors of the journal *Proletarskaia revoliutsiia* (November 1931) appeared, "On Some Questions of the History of Bolshevism" [O nekotorykh voprosakh istorii bol'shevizma]. Finally, in 1938, *The History of the VKP(b): A Short Course* [Istoriia VKP(b): Kratkii kurs], was published, of which, after the war, Stalin was cited as the author. These, of course, are only a few milestones in the development of the cult of personality, the most prominent on the theoretical front, which was manifested in theoretical and political judgments, in the peremptory nature of Stalin's instructions, and the like.

As for the general political evaluation of Stalin's role, here, of course, we need deep scientific analysis, and we need to take comprehensive account of objective and subjective factors. It seems that the following three factors can be taken as starting points. First, the generally accepted role of Stalin as one of the leading figures in the party. Second, the mass-scale repressions and extremely flagrant violations of socialist legality during the years of the cult of personality, which are also inseparable from Stalin's name. Not everything here has been adequately studied, and not everything has yet been made public. And third, the profoundly negative influence of the atmosphere of the cult of personality on all aspects of society, including its spiritual development. "A high price had to be paid for departing from Leninist principles and methods of building the new society, for violating socialist legality and democratic norms of life in the party and society, for voluntarist mistakes, for dogmatism in thought and inertia in practical activity." [5] These words from the Appeal of the CPSU Central Committee to the Soviet people in connection with the seventieth anniversary of the Great October Revolution are, without question, also an evaluation of the situation in the party and in the Soviet state during the period of the Stalin cult.

In speaking of the cult of personality and its negative manifestations in various spheres, we must not fail to note its negative influence on the development of party history, which also requires profound and truthful study. In the speaker's opinion, the discipline of party history is still timid about solving many important problems connected with the personality factor in history, and with its positive and negative manifestations. The lessons of truth in light of the decisions of the Twenty-seventh Congress of the CPSU must be implemented more insistently and consistently. In this connection, we would like to see a more active role for the journal *Voprosy istorii KPSS.*

I. E. Gorelov's paper spoke of the need for a solicitous attitude toward the memories of Russia's revolutionaries, and for rescuing from oblivion the names of many participants in the liberation movement and in the building of socialism. "Not one class in history," Lenin emphasized, "has attained power without advancing its own political leaders, its own progressive representatives, who are capable of organizing the movement and leading it."[6] Purposeful people, people of crystalline honesty and of unexampled courage and heroism, gathered around the leader. The majority endured prison, forced labor, and exile. "These were people who did not waste themselves in useless terrorist enterprises, one by one, but agitated with conviction, unyieldingly, among the proletarian masses, helping to develop their consciousness, their organization, and their independent revolutionary activity."[7] Many of them were killed in the struggle with the autocracy during the revolution and civil war, and were subjected to unjustified repressions during the period of the cult of personality.

In the first years of Soviet power, a great deal of work was done collecting materials on prominent fighters for the revolution. Istpart* and its local branches played an important role here. The appeal of the chairman of Istpart, M. S. Ol'-minskii, "From Istpart to All Comrades" [Ot Istparta ko vsem tovarishcham] emphasized that "the decades of our struggle against the autocracy, followed by years of civil war have taken many of our comrades to their graves. The lives of each one of them is a fragment of party history, and a stone for the building of our communist future. We cannot live without the past, without knowledge of our history, and we cannot know our history without knowing those who were active in it."[8]

The historians of the 1920s and '30s did a great deal preparing and publishing scholarly biographies of the heroes of the Bolshevik underground and the fighters for Soviet power. Such books as *The Grave of Brothers: Biographical Dictionary of Deceased and Fallen Members of the Moscow Organization of the RKP* [Bratskaia mogila: Biograficheskii slovar' umershikh i pogibshikh chlenov Moskovskoi organizatsii RKP], parts 1 and 2 (Moscow, 1922–23); *Bolsheviks of Moscow, 1905* [Bol'sheviki Moskvy, 1905] (Moscow, 1925); *Heroes and Martyrs of the Proletarian Revolution* [Geroi i mucheniki proletarskoi revoliutsii], part 1 (Moscow, 1924); *Political Exile and Forced Labor: Biographical Directory of the Society of Political Prisoners and Exiles* [Politicheskaia katorga i ssylka:

Istpart—acronym for the Commission for the Study of Party History and the October Revolution. Organized in 1920, Istpart was absorbed by the Lenin Institute in 1928. —D.J.R.

Biograficheskii spravochnik Obshchestva politkatorzhan i ssyl'noposelentsev] (Moscow, 1934), and others, are especially valuable. Unfortunately, in subsequent years this necessary work was artificially interrupted. The main cause of this, in this writer's opinion, was the above-mentioned letter by Stalin to the journal *Proletarskaia revoliutsiia*, and later the appearance of the *History of the VKP(b): A Short Course.* However, even today, preparation and publication of biographies of Leninist Bolsheviks, the heroes of the October Revolution and the building of socialism, are not given due attention. The historian's duty is to fill in this lacuna, since an account of the lives and activities of these individuals is one of the best and most efficient means of inculcating communism in Soviet people, particularly the young.

Other seminar participants also spoke during the discussion. Professor O. G. Obichkin, doctor of historical sciences and head of the Department of Party Construction of the Academy of Social Sciences under the CPSU Central Committee, noted that the subjective factor in general, and the personal qualities of participants in the revolutionary movement in particular, played an important role in our party's history. The speaker characterized the basic features of the proletarian Leninist revolutionaries trained during the years of underground work. These features were theoretical tempering, fidelity to one's convictions, and the highest moral qualities. By no means were all able to withstand the rigorous school of underground work, but those who passed through it honestly formed the nucleus of the Bolshevik party, and headed the struggle of the masses in the Great October Revolution and in the years of the building of socialism.

The second generation of leaders was made up of people who entered the party during the revolution and first years of Soviet power. In Obichkin's opinion, these individuals fell significantly short of their older comrades in theoretical preparation, since they often had neither the time nor the opportunity for it. This limited their ideas, and led to dogmatism, an oversimplified approach to the problems of building socialism, an exaggeration of the role of administrative methods, and of tough leadership methods. Although Stalin belonged to the first generation, he later increasingly distanced himself from it, advancing members of the second generation to high positions, and seeking and finding support from them. This, Obichkin thinks, was the most important cause of the slaughter of leading personnel, mainly fighters of Lenin's guard, in the second half of the 1930s. They could not be broken, but they could be destroyed.

In conclusion, the speaker noted that the time has come to abandon the practice in the literature on party history of merely listing the names of party figures, and to show fully and comprehensively what each of them actually did for the revolution and the victory of socialism in our country. It is necessary to publish more biographical works, and to prepare a scholarly biography of Stalin and biographical sketches of those former party members who held leading posts in it, but who later took part in anti-Leninist, antiparty groups; [this must be done] without omitting such figures as Trotsky, Kamenev, Zinov'ev, and others.

In the concept of the "personality factor," said Professor Iu. S. Vasiutin (D. Hist. Sc.), we can trace to this day a close connection between the events of the late 1930s and our own times. The moral situation that developed in the party and country during the years of mass slaughter of leading figures in the party, in the political structure, and in the military, put pressure on the Soviet people for a long time. This situation was to a considerable degree responsible for failures at the start of the Great Fatherland War [World War II], and was felt in the postwar years as well. It also influenced the stagnation and decay of party ranks, which was spoken of so directly and openly at the Twenty-seventh Congress of the CPSU, and subsequent plenums of the Central Committee. This atmosphere was reflected in people's psychology, and particularly among the young. We historians must study these processes deeply, reveal them, and discuss openly and honestly the causes of the appearance of negative phenomena in the 1930s, '60s, and '70s.

Doctor of Historical Sciences, Professor A. A. Chernobaev noted the increased interest of broad circles of the Soviet public in the personality factor in history. Recent publication of numerous articles, short stories, and plays has shown this. Their appearance is a heartening phenomenon and should be welcomed. However, scholars must also have their say—the more so since one cannot agree with all the positions taken in the literary works that have been published. There are quite a few highly subjective evaluations of real historical figures, according to Chernobaev, contained in the novel by Anatoly Rybakov, *Children of the Arbat* [Deti Arbata].*

While working on biographical sketches of the extraordinarily colorful A. Ia. Arosev and A. I. Todorskii, Chernobaev continued, he had to deal with many and sometimes unexpected difficulties. Both of these men had been repressed, and were later fully rehabilitated. However, even now, it is practically impossible to discuss some events in their lives. If the biographies mentioned the years 1937 and 1938 they would not be published. Writers were told to use Aesopian language. Even today it is by no means an easy matter to publish a work in which comprehensive treatment is given of certain historical figures.

Chernobaev attributed the situation to a number of circumstances. One of these is the unceremonious interference of publishers in authors' manuscripts. There is an urgent need to reorganize the work of publishing houses, and to regulate their relations with authors.

A. G. Latyshev, candidate of historical sciences and head of the Department of the International Communist and Workers' Movement at the Moscow Higher Party School, spoke of restoring truth in the history of leaders of many communist parties and prominent figures in the Communist International who fell victim

---

*Set in 1934, this long-suppressed novel presents a chilling portrait of the start of the Great Terror. An English-language edition translated by Harold Shukman was published by Little, Brown & Co. in 1988.—D.J.R.

to the Stalin cult in the 1930s. How, except by excessive fear, can one explain the fact that the anniversaries of prominent internationalists, comrades-in-arms with Lenin, were not observed? For example, May 4, 1987, was the hundredth anniversary of the birth of Hugo Eberlein (Albert), one of the founders of the Communist party of Germany, and its representative at the founding congress of the Comintern, and one of the three permanent members (along with Lenin and the Swiss, Platten) of the Presidium of the First Congress of the Comintern. Hugo Eberlein led a colorful and heroic life. A detailed article was published in *Neues Deutschland*, in which, incidentally, his arrest in 1937 was mentioned. We, on the other hand, did not note this anniversary at all. There are a number of other examples of this kind.

The speaker also noted one other characteristic circumstance. The foreword to the published poems of Nikolai Gumilev* says that his life was tragically cut short in 1921. No matter how distinguished a poet Gumilev may have been, the fact is that he fought against the Soviet regime! In speaking of him, we must not use the same formula that is applied to people unjustly repressed during the period of the cult of personality.

Professor V. M. Ivanov (D. Hist. Sc.) emphasized that filling in the history of the CPSU with individuals' names is one of the most important and at the same time one of the most complex tasks of our discipline. Unfortunately, we often still treat the role of personality in history basically from the point of view of general sociology. For a bad social scientist, this is sufficient, but for history, it is not. We need a deeper, concrete approach to define the contribution made by a given individual to history.

It is Ivanov's opinion that the dialectical method provides the opportunity to take account, in their totality, of aspects of this approach, such as the ontological, the axiological, and the epistemological. Thus far, the ontological approach, which answers the question as to what the given individual did, has predominated. At the same time, unfortunately, we often analyze the past from the point of view of the present, forgetting that the historian must transport himself or herself back into the period under study and illuminate the contribution of a specific individual on the basis of a realistic evaluation of the circumstances of those years.

The axiological approach permits us to shed light on the internal causes that determine the characteristics of a person's activity. V. M. Ivanov disagreed with the unproved assertions of some writers (Anatoly Rybakov, for example) to the effect that Stalin was motivated by the value he placed on absolute personal power. Such an assertion is easily refuted by historical facts on which the ontological approach to the evaluation of this individual is based.

Finally, the epistemological approach allows for clarity in determining how a

---

*1886–1921, a founder of the Acmeist movement in Russian poetry and a prominent figure in Russian modernism.—D.J.R.

historical personality evaluates his or her own activities. Stalin was in the grip of an exaggerated estimation of authoritarian methods, which he contrasted to anarchic methods, which were especially dangerous under those conditions, and which had a strong social base in the person of the petit-bourgeois elements surviving in the country at that time. By virtue of the limited nature of his world view, he did not understand that petit-bourgeois revolutionary ideas could be overcome under socialism only by using democratic methods for which Lenin had fought.

Recently, said Doctor of Historical Sciences Professor L. V. Shirikov, articles have been published whose authors are fighting for the truth in the science of party history, but understand it in a somewhat peculiar way, since they write only of negative phenomena. This approach, in the speaker's opinion, is also manifested in certain papers given at this seminar. In evaluating a major and complex personality like Stalin, stress is laid primarily on his errors and miscalculations, and especially on the repressions of the 1930s. These certainly took place. Quite a few innocent people were killed. But is it fair to connect this fact with the desires and actions of a single individual? Shirikov considers the assertion to be naive that only Stalin was the immediate inspirer and organizer of mass-scale repressions, and passed judgment at his own will. There is reason to doubt the objectivity of such judgments. As proof, Shirikov cited Stalin's report, "On Deficiencies in Party Work and Measures for the Liquidation of Trotskyist and Other Double-Dealers" [O nedostatkakh partiinoi raboty i merakh likvidatsii trotskistskikh i inykh dvurushnikov], and his concluding address at the February-March (1937) Plenum of the Central Committee of the VKP(b), where he spoke of "beating and uprooting" only the real Trotskyists—the enemies of the working class and the betrayers of our Motherland. Shirikov also cited the materials of the January (1938) Plenum of the Central Committee of the VKP(b), which adopted a resolution "On Errors of the Party Organization in Excluding Communists from the Party, on the Formal-Bureaucratic Attitude toward Appeals against Exclusion from the VPK(b), and on Measures to Correct These Defects" [Ob oshibkakh partorganizatsii pri iskliuchenii kommunistov iz partii, o formal'no-biurokraticheskom otnoshenii k apelliatsiiam iskliuchennykh iz VKP(b) i o merakh po ustraneniiu etikh nedostatkov].

All this, Shirikov emphasized, constitutes a set of extremely complex problems that have not yet had scholarly consideration. The events discussed here still contain many things yet unexplored, which sensation-lovers use.

In this connection, Shirikov concluded, it is extremely necessary to prepare and publish a scholarly biography of Stalin, free from subjectivist opinions and judgments made to fit particular situations.

In summarizing the work of the seminar, N. N. Maslov noted that the question of the personality factor in the history of the CPSU is a scientific problem that has not been adequately studied, as is shown by the presence of different approaches and points of view expressed at this meeting.

Emphasizing the usefulness of such a discussion, Maslov noted that not all questions connected with the personality factor were dealt with in the presentations made at the seminar. Not all questions have been unambiguously answered. However, the very fact that such a problem has been discussed shows that the Department of History of the CPSU of the Academy of Social Sciences under the CPSU Central Committee has tried not to avoid the complex and acute questions of the present in the discipline of party history. It also shows that the department is trying to reinterpret the individual periods in it from the point of view of the demands of the present, and to call the attention of party historians to the handling of the most important problems connected with the history of the CPSU.

Notes

1. *Materialy Plenuma Tsentral'nogo Komiteta KPSS, 27–28 ianvaria 1987 goda* (Moscow, 1987), p. 8.
2. See *Kommunist*, 1986, no. 15, p. 14.
3. V. I. Lenin, *Polnoe sobranie sochinenii*, vol. 1, p. 415.
4. Ibid., vol. 38, p. 79.
5. *Kommunist*, 1987, no. 6, p. 5.
6. Lenin, *PSS*, vol. 4, p. 375.
7. Ibid., vol. 20, p. 82.
8. *Pechat' i revoliutsiia*, bk. 2, 1921, p. 246.

Part Three

REWRITING THE HISTORY OF
THE GREAT OCTOBER REVOLUTION

Although less all-encompassing and sensitive than the Stalin question, the Great October Socialist Revolution occupies an extremely prominent place in the Soviet pantheon of holy events. The two discussions of the Revolution comprising this section of the anthology are significant because they trace the evolution of perestroika on this highly visible topic.

The first document dates from the beginning of perestroika within the discipline (January 1987). Octogenarian I. I. Mints, who but recently relinquished his post as chair of the Sector for the Study of the October Revolution at the Academy of Science's Institute of History of the USSR, offers a ten-point agenda for change. Above all, Mints has been a survivor. He contributed to the crisis in the Soviet historical profession in the past, and therefore his statement must be read as a guarded attempt to react to the changing currents. The tone of his comments is typical of the initial period of perestroika when the luminaries from the Brezhnev years were called upon to define the limits of reform. Not surprisingly, Mints's most interesting remarks concern the safest topics; he is least professional in his criticisms of "bourgeois historians" and Soviet scholars who suggest that the diverse tsarist economy included alternatives to the course the country took in 1917, that is, that the Revolution was not inevitable.

Much more penetrating are the remarks of the roundtable held by the journal *Voprosy istorii* (Problems of History) and the Academic Council of the USSR Academy of Sciences in December 1986. The participants need no introduction to Western specialists on the Russian Revolution. Taken collectively, the participants' comments suggest what fresh approaches we can expect to see in future studies of 1917.

P. V. Volobuev, a maverick historian who has had a tough go of things during the past twenty years, made the most stimulating and far-reaching comments at the meeting. The very fact that he and others like him have been playing key roles in the further de-Stalinization of historical writing on 1917 is reassuring. Arguing that "sectarian dogmatism" had gotten the upper hand on vital historical questions, Volobuev charged that "some of the historians present here contributed to the spreading of these dogmatic views," which he sees as being antithetical to party discipline and to good (Marxist) history. It is clear that Volobuev and other specialists on the revolution whose writings have attracted positive attention outside the Soviet Union have reason to be harsh in judging those of their colleagues who have made it so difficult for them. Calls by V. M Selunskaia and others for moderation undoubtedly fell on deaf ears during the roundtable.

Since Mints's ten-point agenda and the *Voprosy istorii* roundtable appeared, several provocative studies have been published that go even farther in rejecting past practices and interpretations, and in adumbrating a program for future research that will strip the October Revolution of its mythical and deliberately falsified constructs. And Volobuev, by the way, has since replaced Mints at the Institute of History.

On Restructuring in the Study of the October Revolution

I. I. MINTS

It is essential first of all to welcome the initiative of the editors of the journal, who supported the proposal of the Scientific Council on the research problem "The History of the Great October Socialist Revolution" for a joint meeting devoted to the theme "The Study of the History of the Great October Revolution: Results and Prospects."

Why is this meeting being held just now? The historiography of the Great October Socialist Revolution includes a multitude of books, articles, memoirs, collections, and documents concerning these grand events. The list of publications grows each year. The central regions of the country, the non-Russian borderlands, and individual cities and villages are objects of study. More and more studies are appearing on the struggle of the Leninist party to prepare and carry through the revolution. Nevertheless, there is an increasing need to determine what still remains to be done.

This is required first and foremost by the seventieth anniversary of the October Revolution, which must be given a worthy welcome. But this is not the main issue. After the Twenty-seventh Congress of the CPSU, the country entered into a phase of revolutionary transformations in all fields of life. The party posed huge new tasks for the social sciences, including historical scholarship, within which the history of the October Revolution occupies one of the most important places. The Appeal of the Central Committee of the CPSU "To the Soviet People" and its decree "On Preparing for the Seventieth Anniversary of the Great October Socialist Revolution" draw conclusions from the history of the October Revolution and indicate the prospects for further study. Guided by these decisions of the party, historians of the October Revolution must critically evaluate what they

Russian text © 1987 by "Pravda" Publishers. "O perestroike v izuchenii Velikogo Oktiabria," *Voprosy istorii*, 1987, no. 4, pp. 3–9. Translated by Stephen P. Dunn.

This article is based on a report presented at a meeting organized in December 1986 by the editorial board of the journal *Voprosy istorii* together with the Academic Council of the Academy of Sciences, USSR, on the research problem "The History of the Great October Socialist Revolution."

have done, and lay out new plans and prospects.

In carrying out this, frankly speaking, difficult task, the party has given us a precise and concrete orientation—to link scholarship and theory with life, with reality, with practice. This means that we are obliged to look at the history of the Great October Revolution through the eyes of a person of our own day, and to see in it those features that may not have been seen earlier, and that are fully recognized—that, so to speak, "work"—for the good of socialism precisely now. After all, V. I. Lenin said that in the course of time the Great October Revolution would reveal more and more new features of itself. If we approach its history from that point of view, then the most urgent and timely directions in its study become obvious. The decisions of the Twenty-seventh Congress of the CPSU and of the January Plenum of the Central Committee concern each and every participant in the restructuring. However, each area has its peculiarities and distinctive features. For historians this is primarily the reconsideration of the subject matter: after all, problems have a way of getting bogged down, getting covered with dust, and lagging behind the tasks of the country's development.

1

In the preamble to his report at the January (1987) Plenum of the CPSU Central Committee, General Secretary M. S. Gorbachev pointedly called attention to the fact that "the turn for the better is proceeding more slowly, the job of restructuring has proved more difficult, and the causes of the problems that have accumulated in society are more profound, than we had earlier thought."[1]

In resolving the cardinal task of our social science—the analysis of "the causes of the problems that have accumulated in society"—historians of the October Revolution are obliged to make their contribution. On this level, one of the high-priority tasks must be the problem of studying the preconditions of the Russian Revolution. We are speaking here not of the discovery of a new approach but of the removal of administrative, routine, and artificial obstacles that hinder study of the preconditions of October—that is, of the need to reconsider the methods of conducting, and to a considerable extent, the results of the "discussion," which we all remember, of the multicomponent* socioeconomic order of Russia in the early twentieth century.

If we look deeper into the causes of the persistence of negative phenomena in the development of our society—the causes of the stubborn passive and active resistance offered to restructuring at all levels—we will have to realize that its

---

*mnogoukladnyi. Uklad, in Soviet-Marxist terminology, is a type of socioeconomic behavior, with the institutional arrangements accompanying it, which may or may not be the dominant and determining one in a given society. A mnogoukladnyi socioeconomic order is one where two or more of these types of behavior, with their institutional correlates, appear with approximately equal prominence.—Trans.

roots lie in the inadequate level of civilization of Russia at the moment of revolution and are determined by typological peculiarities, the "medium-weak" (in Lenin's expression)[2] level of capitalist development of the country, its multicomponent socioeconomic structure, and the capitalist and precapitalist forms of behavior coexisting within it at the time of the October Revolution.

Let us recall in this connection what Lenin wrote in his notes, "Our Revolution Apropos of N. Sukhanov's Notes."[3] The most frequently repeated objection to the view that the October Revolution was timely and necessary—and it remains to this day one of the main arguments of the opponents of that revolution—is that the productive forces of Russia were not yet ripe for socialism. In this article, written in 1923, when Lenin was summing up the experience of the Russian people and noting the future prospects for building socialism, we read:

"The development of the productive forces of Russia has not attained the level that makes socialism possible." All the heroes of the Second International, including, of course, Sukhanov, beat the drums about this proposition. They keep harping on this incontrovertible proposition in a thousand different keys, and think that it is the decisive criterion of our revolution.[4]

The constant and wearisome repetition of the thesis that the development of the productive forces in old Russia was inadequate even affected our own literature. Historians and the editors of publishing houses began to treat the problem of the preconditions of the October Revolution in their own way, under the influence of books on the course of the European revolutions, and having uncritically accepted the experience of the latter: the economy of tsarist Russia had allegedly been evaluated too negatively; tsarist Russia had supposedly achieved significant economic successes, and so forth. The "critics," who in this case turned out to be rehabilitating the role of tsarism and the bourgeoisie, described their approach as a struggle "against slandering" prerevolutionary Russia, and attempts were undertaken to artificially raise the level of tsarist Russia to that of the United States, England, and Germany. It goes without saying that Marxism has nothing in common either with slander or with purification of the truth: its essence is the truth of class relations. Incidentally, even the factual accusation of the "justifiers" of the old regime is untrue: secondary-school and college history textbooks describe the entire course of the economic development of the country correctly, and in adequate detail, as Marxism required.

It never occurred to those who are revising the evaluation of Old Russia that bourgeois historians of all stripes had enthused that they had found an alternative to the October Revolution: no revolution was needed, we could have waited, and tsarism in alliance with the bourgeoisie would have developed capitalism and made Russia the equal of the entire capitalist world. In the article mentioned above, Lenin sharply condemned attempts to justify the old, and revealed that the "critics" lack the dialectical approach to the issue of the revolution's preconditions. Lenin wrote:

> It does not occur to any of them to ask: but what about a people that found itself in a revolutionary situation such as that created during the first imperialist war? Might it not, influenced by the hopelessness of its situation, fling itself into a struggle that would offer it at least some chance of securing conditions for the further development of civilization that were somewhat unusual?[5]

One is struck not only by the need to master dialectics, but by the categorical tone in which Lenin rejects any alternative to the October Revolution: the hopelessness of the position of the masses of the people—that is, not only the inevitability of the revolution, but its obligatory character, its necessity—there was no other way of saving Russia, no alternative. It must be recognized that historians of the October Revolution have not adequately mastered the depth of Lenin's dialectic.

2

At first glance, it may seem self-indulgent to repeat that the October Revolution was a revolution by the people. Is there even one historian of the Great October Revolution, except among its open and devout opponents, who has not written about the popular character of the October Revolution? Nonetheless, a number of considerations compel us to give this problem a leading place. Take a look at most of the books on the history of the October Revolution! Everywhere, people write of the working class as the leader of the revolution. This central theme is thoroughly dealt with. But less is written about the poorest peasant as its ally.* It is true that even here the situation is changing for the better: the first volume of *The History of the Soviet Peasantry* [Istoriia sovetskogo krest'ianstva], published by the Institute of History, USSR Academy of Sciences, has appeared. It is correct and necessary to study further the history of the proletariat and the poor peasantry, which were the moving forces of the October Revolution, calling attention, of course, to new aspects of this problem.

But was the Russian people in 1917 limited to these classes? The founders of Marxism noted as early as the *Manifesto of the Communist Party* that: "All previous historical movements were movements of minorities, or in the interests of minorities. The proletarian movement is the self-conscious, independent movement of the immense majority, in the interests of the immense majority."[6] Lenin developed this idea and emphasized the popular character of the proletarian revolution.

---

*For a more critical discussion of this problem see the Winter 1983–84 issue of *Soviet Studies in History* (vol. XXII, no. 3).—D.J.R.

Of the many statements on this score, I will cite one, written almost a year before the October Revolution—in August and September of 1916:

> The Socialist revolution in Europe *cannot be* anything other than an explosion of that struggle by each and every oppressed and discontented person. Part of the petite bourgeoisie and the other workers will inevitably participate in it— without such participation a *mass* struggle *is impossible*, and *no* revolution is possible, and it is equally inevitable that [these groups] will bring to the movement their own prejudices, reactionary fantasies, weaknesses, and mistakes.[7]

Having emphasized the vast, popular character of the proletarian revolution, Lenin continued:

> But *objectively* they will be attacking *capital*, and the conscious *avant garde* of the revolution, the progressive proletariat, expressing this objective truth in a multicolored, many-voiced, variegated, and outwardly fragmented mass struggle, will be able to unite and direct it, to take positions of power, seize the banks, expropriate the trusts which are hated by everyone (although for different reasons!), and carry out other dictatorial measures, which add up to the overthrow of the bourgeoisie and the victory of socialism, which, however, will not by any means at once "purify itself" of petit-bourgeois slag.[8]

Lenin exposed and sharply condemned those who asserted that it was necessary to wait until the proletariat became the majority of the nation, and then to achieve the transfer of power to the working class. "It's as if," he said, ridiculing the propagandists of the "pure" socialist revolution, "you set up one group of soldiers in one place and said to them: 'We are for socialism,' and then another group in another place and said 'We are for imperialism,' and this would be a social revolution!"[9] Lenin accurately foresaw that the petite bourgeoisie and the semiproletariat masses would take part in the revolution against the oppression by landlords, the church, the monarchy, other ethnic groups, and the like.

To some degree, the inadequacies in demonstrating the popular character of the Great October Revolution can be overcome by studying the urban middle classes, a project begun at the initiative of the Academic Council. Conferences held in the early 1980s in Tbilisi, Kalinin, and Tambov are a good beginning and must be continued; unfortunately, this research has not yet included all social strata of Russia from which active participants in the revolution were recruited. At the same time, we must not forget about the need to distinguish active participants in the revolution as well as its moving forces. By moving forces, Marxism-Leninism means only those classes that have an interest in carrying revolution to its conclusion. Not all participants in a revolution are interested in carrying it to a conclusion. Quite a few of them are only fellow travelers, who often go over to the enemy's side. When we speak of wavering social strata, it suffices to remember the Left SRs, who took part in the insurrection, but then left the ranks of fighters for the victory of the revolution.

There is one other problem that comes to the fore when we speak of the popular character of the socialist revolution in our country. This is the history of mass organizations of the working people (workers, soldiers, peasants, and so forth). It cannot be said that we have ignored this problem. We have quite a few works about the soviets, but few about the trade unions, factory committees, and peasants' organizations, and fewer still about the soldiers' committees and the organizations of the urban middle class. However, it is not just a matter of the number of works available. We have studied the external history of these organizations without paying much attention to how their activity manifested the independent revolutionary activism of the masses, and how they gathered the will of the masses into one body and expressed it in their political actions. Not everything here was simple, particularly during the period when the crisis of confidence in the Soviet leaders who compromised with the bourgeoisie began to mature.

3

The present increase in international tensions requires a new approach to the problem of defending the achievements of the October Revolution. Soviet literature on the history of the imperialist intervention and the Civil War of the USSR is extraordinarily rich: this is one of the major themes of our historiography. However, the speech of the president of the United States in which he called for the organization of a new "crusade" against the USSR, with the aim of "throwing Marxism as a social system into the dustbin of history," compels us to pay particular attention to the history of the first "crusade"—the armed intervention of 1918–20 in Soviet Russia. This is ever the more necessary because Ronald Reagan's declaration expresses not only his anticommunist views, but reflects the policy of the United States toward the Soviet Union. The appeal by the American president is by no means a manifestation of only his personal hatred of socialism. We know that every year seven of the leaders of the largest capitalist countries meet to discuss a unified policy toward the Soviet Union and the other socialist countries, and as a rule all of them support the anti-Soviet actions of the Washington administration. Incidentally, these are the same seven countries that organized the first "crusade" to overthrow Soviet power. It is therefore important to remember how the attempt at intervention against the country of the soviets undertaken at that time ended. It is necessary, as the Appeal of the CPSU Central Committee "To the Soviet People" directs, to expose the policy of social revenge and "crusades" against socialism, conducted by world imperialism.

The progress of science itself points to some deficiencies in the previous treatment of the problem: it was primarily international relations that were studied. It is now necessary to show the role of each power in this anti-Soviet campaign and to count up the cost of the invasion by the interventionists to our people. The Academic Council has prepared for publication two books, *Intervention in the Baltic* [Interventsiia v Pribaltiku] and *The Invasion by the Interventionists in Southern Russia* [Vtorzhenie interventov na iuge Rossii], and it is developing studies of the intervention in Central Asia, in Siberia, in the Far East, and in the Transcaucasus. A collection of new documents is being prepared in collaboration with the Main Archive of the USSR. The problem of the intervention is at present a major concern of the Academic Council.

4

Among the problems requiring work, we should mention that of "The October Revolution, Socialism, and Peace." Our revolution is indissolubly connected with the struggle against war, and for a just peace—peace for everyone. This is vividly shown by Lenin's Decree on Peace, which condemned the imperialist war and called on the people to interfere in the holy of holies—the foreign policy of the imperialists. Let us recall the Brest Peace in 1918. Our party and country made notable sacrifices in the name of saving human life, the lives of workers and peasants. Here is where we find the true humanism of the October Revolution, and that ideal makes up one of the greatest moral values of Leninism. I will not be mistaken if I say that this is the primary source of the mighty influence of the October Revolution on an international scale. The human character and the humanism of our revolution: this is the answer to the question as to why it continues to this day to address the hearts and minds of people all over the world.

5

An important activity of historians of the October Revolution is producing works written in a popular style. Without to any degree abandoning individual or collective research, it is necessary to examine individual problems that have been forgotten or inadequately studied. Some of these are worth mentioning here. A lot has been written in the literature about the attempts of the populist movement to "go to the people." It has been calculated that not more than 3,000 persons actually settled in the countryside at that time. But the "going to the people" by representatives of Soviet power numbered in the tens of thousands. This included the settlements in the countryside of the famine-ridden workers of Petrograd, Moscow, and other industrial provinces; it also included workers sent by party organizations of oblasts and cities to the countryside, and it included the All-Russian mobilizations of workers for work in the countryside. History knows of no other case of a mass "going to the people," which so vividly show the significance of the alliance of the proletariat with the peasantry. There are few books about this, but they are especially important for formerly colonial and dependent countries that have chosen a noncapitalist path of development.

Do our young people know much about the "requisitioning" of the population in Central Asia and the Transcaucasus for labor in the rear echelons of the old army? "Requisitioning" was the term used by the tsarist regime for the mobilization of non-Russians. The "requisitioned" people took part in a joint revolutionary struggle and returned with this experience to their native places, where they became the first builders of Soviet power. Not much has been done with one other theme—"The First Leaders of the Rural Soviets"—and therefore Lenin's instruction that the revolution in the countryside began with the arrival there of soldiers after their demobilization from the army remains undeveloped in terms of concrete historical material.

6

Overcoming the contradiction that has developed between the scientific character of history and the entertaining manner in which it should be set forth has great significance. A peculiar, boring, monotonous exposition of its problems has been developed. It is true that this contradiction is by no means characteristic only of our epoch and of our works. Even Voltaire wrote in his philosophical story "The Simple-minded Person": "History, apparently, pleases us only when it becomes a tragedy that becomes wearisome if it is not enlivened by passions, villainies, and great calamities. Clio must be armed with a dagger, like Melpomene."[10]

Generations of historians have struggled to overcome the contradiction between scientific matter and entertaining matter. This contradiction is not resolved, for example, by filling the works of historians with quotations from *belles lettres*, even though this enlivens a scholarly text. Overcoming these contradictions must be sought in knowledge of a question, in deep study of the problem, and in a truthful and sincere exposition of them. To borrow Goethe's words: "Speech must gush from the soul in order to touch and transport the hearts of people by its true and unfeigned beauty" (*Faust*). One must carefully work not only on analysis of material, but on the style, the exposition, and even the titles of books and articles.

7

It is a serious defect of the literature on the October Revolution, incidentally, that it appears in small editions and is characterized by stereotyped titles, and that adequate information about it does not appear: approximately less than ten percent of the books that appear are reviewed in historical journals and newspapers. Perhaps the editorial boards of journals have set a permanent "quota" for reviews of these publications, and should demand more decisively a serious critical consideration of them from specialists. We once had a special book-review journal, *Books and the Revolution* [Kniga i revoliutsiia]; scholarly supervisors and teachers demanded that graduate and undergraduate students write reviews—and the books became known, while the young authors learned to write and analyze.

8

We have very few books on the great victory of the revolution on the cultural front. In approximately ten years' time, the Soviet regime eradicated one of the plagues of capitalism—illiteracy. Capitalism surpassed feudalism, particularly in questions of literacy: it needed a worker who knew how to use a machine—and that was all. But nowhere did the world of capitalism open up free access to science and the arts. In the United States—the most highly developed capitalist power—not only is there to this day no such access, but there are significant numbers of illiterate people. The eradication of illiteracy in all countries where power has gone to the people has presented itself to the whole world as a characteristic of socialism. In the middle of 1918, Maksim Gorkii proposed to Lenin that the achievements of Soviet power "in A. V. Lunacharskii's department"—that is, in the activity of the People's Commissariat of Education—should be shown to everyone, and primarily the extraordinary scale of work for the eradication of illiteracy among the masses of the people.

9

It goes without saying that the most important part of restructuring the study of the October Revolution is in intensifying the struggle for purifying Marxism-Leninism, so as not to admit any falling away from class positions. An example of deviation from these positions is provided by the statements of some researchers that Freemasonry played some role in the events of 1917. May I remind you in this connection that in the "Program of the CPSU" adopted by the Twenty-seventh Congress of the CPSU, we read:

> The extremely sharp struggle between two world views on the international arena reflects the opposing nature of the two world systems—capitalism and socialism. The CPSU sees its task as that of bringing the peoples the truth about real socialism, the internal and foreign policy of the Soviet Union, and in making active propaganda for the Soviet way of life, showing aggressively and with proper arguments the antipopular, inhuman character of imperialism and its exploitative nature. It will inculcate in the Soviet people a high degree of political consciousness and vigilance, and the skill of evaluating social phenomena from clear class positions, and of standing up for the ideals and the intellectual and spiritual values of socialism.[11]

10

In conclusion, I would like to pause to consider a number of questions that appear from the outside like organizational ones. However, without solving them, we cannot achieve a restructuring within our sector of the ideological front.

The party, in the decisions of its Twenty-seventh Congress, and particularly of the January (1987) Plenum of the CPSU Central Committee, in the appeal "To the Soviet People," points out the importance of strengthening the democratic elements in the life of our society. It seems to me that this relates to us as well. We must increase the activity of the executive bureau of our council, which until now has met only occasionally. It has not yet become an organ that regularly discusses the most important, controversial, and unresolved aspects of the enormous problem that occupy us. The executive bureau must become—not in words, but in action—the organ of the real collective leadership of the council's work and "keep its hand on the pulse" of the study of our problem.

It can be said that much of the research conducted in our field is done by extensive methods. The number of books and articles increases yearly, but unfortunately it cannot be said that their quality is improving, that their argumentation becomes more convincing, or the like. Our executive bureau can play an important role not only in discussing specific topics, but in developing criteria to which work carried out on the new level must correspond.

We sometimes speak with pride of the fact that our council has twenty-four sections in all the union republics and in the most important regions of the RSFSR. However, we must admit honestly that in the past few years negative tendencies in the work of sections have increased. Their activity has fallen off, and as a result fewer investigators are united in the sections. The executive bureau of the council is apparently at fault here, and we must discuss the question of how to aid the sections. But the sections themselves must also critically evaluate their work and together lay out measures to change the situation.

Naturally, the thoughts mentioned above have earlier been developed to one degree or another by historians of the October Revolution. However, in the first place, we must today find new approaches to them, and seek out new and timely themes in them; and second (and this is the main point!) we have an obligation to talk about what, for various reasons, has escaped up to now from the field of our research, and to strive for maximum truth in history.

Notes

1. *Materialy Plenuma Tsentral'nogo Komiteta KPSS 27–28 ianvaria 1987 goda* (Moscow, 1987), p. 6
2. *Leninskii sbornik*, vol. XI, p. 425.
3. V. I. Lenin, *Polnoe sobranie sochinenii* [hereafter, *PSS*], vol. 45.
4. Ibid., p. 380 [we quote here the English translation published by Progress Publishers: V. I. Lenin, *Collected Works*, vol. 33 (1966), p. 478—Trans.].

5. Ibid.

6. K. Marks and F. Engels, *Sochineniia*, vol. 4, p. 435 [we quote the translation in Louis S. Feuer: Marx and Engels, *Basic Writings on Politics and Philosophy* (New York: Doubleday Anchor Books, 1959), p. 18—Trans.].

7. Lenin, *PSS*, vol. 30, pp. 54–55.

8. Ibid., p. 55

9. Ibid., p. 54.

10. Vol'ter [Voltaire], *Filosofskie povesti*, Moscow, 1978, p. 294 (in Greek mythology, Clio is the muse of history and Melpomene the muse of tragedy).

11. *Materialy XXVII s"ezda KPSS*, Moscow, 1986, pp. 165–66.

The Study of the History of the Great October Revolution

Results and Prospects

On December 5, 1986, on the initiative of the journal *Voprosy istorii* and the Academic Council of the Academy of Sciences of the USSR on the research problem "The History of the Great October Socialist Revolution," a meeting of a group of historians was held at the editorial office. V. G. Trukhanovskii, editor-in-chief of the journal and corresponding member of the USSR Academy of Sciences, chaired the meeting. The introductory remarks were made by the chairman of the Academic Council, Academician I. I. Mints.* The editorial board and the Academic Council considered the meeting part of the preparations for the seventieth anniversary of the Great October Socialist Revolution.

No special report was brought up for discussion. The specialists participating in the meeting shared their views on the results and prospects for further developing study of the history of the Great October Revolution. Although there were no polemics on these matters among the speakers, the editorial board and the Academic Council believe it useful to acquaint readers with what most participants in the meeting said. However, the publication of these remarks does not mean the editorial board shares all the opinions expressed in them.

The following people spoke at the meeting.

E. G. Gimpel'son (Institute of History of the USSR, Academy of Sciences): It will soon be seventy years that the historical discipline has been concentrating its attention on the history of the Great October Revolution and the Civil War. Books, articles, publications of documents, and dissertations number in the thousands. We haven't yet made proper sense of this extensive operation, and without doing so it's difficult to plan and move forward. In the Sector of the History of the October Revolution and the Civil War of the Institute of the History

Russian text © 1987 by "Pravda" Publishers. "Izuchenie istorii Velikogo Oktiabria: Itogi i perspektivy," *Voprosy istorii*, 1987, no. 6, pp. 51–72. Translated by Stephen P. Dunn.

*The content of the opening and concluding addresses by I. I. Mints is reflected in his article "On Restructuring in the Study of the October Revolution" (see above).

of the USSR we have tried to make a preliminary analysis of the literature that has appeared over the past five to ten years. Analysis shows that a number of traditional tendencies in the history of the October Revolution are holding their own (the theme of Lenin, the leading role of the Bolshevik party in the revolution, the struggle for Soviet power in the provinces, the alliance between the working class and the peasantry, the army in the revolution, historiography, and others). These are key problems: consideration of them will permit us to understand more deeply the regularities and peculiarities of the socialist revolution in Russia. Further attention to these problems by historians is not only fully justified, but necessary.

The traditional themes also provide considerable opportunities to tap new archival documents, and to explore on the basis of them new aspects even of questions that, on the whole, have been fairly well studied. Here is merely one example. Monographs and articles have been published on the history of the working class during the period from 1917 to 1920. Recently, there was issued a new basic work—the first volume of the *History of the Soviet Working Class* [Istoriia sovetskogo rabochego klassa]. The positive significance of this work of synthesis is, in particular, the fact that it has pointed out the ways to study the problem further: the working class in the national-liberation movement (both by regions and in the country as a whole); the role of the working class in winning the peasant masses away from the petit-bourgeois and bourgeois-nationalist parties; the nonindustrial elements of the working class in the revolution; branch trade unions in revolution and civil war; the first stages in developing the social profile of the working class in a socialist society. Thus, we cannot agree with the opinion sometimes expressed that on the traditional themes everything has already been studied.

Analysis of the literature also shows, in the country as a whole, a sharp reduction in the number of specialists on the history of the October Revolution and the Civil War. From one year to the next, the number of works (books and articles) published on this theme in the center and in the provinces is decreasing. Here are a few figures: on the history of the October Revolution 255 books and 285 articles were published between 1976 and 1980; and between 1981 and 1985, 145 books and 75 articles. The number of publications on the history of the Civil War fell by a factor of 2.5.

But the question, of course, is not only one of fewer works. There is a tendency toward "marching in place," repeating ourselves, publishing works that add nothing to available knowledge. In general, movement follows well-trodden paths and themes already mastered. It is true that in the past decade much work has been done on some previously "forbidden" themes (the history of the petit-bourgeois parties in 1917–20); many works containing critiques of bourgeois historiography have been issued, and studies on the White emigration have begun to appear.

New themes and trends are opened very slowly and timidly, however, even though there are many that have not yet been well studied. Let us mention only some of them: the intelligentsia in the October Revolution and Civil War; the bourgeois-landlord parties, the urban middle classes in the Revolution and Civil War; the antidemocratic regimes on the territories conquered by the White Guard; the revolutionary creativity of the masses in the Revolution and Civil War. We are in debt to many prominent participants in the Revolution whose names have been deleted from history. The publication of sources has in effect been stopped. In the light of the decisions of the Twenty-seventh Congress of the CPSU, such themes as "The Great October Revolution and the Progress of Society," and "Problems of the History of the October Revolution and the Civil War in the Contemporary Ideological Struggle" are especially important.

An important trend by historians of the October Revolution is the creation of works of synthesis on problems that have been well studied and set forth in individual books and monographs. I refer primarily to such problems as that of the petit-bourgeois parties in the Revolution and Civil War, of the establishment of Soviet power in the country, of the construction of the Soviet state in 1917–20, and of the international significance of the October Revolution. Comparative historical works on the Great October Revolution and later social revolutions in the world are also needed. Generalizing works such as *History of the Soviet Working Class* permit us not only to sum up the results of research but also to plan how to study further the history of the Great October Revolution.

Finally, we also have an obligation to the readers of our works. Many of these are written according to an oversimplified model, fail to take account of the psychology of the masses, and are impersonal. In a number of cases, even the unsophisticated reader encounters in them the "silent figure," and avoidance of controversial questions. What should we say of such books, if even in encyclopedias of the October Revolution and Civil War, articles about active participants in these events who later became members of the interparty opposition are lacking, although articles on figures in the bourgeois-landlord camp and in the petit-bourgeois parties are included (and correctly so!)? All this gives bourgeois historians an opportunity to speculate on matters about which it is difficult for us to enter into polemics with them.

Historians of the October Revolution and Civil War, who deal with mass sources, make little use of the opportunities for processing and analyzing these with the help of modern technical means.

Historians have yet to create popular scholarly works on our Revolution and Civil War, written vividly, with emotion, and intended for a broad audience. Great is the role of such works in educating young people in the spirit of Soviet socialist patriotism and political consciousness.

Historians of the Great October Revolution and the Civil War have a lot of work ahead. But we should not underestimate the achievements with which they approach the seventieth anniversary of October. Their arsenal contains an immense literature which, on the whole, gives an accurate Marxist-Leninist inter-

pretation of the greatest event of world history, and defines the general direction
and basic tendencies of world development.

V. I. Miller (Academic Council): For several years now, it has been felt that
our period is a watershed in the historiography of the October Revolution, and
that literally before our eyes, either a whole period in the study of this problem is
being completed, or else one phase of it. In any case, the end of one phase and the
beginning of another is clearly felt. What suggests this? Careful examination of
the historiography of the problem makes it possible to make rather clear-cut
observations. The number of monographic studies on problems that were once
the leading ones in the historiography of the October Revolution—those of the
working class, of the peasantry, and some others—has been sharply reduced.
What has taken their place? The quantity of synthetic works of various kinds has
increased. Six volumes of the nine-volume *History of the Working Class of the
USSR* have been published, as well as two volumes of a multivolume work on the
history of the peasantry, while a two-volume work on the October Revolution and
the defense of its achievements is being prepared for publication. Each of these
publications contains new material that advances study of the given problem. But
still, it is no accident that we call these works of synthesis. Essentially they are
devoted chiefly to summing up the results of research on some aspect of the
history of the October Revolution, and this takes place when the feeling arises that
it is time to sum things up.

The number of historiographic works on the problem has increased markedly.
They can be divided into two categories. On the one hand, there are works in
which the achievements both of the historiography of the October Revolution as a
whole, or of individual problems within it, are analyzed, and in which controversial and unsolved questions are set forth. Such studies, of course, are needed and
useful. But it is no accident that they have appeared almost simultaneously with
works of a more generalizing character. They appear only when their authors
become convinced that the conditions are ripe for them. Unfortunately, historiographic works of a quite different type are also published. They appear when their
authors want to write something, but cannot do this by studying some specific
problem. In this manner, pseudohistoriographic opuses appear, in which they set
forth the content of the works of others, sometimes without having the knowledge
to evaluate them.

The major and general cause of the situation, of course, is not that the history
of October has already been completely studied, but that the methods by which
historians were guided in previous years have been (or are being) exhausted. At
first glance, one fact would seem to contradict this thesis. In the past ten to fifteen
years the study of the history of the nonproletarian parties of Russia, as an aspect
of the history of the Great October Revolution, has been proceeding intensively.
And in the past few years, historians' attention is more and more frequently
drawn to the urban middle classes (both "new," chiefly the intelligentsia and

"traditional"—that is, the artisans, small traders, and other representatives of the urban petite bourgeoisie). However, these phenomena do not contradict the original thesis, inasmuch as the study of the problems indicated is carried on chiefly in a traditional manner—although, of course, it was precisely in the treatment of these themes that those new features that must become a necessary element of the forthcoming stage in the study of the history of October began.

What is the chief problem with our contemporary historiography of the October Revolution? We can find an attempt at an answer to this question in the recommendations made at the conference "The Great October Revolution—The Triumph of Ideas of Marxism-Leninism," held in Kalinin last September [1986]. In dealing with reconstruction of the history of the October Revolution, these recommendations emphasized especially the need to overcome once and for all the illustrative method. In this regard it was noted that this method is now rarely found in pure form, but quite often in the form of a stereotyped exposition based not on analysis of all sources, but on examples taken from an insignificant part of this body. At the conference, the broad use of mathematical methods, which had already been shown to be highly effective, was mentioned as a way of overcoming this defect. It seems to us, however, that traditional methods of study have not lost their effectiveness. At the same time we must not be afraid of statistics and figures (provided, of course, that they are not incomplete).

But editors who try to "free" historians' works from statistical data still exist. Despite this, the attention of historians to precisely this aspect of research and exposition has increased in the last few years. Data on the results of elections to the Constituent Assembly are published regularly (although not yet in full). At the Kalinin conference, four speakers presented papers analyzing the election results alone. Historians are turning more and more frequently to data on the numbers and composition of political parties, the composition of the soviets, committees, and the like. Thus, one of the distinguishing features of the coming period in the study of the October Revolution is manifesting itself even now.

Careful study of the current literature permits us to see other features of the period under way. They include attention to the psychology of the masses—the moods and misapprehensions that frequently determined their behavior during a specific event. Many examples of this can be cited. One of these is the new book by G. L. Sobolev on the role of the Petrograd garrison in the October Revolution, the most interesting pages of which are devoted precisely to analyzing changes in the soldiers' mood. Still another feature that is important not to overlook is the growth of interest in the psychology of leaders, the heads of political parties, their ideologists, and the leaders of mass actions of the working people. In this regard, writers dealing with historical themes are moving ahead of historians. However, historians as well, although with extreme caution, are beginning to turn to this subject matter. It would seem that we have tested instruments for work in this complex field—whole branches of source research and textology, which help us to penetrate into the very thought processes of the author of a specific document—

but we still very rarely use these instruments.

Of course, only the future will show to what degree these features are characteristic of the coming phase of the historiography of October, but it seems to us that without taking account of these approaches, it would hardly be possible to move ahead significantly in the further study of the human factor in the October Revolution.

Now I'd like to turn to a broad range of problems that should attract the attention of historians of October. First among them is the social structure of the population of Russia in 1917. Outwardly, we possess what would seem to be reliable data on the classes making up the majority of the country's population. There is practically no doubt that the proletariat of Russia at the beginning of the October Revolution amounted to fifteen million people—that is to say, approximately ten percent of the country's population. Well, what if we pose the question another way: was Pelageia Nilovna Viasova—Gorky's "Mother"*—part of this fifteen million? We would have to say: no, she wasn't; after all, she didn't work in a capitalist enterprise. But she was a worker's wife and the mother of a worker. In speaking of the numbers of workers in Russia, why do we fail to take account of the members of their families? If we try to determine the total numbers of the proletariat of Russia while taking account of this fact, then it turns out that its proportion of the country's population was not ten percent, but twenty-five percent at a minimum. One other conclusion follows: historians are obliged either to speak of the specific proportion of workers in the self-employed population of Russia (and for this one must determine the total number of the latter), or compare information on the numbers of the proletariat, including members of their families, with data on the population of Russia in 1917 (which, incidentally, they don't yet possess).

The same problems arise when we speak of other classes. In encyclopedia articles on the peasantry, we can still read that this is a class. However, the same articles speak of the stratification of the peasantry, of the presence of a rural bourgeoisie (kulaks), a significant mass of petit-bourgeois, and semiproletarian (poor) strata within it. Besides this, data in the literature usually reflect not the [absolute] numbers of the peasantry or of the class groups composing it, but the number of peasant households of specific types. Therefore, investigators have a lot of work to do in this field. The situation is still worse with regard to the exploiting classes—the bourgeoisie and landlords. In the sole monograph dealing with this problem—P. V. Volobuev's book *The Proletariat and the Bourgeoisie in 1917* [Proletariat i burzhuaziia v 1917 godu]—even approximate calculations of the size of the bourgeoisie are practically lacking. Without a clear conception of the social structure of Russian society, however, historians' arguments on the revolution are of course impoverished.

---

*The reference here is to the protagonist of Maxim Gorky's novel, *Mother* [Mat'].
—D.J.R.

A considerable part of the total body of works on the October Revolution consists of works by historians of the party. And in speaking of the deficiencies in the historiography of the October Revolution, we must not avoid dealing with a number of specific features characteristic of their approach to the study of the socialist revolution in our country. Let us limit ourselves here to two examples— one more general, and the other relatively specific.

In speaking of the size of the Bolshevik party on the eve of the February and October revolutions, we usually use two figures—24,000 and 350,000. However, even in the multivolume *History of the CPSU* [Istoriia KPSS], there is no indication of where these data come from. There is no doubt that their appearance on the pages of our books and articles was preceded by a certain amount of research. But isn't it time to make the technique of calculating available to the scholarly community?

The more specific example relates to S. M. Kvachadze's book *The Bolsheviks of Tbilisi in 1917* [Tbilisskie bol'sheviki v 1917 g.] (Tbilisi, 1977), which contains both new observations and interesting ideas. At the same time, there are passages in it that prompt reflection of a particular kind. The author begins his exposition by relating how the news of the February Revolution reached Tbilisi and how the working people reacted to it. He then details the activity of the Bolsheviks in the city. But even from the first pages, you feel that the author lacks material on the actual social and ethnic composition of the population of Tbilisi, or in other words, on precisely who the masses were for which the Bolsheviks were competing. But it was precisely these data (more than sixty percent of the self-employed population of the city belonged to the middle classes; although the proletariat and the semiproletarian strata amounted to more than twenty-three percent, most of the workers were involved in small-scale production and had not been "seasoned in the factory kettle") which, to a large degree, determined the effectiveness of the Bolsheviks' work among the masses.

The author's way of citing such an important document as the speech of S. I. Kavtaradze, delegate of the Tbilisi Bolsheviks, at the Sixth Party Congress, also makes a strange impression. One can't say that this speech is not dealt with in the book; an extract from it running to almost half a page is given (page 110), but such important passages as: "The Georgian workers have been poisoned by opportunism; they are following Kostrov, the patriarch of defensism" (*Sixth Congress of the RSDRP (Bolsheviks). August 1917. Protocols* [Shestoi s "ezd RSDRP (bol'-shevikov). Avgust 1917 goda. Protokoly] Moscow, 1953, p. 96) or "In the beginning we had [only] one worker, and he was a barber" (p. 95) are omitted. And although the author adduces data to the effect that in July there were 2,675 members in the Tbilisi organization, he omits Kavtaradze's words—"in our military organization" (ibid.). The questionnaires completed by the delegates of the Tbilisi organization to the Sixth Party Congress, which indicate, in particular, that the organization was active primarily "among soldiers" (ibid., p. 37), are not even mentioned in the book. Of course, the growth of the Tbilisi organization to 2,675 members showed significant gains by the city's Bolsheviks. But in order to present a true picture of the political life of Tbilisi it is necessary to indicate that the Menshevik organization at that time numbered approximately 12,000 members.

The defects of one book (and not a bad one) reflect, as in a drop of water, the rather typical features of a certain part of our literature on party history. There can be only one conclusion from this: historians of the party should make use of all available sources, without avoiding those that speak of the difficulties facing the Bolsheviks during the revolution.

V. Z. Drobizhev (Moscow Institute of Historian-Archivists): V. I. Lenin in his speech at the Sixth All-Russian Extraordinary Congress of Soviets of Workers, Peasant, Cossack, and Red Army Deputies, November 6, 1918, gave an excellent example of how anniversaries of the October Revolution should be celebrated. He emphasized the need to try, on the day of the anniversary, "to illuminate the road we have traveled as a whole—to look at what has been achieved in this period, and at the extent to which we have prepared ourselves over the course of this year for our major, real, decisive, and basic task" [*PSS*, vol. 37, pp. 137–38]. The main task of summarizing the work of historians of the Great October Revolution is to extract lessons from the past and to lay out our perspectives.

They have done an enormous amount of work in studying the history of the socialist revolution in our country. At the same time, experience shows that we still have many unsolved problems, which require the concentrated attention of scholars and leaders of scholarly centers. I will deal primarily with a number of questions of an organizational nature.

In the postwar years we have had at our disposal a rather large body of specialists on the history of the October Revolution. The departments of history of Soviet society, created in the 1950s in a number of universities in the country, consisted almost entirely of historians of the October Revolution. Historians of Soviet society of my generation began their careers as specialists on October. The situation has now changed significantly. In the departments of history of Soviet society at universities, teachers' institutes, and other postsecondary institutions in the humanities, specialists in the history of the October Revolution are extremely few in number, and in some departments they are entirely lacking. The same can be said of the institutions of the USSR Academy of Sciences. In practice, at the universities, with some exceptions, no special courses in the history of the October Revolution are given and no undergraduate theses or candidate dissertations are defended. The materials of the All-Union Certification Commission [VAK] also show a sharp reduction in the number of candidate and doctoral dissertations on the history of the October Revolution.

A second organizational question relates to the publication of documents. In the 1950s, when we were celebrating the fortieth anniversary of the Great October Revolution, a large number of document collections were published in the center and locally. They dealt with specific topics or drew from specific archival fonds. For the sixtieth anniversary of the October Revolution there were considerably fewer items published. As for publications of documents for the seventieth anniversary of the revolution, it is hard to name any projects that can be completed in time for 1987. At the same time, the Central State Archive of the Economy of the USSR has prepared for publication a volume of protocols of the Supreme Council for the Economy [VSNKh] for 1917–18. The protocols of the Presidium of the Supreme Council for the Economy reflect the activity of the Soviet state in the socialist nationalization of industry and in setting up a new economic apparatus. Lenin repeatedly took part in the work of the presidium of the Supreme Council for the Economy. However, the matter of publishing the protocols of the Supreme Council for the Economy is not yet closed. The management of the Academy of Sciences' Institute of History of the USSR shows an incomprehensible passivity, or perhaps timidity, in publishing sources on the history of the October Revolution. Even such a first-class source as the protocols of the Council of People's Commissars has not yet been published.

The third question of an organizational character relates to the problem of coordinating research on the history of the October Revolution. The Academic Council under the leadership of Academician I. I. Mints is perhaps the only Academic Council in the field of history within the Academy of Sciences, which coordinates work. But the Academic Council in this case takes the role of advisor rather than law-maker. It would be helpful to make use of the existing experience of historians of the party. The coordinating council based at the Institute of Marxism-Leninism under the Central Committee of the CPSU confirms the doctoral dissertation topics, and the regional party-history councils confirm candidate dissertation topics. We probably need special measures on the level of the Presidium of the USSR Academy of Sciences and the Ministry of Postsecondary Education of the USSR in order that the council under Academician I. I. Mints's leadership might be able to fulfill in its field the role of coordinator both of dissertation research and of monographic works.

A number of problems in the history of the October Revolution require close attention. There is a rather pronounced gap between the study of the economic and social structures of prerevolutionary Russia. The works of historians studying the system of state capitalism (I have in mind here chiefly works by V. I. Bovykin, P. V. Volobuev, V. Ia. Laverychev, K. N. Tarnovskii and others) show the maturity of the material preconditions for the October Revolution. On the other hand, the historians of the prerevolutionary working class, as in the past, emphasize the connection of the workers of Russia with the land, the low level of their culture, and so forth. Thus, a number of problems in the history of the Russian working class that are most characteristic of the end of the nineteenth century, are carried over into the twentieth century. Here we see clear traces of the ideology of zemstvo statisticians, which originated in [Russian] populism. In short, the social prerequisites of the October Revolution are being studied in an entirely insufficient way.

The analysis of the social structure of Russian society at turning points in the country's development is closely related to this range of questions. While we have a rather clear idea about the working class, thanks to the works of L. S. Gaponenko, A. K. Sokolov, and a number of other investigators, we know very little about the social structure of the country as a whole. Works have appeared on the history of the breaking up and collapse of the bourgeois and petit-bourgeois parties, but these valuable monographs and articles are not fortified by a description of the socioeconomic profile of the Russian bourgeoisie, the urban middle strata, and other classes and social groups. At the same time, important sources exist for analyzing these problems (materials of the demographic censuses of 1918 in Petrograd and Moscow, of the census in Kiev, of the census of the exploiting classes in 1919, and a number of other large-scale sources). They would make it possible to produce a comprehensive analysis not only of the working class, but also of the bourgeoisie and the urban middle strata. In this connection, it is very important to trace the dynamics of class relations.

The social shifts of the years 1917–19 were extremely intense. Processing primary material from the 1918 census of white-collar workers of the Soviet state apparatus shows that important sources for cadre formation in the Soviet apparatus included such strata of the population as revolutionary populists, revolutionary students sympathetic to Soviet power and to the working people, and the like. Nonetheless, these problems drop out of the historians' field of vision.

The past decade has seen the appearance of a number of major team-written works connected with the quantitative processing of large-scale sources from the period of the October Revolution. The social and party composition of delegates to congresses of soviets of the RSFSR is being analyzed. The result of this activity makes it possible to present a picture of the true democratism of Soviet power. Unfortunately, the composition of the delegates to the Second Congress of Soviets, which promulgated Soviet power, has not yet been studied. A list of these delegates has been published. However, a great deal of work on the sources is needed to compile biographical commentaries on the careers of the congress's delegates.

Processing the census of the state apparatus in 1918 is practically complete. The results of this work, however, have seen the light of day only in the form of isolated articles. Obviously, it is necessary to set forth the results of this census in detailed monographic form. Numerous censuses and listings of staff members not only of the central state apparatus, but also of local organs of power were carried out in 1918–20. The archives contain extremely rich material in the form of questionnaires, which give a thorough characterization of the "administrative personnel" during the first stages of the existence of the Soviet regime. It would be very useful if the Academic Council, led by I. I. Mints, could coordinate the work of central and local historians so as to give a comprehensive characterization of the makeup of the organs of Soviet power during the first months and years after the October Revolution.

P. V. Volobuev (corresponding member, USSR Academy of Sciences): In light of the demands made by the Twenty-seventh Congress of the CPSU on the social sciences and by the internal logic of the science of history, Soviet historians face the task of reinterpreting what has been done, accurately evaluating the current state of the field, noting its prospects, and determining the directions of research as a first priority. It is necessary to abandon dogmatic stereotypes, and to look anew at problems that seem to have been solved. What has been said applies fully to the history of the Great October Socialist Revolution, whose urgent need of development we all admit.

There is no doubt that much has been done in this regard, and that quite a few questions concerning the history of the Great October Revolution have been correctly and unambiguously solved. A number of valuable monographs have appeared and questions that previously were studied inadequately or not at all have been brought into the orbit of research. At the same time, if we look critically at what has been done, we can't help admitting that our treatment of any given problem over the past ten to fifteen years cannot satisfy us, let alone the mass reader, who reads all kinds of things about history, but our books least of all. The lag in theoretical treatment of the experience of the Great Revolution is especially alarming. In this regard, we have not gone beyond K. I. Zarodov's book *The Three Revolutions in Russia and Our Own Time* [Tri revoliutsii v Rossii i nashe vremia], which appeared more than ten years ago. In the last few years, historiographic generalizations from the work done have also faded away noticeably.

Besides, in a number of directions in the history of the Great October Revolution, we have gone backward, sectarian dogmatism has gotten the upper hand, and deviations from historical truth have made themselves felt in the treatment of certain questions. Quite a few historians think that the words of Politburo member and Secretary of the Central Committee of the CPSU, E. K. Ligachev, in his speech at the All-Union Conference of Department Heads of the Social Sciences in 1986, to the effect that boring repetition of truisms, fear of the new, and dogmatism have become widespread in the social sciences, apply to whomever you like—philosophers, economists—but not to historians. But it's time to admit that they apply in full measure to historians. Each one of us naturally has thought about the causes of the situation that has developed. In general, these phenomena can be considered as a manifestation in historical science of those negative tendencies in public and political life uncovered by the Twenty-seventh Party Congress. But a more concrete analysis is also needed, in particular as it applies to the science of history.

Before the 1970s, Soviet historical scholarship and the treatment of the history of the Great October Revolution, in general, moved ahead, relying on a deeper understanding of the Leninist intellectual tradition. Of course, there were costs involved in this development, but in what science are there not? At the beginning of the 1970s, however, contrary to the outcome of a discussion in the course of which the majority of specialists had expressed themselves rather unambiguously on the basic problems of the revolutionary process in 1917–18 (although in scholarship, questions are not decided by the majority of votes), we were returned in the treatment of these problems, to models already fifty years old, and in particular to the conception of the October Revolution as a "pure" social revolution, with the policy of class alliances characteristic of such a revolution. As a result, on such questions as class and political alliances in the October Revolution, democratic and socialist allies of the proletariat in the revolutionary process of 1917–18, and the democratic potential of the October Revolution, the hegemony of the proletariat, and so forth, a dogmatic sectarian approach prevailed. Thus, the many-sided experience of the Great October Socialist Revolution was greatly impoverished, and its international significance decreased.

Matters got to the point where, in Western communist parties, the authorship of the conception of broad democratic alliances came to be attributed to other, later theoreticians, rather than to Lenin. It is especially regrettable that the study of the problem of the hegemony of the proletariat in the revolution was hindered, because at that point it was being worked out only in a preliminary way.* The question of the role of the majority of the people in the October Revolution was confused. This concept came to be understood not as a political category, but as an arithmetical quantity. A book was extolled in which it was asserted that during the period of seizure of power by the proletariat, it did not have the support of the majority of the people, but acquired it only later, after winning power. The Leninist conception of the October Revolution began to be presented by a number of historians in a distorted form. Unfortunately, some of the historians present here contributed to the spreading of these dogmatic views. Certain researchers in the Institute of Marxism-Leninism under the Central Committee of the CPSU, taking advantage of the fact that this institution is beyond the limits of scholarly criticism, speak out against Lenin's idea of an alliance of the proletariat with the entire peasantry at the political stage of the October Revolution, and demand that the appropriate statements by Lenin be removed from the manuscripts sent to them for refereeing.

We observe a certain indulgent attitude toward dogmatism. At the same time, we must bear firmly in mind that this phenomenon only dresses itself in the toga of party discipline but has nothing in common with it. To the contrary, it is antithetical to party discipline, since it makes knowledge inevitably one-sided and incomplete, and leads in the final analysis to the falsification of history. Both in policy and in theory, it is just as harmful as revisionism.

What must be done in order to correct this situation, and to raise the

---

*See *Soviet Studies in History*, Winter 1983–84, vol. 22, no. 3.—D.J.R.

study of the October Revolution to a level worthy of this event in world history? It seems to me that we need a whole system of measures of both an organizational and a scholarly nature. In the first place, we must study again and again Lenin's conception of the October Revolution as a whole, and not judge it by individual quotations taken out of context. Lenin's intellectual heritage is inexhaustible, and from today's view, aspects are revealed in it that we previously passed by. Lenin's idea of the revolutionary-democratic path to socialism, which he advanced as early as the "April Theses" [Aprel'skie tezisy], has been worked on almost not at all. Both historians and philosophers have failed to study and reveal Lenin's conception of the choice of pathways for the development of society, a conception whose relevance has increased immeasurably in our days.

In the second place, we must create a healthy moral-psychological atmosphere in the social sciences in which competition and comparison between ideas and arguments would become the norm (once again, not in words but in deeds). We mustn't forget that the solution of a single problem can be approached from different angles, guided by general Marxist-Leninist methodology. We need debates and discussions on scientific problems free from external administrative interference. The practice of labeling, accusations of deviation from Marxism (a favorite method of the dogmatists), must be excluded from scholarly life. We now have definite and accurate statements by the party on this vitally important question, but the practice, unfortunately, often remains what it was.

In the third place, the history of the October Revolution deserves not only further comprehensive study, but also preliminary research on a number of its important problems. The opinion as to the limited possibilities for bringing new sources into circulation is apparently justified, but the existing source base in many cases must also be reinterpreted. We need new approaches to problems that already seem to have been studied, and we need to abandon dogmatic stereotypes and those due to inertia.

Which problems have been inadequately studied and need our attention? Here are some of them. We have in effect no works (except for two or three articles) on the ideological struggle—essentially on the general debate in Russia from March to October of 1917 on the question of the possibility of socialism in Russia. At the same time, this struggle and the victory of Lenin and the Bolsheviks in it played a huge role in ideological and theoretical preparations for the October Revolution. Let us take the question of the spread of socialist ideas among the masses in Russia in 1917. There is practically no research on this question, unless we count the team-written monograph by Leningrad historians on the propaganda of Marxism-Leninism among the working people of Petrograd, in which one chapter is devoted to the eve of the October Revolution. We are speaking precisely of the propaganda and dissemination of socialist ideas. It is a strange fact that historians, and particularly historians of the party, have been repeating the same theme for years, but have not gotten around to studying one of the most important problems—the degree of conscious adoption by the masses of the idea of socialism. What about the problem of the unified revolutionary-democratic front that developed in the days of struggle against Kornilov? It has only been posed quite recently in the works of some historians from Leningrad, but has not yet been studied in breadth and in depth. Besides, some historians are inclined to deny altogether the existence of such a front in 1917.

The treatment of such a question as the experience of the Bolsheviks in leading the masses to the socialist revolution also leaves much to be desired. We still underestimate the enormity of the democratic task which went beyond the bounds of the antifeudal revolution, and which had to be solved in 1917. The Bolsheviks were able to lead the masses into the struggle for socialism precisely by way of the struggle for democratic demands, and for the development and deepening of democracy.

The question of historical alternatives in the March-October period of 1917 also deserves special attention. The point is that quite often the predictable nature of the October Revolution is replaced by the idea that it was predetermined, or in some way "programmed" from the beginning. To the contrary, between March and October of 1917 a sharp struggle between the various forces in society over the choice of one or another path for the political and social development of Russia was in progress, and at any given moment there were various possibilities and tendencies for development. In June 1917, when the revolutionary movement in the country oriented toward socialism was gaining momentum, Lenin wrote "What our revolution will yield tomorrow—a return to monarchy, a strengthening of the bourgeoisie, a transfer of power to new classes—we don't know, and nobody knows" [PSS, vol. 32, p. 252]. For this reason, in our new research we should not smooth out or oversimplify the difficult course of the struggle of the working class and its party for the socialist alternative, but portray it in all its complexity and richness, and with all its contradictions.

As far as controversial problems are concerned, we should mention two. One of these has to do with the regrouping of class and political forces during the October Revolution. This is occasioned by the fact that in the past ten to fifteen years this question has become overgrown with dogmatism and has become thoroughly confused. The other has to do with the history of the Civil War. Owing to the fact that some staff members of the Institute of Marxism-Leninism and the Institute of the History of the USSR have acquired other ideas about the class nature and political behavior of the officer corps in the three Russian revolutions from those they had previously (the officer corps's support of the bourgeois Provisional Government has even begun to serve as a sign of its progressive orientation), a discussion of this problem should be held in the scholarly press, and the Leninist, Bolshevik views on this currently very urgent problem should be restored.

Thus, we must bring back to life the spirit of competition and struggle of ideas in the science of history as a condition for its creative development. Fidelity to philosophical and methodological principles will remain in this regard the guiding principle of Soviet historians.

V. M. Selunskaia (Moscow University): The October Revolution is the major event of the twentieth century. Soviet historiography must preserve this fact in the people's historical memory, reconstructing an increasingly complete, adequate, and objectively truthful image of the first victorious socialist revolution in all its complexity and with all its contradictions.

Soviet historians understand that the science of history must not remain aloof from the process of restructuring begun by the party. On the contrary, it must use its potential to the maximum degree in order to place historical knowledge at the service of the general process of speeding up the country's socioeconomic development, and in order that the historical memory of the Soviet people will nourish socialist patriotism, and that the energy of historical knowledge will be transformed more and more intensely into social action. For this purpose, the science of history itself, in which, during the last decade and a half, retrograde phenomena have accumulated, tendencies toward glossing over reality have been reborn, and dogmatic stereotypes have become established, must actively include itself in the restructuring and must decisively veto everything that hinders the development of scholarship and prevents it from actively participating in solving the urgent tasks facing the people as a whole.

In the work directed toward overcoming negative phenomena in the study and interpretation of the history of the October Revolution, we must not permit the rejection of what has already been achieved in Soviet historiography, the reduction of it to "Stalinist models," the pressing of various "sore points." Such an approach cannot become the basis of further constructive work. In the history of Soviet society, the history of the Great October Revolution is the most thoroughly researched theme. It is moving forward in terms of monographic study and in terms of the volume of the source base that has been utilized. It is being advanced historiographically, and in the degree to which it has been populated by human beings and has been personified.

The Twentieth Congress of the CPSU and the subsequent decisions of the Central Committee became a serious and powerful impulse for developing the historiography of the October Revolution. The second half of the 1950s was legitimately the starting point of a new period in the development of Soviet historical scholarship. Soviet historians, in the future as well, must calculate the process of overcoming the long and painful dogmatic stagnation in the social sciences from this starting point. Unfortunately, this progressive process has been slowed down significantly in the past decade and a half and, in a number of areas of the social sciences and in a number of subdivisions of the history of Soviet society, it has even been interrupted. As for the study of the October Revolution, I believe that here it would be more accurate to speak of a slowing down, of a decrease in intensity, and of the creation of stagnant areas which, as it were, become surrounded by a picket fence of evaluations and conclusions permanently set up. A field of heightened tension for researchers was created.

Our task consists of preserving the continuity and healthy development of the historiography of the October Revolution since the Twentieth Congress, while critically analyzing and clearly determining what has actually enriched it during this period, which controversial questions are actually in need of further reinterpretation and deeper research, and which ones, on the contrary, should be considered as directions mistakenly or unreasonably introduced into the mainstream of the historiography of the October Revolution. If today we make our plans for restructuring without doing this beforehand, then we will inevitably repeat ourselves and old grudges and offenses will float to the surface; we will busy ourselves with problems that are not genuine but illusory, and the desired acceleration and improvement in the quality of research will not be achieved.

Over the past quarter of a century we have made significant progress in working on the history of the October Revolution, in studying the prerequisites of the revolution, and its main moving force—the Russian proletariat—and in shedding light on the formation, activity, and collapse of the counterrevolutionary forces. The limits of the big picture of the revolutionary transformations on the scale of the country as a whole have been pushed back, and this has permitted us to take a deeper approach to the study of the international significance of the Russian Revolution, in the dialectical interrelationship of its general regularities and its specific character. Interesting new works describing the social aspect, psychology, and moral status of the active forces in the first socialist transformations have appeared. However, we cannot say that we've done all we could.

Regarding the problem of the prerequisites of the socialist revolution, the theme of Russian capitalism in its division among regions and branches has not yet been adequately worked out. The point is by no means that we have "forgotten about the existence of several structures [mnogoukladnost']," and that "the conception of the existence of several structures" must serve as a basis for further developing this large and complex problem. The problem is in working out the concept of a "capitalist country at an intermediate stage of development" in a concrete historical way, and in showing Russian capitalism in its fullness, both in its higher, monopolistic forms, and in its lower ones—simple commodity production—with the degree to which these are interrelated and interact, with precapitalist structures in the basic, large socioeconomic regions of the country. We must show not only the backwardness of Russia before October relative to the highly developed capitalist countries (which has already been done to a considerable degree in our literature), but we must also give the entire complex of arguments showing that there is no basis for classifying Russia among the developing countries that are just embarking on capitalist modernization.

Inadequate development of the problem of the relationships among classes, social strata, and groups within the totality of the new moving forces of the revolutionary process remains a major defect in the historiography of the October Revolution. This is connected with the complexity of the problem itself, since the allies of the proletariat of Russia at various stages of the revolution and in different spheres of the revolutionary-transformational process were dissimilar, both in social classification and in political inclination.

Familiarity with the plentiful literature devoted to the alliance between the working class and the poorest section of the peasantry, the working peasantry in general, and the nonproletarian working masses of the city and countryside during the October Revolution, suggests we have not yet developed the very concept of "an alliance of class forces." Certain historians consider this to be derived from exclusively subjective factors of the historical process, while others consider it to be derived from objective factors; as a rule, the degree of the objective growth of sentiments favoring an alliance is ignored, as are the qualitative stages of the revolutionary-transformational process in particular spheres, and the regrouping of contending forces during transitions from one stage to another of these transformations are not differentiated. The differences between the main strategic line of the proletarian revolution (the struggle for power between the classes at opposite ends of the spectrum) and its collateral revolutionary-democratic tasks, in the solution of which, as we know, the number of "temporary and unstable" allies of the proletariat increases, are not taken into account.

The traditional specialization of scholars that has developed creates a certain difficulty in treating the problem of alliances and interactions among classes and social groups. For this reason, specialists in the history of the working class, in solving the problems of its relationship with the peasantry, the intelligentsia, and the petite bourgeoisie, are not always able to take account of the specific character and the nuances of these relationships.

The question of social policy in the first year of the dictatorship of the proletariat seems to have become quite timely, but has not been studied adequately. Through this policy the demands of the insurgent people for establishing social justice in the laws and actions of the Soviet workers' and peasants' government were realized. To develop this theme requires a broad approach, and requires us to overcome the established practice of limiting social policy to questions of social security, new labor legislation, the organization of food supply and the like. We need to take into account the current broad arena of social policy of the socialist state, and to analyze the sources from which its basic components were formed, both in the revolutionary legislation, and in the social practice of the revolutionary transformation of relationships of production, of the way of life, and of the intellectual and moral spheres.

The social profile of the Russian proletariat has been reconstructed by Soviet historical scholarship only in its most general features: so far, only crude outlines have been laid down. As a consequence, in many spheres, its leading role in the revolutionary process remains inadequately explored. Essentially, we still face the task of studying in depth Lenin's conception of this problem and the sources, so as to reconstruct the social portrait of the leading class of the revolution in all its essential features, with the strong and weak points of its concrete historical and regional and ethnic peculiarities.

Historians have accumulated considerable positive experience in studying the transformation of the proletariat from a "class in itself" to a "class for itself." On the other hand, the transformation of the Russian proletariat from an oppressed class into a ruling class has not been studied so solidly. This process has at least three aspects requiring study—the sociopolitical, the socioeconomic, and the sociopsychological. Both in objective reality and as reflected in history, these three aspects of a single process developed in connection with each other, but not to an equal degree. The sociopolitical aspect has been most studied. However, even in the examination of this, there are large lacunae and mistakes. One of the important aspects of the sociopolitical dimension of the transformation of the proletariat from an oppressed into a ruling class is the development of the hegemony of the working class during its conquest of state power into the dictatorship of the proletariat, in which the hegemonic class is organized into a socialist state. Large and detailed works have been devoted to this question. On the other hand, the first experience of the realization of a legislative initiative by the victorious class, the accumulation of the creative energy of the proletariat in revolutionary laws expressing the conception of social justice of those who yesterday were oppressed—this theme still awaits its students.

The least-studied feature in the social portrait of the working class is its intellectual and moral aspect, its political culture, and its revolutionary ethics. Although the first furrows in this almost virgin field of study have already been plowed, we cannot say that study of this great problem has taken place. There are considerable difficulties here, both in methodology and in terms of sources. There is a tendency toward idealizing and prettying-up the portraits of the heroes of October, as well as a tendency in the opposite direction. One thing is beyond doubt: the sources for the birth of the new man, the formation of his socialist ideals, value-orientations, and demands for social justice and social equality lie in the revolutionary practice of those years. We must actively develop the biographies of the heroes of October, the progressive workers, by tracing their fates and showing their social consciousness in its dynamics, their devotion to socialism, their thirst for knowledge, and their hatred of everything that undermines socialism. Such work is needed in order to instruct today's youth with concrete examples from history. It is necessary to show the formation of the social consciousness of the leading class in its struggle with serious difficulties (a low level of culture, the influence of anarchism, syndicalism, and of *proletkul't** and the petit-bourgeois morality of the artisan and trading class), the concrete histori-

---

*Proletarian culture—a voluntary worker's organization (1917–32) active in several cultural fields, primarily literature and the arts. It was supposedly criticized by Lenin and the party as having the wrong attitude toward the cultural heritage of the past.—Trans.

cal experience of the struggle against these tendencies, the process by which they were overcome at definite historical stages, and the reasons for possible recurrences of them.

And if there are so many lacunae in the study of the social aspect of the proletariat in Russia in the October Revolution, there are still more in the history of the Russian peasantry and intelligentsia in that complex revolutionary epoch.

Today we are clearly aware of the justice in the demands made by the party on social scientists to intensify and improve the quality of our treatment of urgent historical problems. The process of democratization of public life now developing in the country must involve the historical discipline in a fundamental way. An atmosphere of collectivism, comradeship, mutual aid, and a party attitude toward criticism must become the norm for relationships among Soviet historians. We must not permit offenses against the dignity of participants in debates—especially those who are in the minority. It is also desirable that publishers not impose imperative quotations on us, not cross out or insert names contrary to the will of the author, not break up the conceptual fabric of the text, and give the author the opportunity to employ to the full his rights as author and his responsibility for the professional competence of his work.

A. L. Litvin (Kazan University): The history of the Great October Revolution and the defense of its achievements are the subject of hundreds of document collections and other publications. Among them, few are taken from archives. At present, we clearly need a working over of sources in which the authenticity and reliability of publications would be determined and in which the history of the appearance of a particular document would be given. Making a fetish of archival data or of a published document is often the result of mistaken conclusions of studies of various kinds. The history of a document helps to explain the reliability of the information it contains.

It was no accident that Lenin, in telegrams sent to the provinces in connection with violations of revolutionary legality, or with crimes committed by officials, qualified the proposed punitive measures by adding the phrase "if it is confirmed." Let us cite just one example. On February 10, 1919, Lenin, in an instruction to the Simbirsk Guberniia Executive Committee and the Simbirsk Guberniia Cheka, proposed that if the facts were confirmed, severe punishment should be meted out to the members of the Committee of the Village Poor of Mediany, Chimbelevo Volost, Kurmysh Uezd, for nationalizing women. Exactly a month later, on March 10, 1919, the chairman of the Simbirsk Guberniia Cheka, A. M. Levin, reported to Lenin: "Investigation has established that there was no nationalization of women by the Committee of the Poor in Mediany." The declaration by those who complained to Lenin proved to be a fabrication (see *V. I. Lenin and the Cheka: A Collection of Documents (1917–1922)* [V. I. Lenin i VChK. Sb. dok. (1917–1922)], Moscow 1975, p. 158). Few such cases are known, but they do indicate such a form of class struggle as disinformation, the slandering of people devoted to the revolution and its ideals, [and] the complexity of human relationships.

In many monographic studies on the October Revolution and Civil War, the names of prominent figures in the Soviet state and military commanders are mentioned. Sometimes, in a local example, the previously unknown name of yet another person who fought for Soviet power is mentioned. Nevertheless, we should surely speak, not about how to mention as many names as possible, but about how to give a characterization that will be remembered even of those who are already known. We should not spare details such as the relationships that had developed at that time in the headquarters of the High Command of the Red Army, the military revolutionary councils of individual fronts, and so forth. In 1962, an article appeared by P. Kolesnichenko "On the Question of Conflict in the Military Revolutionary Council of the Southern Front (September–October, 1918)" [K voprosy o konflikte v Revvoensovete Iuzhnogo fronta (sentiabr'–oktiabr' 1918 goda)] (*Voenno-istoricheskii zhurnal*, 1962, no. 3). This article has its defects, but the author showed how the personal qualities and individual subjective actions of members of the military revolutionary council of the front harmed the cause and created conflict, at a time when unity and discipline in routing the enemy were required.

The study of such facts should be continued not only in order to show that period as a time of human passion and arguments on matters or principles, but also in order to understand it better, and to present clearly the Leninist style of leadership in defending the country by people to whom the party entrusted important sectors of the front, where the fate of the revolution was often decided. It seems to me that we should not give what we call "the human factor" entirely over to the discretion of writers: it should also be worked on by professional historians.

The special encyclopedic handbooks *The Great October Socialist Revolution* [Velikaia Oktiabr'skaia sotsialisticheskaia revoliutsiia] (Moscow, 1977), *The Civil War and the Intervention in the USSR* [Grazhdanskaia voina i voennaia interventsiia v SSSR] (Moscow, 1988 [*sic*—should be 1983.—D.J.R.]) contain data on many revolutionaries and counterrevolutionaries. Only information on representatives of opposition groups is lacking. A considerable literature exists on the party's struggle with Trotskyism and with representatives of right-wing deviationism, and the same thing is written in textbooks for postsecondary school students on the history of the USSR. But they do not answer the question that has become standard for students: if Trotsky, Zinoviev, Rykov, Bukharin, and others were always in opposition to the Leninist course of the party and were its enemies, then why were they entrusted with high posts in the party and state at least during the first decade of the Soviet regime? Usually, the teacher answers this question insofar as his competence permits. But surely the time has come to write special articles, and to explain in textbooks the causes of these phenomena, and to show that the appearance of an opposition is to be expected at important, revolutionary turning points in history in order to avoid idle speculation and incompetent explanations.

In the localities, and in the country's colleges, a large contingent of historians known for their research on the October Revolution and the Civil War is at work. The Academic Council of the USSR Academy of Sciences, under the leadership of I. I. Mints, is carrying out a major job of coordination. The Sector of History of the October Revolution and the Civil War of the Institute of the History of the USSR, Academy of Sciences, has kept aloof from it. It seems to me that joint team-written works and the creation of summary, historiographic works about the history of the first years of the Soviet regime in various regions of the country would further promote successful research.

P. A. Golub (Institute of Marxism-Leninism, Central Committee of the CPSU): At the Institute of Marxism-Leninism, we have completed a work of synthesis, *The Historical Experience of the Three Russian Revolutions* [Istoricheskii opyt trekh rossiiskikh revoliutsii]. The third volume, which analyzes the experience of the Great October Revolution, is to appear very shortly. The results of the work of a large team of writers uniting specialists from a number of scholarly institutions, are of interest because of the discussion concerning the present condition and problems in the further treatment of the first victorious socialist revolution in history.

One of the distinguishing features of the new book on the Great October Revolution, and of the entire publication, is that it analyzes the revolutionary process in terms of particular historical problems. The application of this approach to the study of the problems of the preparations for, and victory of, the October Revolution in their dialectical interconnection, has helped to reveal "blank spots," and to deepen significantly the understanding of the question traditionally studied, and to approach the solution of a number of new problems.

As for the "blank spots," they relate primarily to the study of the theoretical activity of Lenin and the Bolshevik party during direct preparation for the victory of October: the sociopolitical conditions of the revolution and their role in transforming Russia into the weakest link in the world imperialist system; the growth of the bourgeois-democratic revolution into a socialist one, its basic conditions and the distinctive features of its implementation in Russia, the action of the mechanism of transformation; the comparison, by experience, of the October Revolution with the peaceful and so-called parliamentary paths to the victory of the revolution; the lessons of the Bolshevik party's struggle for creating a broad front of democratic forces against the bourgeois regime; the experience of establishing Lenin's party as the ruling one; the socioeconomic and ideological-political factors in providing for the defense of the victorious revolution; and a number of others.

The scientific and political importance of these questions is beyond doubt, but their study is either still in the initial stage, or else has not yet really begun. For this reason, we cannot accept the opinion that the October Revolution has already been studied "thoroughly." This revolution is such a large-scale, many-sided, and powerful event in its influence on the fate of humanity, that the sources and causes of its action, increasingly revealed over the course of time, will long remain an object of persistent analysis and generalization.

The approach to the subject-matter in terms of particular problems required the authors of this new book on the Great October Revolution to utilize the full wealth of Lenin's ideas, conclusions, and evaluations on the root questions of developing the revolution. Presented in the form of a system, indissolubly connected with the solution of specific historical problems, and taken as a unified whole, they made possible a significantly more complete revelation of Lenin's conception of the Great October Revolution, and this in turn is of fundamental importance for a deeper analysis of the experience of our revolution.

All revolutions, as we know, are preceded by ideological preparation. But the preparation in terms of ideas and theory that preceded the October Revolution has no equals either in scope and depth or in its class tendency. This is one of the main sources of its triumphant success. The huge ideological and theoretical work performed by Lenin's party on its way to the October Revolution, and after it was realized, promoted decisively the formation of the subjective factor of the revolution, the development of a scientifically based program of action in the political and economic areas, in agrarian, ethnic, military, and other questions, and of the strategy and tactics of the revolutionary forces in the struggle for establishing and consolidating the Soviet regime. This gave the revolutionary movement a conscious, purposeful, stable character and set it apart from a number of other revolutions that to a larger degree developed spontaneously, and, having won, did not know how to use the power they had obtained.

For all the importance of this cardinal question, our historiography has not produced a special work dealing in summary form with the theoretical activity of Lenin's party during the October Revolution. The team of authors for the book tried to fill in this lacuna to the extent possible, and to evaluate the importance of the extremely intense theoretical work of the Bolshevik party in 1917. The book emphasizes that the party, in response to the demands of revolutionary practice after the February Revolution, furthered the working out of many cardinal questions of revolutionary theory. In particular, the conclusion is drawn that it was precisely Russia that was destined to lay down the first path to socialism, and this enriched and made more concrete the conceptions of Marxists concerning the paths of development of the revolutionary process on a world scale, and opened before the proletariat of Russia a clear prospect, making significant corrections in the strategic orientation of the world revolutionary movement.

It was precisely after the February Revolution that Lenin and the Bolshevik party significantly advanced the theoretical treatment of the question of the soviets as a new type of state power, concluded that a republic of soviets was the best state form for a proletarian regime, gave a comprehensive validation of the advantages of proletarian over bourgeois democracy, determined the paths by which the bourgeois state could be broken up and the socialist one constructed, and formulated the basic principles of Soviet statehood. Marxist theoretical thought in that period made a large step forward in the further validation and concretization of the growth of the bourgeois democratic revolution into a socialist one, in the treatment of the paths of peaceful development of the revolution, in the doctrine of the armed uprising, in the question of the correct relationship between the actions of the political army of the revolution and those of its armed forces.

The treatment of such questions as that of the correlation of socialist and democratic tasks in the proletariat's struggle for power; that of recruiting to its side the nonproletarian majority of working people; that of validating bloc tactics and agreeing with the petit-bourgeois parties and the masses with a view to solving the main task—the question of power; that of the necessity of implementing a program of transitional measures during the movement toward socialism, that of the role and place of the democratic majority of the army in the revolution; that of the question of peaceful and nonpeaceful forms of class struggle, that of the conditions for their correct application; and that of the need to prepare the proletariat for any form of struggle and for a swift change from one form to another in accordance with the changing situation—all of these were of immense significance for the October Revolution's success.

A primary role in consolidating the power of the victorious proletariat was played by the theoretical validation of the program of the first revolutionary transformation, the plan of attack in the building of socialist society, the defense of the socialist fatherland, the paths toward constructing the armed forces of the Soviet state, the policy of "War Communism"; the principles of Soviet foreign policy, and above all, the principle of peaceful coexistence.

The high degree of theoretical "armament" of the revolutionary forces that accomplished the October Revolution is a most important distinguishing feature of its historical experience, and the team of authors strove to reveal the influence of this factor as fully as possible.

In validating the historical conformity of the October Revolution, the book details the degree of maturity of the sociopolitical conditions as a component part of the objective factors that predetermined the inevitability of a gigantic revolutionary explosion in Russia. Unfortunately, our historiography has at its disposal only two or three specialized articles on this subject. At the same time, bourgeois falsifiers try to concentrate all their attention on the economic conditions of our revolution, and, since Russian capitalism was on a lower level of maturity than the more highly developed countries, they conclude that the conditions for the victory of October were "immature," and the victory was "accidental." In the same connection, a detailed factual description is given in the book of the maturity of the subjective conditions for the revolution's victory—and of the ideological and organizational preparation of the proletariat and its allies for winning power.

From this point of view the authors describe the national crisis in the country in the autumn of 1917, which combined a high degree of maturity in both objective and subjective conditions. Guaranteeing the maturity of the subjective factor was the chief concern of the Leninist party on the road to October. And although the masses' determination to overthrow bourgeois power was caused primarily by their own practical experience, the role of the party in deepening this determination, in inculcating a higher revolutionary consciousness and in guaranteeing the organized character of their action was decisive. The party not only scientifically validated the course toward a socialist revolution, but also was able to arouse the masses for its implementation. It is important to note this last fact, because there are cases in history when underestimating the importance of work with the masses has defeated proletarian parties even in the presence of a correct strategy.

The need to reveal a general formula for the changing over of a bourgeois democratic revolution into a socialist one, to fill this formula with concrete content, and to show the principal factors determining this difficult, ambiguous, and extremely intense process, has long since matured. I believe that the new book takes a definite step forward in this direction. A special place in this connection is allotted to the period of the peaceful development of the revolution, to its conditions, and also to what interrupted it. The book summarizes the essence of the struggle of the Bolshevik party for the conquest of power by the proletariat through peaceful means, compares it with the so-called parliamentary path to power, and shows the invalidity of these conceptions.

Among the new topics considered by the authors is the validation of the question of two political camps after the February Revolution, which is of fundamental importance for characterizing the disposition of class forces in that period and of the change in it between February and October. There is a special study of the counterrevolutionary camp, its variegated social makeup, the types of counterrevolution according to class (landlord-monarchist, bourgeois, and petit-bourgeois), the peculiarities of their tactics in the struggle against the revolution, and the revolutionary camp's implementation of countermeasures. This helps in revealing the struggle's drama, the sharpness of its conflict, and in overcoming the impersonal and schematic quality of our works on the October Revolution.

The treatment of the indissoluble connections among the three Russian revolutions,* and of the significance of the revolutionary heritage of the two bourgeois democratic revolutions in preparing for the October victory is a weak spot in the literature on the October Revolution. In the three-volume work devoted to the Russian revolutions, the team of authors has tried to fill in some measure the significant lacunae.

Among the problems relating to the stabilization of the victory of the proletar-

---

*1905, February 1917, and October 1917.—D.J.R.

iat of Russia, that of transforming the Bolshevik party into the ruling party is analyzed in detail for the first time. The summary of the extremely rich and valuable experience of the restructuring of its activity in the initial period of Soviet power has great international significance. However, this is one of the least-studied questions in our historiography. Fundamentally new features have been brought into the treatment of the problem of defending the revolution, particularly in revealing the role of socioeconomic and foreign-policy factors in strengthening the capacity of the Soviet state, and in validating the transition from the universal arming of the people to the formation of a new type of standing army. The book gives a clear-cut Leninist evaluation of the policy of "War Communism," as one that was necessary under civil war conditions, and this is of fundamental significance in view of the attempts to depart from the Leninist evaluations of this policy.

Thus, the approach to the study of the history and experience of the Great October Revolution in terms of specific problems has fully justified itself and has opened new horizons for investigating the main event of world history. It is necessary to move ahead more energetically along this path.

N. N. Demochkin (Moscow Textile Institute): The process by which the Bolshevik party won over the soviets remains inadequately studied. But the ability to link up and to get close to the broad masses of the working class and all working people who had allied with them during the development of the bourgeois-democratic revolution into a socialist one, determined the success of the proletarian revolution. The party allotted a special role in solving this task to the soviets, which had been created during the February Revolution by the revolutionary creativity of the masses. From the moment of their formation, the soviets became the basic organization of workers, soldiers, and peasants, the school in which they learned politics, and the most important point of support for the Bolshevik party in developing the revolution. For this reason, a thorough study of the activity of the Bolshevik party in strengthening its influence in the soviets, and later, under the conditions of the immediate preparation of the October Revolution, the change in their political direction and activity, and also in their reception of Bolshevik resolutions, is of great scholarly and practical importance.

In the literature, the initial process of Bolshevization of the soviets after the defeat of the Kornilov insurgency is usually considered from the example of changes in the party composition of only a few soviets. Such an approach does not reveal fully Lenin's position to the effect that in the course of the Bolshevization of the soviets, the masses "turned away from the petit-bourgeois leadership, and passed over to the side of the proletarian revolutionary struggle for the overthrow of the bourgeoisie" [*PSS*, vol. 37, p. 281]. In September and October of 1917, under pressure from the revolutionary masses, new elections to the soviets and their executive committees were conducted across the country. The elections promoted the uninterrupted growth of Bolshevik influence in the soviets of Petrograd, Moscow, the central industrial region of the country, the Middle and Lower Volga regions, the Ukraine, the Urals, Belorussia, and Siberia. According to our calculations, in October 1917 there were Bolshevik fractions in 191 soviets, including 56 soviets in guberniia and oblast capitals—that is to say, in the majority of the guberniias and oblasts. This affected the party composition of oblast and guberniia congresses of soviets that took place in September and October 1917, and the decisions taken by them on the question of power, and also on the party composition of the delegates to the Second All-Russian Congress of Soviets. According to data which are by no means complete, out of twenty-one oblast, guberniia, and okrug congresses of soviets, conferences, and consultative meetings that took place in September and October, representatives of more than 700 soviets were present. More than 500 soviets, whose delegates participated in these congresses, favored a transfer of power to the soviets.

According to the data of a survey of delegates to the Second All-Russian Congress of Soviets on the attitude of local soviets toward state power, 505 soviets supported the Bolshevik slogan, All Power to the Soviets! If we include the soviets that accepted the Bolshevik resolution on power, but whose representatives were not present at the Second All-Russian Congress of Soviets, then, according to our calculations, more than 700 soviets of workers', soldiers', and peasants' deputies came out in favor of a transfer of power to the soviets. Of the 974 soviets active in the country at the beginning of October, more than 600 supported a transfer of power to the soviets, including the majority of the amalgamated guberniia and oblast soviets, and the soviets of workers' deputies in provincial capitals. One hundred guberniia and uezd peasant soviets also spoke in favor of soviet power (455 soviets of peasants' deputies existed at the time of the October Revolution).

The Bolsheviks' intense struggle for the soviets from the February to the October Revolutions tipped the balance of forces in their favor. This affected the party makeup of the Second All-Russian Congress of Soviets. According to corrected data, among the 900 deputies to the congress there were 490 Bolsheviks—that is, at least fifty-four percent—and, together with the "Left" SRs, who also supported a transfer of state power to the soviets, they made up the vast majority of delegates (more than seventy-three percent). Unfortunately, these data, which were published in the journal *Voprosy istorii KPSS* (1977, no. 7) are not used in the literature.

The experience of the Bolsheviks' struggle for the masses during preparation for the October Revolution shows that necessary conditions for the creation of a mass army of the socialist revolution are: first, the winning over by the party of the majority of the working class and the achievement of unity in its ranks; and second, the uniting around it of broad strata of the politically active nonproletarian working population—primarily the poorest peasants—and the creation of a broad popular front. The entire struggle of the Bolsheviks for the masses and for drawing the soviets to their side, shows convincingly that without uniting the proletarian majority around its militant avant-garde, without overcoming the political division of the proletariat, and without its willingness to follow the communists, it is impossible to create a mass political army of the revolution. Unless this task is solved, there is no chance of overthrowing the bourgeoisie in practical terms. This important problem still awaits further and deeper study.

G. Z. Ioffe (Academic Council): The party is now charging the social sciences to make themselves more relevant in regard to society and to get involved more directly in practical matters. For the science of history this means to accept without reservation the ''challenge'' presented by the increased interest, during the last few years, of the common reader in the past. It seems to me, to put it mildly, we were entirely unprepared for this challenge.

I have been struck by one fact. Recently, *Literaturnaia gazeta* published a rather angry article about the start of subscription taking for the works of S. M. Solov'ev and V. O. Kliuchevskii, and the expected opening of subscriptions for works by N. M. Karamzin. The author of the article was demanding an unlimited subscription on the basis of the unprecedented interest of Soviet people in history and in the works of the prerevolutionary scholars. Let's think about this. The struggle with bourgeois and émigré historiography has been conducted for several decades and the correctness of our Marxist-Leninist interpretation has been established. A number of works have laid down this conception—for example, the twelve-volume *History of the USSR* [Istoriia SSSR] (in two series). But would such a fuss be made by readers if a subscription were open for this and other works of ours, including those on the history of the October Revolution?

So what's the point? Is our conception bad? Certainly not. It is precisely the conception that opens to historians enormous possibilities, so to speak, both in form and in content. But have we taken advantage of these? Here is a minor example: I happened to read a review by an American Sovietologist of a book about the October Revolution by one of our historians. The reviewer recognized that the author had followed the Leninist approach faithfully, and that there were in his book many quotations from Lenin and evaluations by Lenin. But what it didn't have was precisely what makes Lenin and Leninism attractive—its emotional tone, its passion, its sincerity, its conviction. A pretty good point! Evgenii Evtushenko once wrote that ''if the material hasn't been experienced, you will not make anyone else experience it with you'' [*Literaturnaia gazeta*, July 10, 1981]. It's been said that in order to write well you have to mix at least a little of your own blood with the ink.

The Leninist approach to the history of the October Revolution is foreign to the two-dimensional, tired pattern, in which the description of events is fitted in order to reach conclusions that were known to the reader to begin with. The revolution, for Lenin, is a living, swift social torrent, filled to the brim with struggle, victories, defeats, tragedy, and flights of spirit. The revolution, for

Lenin, was what life can be only at the moment of greatest social tension. In January 1918 he said:

> There's no question but that the socialist revolution cannot be offered to the people in a clean, smooth, impeccable form; it can't help but be accompanied by civil war, and by sabotage and resistance. And those who try to convince us otherwise are either liars or people wrapped up in cocoons [*PSS*, vol. 35, p. 240].

This is the truth, of which Lenin said that it "shouldn't depend on the person whom it's supposed to serve" [*PSS*, vol. 54, p. 446]. If our books on the October Revolution had in them that kind of truth, their moral and ideological power would be increased manyfold, and we wouldn't now be noting with sadness the decline of interest in the history of October and the loss of confidence in historians.

The monotony of subject matter, the repetition, the "regurgitation" of the same topics, etc., have been justly spoken of here, and at the same time, we've also spoken of the avoidance of controversial problems and questions that interest the public. Let's answer honestly the question of what caused this situation. There are, of course, many causes, but right now we should isolate two of them: first, the fear of labels and nonacademic conclusions that for such a long time hounded historians. Alas, not all of them are fighters by character, and many prefer to avoid conflict, remembering the fates of their predecessors or colleagues. And if we really want to open up space for genuinely creative forces in the science of history, then we must decisively end such a situation. In the second place, historians lack a creative environment. It sounds strange, but we silently accept "scholarly subordination," "scholarly hierarchy worship." There are quite a few people who are beyond criticism; too often the same names show up on the title pages of books as "responsible editor." The absence of really sharp, lively debates is of course still worse. And those that take place often suffer from scholasticism. For example, the fierce argument on the problem of "the October Revolution and the Officer Corps" hasn't yet died down. But how much scholasticism, how much readiness to "brand" and to stick on labels there is in this argument.

Let's remember in this connection the admission of Marshal of the Soviet Union G. K. Zhukov, which he made in a conversation with Konstantin Simonov. Speaking of 1917 Zhukov said:

> In those young years of mine, I could have turned away from the right path. This possibility couldn't be excluded. And who knows what would have happened if I had not been a common soldier, but an officer, who had distinguished myself in battle and received other ranks, when the revolution had broken out. . . . Where would I have ended up under the influence of various circum-

stances—where would I have been? Would I perhaps have lived out my days in emigration somewhere? [*Ogonek*, 1986, no. 48, p. 7].

What does this ostensibly minor example show? It shows that in analyzing the various economic and social factors shaping the course of history, in our statistical computations and calculations, etc., we must not lose sight of the individual and his specific circumstances. He is our chief hero. And his course in the revolution was not simple.

Only thus, I think, will we be able to restore the shaken confidence of the reader in historians and their work. Apparently the scientific and ideological urgency of this task is recognized by everyone today.

One last thing. It has been said here that we have already almost exhausted the various sources for the history of the Great October Revolution. Anyone who works in libraries or in archives knows well that it is hard to agree with this.

Iu. I. Korablev* (Scientific Council): The basic purpose of our meeting is to share our views on the defects and problems in the study of the history of the October Revolution. This, of course, does not mean that there have not been achievements. Among the works that have appeared lately are the following: I. I. Mints's *The Year 1918* [God 1918-i], books by A. Ia. Grunt, A. M. Sovokin, V. I. Startsev, the monograph of the Ukrainian historians, *In the Fire of Three Revolutions* [V ogne trekh revoliutsii], the collection of articles, *The Historical Experience of the Great October Revolution* [Istoricheskii opyt Velikogo Oktiabria], and other works containing new factual material and profound conclusions.

However, we should recognize that the literature on the history of the October Revolution that has appeared over the past ten years suffers, as previously, if we can express it so, from a "glossing over" of the historical canvas. In order to show the revolutionary process with all of its complexities and contradictions we must abandon the usual approach, which oversimplifies the events of those days. This requires a restructuring of thought and a search for new approaches. Where shall we begin? Those people are right who propose that we first of all study the heritage of Lenin more deeply, emphasizing in the process his conception of the history of the Great October Revolution as a people's revolution, a revolution for social justice, which delineated for mankind the road to socialism.

It would be very useful for us to prepare and hold, in collaboration with philosophers, a conference, or more correctly, a theoretical seminar, where the most important problems of the Leninist methodology of the study of revolutionary experience would be discussed. I have in mind such problems as the dialectic of the objective and subjective factors in the Revolution, the relationship between spontaneous and conscious elements in the masses' struggle, and especially the

---

*Due to illness, Iu. I. Korablev was not able to be present or speak at the meeting. The editors have taken the liberty of including here the text of his address, which was submitted to them.

role of the subjective factor, its reciprocal action on the objective prerequisites of the Revolution, on the activism of the masses, and on their unwillingness to live in the old way. Incidentally, we often treat the subjective factor as only the condition and action of revolutionary forces. Wouldn't it be more accurate, in the light of Lenin's methodology, to consider it as a unity of opposites—that is, the forces of revolution and counterrevolution, the struggle between that which determines the success of one or the other at each stage of the historical process? For a long time, the history of the counterrevolution was neglected. Recently special works by G. Z. Ioffe, N. G. Dumova, V. D. Polikarpov, N. Ia. Ivanov, and others on the counterrevolutionary forces have appeared. But there are still very few works like A. Ia. Grunt's monograph, which study the dialectic of the revolution and the counterrevolution on the basis of Lenin's well-known position to the effect that there are no revolutions without counterrevolutions.

It is hard to raise the level of research, to freshen and revivify the literature on the history of the October Revolution without making a broad search for new sources, and also without a new interpretation of many documents and materials already utilized. Historians frequently complain about the difficulty of access to archival documents. True, some believe that everything important has already been published and that the probability of new archival finds is extremely small. In any case, the number of visits to the archives by historians studying the twentieth century has decreased noticeably in the past few years. Let's put it bluntly: if there are now untouched or inadequately used strata of sources, then this is primarily because of the lack of enterprise of historians, and of a certain loss by many of them of the taste for detailed archival research. The use of such major publications as the ten-volume series of documents and materials on the history of the October Revolution, the edition of documents of the Petrograd Military Revolutionary Committee, the correspondence of the Secretariat of the Central Committee of the RSDRP(b), and others, is limited, and for the most part purely illustrative and episodic in character.

As for the possibility of new finds, as the saying goes, "seek and ye shall find." Here's one example: in the Central State Archives of the Soviet Army investigators have found the minutes of the meeting of the Third Petrograd Congress of Bolsheviks of October 11, 1917, where the question of the Red Guard and its readiness for an uprising was discussed. Up to now, it has been thought that the minutes of the conference on October 10–11 did not survive. They have now been published. Several years have passed, but for some reason they are not being used. Another example: among the finds of the last few years in the same archives is a summary of answers by delegates to the All-Army Conference on the Demobilization of the Army, assigned to work on the appropriate commissions, to questions posed in writing by Lenin. Accordingly, the note in vol. 35 of *The Complete Works of Lenin* to the effect that "neither the answers to the questions nor material summarizing the answers have been discovered in the archives," has lost its meaning. The document has been put into circulation, but researchers rarely use it.

Further searches and scrupulous source research on all documents and materials, in particular, the effort to date hour by hour (and sometimes minute by minute) documents relating to October 24, 1917, should answer the excessively long-drawn-out argument among historians as to when the armed uprising began—on the morning or in the evening of October 24. The value of such research is shown, for example, by the article of Kh. M. Astrakhan, "On the Initial Phase of the October Armed Uprising in Petrograd" [O nachal'nom etape Oktiabr'-skogo vooruzhennogo vosstaniia v Petrograde"] (in the collection, *The Historical Experience of the Great October Revolution* [Istoricheskii opyt Velikogo Oktiabria], from which we can see that not even all the published documents have been used to establish the events of the first day of the uprising.

In one of his conversations, Lenin said that there would come a time when the October armed uprising would be studied not day by day but hour by hour. Since then, hundreds of works have been published and the events of those days have been examined by historians not only hour by hour but also minute by minute. Nonetheless, we can hardly say that Lenin's prophecy has come to pass. The author of one of the two existing monographs on the October uprising, E. F. Erykalov, believes that "many questions need further investigation," and, in the opinion of E. N. Gorodetskii, a number of questions "still await their solution." Let's mention one of them. We still know very little about the soldiers, sailors, and Red Guards who gave their lives in the struggle for the victory of the armed uprising in Petrograd. We know that it was almost bloodless; only about 15 people died in those days. When the mutiny of Kerensky and Krasnov was defeated, the losses on the side of the revolutionary troops amounted to no less than 200 persons. Only the names of 40 of those who were killed have been established, not even the surnames of all of those who died in the storming of the Winter Palace have been discovered. Work in this direction must be continued. This is our duty to the memory of those people who gave their lives in the cause of the socialist revolution.

In the 1920s, three editions of the book, *A Monument to the Fighters of the Proletarian Revolution* [Pamiatnik bortsam proletarskoi revoliutsii] which dealt with the Bolsheviks who had been killed, were published. In the 1930s and 1940s there were almost no similar publications and books about prominent participants in the revolution. The struggle of the masses began to be treated impersonally in the literature. Hundreds of names of active participants in the revolution, the first builders of the Soviet regime and the Red Army, the heroes of the Civil War, were deleted from the history of the revolution altogether. Those who at various stages made mistakes or became confused were omitted from the list of participants in the Revolution. Lenin's appeals to gather and publish documents and reminiscences and books about revolutionaries whose lives and struggle could teach young people how to live and act were ignored. As a result, the history of the October Revolution took on in most books the character of a lifeless diagram. As

E. N. Gorodetskii justly noted, the history of a mass movement was increasingly replaced by the history of a movement of ideas without the living bearers of these ideas.

After the Twentieth Congress of the CPSU, in the 1960s and 1980s, historians did a good deal to overcome the depersonification of the revolutionary process. Many glorious names returned to print. The remnants of the Stalin cult in regard to treating the role of individual participants in the revolution were liquidated. More than 140 reference books on participants in the revolution at the center and in the provinces were issued. In 1985, the Institute of the History of the party under the Moscow City Committee and Moscow Committee of the CPSU issued the book *Comrades in Arms* [Soratniki] containing 400 biographies of active participants in the revolution in Moscow city and Moscow Oblast. Each biography provided references to the sources and other relevant literature. Nevertheless, what has been done is far from adequate. The published biographical materials still relate to a small portion of the active participants in the revolution. Many participants remain undeservedly forgotten. In studies on the October Revolution we find, as a rule, only a list of surnames with the notorious phrase "and others" appended to it.

But we should write more about people, and show what qualities enabled them to draw over the masses, and to overcome unbelievable difficulties. This is of immense importance for inculcating historical knowledge. At conferences we have repeatedly discussed the question of the need to prepare a single biographical dictionary of the participants in the October Revolution, and to expand the range of the biographical articles in the encyclopedia of the October Revolution and Civil War. The fact that neither one nor the other yet exists is due not so much to the sloth of historians as to the inertia of the past, when participants in the Revolution were looked at for many years through the prism of the prejudices of the later 1930s.

Among other problems requiring more attention, we should mention the social policy of the Soviet regime, which began for the first time to implement the principles of social justice. In general works, this most important branch of state activity under the dictatorship of the proletariat is usually reduced to a list of decrees. On the other hand, the special works on the activity of the Soviet regime in providing for the welfare of the working people can be listed on the fingers of one hand. Over the past twenty years, only two such works have appeared: that of L. K. Baeva on the social policy of the Soviet regime, and M. P. Pol'skii on the organization of public feeding of workers. The party, which is now paying great attention to social policy, is relying on the experience of solving social problems in our country, which was started by the Great October Revolution. Historians are obligated to disseminate this experience, and this task has international significance.

Quite recently, a new theme, "The October Revolution and the Acceleration of the Progress of Society," has been formulated. M. S. Gorbachev has repeatedly noted that we are continuing the policy of acceleration established by the October Revolution. Even before the October Revolution, Lenin opened up the possibilities of accelerating the revolutionary process under conditions in which the objective preconditions for the transition from capitalism to socialism were mature. These possibilities, he indicated, were connected with the readiness and ability of the working people to take revolutionary action, their level of consciousness and organization. Their experiences of struggle, the degree to which the strategy and tactics of the party were scientifically validated, and its ability to determine that the "time was ripe," and compelled it to take a bold step into the future. It would hardly be an exaggeration to say that the demand Lenin made in his letter of October 24, 1917, that power be seized immediately ("History will not forgive delay on the part of revolutionaries. . . .") was not only a brilliant example of precise determination of the moment when the revolution must and will prevail, but also an acceleration of the transition of our country to socialism, and of humanity to a new epoch. It is necessary to uncover the historical roots of the concept of acceleration, worked out by the April (1985) Plenum of the Central Committee of the CPSU and the Twenty-seventh Party Congress, and to show the great role of the leader of the Revolution in working it out and implementing it, in accelerating the transition of Russia from one social order to another.

K. V. Gusev and L. M. Spirin (both of the Institute of Marxism-Leninism, Central Committee of the CPSU), V. D. Polikarpov (Institute of History, USSR Academy of Sciences), and E. M. Shchagin (Lenin Pedagogical Institute, Moscow) also spoke at the meeting.

In his concluding remarks, Academician I. I. Mints called for a more profound study of the Great October Revolution and its further discussion in the pages of this journal.

Part Four

THE CHALLENGE FROM THE PUBLICISTS

Although elements within the Soviet historical profession had expressed dissatisfaction with the status quo before 1985, and despite reformist currents that had
always been part of the discipline, the historians were slower to respond to calls
for change than public affairs writers, journalists, and professional writers of
imaginative literature. Moreover, the publicists posed a serious challenge to
Soviet historians, for in a country whose official history had been falsified,
discussions of reform ineluctably lead to historical revisionism. The more exciting and controversial writings of the publicists issued during the early phase of
perestroika did a great deal to shake up the historical profession, for the publicists
had denied historians their readers by boldly treating moral issues that people
longed to address publicly. Historians bent on change could now argue the need
for responding to the publicists, and for dealing with the controversial and even
taboo subjects the publicists addressed.

This section of the anthology comprises three representative examples of the
various types of publicistic writing. The first, ''Roots,'' by the economic journal-
ist Vasilii Seliunin, which appeared in *Novyi mir* (New World), is one of the most
original and startling essays of its genre. A champion of the resurrection of NEP,
Seliunin manages to touch upon many matters of dispute in Soviet history and
even a few sacred cows in his emotionally charged, eloquent essay. After tracing
the negative impact of extreme political and economic centralization on Russian
history, Seliunin turns to a frank assessment of the formative years of the Soviet
state. He criticizes Lenin for resorting to the use of revolutionary terror in 1918,
arguing that Lenin introduced it as a matter of principle, and not in response to
difficult circumstances. In insisting the kulaks had been liquidated as a class
during the Civil War (and hence that collectivization was not needed), he pins the
blame for the famine of 1921–1922 on Bolshevik requisition policies. He likewise
touches a raw nerve in suggesting that Stalin's measures to some extent represent
a continuation of the Leninist tradition, for it was Lenin who introduced forced
labor and concentration camps. In the author's view, Lenin's saving grace is that
he was able to see the faults in his earlier policies and alter them.

The NEP is Seliunin's hero, and he argues passionately that the greatest lesson
that can be learned from the experience of the 1920s is that it shows the possibility

of revolutionary change from above, literally in a few months. In rejecting mandatory planning and ruination of agriculture, he maintains that forced labor has always been unproductive. Bureaucratic management represents the main obstacle on the road to perestroika. His jarring conclusion is intended to mobilize the forces of reform: "To lose time is to lose everything."

The journal *Ogonek* (Little Light) has also become associated with the cause of perestroika. In December 1987, a few weeks after Gorbachev spoke favorably in public about N. I. Bukharin, it published an interview with Bukharin's widow, Anna Larina. By then Bukharin, "the favorite of the entire party," as Lenin called him, had been legally rehabilitated. Full rehabilitation came in February 1988 and shortly thereafter he was reinstated in the party. The symbolic importance of Bukharin's rehabilitation and of this interview must be stressed: the latter put historians on the defensive, for they had not yet dealt with him impartially.

Glasnost' has created conditions in which it is much less dangerous to speak up, and many prominent individuals in the political and cultural spheres have taken advantage of the opportunity to inform the public and to set the record straight. An example is Fedor Burlatskii, Nikita Khrushchev's speech writer and advisor, later discredited during the Brezhnev years, who has experienced a stunning comeback since 1985. Burlatskii's reminiscences and commentary on Khrushchev merit attention not only because they resurrect Khrushchev, who was so maligned until recently, but also because of their didactic message: Khrushchev's reforms failed because he depended on the party for their implementation. This theme certainly vindicates Gorbachev's efforts to go outside the party and to enlist the support of the Soviet intelligentsia and people in general. Apart from Burlatskii's opportune explanations for Khrushchev's failures, the author maintains that although the people backed Khrushchev's efforts, they remained silent and restrained in promoting his agenda because there was no glasnost'. Burlatskii's criticism of Khrushchev for doing little to undermine his own personality cult, despite the fact he had done so much to destroy Stalin's, likewise must be read as a message to today's leaders to be satisfied with a life-like public image.

Roots

VASILII SELIUNIN

1

My sister's husband and I had picked out the place. A bulldozer operator from the timber enterprise who was passing by turned off on his own initiative and cleared a road through the snow. All he asked was: "Who are you burying?" Upon learning that we were burying my mother, he refused to take anything for his work and drove away. My mother would have a good place—tall birches and a fir tree that was straight as an arrow. . . .

I had visited my mother three months before she died. She was born in 1900 (and hence was as old as the century). As was the habit of peasants, she would get up early and bustle about until evening, cooking, feeding the piglet, while still managing to find time to knit mittens for me, and in addition to everything else, to caress and care for her great granddaughter. Thinking came easy to me in this house with its simple cares and firmly established order. Things I had thought over passed this test hundreds of times. The petty and the pretentious winnowed itself away and all that fell to the bottom of my soul was the dry, rather bitter residue of truth.

Much of what would be recounted below I managed to read to my mother in different years. She knew how to listen—a rare gift these days. From time to time, she would interject: "That is true, my son. That's how it was," even though she could not possibly know how it was—the events of distant centuries were compared or writers whose works she had not read were quoted. Other times she would look at me not so much with reproach as with the helpless desire to understand. This was for me a verdict: nonsense, daubing.

I loved this roof, my parents' last, for the fact that everyone under it had enough to eat, shoes on their feet, and clothes on their back. "Man is higher than satiety"—only someone who had never known hunger could blurt out such nonsense. In our area there was no one who had not drunk from this cup. The family moved here to the Murashi Timber Enterprise from the tiny Viatsk village

Russian text © 1988 by "Izvestiia" Publishers. "Istoki," *Novyi mir*, 1988, no. 5. Translated by Arlo Schultz.

of Fomintsa, which was named after my great grandfather Foma Andreevich. To go there because it is not far, to get in touch with one's roots. As the poet so beautifully phrased it: when your life is spent, the love of hearth and home and the love of your forefathers' gravesites swallow your soul. The only problem is there is nowhere to go. Little is left of the villages in these places; the fields are covered with birch groves. The land of your forefathers lives only in the memory of your heart. Many things are imprinted here that would be better forgotten—only it is not easy to forget. I remember the first shock I experienced of the type that signals the end of childhood. They were threshing rye. We schoolchildren were detailed to driving the horses in harness while my mother and the other peasant women were raking straw away from the threshing machine. There was no one to leave the children with at home and they were placed on fresh straw near the threshing floor—so they were not without supervision. After the Viatsk fashion, they were called sitters: they were five years old but still could not walk. They had thin legs, large heads, and swollen stomachs—in a word, they had rickets. I watched them crawl swiftly to the threshing machine and stuff handfuls of grain into their mouths. But this was bad for them. The grain could make them swell up and also injure their intestines. Their mothers would drag them farther away, but they, accursed kids, would crawl back to their immeasurable repast. . . .

Our bread was baked with sawdust, with clover tops, and when it included mashed potatoes, it was a real treat. The most repugnant thing in childhood was going to the outhouse: the sawdust and the undigested grass scratched the anus to the point of bleeding.

Such are my roots.

Of course, each year was not alike. There were also somewhat better times. But starting in 1932 (I remember this famine clearly), we did not eat our fill very often. Whether the harvest was good or bad did not matter much: we had to feed the state. And so it was to the end until the breadwinners ran off in every direction. After the war, when my stint in the army was drawing to an end, my mother wrote to me: "Go wherever you want but don't come home. You'll perish here." Mothers probably didn't find it easy to write such epistles.

But she didn't like to complain. During my entire life I can recall hearing her complain only once, when I was a student and came home during vacation. "You, Vasen'ka, are now a scholar. You've been going to school for many years. Now tell me why Stalin doesn't allow us to cut grass with a scythe? We can tear it up with our hands, but we can't use scythes if it's for our own cow. Haven't we earned the right from him? Just look what happens to our hands. . . ."

There was something to look at. Just about that time, Fadeev the writer had artistically described a mother's hands—her kind, affectionate, working hands. Actresses with laureate badges pinned to their velvet dresses read these sincere words from the stage, and school pupils inserted them in their compositions. My mother's hands were hard as hooves.

Her question was simple, but the answer to it was not. I don't know if I will live long enough to think this question through all the way to the end, but I have to answer it before it's too late. Of course, it wasn't just the prohibition against scythes. That's not so difficult to explain. They didn't send authorized agents out to the collective farm hayfields, and so everyone—young and old—turned out: nine ricks to the collective farm, one rick to you. This wasn't enough. Naturally, anyone who did not take good care of his Daisy (cow) would hardly make it through the winter with his entire family, could hardly stick it out until better times, when horsetails pushed their way up through the still barren soil (at least they were something to eat!). But allowing people to cut scrubland grass with a scythe will not encourage them to work in artels. Even then, people were permitted to tear up grass with their bare hands—they really could do this. And at the same time, the peasant women managed to carry away a good deal of grass stuffed in their aprons during the summer.

Why stir up the past? Well-educated people explain that enemies are drawing us into discussion about the past as a distraction. It goes without saying that the enemy is cunning. You can't deny him that. Only how can you learn from history if we again start covering up lines from history with our finger: read this but don't read that? And most importantly, does everything we have experienced belong [merely] to history?

. . . A whole era passed into oblivion together with my mother. We will hope that it is gone for good. Her generation dragged History wherever it was prescribed, along with itself, over ruts and potholes. And even if their sufferings were forged as planned into the might of the state, all the same the doubt about the price that had to be paid gnaws at us. How could it happen that man, the crown of creation, was merely the material, the resource for social experiments on earth, which nurtured the soil for the universal prosperity that was to come? We are told that what has been has been, that the ultraleft idea of the creative role of violence, of noneconomic coercion to work was always alien to our objectives, and then only under particular historical conditions, due more to subjective mistakes and distortions, was it actually implemented for a certain period of time. But the question is so important and of such enormous relevance for the present that we cannot in any event place our trust in words.

2

Thinkers in distant epochs and socialists of feeling have been justly indignant: What kind of society is it where a glass cutter dreams of hailstorms that break windows or a gravedigger dreams about epidemics? It is a different matter where property and products of labor become common. One asks, however, why these products will be abundant. Wealth is created by labor and only by labor. But what force compels people to work? The thinkers naturally could not skirt this fundamental question.

Let us look at Thomas More's *Utopia*. One of the disputants reflects:

". . . men shal never there live wealthelye, where all thinges be commen. For howe can there be abundaunce of gooddes, or of any thing, where every man withdraweth his hande from labour? Whome the regard of his owne gaines driveth not to worke, but the hope that he hath in other mens travayles maketh him slowthfull." The answer is as follows: the blessed society must have civilian overseers or, as More calls them, Syphograuntes. "The chiefe and almooste the onelye offyce of the Syphograuntes is, to see and take hede, that no manne sit idle: but that everye one applye hys owne craft with earnest diligence. . . ." [The above passages are taken from the English version—*Trans.*]

Utopian or not, his formulation of the question and his answer to it were sound: noneconomic coercion takes the place of gain. The founders of scientific socialism provide no such simplicity and clarity in addressing the problem. In his dispute with Dühring, Engels decisively rejected the assumption that differences in pay will persist in socialist society. In the famous example involving the person pushing a wheelbarrow and the architect, the unequivocal solution was that both should receive the same pay. Why? The answer is very simple: the architect's higher qualifications are not his personal merit. "In a society of private producers," Engels writes, "the cost of training a worker is borne by private persons or their families; it is also primarily for this reason that private persons enjoy a higher price for their trained labor power: a skillful slave is sold for a higher price; a skillful hired worker receives higher pay. In a socialistically formed society, this cost is borne by society, and hence the fruits, i.e., the greater amount of value created by complex labor, belong to society. The worker himself is not entitled to lay claim to additional pay."[1] Differences in the remuneration of simple and complex labor were of no practical interest to Engels: not everyone will be an architect or a wheelbarrow pusher in the new society. Everyone will be able to do everything—the architect, for example, will spend two hours a shift instructing others in his specialty and will spend the rest of the time pushing a wheelbarrow or, we would add, sorting vegetables in a storehouse. The question of what to substitute for the old stimuli and what force to use to compel the worker to work is skirted here.

Marx's reasoning is more solid. He admits the possibility of differences in pay depending on the quantity and quality of labor: ". . . each individual producer will receive back from society, after all deductions, just as much as he himself has given it. . . . Therefore *equal right* here is still essentially a *bourgeois right*."[2] A bourgeois right under socialism? Clearly, such an unnatural thing can be permitted only for a very short time.

What, then, will be the constant stimulus? Many thinkers from the past believed that, in time, it would not be needed at all: labor would become the primary vital necessity, a play of physical and spiritual forces. The might of such theories lies in their irrefutability. It can always be said that their time is yet to come, and if it has not yet come, we ourselves are to blame—we have not learned to find rewards for labor in the actual labor process. While the goal is unquestionably a noble one, we are presently hardly any closer to it than we were twenty, thirty, or however many years ago.

If we have not been able to find a satisfactory solution to the problem even today, imagine the difficulties the first builders of the new society confronted! In accordance with the behests of the founders, everyone now was to do an equal job for equal pay.

History had never known such an experience. More precisely, there was purely negative experience: at one time, the Jacobins—in Lenin's words, "the most vehement, the most sincere revolutionaries"—had racked their brains over this problem.[3] In his search for practical solutions, Il'ich referred to them more than once, compared the French Revolution with our revolution, and reflected on the boundaries to violence in economic construction.

Conscious participants and leaders of that far-off revolution did not by any means initially advocate violence, to say nothing of terror. Educated by the Enlightenment, they relied more on reason. Liberty, equality, and fraternity seemed to them to be such obvious values that there was no need to defend them. One only had to establish them, and then there would be no madmen who would oppose such attractive things. It was Marat's belief that "a few heads chopped off at the right time will save a great nation from the misfortunes of poverty and the horrors of civil wars." This was written in early 1790. But a half year later, Marat would demand five to six hundred decapitations, in another half year—five to six thousand, and in 1793—a little over a million. And these were not exercises in rhetoric—the guillotine was in excellent working condition. You have only to read the essays of Gracchus Babeuf, which were recently published in our country. This man's testimony is all the more important because he was a participant in all phases of the revolution. Moreover, he belonged to the extreme left flank in the array of forces and, therefore, could hardly be suspected of prejudice in his criticism of Jacobinism. In the book, which was written immediately in the wake of the events, he described the activity of Carrier—one of Robespierre's closest collaborators.

I cannot refrain from presenting an excerpt from this work. (May the reader not be dismayed by the large number of ellipses—after each fact, the conscientious author named witnesses.) Babeuf asks:

> Was it really necessary to carry out twenty-three mass drownings in Nantes, including the one in which six hundred children lost their lives, in order to save the homeland? Was there a real need for "revolutionary marriages" where girls and boys were stripped naked, bound in pairs, deafened by saber blows to the head, and cast into the Loire? . . . Was it necessary . . . that ten thousand citizens perished in Nantes prisons from emaciation, contagious diseases, and all manner of adversities and that thirty thousand were shot or drowned? . . . Was it necessary . . . to hack people with sabers in the department square? Was it really necessary . . . to execute by firing squad infantry and cavalry detach-

ments of the mutinous army that were prepared to surrender voluntarily? Was it really necessary . . . to drown or shoot another five hundred children—the *oldest were under fourteen*—whom Carrier called "vipers that must be smothered?" Was it really necessary. . . to drown between thirty and forty women in the ninth month of pregnancy and to show the horrible spectacle of the still quivering infant corpses thrown into vats filled with excrement? . . . Was it really necessary. . . to force the fetus from women near their term, carry it on a bayonet, and then throw it into the water? . . . Was it really necessary to instill in soldiers in the Marat company the terrible conviction that each of them should be capable of drinking a glass of blood? . . .

It would seem that we are like Hecuba and that we should stock up on validol before we read such things. Today's critics of red terror, which was introduced in 1918, would do well to refresh their memory with respect to this testimony. For the topic of our discussion, it is important [to remember] that purely economic tasks were one of the primary goals of violence. Gracchus Babeuf—a communist utopian by conviction—while passionately condemning the famous terrorist, was on one key point inclined to vindicate him:

> Numbered among Carrier's crimes is the fact that he crushed petty trading and the mercantile . . . spirit in Nantes, that he ordered the arrest of all speculators without exception and all those who engaged in this scandalous trade since the beginning of the revolution within the Nantes city limits; the fact that he ordered the arrest of all middlemen, all people of both sexes who bought and resold items of primary necessity, and extracted shameful profits, selling them for prices exceeding the *maximum* established by law. There is no doubt whatsoever that if all democratic principles and the highest law of the good of the people have not yet been repealed, these facts taken by themselves not only cannot be blamed on Carrier but by their nature can win him laurels among republicans.

The essence of the matter is concealed here by expressive terms: "shameful profits," "scandalous trade," "petty trading," etc. We must without fail force our way through this abusive language and get to the sense of the events. The revolution, in Marx's words, wiped "all feudal ruins from the face of France as if by magic."[4] Room was opened up for a new mode of production—the capitalist mode; henceforth, development was not restrained by feudal fetters. And peasants—the largest class in society—made use of their unprecedented opportunity to produce for sale at a gain or, if you wish, for the sake of shameful profits. But the extracted profit means inequality. Inspired by the ideas of the Enlightenment philosophers, but most of all by the urgent necessity of feeding the army and the cities, the Jacobins instituted ferocious measures against speculators (i.e., against the market, without which commodity production is inconceivable) and regulated consumption with laws on maximum profit. Only through violence was it possible to take the fruits of the peasants' labor from them without compensating them. Terror gave rise to the *Vendée*, with which the revolutionaries tried to cope by means of still more brutal terror.

The Jacobins lay down across the path of life and in so doing signed their death sentence. They departed the arena of history leaving behind them not only mountains of corpses, but also a new France that was adapted to the only effective mode of production of the time. Terror and violence for economic purposes were but a deviation from the tasks of the revolution, an episode.

The situation in socialist revolutions was much more complex. The annihilation of "shameful profits" and the eradication of commodity production and private enterprise here were not a deviation from the goal; on the contrary, they were the goal. Generally speaking, it was not so very difficult to get rid of the landowners and to nationalize large enterprises, but this did not by any means solve the problem. "What does the suppression of the bourgeoisie mean?" Lenin asked.

> The landowner could be suppressed and destroyed by abolishing landed proprietorship and transferring the land to the peasants. But can the bourgeoisie be suppressed and destroyed by the abolition of big capital? Anyone who knows the ABC of Marxism knows that the bourgeoisie cannot be suppressed in this way, that the bourgeoisie is born of commodity production; the peasant who has a surplus of hundreds of poods of grain which he does not need for his family and does not deliver to the workers' state as a loan to help the hungry worker, and who profiteers under the prevailing conditions of commodity production—what is he? Is he not a bourgeois? Is the bourgeoisie not born in this way? This is a terrible thing, this is a danger to the social revolution! (vol. 39, pp. 421, 422)

The danger was indeed menacing. To Lenin it was even conceivable that the revolution could slide from a socialist to a bourgeois level. Everything depended on conquering the spontaneity of the petit-bourgeois element: "If we do not conquer it, we shall slide back down as the French Revolution did. This is inevitable, and we must not let ourselves be misled by phrases and excuses" (vol. 43, p. 141).

Various means could be used in the struggle. "A hundred and twenty-five years ago," Lenin wrote,

> it might have been excusable for the French petite bourgeoisie, the most ardent and sincere revolutionaries, to try to crush the profiteer by executing a few of the 'chosen' and by making thunderous declamations. Today, however, the purely rhetorical attitude to this question assumed by some Left Socialist-Revolutionaries can rouse nothing but disgust and revulsion in every politically conscious revolutionary. We know perfectly well that the economic basis of

profiteering is both the small proprietors, who are exceptionally widespread in Russia, and private capitalism, of which *every* petit bourgeois is an agent'' (vol. 36, p. 297).

As early as November 10, 1917, profiteers were declared enemies of the people, and three months later, a decree signed by Lenin contained unequivocal instructions: "profiteers . . . are to be shot at the place of the crime.'"[5] Understandably, in the absence of organized state trade, any sale of food was considered profiteering. "Not a single pood of grain," the authorities decreed, "must remain in the hands of the holders, with the exception of the amount required to sow their fields and to feed their families until the new harvest."

> . . . All persons possessing surplus grain and not hauling it to grain collection points are declared . . . to be enemies of the people and are to be delivered to appear before the revolutionary court in order that the guilty be sentenced to a minimum of ten years in prison; they should be banished from the commune permanently, and all their property should become subject to confiscation. . . .[6]

It is the customary belief that these stern measures were inspired by famine and devastation. But as we have seen, a point of principle was involved: unless commodity production and the market accompanying it were destroyed, the October Revolution would, in a manner of speaking, decline to the level of a bourgeois revolution. But common sense suffices to realize that food produced in the nation will also be eaten by its population. It was not famine that inspired requisitioning, but more likely requisitioning that caused the famine: mass requisitioning brought famine as its result. The peasants were called upon to feed the country for nothing, without any gain for themselves. The peasant answered these measures at best with a reduction in his sowings, and at worst with a sawed-off shotgun.

Most historians—both Soviet and foreign—have reduced the Civil War to a confrontation between the Whites and the Reds, with the only difference being in their evaluations. The facts, however, show that there was a third force—the peasants' insurgent movement—against which the main blow was struck. It allied itself at various times and with varying degrees of intensity with the Whites and then with the Reds, while remaining a relatively independent force. Foreseeing the events long before the revolution, Lenin wrote: At first, we will support the peasantry *en masse* against the landlords, support it to the hilt and with all means, including confiscation, and then (it would be better to say, at the same time) we will support the proletariat against the peasantry *en masse*" (vol. 11, p. 222). In the struggle against the landowner, the interests of the peasantry coincided entirely with the interests of the new power. This is a fact that was understood even by the White generals. For example, in a letter from Kolchak to Denikin, the ill-starred admiral condemned a land policy "that creates in the minds of the peasantry the notion that the landowners' holdings are being restored." No sooner did this danger disappear than the gray army turned the front around. At the height of the Civil War, Lenin noted with alarm that "the peasantry of the Urals, Siberia, and the Ukraine is turning to Kolchak and Denikin" (vol. 40, p. 17). Resistance increased as the White movement was being defeated. The headquarters on the eastern front reported from the Volga region in 1919, for example: ". . . the peasants have become brutal. With pitchforks, pickets, and with guns they are singly and in mobs attacking machine guns, notwithstanding the piles of corpses. Their fury is indescribable." According to historian M. Kubanin's calculations, 25 to 30 percent of the population in Tambov Province took part in the rebellion. He concluded: "Unquestionably, 25 to 30 percent of the rural population means that the entire adult male population has joined Antonov's army." According to archival documents published in 1962, the peasant army in the Tambov region incorporated eighteen well-armed regiments. Regular forces under the command of Tukhachevskii had to wage a real war here that was no less intensive than the war against Kolchak's forces. Lenin himself explicitly stated that petit bourgeois spontaneity was more dangerous than all the White armies combined.

The logic of the struggle demanded that violence be countered with violence. The difficulty was that peasant uprisings had to be put down by an army that was made up primarily of peasants. Consequently, there was a need for some type of forces that were unconditionally dedicated to the revolution and that were ready to carry out any order. One such force was cited in a brief report on the total defeat of a peasant uprising in Livny:

> The town suffered comparatively little. The dead and wounded are presently being picked up from the streets. Losses among reinforcements arriving later are relatively small. Only the valorous internationalists have sustained extremely heavy losses. But there are literally mountains of White Guardists. All the streets are littered with their bodies.

The reference is to former prisoners of war who voluntarily joined the Red Army. They numbered up to three hundred thousand (specialists consider such a large number of foreigners in the fighting army a unique phenomenon in contemporary history). They showed themselves to be very reliable in putting down peasant rebellions, and in halting attempts at desertion from the army itself when it was thrown into battle against the "third force." Special units also operated successfully.

However, it is easy to understand that the final solution of the peasant question could not be reached by military means alone. The goal was to eliminate commodity production in the countryside. Kulak commodity farms, which employed hired labor, proved to be the strongest. The kulaks, according to Lenin, "are the most brutal, callous, and savage exploiters" (vol. 37, p. 40). "And if the kulaks are not dealt with properly," Vladimir Il'ich stated, "if we do not cope with the parasites, the return of the tsar and the capitalists is inevitable'' (vol. 37, p. 176). He gave the instruction to propagandists on their way to the provinces: ''. . . the kulaks and sharks must be pulled up short'' (vol. 35, p. 326). Here the authorities could rely only on the poor in the countryside, and it constituted a negligible minority in the rural population (let us not forget that peasants received land as a result of the revolution). Committees of the Village Poor were created in June 1918. With their help, fifty million hectares of land were taken away from the kulaks. This was approximately one-third of the arable land of that time. The material base of the kulak economy was thereby destroyed. The facts incontrovertibly show that the liquidation of kulaks took place specifically during the years of War Communism and not in the late twenties and early thirties.

However, the middle peasant also wanted to trade in the products of his labor, but trade, according to the views of that time, led straight to capitalism. The belief was that grain which the peasant did not turn in under forced requisitioning during the period of War Communism, even though the fruit of his own labors, was appropriated by the peasant who thus became a class enemy. ''If the peasant is installed on his plot of land,'' Lenin maintained,

> and appropriates his surplus grain, that is, grain that he does not need for himself or for his cattle, while the rest of the people have to go without bread, then the peasant becomes an exploiter. The more grain he clings to, the more profitable he finds it; as for the rest, let them starve: 'The more they starve, the dearer I can sell this grain.' All should work according to a single plan, on common land, in common factories and in accordance with a common system (vol. 41, pp. 310–11).

Consequently, the genuine resolution of the tasks of the socialist revolution was seen to lie in bringing the peasantry to work on common land. Indeed, this was part of the Bolshevik party program. As far back as 1902 Lenin explained: ''A Social Democrat . . . would advocate nationalization of the land only as a means of making the transition to large-scale communist, and not small individual, farming'' (vol. 6, p. 339). Soon after the October Revolution, Vladimir Il'ich took into his own hands ''the gradual but steady transition from small individual farms to collective farming'' (vol. 37, p. 364). In January 1918, he was already participating in the drafting of the ''Basic Law on the Socialization of Land.'' As S. Ivanov, a member of the drafting commission, relates, ''Comrade Lenin was the only one who actually worked in the commission. We just voted.'' In the course of the discussion, a dispute arose—at this point, only about landowners' land and not about kulak-owned land. The Socialist Revolutionaries insisted on the division of land among the peasants, which would have strengthened the economic base of the petit–bourgeois element. Lenin, on the other hand, spoke out in favor of the creation of state farms on land formerly belonging to landowners. It was this idea that carried.

In December 1918, Lenin established a special commission to draft the Statute on the Public Cultivation of Land. (P. Pershin, one of its members, relates that the finished draft was edited by Vladimir Il'ich personally.) At his orders, land was allocated first of all to collective farms; they were supplied with equipment taken from well-to-do peasants without remuneration, and from middle and poor peasants for an amount that did not exceed the fixed prices, i.e., for a symbolic sum. The "Statute on Socialist Land Policy and on Measures Governing the Transition to Socialist Agriculture" was promulgated in February 1919. This document stated that all types of individual land tenure were to be regarded as transitory and outmoded—they would be replaced by state farms, production communes, and other associations for the joint cultivation of the land.

Notwithstanding the obvious advantages (better land, free equipment), the peasant did not join these associations. Nevertheless, in a short period of time it was possible to create more than five thousand state farms and approximately six thousand collective farms. But, as Lenin admitted, "the collective farms are still so unorganized and are in such a lamentable state that they deserve to be called almshouses" (vol. 42, p. 180).

The best minds of the time tried to discover why something as good as collectivization had ended in total failure. Their reasoning was this: the simple combination of land and primitive equipment is not sufficient to secure qualitative progress in the development of production. But if we could give the countryside a hundred thousand tractors, then every peasant would say: I, too, am for the commune. But this equipment was not yet available, and would not foreseeably be available for another ten years.

With the benefit of hindsight, we today cannot consider such an explanation sufficiently complete. Mechanization, chemicalization, reclamation, intensive technologies—all this means hopelessly little for success. Lev Tolstoy understood that the most important thing was "not nitrogen and not oxygen that are in the soil and air, not a special plow and manure—the main implement that puts nitrogen, oxygen, manure, and the plow into action is the working peasant." But his interest was ignored—emphasis was placed on brute force. It seems to me that here lie the deep roots of many of the difficulties the country has experienced.

Incidentally, noneconomic coercion at that time was applied not only toward the peasantry. Any revolution is worth something only when it is able to defend itself. This is axiomatic. Only a pharisee today would condemn punitive measures taken against counterrevolutionaries. Yet, on the third day after the October *coup* the opposition press was shut down, and the decree correctly stated that this weapon "is no less dangerous at such moments than bombs and machine guns." And an apparatus of violence was created in the form of the Cheka. But Lenin once again stated it right: "The power of the working people cannot exist without such an institution" (vol. 44, p. 328). On January 31, 1918, the government decreed "the adoption of measures to increase the number of penal institutions." Somewhat later it was deemed essential "to secure the Soviet republic against its class enemies by isolating them in concentration camps." Dzerzhinskii's explanation was logical:

. . . the need for self-defense was so great that we could consciously close our eyes to some of our mistakes, as happened during the period of red terror, . . . as long the republic was preserved. This is why the law gives the Cheka the possibility of administratively isolating those violators of labor discipline, parasites, and suspected counterrevolutionaries against whom there is not sufficient evidence for judicial punishment and where any court, even the most severe, would acquit all or most of them.[7]

The economist's ear, however, discerns a certain dissonance in this pronouncement: in addition to "suspected counterrevolutionaries," violators of labor discipline should be put in concentration camps. In another document, Dzerzhinskii offers a very broad interpretation of the camps' purpose: "In addition to court sentences, we must retain administrative sentences, and specifically the concentration camp. . . . I propose retaining these concentration camps in order to use the labor of those arrested, for those gentlemen who live without working, for those who cannot work without a certain measure of coercion. If we take Soviet institutions, a measure of punishment must be applied for an unconscientious attitude toward work, for negligence, for tardiness, etc. We can even use this measure to bring our own personnel up to the mark."[8]

As we see, the boundaries of violence were expanded infinitely—they were initially used to suppress enemies of the revolution, were then applied against potential enemies (the red terror), and finally became a means for solving purely economic problems. In 1920, Trotsky proposed putting this matter on a firm, long-term footing, transforming the country into a gigantic concentration camp or, more precisely, a system of camps. At the Ninth Party Congress, he proposed a program that was without precedent in history: workers and peasants would become like mobilized soldiers who would be formed into "labor units resembling military units." Each should consider himself to be a "soldier of labor who cannot freely decide whether or not to carry out an order. If he fails to do so, he will be a deserter subject to punishment."[9]

Would such labor be effective? Capitalism was victorious over the formation that preceded it because it replaced the stick, the dependence of the serf, and the will of the seignor with a more effective work incentive: personal gain and the right to sell one's labor power. Camp labor law in practice would have meant a step backward in the history of mankind. Trotsky decisively objected: "If we take at face value the old bourgeois prejudice—or not the old bourgeois prejudice but the old bourgeois axiom that has become a prejudice—that forced labor is unproductive, then this applies not only to the labor army but also to labor conscription as a whole, to the foundation of our economic construction, and hence to socialist organization in general." (How candid: forced labor is the basis of socialist organization!). According to Trotsky, the "bourgeois axiom" is true only when applied to the past: "We say it is untrue that forced labor is unproductive under all circumstances and under all conditions."[10]

According to modern historians, the congress rejected Trotsky's military-bureaucratic strategy for economic construction. But this was an obvious historical erasure (a common occurrence in old Russia. Herzen wittily observed: "The Russian government, a *Providence* in reverse, is more oriented toward a better past than a better future"). Let us turn to the basic resolution of the congress: "On the Immediate Tasks of Economic Construction":

> Approving the theses of the Central Committee of the Russian Communist party on the mobilization of the industrial proletariat, labor conscription, the militarization of the economy, and the use of military units for military needs, the congress resolves:
> . . . to register all skilled workers with the aim of drawing them into productive work with the same consistency and strictness as has been and is the current practice toward persons of the command staff for the needs of the army.
> Every skilled worker must return to work in his specialty. . . .
> From the very beginning there must be correct organization of mass mobilization under the labor conscription program, i.e., the most precise possible correspondence in each case must be established between the number mobilized, the place of their concentration, the scale of the labor task, and the number of necessary implements. It is equally important to provide labor units formed from the ranks of the mobilized with technically competent and politically stable instructors and with communist labor cells selected beforehand under the party mobilization program, i.e., to follow the same path we followed in creating the Red Army.[11]

The resolution also recommends "the use of a system of tasks, the nonfulfillment of which will result in a cut in rations." And since "a considerable part of the workers—in search of better food conditions and frequently with the aim of profiteering as well—quit their jobs at enterprises and move from place to place, thereby inflicting further blows on production," this must be halted in the "stern struggle against labor desertion, in particular by publishing lists of deserters deserving punishment, by forming deserters into punitive work teams, and finally by confining them in concentration camps."[12]

Do not think that these were merely temporary measures. The resolution "On the Transition to the Militia System" explains: since the Civil War is drawing to an end and the international position of Soviet Russia is favorable, for the future period, "which may be of a prolonged nature," a militia-like economy shall be introduced, the essence of which "must consist in bringing the army closer to the production process in every way so that the available labor of certain economic regions is at the same time the live human power of certain military units."[13]

These documents are all the more instructive in that they reveal to the fullest the connection between the economic mechanism and the rights of the individual. Capitalist commodity production means that whoever has money is free to engage in a profitable venture, to acquire property, to take risks, and to bear economic responsibility for his actions. Any person is entitled to dispose of his own property even if this property is only a pair of working hands. While this is unquestionably a severe system, it does not have to use threats and militia overseers to get people to work. The state, for example, does not have to stop strikes because the losses resulting from them are borne by the private entrepreneur. While not guaranteeing employment, the state has the obligation to give a person the full initiative to become rich or to starve, as the case may be. Personal rights are the other side of merciless economic freedoms. Contrary to this, when the means of production are entirely owned by the state, there is the temptation to expropriate the individual himself, his physical and mental powers in order to organize work under a unified plan and system. Under these conditions, it is admissible to view man as a tiny screw in a gigantic machine that is preparing future happiness for everyone. It would be strange to speak about the personal rights and civil liberties of a tiny screw and equally of the screwdriver that drives it into its proper place.

Trotsky's martinet dreams of the time were not fated to come true—they were imperatively rejected by events. The economic results of War Communism left no doubt that the "bourgeois axiom" of the ineffectiveness of forced labor was true. In 1920 coal production was more than three times lower than in 1917; steel production—sixteen times lower; the production of cotton textiles—twelve times lower; sugar production—ten times lower, etc. Per capita annual steel production dropped to 1.5 kilograms, and one pair of shoes was produced for every fifty members of the population. In the same year, 1920, Moscow workers performing the most difficult physical labor received 225 grams of bread, seven grams of meat or fish, and ten grams of sugar per day. The crop failure of 1921 brought the country to the edge of an abyss.

3

Unlike Trotsky, who saw the root of all evil in the general lack of discipline and who planned to use police methods to overcome slipshodness, Lenin quickly realized the groundlessness of the economic policy of War Communism:

> . . . we made the mistake of deciding to go over directly to communist production and distribution. We thought that under the surplus-food appropriation system the peasants would provide us with the required quantity of grain, which we could distribute among the factories and thus achieve communist production and distribution (vol. 44, p. 157).

On March 1, 1921, the Kronstadt sailors revolted. Workers from Petrograd and other cities as well went out on strike simultaneously. "This is something quite new," Lenin reflected:

This circumstance, in the context of all the crises, must be given careful political consideration and must be very thoroughly analyzed. There is evidence here of the activity of petit-bourgeois anarchist elements with their slogans of unrestricted trade and invariable hostility to the dictatorship of the proletariat. This mood has had an extensive influence on the proletariat. It has had an effect on the factories in Moscow and a number of provincial centers (vol. 43, p. 24).

The political demands of the strikers were especially alarming to Il'ich: "There is no doubt that some discontent and stirrings have recently been in evidence among non-party workers. Non-party meetings in Moscow have clearly turned 'democracy' and 'freedom' into slogans designed to bring the overthrow of Soviet power" (vol. 43, p. 31).

Lenin expressed these ideas at the Tenth Party Congress in March 1921. At his insistence, the congress adopted a key decision to replace requisitioning with a fixed tax on peasants. There was not as yet a whole system here. The measure was considered *temporary*. Not by chance was it introduced in March so as to inform the peasants before they began their sowing: expand your sowings, this year there will be no requisitions. At the same time, there was no plan for the unrestricted sale of grain that remained after taxes. "Unrestricted trade," Lenin emphasized, "even if it is not as bound up initially with the White guards as Kronstadt was, will inevitably lead to White-guard rule, to a victory for capital and its complete restoration" (vol. 43, p. 25). But these were rearguard battles. The fixed tax amounted to approximately one-half of the previously planned requisitions. Clearly, the bulk of food would be forthcoming only from the unrestricted sale of the products of rural labor. Literally two months later, in May 1921, a party conference announced NEP as a system of measures, as a course that was being taken in earnest and for a long time to come. In the course of a year, the entire economic mechanism of "War Communism" was dismantled and replaced by the New Economic Policy, the principal features of which are similar to those of the new economic mechanism that is being born today.

In this lesson I see support for our present restructuring. There lie before us changes that are no less revolutionary—the working people do not wish to live in the old way any longer, and the administrative apparatus can no longer manage in the old way. While the directions of the radical reforms being undertaken today are in general clear, even ardent advocates of restructuring are saying that the democratization of public life and economic innovations must be introduced gradually, over a period of years. But such a variant is highly improbable—there is simply not enough time, it has been exhausted and licentiously dissipated over the decades of stagnation. According to estimates, unless there are major changes, our economy will break down in the mid-nineties with all the attendant social, international, military, and other consequences. Then it will be too late to worry about democracy—dictatorship is more in keeping with periods of economic decline. Up until recently we have only been able to observe with sadness and alarm the facts attesting to this vector of the nation's development. In April 1985, we were given a chance for salvation. The chances have now grown, and it would be a crime to let them go by. The experience of the early twenties is good in that it proves the possibility for revolutionary change from above literally in a few months.

The second lesson for us is the astonishing speed with which starting impulses are sent to the economy. It was specifically because the changes were rapid and radical that the old economic mechanism did not hinder the new one. The crop failure of 1921 is not taken into account here—this was a natural disaster and was in large measure the consequence of experiments under War Communism. But here is something instructive: peasant uprisings ceased during the terrible famine—there was no reason to revolt, since the well-being of the family would depend henceforth on their own labor. Economic measures were more successful than executions in eliminating social tension. There was already a good harvest in 1922. The Twelfth Party Congress even ordered efforts directed toward the search for an external market for grain (isn't it pleasant to recall that such a thing happened in our contemporary history?). In only four to five years, the prewar level in industry and agriculture was reached. In 1928, it was surpassed by 32 percent in industry and by 24 percent in the countryside. Compared with 1921, national income rose 3.3 times and industrial production increased 4.2 times, with output in heavy industry increasing 7.2 times. The real pay of workers surpassed the prewar level. It was estimated that starting in 1924, people ate as good as they ever had before that time. Throughout the nation as a whole, the average worker consumed seventy-two kilograms of meat per year, for example. This is impressive even by today's standards.

Economic successes went hand in hand with the democratization of public life. (This could not be a more relevant fact for the current watershed events.) The boundaries of violence were sharply reduced, and legality was strengthened. Lenin provided the following justification for this: "The closer we approach conditions of unshakable and lasting power and the more trade develops, the more imperative it is to advance the firm slogan of greater revolutionary legality, and the narrower becomes the sphere of activity of the institution which matches the activities of those who plot against us blow for blow" (vol. 44, p. 329). The country received criminal and civil codes. Revolutionary tribunals were replaced by courts. The procuracy and the legal profession were established. The role of trade unions changed. While in March 1918 Lenin had flatly declared, "Trade unions . . . must become state organizations" (vol. 36, p. 160), the party now thoroughly reexamined this position. The Eleventh Party Congress (1922) obligated them to "protect the interests of the working masses in the most direct and immediate sense of the word." Protect against whom? Not only against the private trader, but also against the "bureaucratic distortion" of the state apparatus.[14] How far personal freedoms went can be seen in the open publication of works of literature, art, sociology, and politics, the mere possession of which subsequently would cost some people their heads. But there were no social cataclysms.

There definitely was no need of outside economic coercion as a stimulus either in the private or the state sector of the economy. As far as the private trader went, everything was clear. He had almost been entirely eliminated starting in 1917, but now he bounced right back. Without state investments, without the tutelage and painstaking efforts of the authorities, he restored trade and the service sphere. Private peasant farms kept the country plentifully supplied. What is more, from the mid-twenties up until collectivization, the country exported up to 150 million poods of grain a year. Foreign currency proceeds poured into the treasury.

And our own money became real. At the beginning of 1924, there were over 1.3 quadrillion rubles in circulation; the purchasing power of the ruble had fallen 28 million times. But in 1925, after the monetary reform, our *chervonets* was higher than the pound sterling on the London exchange, much to the dismay and alarm of the haughty English. Now that monetary circulation was sound, the state no longer received great quantities of worthless Soviet notes in the form of taxes as before, but became the proprietor of real resources that it could invest in the development of types of production it desired, especially heavy industry. During those years, the famous GOELRO plan [for electrification of the nation] was implemented. Receiving money from the treasury for the construction of a plant, the client purchased materials and equipment on a contract basis—the state did not take them from the suppliers without compensation, as had been the practice during the period of War Communism, and did not alienate funds for receipts as was the case later. Upon completion of construction, the electric power plant operated in the usual commercial way. Heavy industry developed at a relatively more rapid rate: according to the official statistics, in 1923–28 the manufacture of producer goods increased by an average of 28.5 percent a year, while consumer goods production increased at the rate of 21.4 percent a year.

The small urban entrepreneur was thoroughly aware of the instability of the legislation permitting private trade and was reluctant to invest his income in industrial enterprises. And anyone who did take the risk tried to "eat up" his profits as fast as possible or else turn them into gold against a rainy day. Trade was the sphere in which the private dealer truly expanded: his initial investments were minimal, the payoff was rapid, he took his money and would not be bothered if they closed him down. The peasant—the nation's breadwinner—also constantly felt inconvenient restrictions. But what if the obstacles were removed? This idea was put forth by Bukharin, who was, it must be said, a curious individual. A "left-wing communist" during the years of War Communism, the author of the first noncommodity conceptions of economic development on our soil, an advocate of the abolition of money, he went through a rapid evolution because he sought answers to the main questions of the day in real life.

In a speech at a meeting of Moscow party activists on April 17, 1925, Bukharin explained NEP as follows: "We still have certain vestiges of War Communism that hinder our further growth. . . . The most prosperous peasants and the middle peasants who are also trying to prosper *are today afraid to accumulate*. One gets the impression that the peasant is afraid of putting an iron roof on his house for fear that he will be declared a kulak; if he does buy a machine, he will do it in such a way that the Communists will not see it. Higher technology thus becomes conspiratorial. . . .

We should in general say to all the peasantry and all its strata: enrich yourselves, accumulate, develop your economy." (Bukharin would later be reminded of this appeal.)

But of what benefit was all this to industrialization? According to Bukharin, the benefit was twofold. As the countryside grew richer, it would increase its demand for the products of industry, which would lead to the rapid growth of the latter. The peasants' bank deposits would become an additional resource for economic development.

Many restrictions were removed during this period. Commodity production inevitably led to the stratification of property in the countryside—some farms went under while others grew stronger. In early 1925, the leasing of land and the hiring of labor were allowed and all obstacles to unrestricted trade were removed. Objectively, the trend was in the direction of very efficient farms like the American farms.

To Bukharin's way of thinking, economic freedoms were useful not only for the countryside: "We must learn *how to manage sensitively* [kul'turno] *under the complex conditions of the reconstruction period*. . . . We must put into operation the maximum of economic factors working for socialism and make them flexible. This presupposes a very complex combination of personal, group, mass, social, and state initiative. We have *overcentralized* everything. . . . Should we not take a few steps in the direction of Lenin's state-commune?" This is a passage from "Notes of an Economist," printed in *Pravda* on September 30, 1928, i.e., literally on the eve of the first day of the First Five-Year Plan (the fiscal year at that time started on October 1. This is the day when accelerated industrialization is calculated to have started). By publishing his "Notes," Bukharin was still attempting to influence events.

Thus, we have before us an entire plan of socialist construction. For all its practicality, Bukharin's conception had one debatable point: How viable was the aforementioned "complex combination?" How would private farms get along with state industry? Was it at all conceivable to consider the proprietor part of socialism? Naturally, the author of the plan was fully aware of these debatable points. He saw the resolution of the contradiction in the belief that the countryside would arrive at socialism through the gradual voluntary cooperation of peasant farms. Here, he based himself on Lenin's last works, on Lenin's idea that under conditions of Soviet power the simple growth of the cooperative system was identical to the growth of socialism.

However, NEP faced menacing opposition from the very outset. Trotsky, the theorist of barracks socialism, said threateningly as early as 1923, at the Twelfth Party Congress: "The age of the growth and development of the capitalist element is beginning. Who knows whether in the next few years we will not have to defend every inch of our socialist territory, i.e., every particle of the state economy under our feet with our teeth and our claws . . . ?"[15]

In conformity with these postulates, another plan for national development contrary to all the points in the Bukharin plan (i.e., essentially Lenin's conception of NEP) was devised. I refer to Preobrazhenskii's article: "The Law of Socialist Accumulation" (he later made it over into a small book, the conspectus of which passed from hand to hand with the author's knowledge; Preobrazhenskii energetically propagandized his theory from the rostrum). Here is the course of his reasoning. It is absurd to think that the "socialist system and the system of private commodity production . . . can coexist. . . . Either socialist production will subordinate the petit-bourgeois economy to it or socialist production itself will be absorbed by the commodity production element." Future industrialization and the nation's accelerated development were conceivable only if the state sector "devoured" private trade. (According to Bukharin, as we recall, the complex combination of personal, group, and state initiative would be preserved.) Means for industrialization would for the most part have to be taken from "outside the complex of the state socialist economy." But from where specifically? "Such a country as the USSR," Preobrazhenskii declared, "would have to go through a period of primitive accumulation, drawing very generously from the sources of *presocialist forms of the economy*. . . . The task of the socialist state is not to take less than capitalism took from petit-bourgeois producers, but to take even more." To put it more simply, he proposed to develop the economy at the expense of the peasantry's ruination. This, according to Preobrazhenskii, was also good because the individual farm was not inscribed in socialism.

An eyewitness described with relish the reaction of Rykov, the erstwhile chairman of the Council of People's Commissars (*Sovnarkom*) to this plan. Aleksei Ivanovich, who was angry and therefore stammered more than usual, cried: "Preobrazhenskii's theory is outrageous. The devil knows what it is! . . . Is it possible to conceive of anything that would be more mortally compromising to socialism? . . . To him the countryside is nothing more than a milk cow for industry."

The matter was not simply limited to mental errors. Piatakov, the deputy chairman of VSNKh [Supreme Council of the National Economy], who shared the ideas of Preobrazhenskii, then and there suggested a mechanism for collecting tribute from the peasantry: high prices on industrial goods coupled with low prices on agricultural products. This was more than a proposal. On July 16, 1923, he issued an order jacking up prices, which was promptly carried out. For example, the profit in prices on cloth was 137 percent. This was clearly more than the urban and the rural population could afford to pay for cloth. There was a sharp jump in prices on all agricultural equipment. The result was paradoxical: the still weak industrial sector was struck by a sales crisis amidst an acute shortage of goods throughout the nation, and production was paralyzed. F. E. Dzerzhinskii, who had been appointed chairman of the Supreme National Economic Council, took drastic measures. At his initiative, wholesale prices were cut sharply in 1924, thereby normalizing the situation. By that time, this distinguished statesman was far removed from foolish ideas about forced labor in camps. N. Valentinov, one of his close colleagues on the Supreme National Economic Council and who subsequently emigrated, published in the West quite an objective book about that period. He recalled the terror with which the appearance of the feared leader of the Cheka was awaited at the Supreme National Economic Council, but Dzerzhinskii proved to be a charming leader and an able implementer of the New Economic Policy. In a talk with Valentinov, Dzerzhinskii explicitly distanced himself from his earlier views from the War Communism period: "Good work cannot be inspired by fear alone. There must be a desire to do good work. There must be all manner of other incentives to perform good work. . . ."

There probably was no more ardent opponent of the ultraleft plan for the ruination of the countryside than the leader of the Supreme National Economic Council. On July 20, 1926 (a few hours before his end) he shook with indignation as he listened to complaints by Kamenev and Piatakov at a plenum of the Central Committee that the countryside was becoming rich. "What misfortune for you!" Dzerzhinskii said ironically. "Our statesmen and representatives of industry and trade are shedding tears over the well-being of the peasant." He called Piatakov's program for raising wholesale prices senseless, anti-Soviet, and antiworker. "It is impossible to industrialize," Dzerzhinskii insisted, "if one speaks with fear about the well-being of the countryside."[16]

And so, the two plans collided. Of course, it is senseless after the fact to try to imagine "what would have been, if." However, there is no absolute determinism or doom in the fate of an individual or in the fate of peoples. This is a dangerous misconception which the powers that be have always used to their advantage at virtually all times: the events are predetermined, it is practically impossible to exert a serious influence on them, so reconcile yourself and submit. Such fatalism disarms a person and paralyzes our only reliable weapon—reason. Life is always a crossroads. History is realized potential—one of a number of unrealized possibilities, but nothing more.

In critical periods, at times when alternate variants of development are still possible, is it a matter of indifference which side the apparatus of power takes, on which side of the scale it places its leaden weight? Does such an apparatus always best express the interests of the nation? Were that so, we today would not have the right to complain about the recent period of stagnation.

In the twenties, one person efficiently concentrated in his hands unlimited power, a person who had an excellent knowledge of its value—the unforgettable Stalin. He was little concerned with the disputes arising at all the congresses and meetings of that time. He understood the most important thing: the country is governed by those who have in fact appropriated the executive apparatus of state, by those who control this apparatus. He also accurately guessed something else: it is best to take military organization with its discipline and one-man rule as the model for the hierarchical apparatus. In 1921 he wrote with rare candor in a draft of the pamphlet *On the Political Strategy and Tactics of the Russian Communists* [O politicheskoi strategii i taktike russkikh kommunistov]: "the Communist party is something like an order of *sword-bearers* within the Soviet state that directs the organs of the latter and is the personification of their activity." (I remind the reader that the sword-bearers were the militarized religious fellowship that preceded the Livonian Order.) Naturally, any manner of conflicting opinions within the order was inadmissible and factionalism was criminal.

According to the decision of the Tenth Congress, membership in any faction would lead to "unconditional and immediate expulsion from the party." Many distinguished party members complained that a hierarchy of secretaries had come into being who decided all questions, that congresses and conferences had become passive assemblies, and that party and public opinion were suppressed. At the Thirteenth Party Conference in January 1924, Stalin answered these critics, saying that the party cannot be a union of groups and factions, that it must become a "monolithic organization cut from one piece."

In another speech, Stalin declared all other institutions (the soviets, trade unions, the Komsomol, women's organizations, etc.) to be drive belts, "tentacles in the party's hands, with the aid of which it conveys its will to the working class and the working class is transformed from a diffuse mass into the army of the party." That is to say, the soviets represent no kind of authority but are merely a drive belt. "The dictatorship of the proletariat," Stalin taught, "consists of the party's guidelines plus the implementation of these guidelines by mass organizations of the proletariat plus their realization by the population."

What kind of "guidelines"? Whose are they specifically? It is sufficient to ask these questions to see clearly that the party itself also becomes a drive belt—the main one in the transmission. The mechanism of power described by Stalin presupposes only one machinist who actually controls the unit.

There were people who understood the threat that this posed. In a personal letter to Kuibyshev, Dzerzhinskii astutely predicted: "I am absolutely confident that we can cope with all our enemies if we find and adopt the right policy in managing the nation and the economy. If we do not find this policy and tempo . . . the country will then find its dictator, who will turn out to be the gravedigger of the revolution, regardless of the fine feathers he may wear. . . . " However, it was not the farsighted who determined the course of events.

Naturally, the plan of Preobrazhenskii and other leftists did not explicitly call for the physical extermination of the most active part of the rural population for noneconomic coercion to work. But all this was contained in embryonic form just as the acorn contains all the properties of the oak tree. After liquidating the authors of this theory in the usual fashion, Stalin put their ideas into practice. Naturally, the appropriate methods were required to attain the objective. There were no differences between the goal and the means, just as they do not exist at all in life. After all, the means are the goal in action, in movement, in everyday practice. The goal cannot manifest itself in any other form than through the means.

The turn toward industrialization started with a clear break with the NEP mechanism. In 1929, the power apparatus shut down all private enterprise. The private trader could no longer obtain bank loans, he was smothered with taxes, and he paid the highest transportation rates. The authorities either requisitioned or simply closed down private mills and dissolved many contracts for the lease of state enterprises.

The apparatus methodically and purposefully forced the peasantry up against the wall by reinstituting methods typical of War Communism. In view of the deliberately nonequivalent exchange and the deliberately depressed prices of grain, meat, milk, and other products, the peasant understandably did not wish to sell the fruits of his labor to the state. Stalin personally took charge of procurement. In early 1928, a directive ordered that grain be taken from the peasantry ''at any price.'' Stalin personally went to Siberia. At a meeting with local leaders, he accused the kulaks of undermining the procurement program and demanded that they be brought to trial for profiteering. The property of the condemned was to be confiscated. As under War Communism, Stalin proposed giving one-fourth of the confiscated grain to poor peasants (practically speaking, to the informers). Stalin ordered the removal of party and soviet officials who failed to carry out these repressive measures.

A wave of general searches swept the nation just as in the days of War Communism. The authorities prohibited the sale of grain at markets, and armed antiprofiteer roadblocks were set up in many localities.

Forced collectivization completed the total destruction of rural commodity production.

A series of stiff measures also destroyed the commodity model in state industry. In 1932 the Seventeenth Party Conference emphasized the ''total incompatibility of the policy of the party and the interests of the working class with bourgeois-NEPman distortions of the principle of cost accounting, which were expressed in the squandering of public and state resources, and consequently in the wrecking of established economic plans.'' Wholesale trade and economic responsibility for the results of labor were labeled distortion and squandering at the conference. From here dates the central allocation of resources, a system that has had a ruinous impact on the economy to this very day.

It is said that victors are not judged. But in economics it is obligatory that results be compared with the price paid for them. Only by analyzing this point can we see what in reality was a victory or a defeat. Let us ask the seemingly simple questions: What were the parameters of the First Five-Year Plan and what were its economic results?

The State Planning Committee and the Supreme National Economic Council prepared different variants of the plan beginning in 1926. The planners of that time should not be confused with today's planners who do not forecast the weather but rather prescribe what it should be. They had not developed the discipline of forcing the barometer arrow to point to "clear" even when a storm was approaching. In the plans they recommended maximum proportionality and balance—between accumulation and consumption, between industry and agriculture, between industry groups A and B, between money incomes and the supply of goods.

Cautious specialists headed by Krzhizhanovskii developed two variants of the plan—the minimal (or as they called it, the initial) and the optimal variant. According to the optimal variant, industrial production was to increase by 180 percent in five years (i.e., almost threefold!), including a 230 percent increase in the production of the means of production. Labor productivity in industry was supposed to be raised by 110 percent. Agricultural output was to increase by 55 percent. They programmed in a rapid growth of real wages and a twofold increase in national income.

The targets did not seem to be fantastic—they approximated the actual growth rates in previous years. Nevertheless, to be on the safe side the planners reduced the targets of the minimal variant by twenty percent. This was understandable: as the plan's authors warned, the maximum variant was based on the assumption that all five future years would be years of good harvests, that foreign countries would supply machinery on credit, and that defense spending would be lower. But Stalin personally intervened in the matter. He ordered that only the optimal variant should be considered.

The plan was approved by the Fifth All-Union Congress of Soviets in May 1929. This act had no practical significance, for the plan was considered to have been in effect since October 1, 1928. But this was not an end to the matter—the plan was shaped and reshaped. Stalin issued the call: "The five-year plan in four years." In the second year of the five-year plan, industrial output was slated to increase by 31.3 percent, which was roughly 1.5 times higher than the maximum projection in the initial plan. But even this was not enough. Stalin declared that many branches of industry could fulfill the five-year plan in three years.

Finally, on January 7, 1933, Stalin declared that the five-year plan had been fulfilled in four years and three months. After that day, it seemed that no one ever compared targets and results again. Let us do so here. The increase in industrial output in 1928–32 was not 180 percent, as the specialists had calculated, but 100 percent. The average annual increase compared with that of the NEP period dropped from 23.8 to 19.4 percent throughout industry in general while the growth rates of light industry declined to almost half of the previous level. Such are the official statistics.

Someone may object that even though the plan was not fulfilled, even though the industrial growth rates slackened compared with the preceding period, nevertheless there was striking success. Is it a bad thing that industrial output doubled in only four years? This in itself would not be bad, but the question is how this figure was obtained. Total industrial output is expressed in rubles (otherwise, it is impossible to total bread and tractors, aircraft and electric power), then production volume is compared by years and the growth rate is arrived at. This method is valid only if the value of the same products is calculated for all years at the same prices. But wholesale prices in the First Five-Year Plan rose precipitously, and this was not taken into account. Therefore, the total increases announced for production were unduly high.

It is easiest to evaluate the fulfillment of the First Five-Year Plan in physical indicators. Pig iron production was supposed to be raised to 10 million tons; actual production was 6.2 million tons. Electric power production was not 22 billion kilowatt-hours but 13.5 billion; fertilizer production was 0.9 million tons instead of 8 million, etc. Compared with the NEP period (1923–28), the average annual increase in steel production declined between 1929 and 1932 from 670,000 to 400,000 tons; footwear production declined from 8.5 million to 7.2 million pairs a year. Textile production had previously grown at an annual rate of 400 million meters, sugar—by 179,000 tons, but during the First Five-Year Plan, the production of these goods, like many others, declined in absolute terms. How then is Stalin's declaration of the fulfillment of the five-year plan at the end of 1932 to be understood?

The Second Five-Year Plan initially called for raising the production of electricity to 100 billion kilowatt hours, for increasing coal production to 250 million tons, and for raising pig iron production to 22 million tons. These levels were not reached until the 1950s. In 1938–40, industry was in general marking time—there was no practical increase in the production of pig iron, steel, rolled metals, cement, and oil, and a number of enterprises even regressed.

The economist G. Khanin recently used new methods to recalculate the most important economic growth indicators for the period between 1928 and 1941. He found that national income during this period had grown not 5.5 times, as the statistics claim, but by 50 percent; the productivity of social labor increased 36 percent rather than 4.3-fold, etc. During these years, enterprises were constructed at a rapid pace and entire new branches of industry came into being. Productive fixed capital in the national economy almost doubled, but at the same time output per ruble of capital declined by one-fourth. The expenditure of materials per unit of final output increased by 25 to 30 percent, which largely negated production increases in raw materials. This period gave birth to the disproportions that are still tearing our economy asunder today: between heavy and light industry, between transport and other branches of material production, between money incomes and goods on which to spend them.

The ruination of agriculture was the most serious legacy of the thirties. In 1929 Stalin promised: the Soviet Union "in some three years will become one of the largest grain-producing nations if not the leading grain-producing country in the world." Three years later, as is known, a famine descended upon the land, taking the lives of millions of people. Not until the year 1950 did grain production finally surpass the level attained under NEP. The number of livestock diminished by roughly one-half between 1928 and 1933. It was not until the mid-fifties that the number of cattle and sheep reached the 1926 level, and then only thanks to personal household plots.

The destruction of commodity production was accompanied by the objective demand to replace economic work incentives with naked coercion, significantly to strengthen, as the journal *Bol'shevik* wrote, that side of the dictatorship "that is expressed in the application of violence not limited by the law, and in the necessary cases to use *terror* against class enemies." Much has already been written about the violent nature of collectivization. In March 1930, when it became clear that the collective farms would not make good on the sowing campaign, Stalin published the article "Dizzy With Success." After shifting the blame for "excesses" on those who carried out his orders, he authorized people to leave the collective farms. But the ones who left did not have their livestock and equipment returned to them, and they received the poorest land. In the summer of 1930, however, Stalin declared: "There can be no return to the old ways: the kulaks are doomed and will be liquidated. There remains only one way, the collective farm way." Years later he said in a conversation that millions of peasants had been physically exterminated in the collectivization process. The actual figure is still unknown.

As one wise man observed, 1929 was justifiably called the year of the great breakthrough. Only he did not mention what was broken: the people's backbone.

The methods of War Communism were essentially reborn in economic construction. The personality of the leader unquestionably influenced the choice of specific methods. Stalin was by nature mistrustful of all innovations and had no wish to implement Trotsky's brilliant plan for the militarization of labor. The classical form of coercion—work performed by convicts under guard—was dearer to his heart. They developed Kolyma and the polar regions of the Urals, they developed Siberia and Kazakhstan. They built Noril'sk, Vorkuta, and Magadan. They constructed the canals and the northern roads—more than anyone can count. On one of my journalistic trips through the north, an eyewitness who had miraculously survived told me how the Kotlas–Vorkuta road was built. A worker in the polar regions was supposed to be given at least a quilted jacket, felt boots, and mittens. None of these things were available. A prisoner here was used only two weeks—experience showed that this was the length of time he was able to work in the clothing he was wearing when he was taken from his home. He would then be sent, frostbitten, to rot in a camp and would be replaced by the next wave of "pathfinders." Until recently, it was even forbidden to mention this. Fortunately, the times are now different. The dam of silence has been broken. However, behind the tragedies of Sergei Mironovich [Kirov] and Nikolai Ivanovich [Bukharin] we must not forget the sufferings of Ivan Denisovich. A people that forgets its history is doomed to repeat it.

There was no shortage of labor power in the camps. The law of August 7, 1932, stipulated death by firing squad as punishment for the theft of collective farm property, or ten years in prison in the event of mitigating circumstances. At the end of 1938, people who were late to work had fines deducted from their pay; if they were late three times in the course of a month, they were brought into court. From June 1940 on, no one could change jobs of their own volition or refuse to work overtime under fear of imprisonment.

After the war, I worked for a blended-yarn fabric combine in Barnaul. The greater part of my dormitory bunkmates had been in prison—for stealing a piece of cloth, for fighting, for all kinds of things. One of the people I attended evening school with worked for the city military registration and enlistment office, and he once told me in secrecy that about half of the inductees had a record of convictions. And inductees are just kids. . . .

The life of those "at liberty" often differed little from the life of prisoners and exiles. The Viatsk wilderness, which is dear to my heart, was for long years a place of exile. Before and after the war, they transported people to us from places many had never even heard of. One of the neighboring collective farms was thus called "Natsmen" [national minority]. I have always been thankful to my small birthplace because it simply and naturally inspired the precious feeling of internationalism in one's soul. Our own people and the exiles did the same kind of work, were equally hungry, equally tried to steer clear of the higher-ups, and buried the dead in the same cemetery. The young people intermarried, and no one was interested in the blood mixture of their offspring. There were no reasons for ethnic enmity just as there are none today. In our common fatherland, we are bound together by our misfortunes and our victories.

I remember when we were ordered to settle a single peasant man in our village. From the look of him, he was a Tatar, but it was not customary to ask a person who he was or where he was from: since the authorities weren't sending him any further, that meant he was within his rights. But then he up and died. As they were burying him, the peasants started arguing over whether to put a cross on his grave. It just didn't seem human somehow, an unmarked grave, as if they were hiding him in the ground. So they put up a cross, reasoning that if it came to that, his god and our god would work it out up above. . . .

It is no joy to write about all this—my cheeks quiver. But I must. I must because now there are many who say nostalgically: Oh, what order we had under the great and wise one—if only we could have that again! I testify here that this is not how things were. Forced labor at all times and among all peoples has always been unproductive. In 1937, when the country was paralyzed with fear, millions of collective farmers did not work the mandatory minimum number of workdays that they in general could have. Later, they were exiled to uninhabited places, which was not so very terrifying—it was the same everywhere. So, we should not look back in our present searching. There is little good there, those sources do not slake our thirst; they have either dried up or turned foul.

4

We are now searching for other work incentives in the justifiable belief that personal interest is more reliable than fear and outright coercion. But what does personal interest mean?

One is now apparently permitted to operate one's own business. An exotic theme, the opening of a cooperative snack bar on Kropotkin Street received almost as much attention in the newspapers as the commissioning of the Bratsk Hydroelectric Power Plant. But before we accept and recognize material values, we should ascertain their creator's motivations. It is assumed that personal interest is one thing and that public, state interest, is something altogether different.

This indeed seems to be the case. It is not the private trader who should decide what and how much to produce. Individual businesses are useful as a support to large-scale production, but the state must measure out private initiative and strictly define its boundaries so that too much effort is not diverted from activities on a nationwide scale. And what about personal interests? Is there a place for them? There is. They are included in the fulfillment of plans: collectives that produce the planned product of the best quality at the lowest cost and deliver it to the customer precisely on schedule should be generously paid with both money and social benefits. Negative deviations from the plan should also be punished by the ruble. For example, the bonus fund should be reduced by large amounts for failure to meet mandatory delivery schedules; products rejected by State Acceptance or the customer should not be paid for at all; the treasury should not compensate losses if the cost of a product is higher than the price that is established at the top. In such cases, there will simply be nothing with which to pay for labor—slipshod workers, negligent suppliers, and squanderers must straighten up or run the risk of the enterprise being shut down.

Such is one conception of restructuring. There is also another one which maintains that historical experience has not revealed the special advantages of mandatory planning. [Yet] the tragic losses that society bears in strict correspondence with the plan are there for everyone to see. For example, billions and billions were spent on the construction of the Baikal-Amur Mainline (BAM), but there is nothing to haul over the new railway. It will go out of commission without ever having served us. Another example: for decades the treasury has generously allocated funds for increasing the production of agricultural combines. We are presently producing more combines than any other country. But what is the result? At least a third of the new machines are not needed—collective and state farms refuse to buy them even at half-price. These are not isolated instances. Hundreds of billions of rubles' worth of all kinds of products are immobilized in surplus inventories—they are not needed even though they were produced under the plan. On the other hand, there are the accursed shortages of both producer and consumer goods.

The number of examples could be multiplied. And the point here is not mistakes or the inexperience of planners—they have had time in which to acquire experience. The idea that the proportions and priorities of economic development and the scale of production of at least the most important products can be scheduled from above in a greater or lesser degree of detail has been proven false. This is confirmed not only by the results but also by the planning techniques themselves. In determining the perspectives, planners painstakingly consider world trends in economic development. If the people on the other side of the hill are intensively developing their chemical industry, then we, too, have to become involved in chemicalization. If electronics is in vogue, then that's what we have to get into. We are continually looking over our shoulders to see what kind of hats the bourgeoisie is wearing. But after all, "their" proportions and priorities do not form according to a plan. And just as soon as we take them for our model, we thereby tacitly admit that there exists a more effective mode of regulation or self-regulation of the economy than ours. We will then be consistent: mandatory planning is neither an invariable symbol nor an advantage of our economic system. And if this is so, what is the benefit of encouraging the exemplary fulfillment of plans? It will probably provide a certain work incentive, but this is not enough.

There is a need for new economic thinking here. Let us agree on a simple thing: any product or service that satisfies sensible needs, be it the product of an individual or an enterprise, is beneficial regardless of whether it is produced on the basis of a directive from above or initiative from below. The national economy must be a combination of three equal entities: cost-accounting state enterprises, cooperatives, and private trade. The working people themselves should select the sector in which they wish to work. Private traders should in particular be encouraged to operate in unprofitable spheres of production and services (while regulating the use of hired labor). Trade, personal services, and small-scale industrial enterprises should be leased to cooperatives. Cooperatives of equipment operators—who should be given as much land as they can cultivate—can take root in the countryside alongside family farms. They should be allowed to lease or purchase implements of labor as they wish.

Naturally, the state sector must remain the basic sector of the economy. [But] it must also work under the conditions of commodity production. This means observing several very simple rules. The production program should not be handed down from above but compiled from customers' orders. It is no longer necessary to distribute products—the contract concluded between partners makes it clear for whom they are intended. The wholesale price must not be assigned but be established via agreement between seller and buyer. The collective will defray all costs—including production development costs—from its income. Once you have paid your taxes and paid off your loans, the rest is yours. Decide for yourselves how much you want to allocate for maintaining and expanding production and how much you want to pay out.

In short, the new economic thinking presupposes that everyone will feed himself as best he can, the important thing being that he pays taxes on personal and collective income. Is this anarchy? Not at all. In this model, real centralism is possible. It consists not in total mandatory planning but in the state's guidance of the development of the economy in the necessary direction.

Here is a small example that will make many things clear. In socialist Hungary the state supports the "Ikarus" bus program, as well as many others. However, it does not expressly dictate the number of vehicles the manufacturer must produce for a one-year or five-year period. Rather, indirect methods are employed: taxes payable to the treasury are reduced for a certain time, loans are granted at a lower interest rate, and nonreturnable subsidies for capital investments in plant are not excluded. Everyone can see that these methods are working—the number of "Ikarus" buses is increasing on our streets as well. And this is centralism in fact: the planned increase in the production of a given product and the planned structural shift toward the production of a product that is beneficial to the nation have been achieved.

In a similar situation, we would by habit have planned the increase in units, we would have obligated construction firms to commission new capacities and machine builders to supply additional equipment. . . . Everything would seem to have been taken into account, but when the deadline comes it would turn out that the plan is one thing and reality is another. This is not an abstract supposition. I remind you that the last three five-year plans have not been fulfilled, and the degree of deviation from the plan up to now has grown. Given the formal dictatorship of the plan, the economy is developing in increasingly anarchistic fashion, real centralism in management is weakening, and we are losing control over events. Today, you could say, management of the American economy is more centralized than ours.

You will agree that these judgments sound rather strange. Why? Changes in life must be preceded by changes in thinking. It appears that a danger to restructuring is lurking here. People are having a hard time grasping its radical variant, the only variant that is capable of normalizing the economy (and not just the economy). We are too much in the grip of the prejudice that the power of the state over the productive forces is an unconditional blessing and an imperative demand of the historical process.

This prejudice has been with us not for seventy years; it is much older.

5

War Communism had its roots in our country's history. In the past as well, the central authority in Russia for long periods of time directly ordered everything that lay, stood, crawled, walked, swam, or flew. The science of history is always a battlefield. Fulfilling their social mandate, our historians have tried to prove that economic, military, and all other successes were achieved precisely in such periods. Until recent times, for example, Ivan the Terrible has been highly revered. Nikolai Cherkasov, who played the leading role in Eisenstein's famous film, described in his memoirs important details of a meeting between Stalin and figures from the world of the arts: "Discussing Ivan the Terrible's mistakes, Iosif Vissarionovich remarked that one of his mistakes was that he did not liquidate the five large remaining feudal families and that he did not carry the fight against the feudal lords through to the end—if he had done so, there would have been no Time of Troubles in Russia. . . . And then Iosif Vissarionovich added with humor that 'here, Ivan was hindered by God: Ivan the Terrible liquidates one family of feudal lords, one boyar clan and then spends an entire year repenting and praying for forgiveness for his sin at a time when he should have acted more decisively! . . .'''

The goal of these scholarly exercises is obvious: it was necessary to prove that the fighter against an outmoded order, regardless of the era, must liquidate his opponents—history does not forgive spinelessness. It would appear that some historians are following these invaluable precepts to the letter to this very day. A textbook used in higher education proclaims Ivan the Terrible's supporters, noble landowners who supported serfdom, to have been a "progressive stratum of the feudal class that was involved with the solution of important economic and political problems." Such opinions can be confirmed or refuted only by analyzing property relations starting with ancient times. We will see that this search will reveal the living sources of today's conflicting ideas about the avenues of change in society.

Prebourgeois production relations began forming in our country an entire century before the era of Ivan the Terrible. The peasantry was making the transition to commodity production. This process was especially rapid on hereditary estates, i.e., on the lands of the selfsame boyars, the nonliquidation of whom the coryphaeus of all the sciences would lament centuries later. The owners of latifundia usually did not work their own farms—they preferred to lease their land to peasants and tried to collect payments in money rather than in kind. "The agricultural labor of the free peasant working on state or private land," wrote Kliuchevskii, an expert on property relations, concerning that time, "remained the basis of the national economy." The historian goes on to explain: "The peasant negotiated with the landowner as a free, juridically equal person." Commodity production and its property stratification created a market for labor power. Successful proprietors hastened to invest their money in business and small trade. Cities grew rapidly: there were about one hundred cities in the second half of the fifteenth century; by the mid-sixteenth century there were already one hundred sixty. "Peasant traders," i.e., wealthy peasants and merchants, founded solid enterprises. The Stroganov industrialists, for example, employed more than ten thousand hired workers at their saltworks in Sol'-Vychegodsk. The number of "nepashnye liudi"—craftsmen working for the market—increased in the countryside. Hence the origin of the Russian third estate, which, with a certain confluence of circumstances, could have directed the nation along the capitalist path. Our country then would not have lagged behind other powers in terms of the type of production relations.

However, in addition to hereditary landholdings, at that time there also existed a fundamentally different form of ownership—*pomest'ia*, i.e., lands that were granted to noblemen by princes. These plots of land were relatively small, were granted only for the term of service, and were not passed on by succession. Therefore, the landowner [*pomeshchik*] considered it more advantageous not to lease land to tenant farmers, but to force peasants to work his land under the corvée system. *Pomest'e* noblemen, unlike hereditary landholders, were specifically interested in the forcible attachment of peasants to the land, in other words, in serfdom.

"But the corvée system," writes N. Nosov, a well-known researcher of property relations,

> even though promising the feudal lords the production of commodity grain in the fastest and most effective way (and this made it especially advantageous in their eyes), in the broad economic perspective was more conservative than the system of rent based on money. The corvée system led to the ruination of individual peasant farms and, above all, undermined the motivation of the peasant to increase the productivity of his labor and to turn the results of his labor into a commodity.

". . . In the late fifteenth and early sixteenth century," the author continues,

> the question was still being decided as to which socioeconomic road Russia would follow: the road of the *pomest'e*-serf-owning economy, in which broad strata of the ruling class, especially the *pomest'e* nobility, were particularly interested, or on the contrary the path of relaxation of feudal relations and broad development of a free, small-commodity economy in the city and the countryside. Urban dwellers and peasants were interested in the latter. Also inclined toward this path was a certain group of powerful feudal lords who were connected with the rising merchant class (like the Novgorod boyars had in the past, for example) and who counted on achieving greater economic gains through urban and peasant small trades and commerce.

The outcome of the struggle in this instance also depended in decisive measure on which side the authorities would take. Under Ivan the Terrible, the state supported the advocates of serfdom. The tsar called to life and nurtured the punitive corps—the infamous *oprichnina* (which, Cherkasov reports, was highly praised by Stalin). With the support of the latter, Ivan the Terrible expropriated (1) the inherited property of powerful feudal lords (and exterminated the latter) and (2) labor power, i.e., he transformed the peasants into serfs. The productive forces became statized, and the *pomest'e* became the basic form of land tenure. This was a turning point in our history. "Even if serfdom (in the social and not just the peasant sphere) and the autocracy (in the political sphere) triumphed in Russia as a result of the *'oprichnina'* and the 'great peasant misfortune' at the end of the sixteenth century, this still does not prove that the Russian people could not have followed another road. But nevertheless this was the basic 'objective' reason for much of the economic and cultural backwardness of serf-owning tsarist Russia," Professor Nosov concludes.

This is precisely stated, isn't it? It suggests that Stalin's idol fought not against feudalism, but for feudalism against the embryonic capitalist mode of production. It turns out that the selfsame "unexterminated" patrimonial landholders, and not the pro-serfdom nobles, were the "progressive stratum of the feudal class."

The autocracy was strengthened by the expropriation of its subjects. Incidentally, Ivan the Terrible himself understood this just as well as we do. After suffering his military failures, he appealed for aid, as we know, to the queen of England. Upon being refused, the tsar gave the queen a dressing-down: "We expected that you would be the sovereign in your own kingdom and that you yourself would rule. . . . But there are many people who rule besides you, not only people but traders. . . . But you are like a bad (common) girl in your maidenly office."

Retribution for the reactionary turn of events was not long in coming. As a result of Ivan the Terrible's military adventures, the country lost its outlet to the Baltic Sea, lost important cities, and became a target of intervention. The economy was thoroughly ruined. Even today, the sad documents of that time have a heartrending effect:

> In the village in Kiuliaksh, Ignatok Aut'ianov's *luk* (plot—*V. S.*) is empty. It is desolate because of the *oprichnina*—the *oprichniki* plundered the *zhivot* (property—*V. S.*) and whipped the livestock to death. He himself died, and the children ran off to somewhere unknown. . . . In the same village, Eremeik Afanosov's *luk* is empty. It is desolate because of the *oprichniki*—they plundered the *zhivot* and killed him; he has no children. . . . In the same village, Melenteik's *luk* is empty. It is desolate because of the *oprichnina*—the *oprichniki* plundered the *zhivot* and whipped the livestock to death; he himself ran off to some unknown place.

While historians debate over Ivan the Terrible, Tsar Peter, the continuer of his work, inevitably receives a positive evaluation. The opinion is that Peter transformed Russia according to European models. This legend crumbles just as soon as we begin looking at the property relations of the time. It was under Peter that the statization of the productive forces reached its high point. By the end of his reign, there were 191 manufacturing enterprises, 178 of which were founded under Peter. Precisely half of them were built with state funds. In metallurgy, for example, fourteen state plants and only two private plants were built between

1700 and 1710. To be sure, the tsar occasionally transferred state plants to private hands or to companies, but, as Kliuchevskii noted, "the factory and the company acquired the nature of state institutions." There was one other difference between industry created under Peter and European industry. Free working hands did not exist in this country of serfs, and the autocracy solved the problem simply: peasants were assigned to state enterprises. What is more, by an edict of January 18, 1721, the tsar abolished the law that only landowners and the state could own serfs and gave this right to merchants. The autocracy transposed the traditional forms of serfdom into industry, and something unprecedented in history was born—a working class consisting of serfs.

When the national economy is viewed only as an instrument, as an implement of war, even real attainments are invariably unstable. The navy created under Peter won glorious victories. In the Baltic alone, Russia maintained 848 ships and 28,000 crewmen. But a few years after Peter's death, only a few ships were able to put out to sea. The navy was needed to conquer the Baltic lands. Once the job was done, the tool could be discarded.

The fate of the nation's metallurgy is instructive. *Memory* [Pamiat'], a novel-essay written by the now deceased V. Chivilikhin, was read by the public not so long ago. I knew the author—at one time we were bunkmates in a university dormitory. A faithful admirer of Stalin, by the logic of things he also worshiped Peter. Chivilikhin wrote:

Metal? By all means! It is common knowledge that metal is the bread of industry, the basis of economic development, and Peter I was among the first to understand this. As if possessed, he raced about Russia's orefields, infecting Russian industrialists with his energy. In 1702, Peter transferred the state-owned Nev'ianskii Plant together with land, timber, and Mt. Blagodat' to Nikita Demidov. Production of the best military guns in the world was quickly organized at the plant, which produced as many as 100,000 guns a year, such that the Battle of Poltava could be said to have been won by shops in the Urals. In a historically brief period of time, the Demidovs—without telephones or radio, without all-terrain vehicles or helicopters—set up twelve metallurgical plants in the Urals.

The Urals held the world record for pig iron production per furnace and for economic indicators of expenditure of fuel and raw materials. Demidov iron—"Russian sable"—went to Europe. By 1718—seven years before Peter's death—Russia occupied first place in the world in the production of pig iron, leaving behind England, Germany, France, and America, to say nothing of other countries. We produced one-third of all ferrous metal on the planet! In the eighteenth century, England herself bought several million poods of iron a year from us.

Naturally, the author does not report that the state-owned Nev'ianskii Plant was transferred to Demidov not only "with land, forests, and Mt. Blagodat"' but also with serfs. From prerevolutionary historians, we know that miners at the Demidov plants were chained to their wheelbarrows and were in fact buried alive underground. Very well, human material is a renewable resource. Women will bear more. But how can one understand the subsequent decline of metallurgy? "Peter's descendants," Chivilikhin explains, "exploited their rich legacy for decades but after a certain time ceased to care about multiplying it." A very practical explanation! If there is a master in charge, there will be success. When the state relaxed its attention and guardianship, things fell to pieces. This isn't history, this is the latest news, the focus of current disputes. . . .

M. Tugan-Baranovskii, a very qualified researcher and author of *The Russian Factory* [Russkaia fabrika], asked the same question long before Chivilikhin did, but from him we get a totally different answer. At the end of the eighteenth century, Russia and England each produced eight million poods of pig iron, but half a century later the English produced 234 million poods while our forefathers produced sixteen million. "What produced such a sad plight for the iron-producing industry?" the historian asked, and he answered:

> At any rate, it was not for lack of government aid and tutelage. Iron was one of the most essential products for the state. Therefore, the government spared no resources. . . . Private metallurgical plants in the Urals received no less than fifteen million in loans from the government. What is more, these plants were deeded enormous state farm and forest land and hundreds of thousands of peasants—all this without the slightest payment by owners of the plants. Why then did iron mining in Russia not only fail to grow but even decline in comparison with the population? Specifically, as a result of too much government tutelage and support.

Having cost-free plants, cost-free working hands, and having created a forced labor apparatus, our metallurgical plant owners, unlike the English, were not the least bit concerned with technical improvements. "The entire iron-manufacturing process, starting with timber felling for blast furnaces, the transporting of materials, the extraction of ore and ending with iron and pig-iron castings, was performed by workers under the threat of severe punishment, without any hope for improvement in their material lot," the historian noted. "As long as the worker at iron plants worked under the cudgel, his labor productivity could not progress. No kind of benefit could take the place of the condition necessary for industrial progress—free labor."

The economic depravity went so far that even freedom could not help Urals metallurgy. After the reform of 1861, the region went into decline. Once again, from Tugan-Baranovskii:

> A worker who had received all his provisions free of charge, who had been maintained entirely by the plant administration, which kept the large working

population of plants in a state of subjugation and forced it to work by measures of extreme severity, became entirely unaccustomed to free activity and totally lost his head after liberation. Having been given the opportunity to quit the heavy work at the plants, with which such hateful memories of the past were associated, the workers left the plants in droves and moved to other provinces. . . . The former plant workers were so eager to leave the hateful plants that they sold their farmsteads, homes, and gardens for next to nothing, even giving them away.

All this is very reminiscent of the ruination of the countryside in my birthplace. After the death of Stalin there was no hunger and there was joy in living. But just as soon as passports were freely issued to collective farmers, the villages were literally depopulated—no one had any need of houses even if they were free.

Let us return to history. A researcher views state tutelage of the economy as a misfortune. But what if it had not existed? Would things have necessarily gone better? On this score, history itself posed a graphic economic experiment: the treasury spared no money for the production of the cloth needed for state uniforms but took no interest in the production of chintz. Let us see how the sub-branch progressed. From an edict issued in 1740, we learn that notwithstanding injections of capital and the strictest orders and regulations, "cloth for uniforms, which are made at Russian factories and are used by regiments, are very poor and do not wear well. . . ." In edicts dated November 25, 1790, and November 20, 1791, the government divided cloth-mangfacturing enterprises into two groups. The first included so-called obligated factories—when founded, they received a grant from the treasury, had serfs, and were supposed to deliver their product to the state. The second group—free factories—was created on the basis of private money and employed free hired personnel. It was soon found that the obligated factories did not fulfill their quotas. The free factories were more successful, but this meant little to the state, and in 1797 they were forbidden to sell cloth freely and were required to supply it to the state. The supplier was fined for every yard that was sold without what we today would call an allocation schedule. The cloth was immediately confiscated. In 1809, the government allocated two million rubles for the organization of new factories. But to no avail—there was not enough cloth, even of inferior quality, for the army. Only in 1816 did the state decide to end its tutelage over production, and six years later the supply of cloth exceeded demand.

But what became of chintz during this time? The treasury provided not a single penny for its production, but at the same time neither did it impose its directives and pricing policies. Production grew by leaps and bounds. In Ivanovo at the beginning of the nineteenth century there were cotton enterprises with a work force of a thousand or more workers. Factory owners earned five rubles on the ruble. Old Russia to this very day is scornfully called "chintzy." And yet, objectively, this branch operated under worse conditions than the cloth-making branch. Imported cotton was the raw material here, whereas the country was even exporting wool. Peasants on quitrent worked for hire at chintz factories. In addition to the cost of labor power, the factory owner in one way or another paid their quitrent and, in addition to this, since he as a rule was also a peasant himself, paid an enormous quitrent to his landlord. It would seem that the surplus product as the source of expanded reproduction should remain slightly less than at state enterprises with "free" labor power. Well, who would have thought it possible? . . .

The great reforms of the 1860s finally created the main conditions for the industrial development of the nation—a manpower market. A thankful economy, literally freeing itself of its weights, performed very well. Metallurgical production moved from Urals plants that had fallen into decline to the southern part of the country where it operated on a new, purely capitalistic basis. While prior to 1887 there were two plants in the south, in 1899 there were seventeen with twenty-nine blast furnaces in operation and twelve under construction. These furnaces were 1.5 times more powerful than English furnaces of the time. In thirteen years (1887–99), pig iron production in Russia increased fivefold—from 32.5 to 165.2 million poods. The absolute increase (132.7 million poods) was higher than in any European country except Germany. Our country overtook France and Belgium in the production of pig iron and was in fourth place in the world on the eve of the twentieth century.

The rate of railroad construction staggers the imagination. Between 1866 and 1875, Russian railroads grew by 1,520 kilometers a year on the average—double the present rate. And in the last eight years of the nineteenth century, 2,740 kilometers of mainline track were commissioned each year (today, we build approximately this much during a five-year plan period).

In 1913 our country was fifth in the world in the volume of industrial output and, judging by its growth rates, had every expectation of winning new victories in the competition between the powers. Of course, the rates are especially impressive because the count commenced from a low level. But even the absolute increases were impressive. Thus, in 1911–13, coal production increased by approximately eleven million tons (in 1981–85, i.e., during the entire past five-year plan, it increased by 9.6 million tons), and pig-iron production increased by 518,000 tons annually, which is entirely comparable with current increments. I should note that industry progressed on the basis of intensive factors characteristic of a commodity economy. Between 1887 and 1908, industrial output increased 3.7 times while the increase in the number of workers was less than double. As you can see, old Russia left us a rather good legacy in industry.

Economic historians long ago observed that Russia was always more inclined to state economic regulation than the West. However, researchers differ in their evaluation of this phenomenon. In his voluminous work *Russia Under the Old Regime*, the not-unknown Richard Pipes argues that from the days of Kievan Rus' our country has never known any form of private ownership, that the princes and later the tsars viewed the expanding state as their patrimony. According to Pipes, the dominance of sovereign, essentially state ownership formed the stereotype of the Russian: lumpen in an economic sense, he was invariably a slave to the state in the political sense. Pipes believes that the history of Russia was not development, not a continuous process, but was rather a repetition, a variation on one and the same dismal theme similar to that which took place in the somnolent states of oriental despotism.

I hope that our study of ownership relations has convinced the reader that our history does not wish to fit the picture painted by the American. He absolutized and extended to an infinite number of centuries what essentially were limited periods in which the state indeed attempted to centralize economic management. At the same time, analysis refutes the popular opinion that the productive forces flourished during these periods. No, at best there were short-term breakthroughs in narrow sectors of the economy that were directly connected with military needs. On the other hand, when room opened up for initiative from below, our economy developed at a good tempo.

Unlike industry, agricultural production continued to suffer through a long period of stagnation following the reforms of 1860. The renowned Russian commune [*obshchina*] played a negative role here. It was imposed from above or at least strengthened after the coup by Ivan the Terrible's *oprichnina*. As already stated, the nonhereditary landowner [*pomeshchik*], unlike the hereditary land-holder [*votchinnik*] did not lease the land out but used peasant hands to till the soil. But how would the peasant be fed? If forced labor was inefficiently used, even the modest cost of its maintenance would cut the noble's income in half. On the other hand, as soon as a peasant was given even a small piece of land, he would put his all into it and shirk his corvée obligations. The commune was the ideal solution. Plots allocated for feeding the serfs belonged not to families but to the rural society, to the *mir* [peasant commune], to the entire village. Collective land tenure clipped the wings of the energetic and the enterprising and implanted a dismal, wretched equality. But this was the aim of the serf-owner. He was interested in obtaining labor power for nothing, not in successful competitors. The commune as a whole bore responsibility for the corvée—if someone became too engrossed in his personal farm, his neighbors would have to work in his stead. The commune also proved to be very convenient to the state: taxes and duties were imposed on the commune, and it apportioned them among the families. The *mir* paid assessments for peasants who disappeared into a common fund, so that the peasants kept track of one another better than the authorities.

The dispute over the fate of the commune became especially intense when the nation turned toward capitalist development. And this is understandable: after all, this conservative institution was essentially inimical to private ownership, without which there is no capitalism. The reform of 1861 preserved the commune—it was convenient for landowners to receive redemption for land whole-sale from the *mir*, and the state correctly saw in the commune a condition for preserving the autocracy. At the turn of the century, a reactionary figure wrote: "Everything that is still sacred, ideal, patriotic, and heroic in Russia stems invisibly from the commune."

Nonhereditary landowners and the tsarist bureaucracy defended the commune from the right. However, it also had defenders on the left—on the part of socialists who saw in the commune the nucleus of future collectivist society. Utopians were not the only ones who cherished this hope. In 1902, Lenin declared very resolutely: ". . . we shall unreservedly defend the commune as a democratic organization of local government, as a cooperative or a neighbors' association, against all encroachments on the part of the bureaucrats" (vol. 6, p. 344).

But events took their own course: it was unthinkable to combine the development of industry with the stagnation of agriculture. The demand of the time was best expressed by P. Stolypin, a prominent statesman of prerevolutionary Russia. In 1902, while he was still the governor of Grodno, he warned: "It is impossible to preserve the existing forms of land tenure that have been hallowed by centuries, because they will ultimately lead to economic collapse and the total ruination of the country." Later, as head of the government, he formulated his agrarian policy in a speech to the Third State Duma as follows: ". . . the creation of small-scale personal land ownership, the real right to withdraw from the commune, and the resolution of problems connected with reformed land tenure—these are the tasks that the government has considered and still considers as matters vital to the existence of Russia as a power." It is curious that Stolypin was almost the first to grasp the relationship between forms of ownership and personal rights: "As long as the peasant is poor, as long as he does not have his own land, as long as he is gripped in the vise of the commune, he will remain a slave, and no written law will give him the benefits of civil liberty."

The head of government, retreating and maneuvering, succeeded in implementing his program despite desperate opposition from the right and the left. In Lenin's assessment, "Stolypin had a correct grasp of the matter: unless the old system of landownership was broken up, Russia could not develop economically. Stolypin and the landlords boldly took the revolutionary path, ruthlessly breaking up the old order, handing over the peasant masses as a whole to the mercy of the landlords and kulaks" (vol. 16, p. 424). The reforms inaugurated by Stolypin gained momentum. By the summer of 1917, 62.5 percent of all peasant land was under private ownership or in personal holdings, i.e., did not belong to the commune.

On the eve of the world war, Russia already occupied second place in the world in grain exports. With economic success, public opinion inclined more and more toward Stolypin's policies. A. Izgoev (one of the authors of the famous *Vekhi*, [Landmarks]), a well-known publicist of that time, wrote optimistically:

> The dispute is now being weighed by fate. The law of the commune has been
> irreversibly condemned, and all attempts to restore it to its dominant position

are doomed to failure. . . . . Russia must be reformed on the basis of private ownership, and for this reform to work to the greatest advantage of the peasant masses will require the energy, knowledge, and ability of democratic public figures.

But history thought otherwise. The dispute had by no means been weighed by fate. After the October Revolution, those seeking a transformation rejected the capitalist road of development for Russia and again turned to the commune. During the years of War Communism, as we remember, fifty million hectares were confiscated from the kulaks. This land was not divided among the peasants but for the most part was given into communal use. This nullified the results of the Stolypin reforms and essentially restored land tenure forms characteristic of old Russia.

It goes without saying that it was not just the convenience it offered for requisitioning that provided the attraction of the commune—it was believed to contain the embryo of the future collective socialist economy. This is not my conjecture. Even at the Tenth Party Congress, which decided the question of the New Economic Policy, Lenin insisted on the conversion of small farms "to socialized, collective, communal labor" (vol. 43, p. 26). Later, researchers repeatedly emphasized the continuing relationship between the commune and the collective farms. For example, S. P. Trapeznikov, the Soviet scholar and organizer of science, explicitly stated: "The Soviet revolution has prepared land communities for transition to a higher form and has made them support points for the socialist transformation of the nation's agriculture."

In a word, the utopian hopes for the commune held by the last century's thinkers did not prove to be so very utopian. Prince V. L'vov (the head of the Provisional Government for a short period of time), who suddenly grew wiser in emigration, wrote in a pamphlet published in 1922:

> . . . the old Slavophilism and new Soviet power are extending their hands to one another. . . . While idealizing the commune, the Slavophiles themselves did not live in one. If they had been more consistent, they would have come to Soviet power, which is the communal government of the state. . . .
>
> How did the Slavophiles picture the state structure of Russia?
>
> In the form of self-government that overcame all manner of political and partisan struggle and that combined the entire common effort in the name of a single common ideal. Was this not the goal that Soviet power set for itself? . . .
> Thus, having cast off the armor of European patterned cloaks, Russia stands before the world in the new clothing of its national being and general service to mankind.

As you see, Prince L'vov saw the same roots as the eminent scholars of today. In addition to this, the ex-premier directly adduced from communal relations the moral-political unity of society as the antipode to "patterned" bourgeois democracy. . . .

History teaches that the commune has never succeeded in securing work incentives and economic successes: equality and social justice of the communal type have invariably involved the suppression of the individual. Nor have the advantages of "socialized, collective, communal labor" been proven today even though all conceivable and inconceivable variants have been tried.

6

In one exceptionally important realm of life the legacy of centuries has weighed quite heavily on post-revolutionary history, forming a monolithic wall that we have not yet been able to penetrate or overcome. This is the wall of bureaucratic management—the main obstacle on the road to change.

It is commonly thought that Peter I implanted Western bureaucratic models onto Russian soil. But this isn't quite the case. Naturally, state enterprises in all countries are managed by state employees. But since industry under Peter was predominantly state industry, the scope of authority of the Russian bureaucracy was from the very beginning wider than in the West. The Berg Kollegium and Manufaktur Kollegium (forerunners of the economic ministries) directly dictated the product mix and set prices. This is understandable. After all, industry worked primarily for war. Even small craftsmen were not left outside the sphere of centralized government. The Edict of 1722 unified them into shops for the purpose of organized utilization in manufacturing products required by the army and navy. The authorities even crept into economic areas where they clearly could not influence events. The Edict of 1715 called for doubling the sowings of flax and hemp and for raising these crops in all provinces throughout the nation (as yet there was no discussion of corn). The state sent instructions concerning the care of livestock, periods for carrying out agricultural work and fertilizing the fields, and the use of scythes instead of sickles to harvest wheat, etc., to the estate stewards, going over the heads of the nominal owners of the estates.

When the state expands the number of objects under its control immeasurably, the bureaucratic apparatus proliferates. In Petrine times, there were 905 bureaus and offices. After the death of Peter, four of his associates (Menshikov, Osterman, Makarov, and Volkov) testified: "Over the peasants today there are ten or more commanders instead of one as in the past, namely: military commanders, all the way from soldier to headquarters and the general staff; and civilian commanders—from fiscals, commissars, forest masters, and the like to governors, some of whom today can be called not shepherds but wolves that have begun stealing into the herd." Given such complex structures, it would have been impossible to define precisely areas of influence and to demarcate lines of authority.

Frequently, three ramified state apparatuses—the military apparatus, the civilian apparatus, and the secret police—were engaged in the same affairs independently of one another. Under these conditions, there was an objective need for a supreme arbiter whose unequivocal pronouncements would be equally obligatory for any government link. Call him emperor, dictator, father of the people or whatever, his place in the administrative structure would remain unchanged no matter. Even simple questions have to be resolved at the top of the hierarchical pyramid. This feature of excessively centralized government explains the delight that his descendants have taken in the fact that Peter was personally involved in every possible nuance of life and wrote edicts on virtually any subject.

The fact that the old state machine was smashed after October 1917 did not mean that the roots of bureaucratism had been torn up. The danger of such may even have intensified, since the entire economy was once again included in the sphere of [central] administration. The colossal effort to regulate the economy, which, albeit imperfectly, is performed by the market in commodity production, suddenly had to be transferred to the government apparatus. The situation was complicated by the fact that the economic model of War Communism excluded any kind of independent economic activity. Industry, for example, was essentially one superenterprise managed from the center.

A countless number of organizations had to be created to deal with pressing problems. Iu. Larin, a famous economist of the time, labeled the erstwhile system of economic management the All-Russian *Chekvalapstvo*—the Extraordinary Commission for Felt Boots and Bast Shoes. It is important to note that for all the peculiarity of such institutions, they could not fail to arise. The army and the labor camps needed footwear. But imagine a messenger from the center with extraordinary authority in this regard. He has a specific target, and in order to fulfill it, he tries to take people from other production about which another authority is concerned in turn. The result is the announcement of a need for a new, superextraordinary commission. . . . Noneconomic coercion to work required an apparatus of overseers. We can add to this an apparatus for requisitioning, for the distribution of vital necessities, and a host of others.

Lenin was the first to understand the danger and to declare war on bureaucracy—otherwise, [he feared], the revolution would be drowned in ink. It was the great service of Il'ich that he veered the nation sharply in the direction of NEP, under which objective conditions arose for bridling bureaucracy. By the summer of 1922, the work force in the central economic agencies declined from 35,000 to 8,000, and in the provincial national economic councils—from 235,000 to 18,000.

But in 1927, when NEP was on its way out, the status of the enterprise changed through legislation. Under its new statute, the goal of the enterprise was to fulfill a plan handed down from above, and not to realize a profit as stated in the Statute of 1923. A higher organ would henceforth hand down construction targets, appoint and fire administrators, and dictate prices. The vertical management system (people's commissariat—main administration—enterprise), which was ideally suited to command management, began to take form rapidly beginning in January 1932.

With the disintegration of NEP's economic mechanism, the directive once again took the place of interest. Let us take a random look through a collection of decrees dealing with economic issues. Here we have the August 1, 1940, Decree of the Central Committee of the All-Union Communist Party (Bolsheviks) and the Council of People's Commissars, "On the Harvesting and Procurement of Agricultural Products." Section VII of that document regulated the harvesting of tobacco in the most detailed manner:

> 1. To establish that the harvesting of tobacco must be carried out with the existence of full technical ripeness strictly in stages, without permitting the overripening of tobaccos or the harvesting of underripe leaves.
>
> 2. To secure the timely and consistent performance of work relating to tobacco harvesting (breaking, threading, drying, processing) without allowing interruptions in these operations. . . .
>
> 4. To complete the tobacco and makhorka harvests by the following dates:
>
> (a) makhorka—no later than September 10 in all areas with the exception of the Altai and Krasnoiarsk territories and Novosibirsk Region, where the harvest must be completed no later than September 1.

And so forth.

The instruction was signed by Stalin himself—he was also an expert in tobacco harvesting. The directive had to be duplicated and delivered to every collective farm. The execution of each point had to be monitored (as well as the entire decree, which was a whole pamphlet), and reports had to be compiled regularly. . . . Note also that the first point might contradict the fourth: it was ordered that the harvest be completed before September 10, but what if the tobacco was not yet ripe by that time? The authorized representative would probably begin to press for the deadline, but the collective farm chairman would be inclined to wait. The result would be something like a court of arbitration. It is easy to imagine the number of civil servants that would be fed . . . not by the tobacco harvest but by the paper accumulated on this problem. We should not see in this example of *Neochekvalapstvo* Stalinist eccentricity. Without the paper bearing his signature, without the army of overseers, the erstwhile collective farmer would hardly remember tobacco plantations.

Beginning in the thirties, the administrative apparatus grew faster than any other group of working people. Ten years ago, planners and accounting clerks alone numbered 5.5 million. Reporting this figure in the press, Academician N. Mel'nikov added with pride: "No other country in the world has such cadres. . . ." It is indeed possible today that the rest of the world does not have nearly as many of "such cadres"—between 1976 and 1983 alone, the number of administrative personnel increased by 3 million persons, passing the 17-million mark.

When the economic mechanism incorporated noneconomic coercion to work as an obligatory element (the "subsystem of fear," as the management expert G. Popov expressed it), management based on orders influenced life to a certain degree, even though at that time it operated with terrible ineffectiveness. Today, this is an apparatus that knows its shortcomings but does not know how to eliminate them.

In management theory there is the concept of a "self-sufficient system." When an organization takes excessive management functions into its hands, the number of administrators sooner or later reaches a certain critical magnitude, and the apparatus begins to work for itself: the higher-ups write, and those at the bottom make formal replies. Real life is ignored because it only gets in the way of the smoothly functioning mechanism. This is something like those black holes in the universe—congealed masses of matter so monstrously dense that no signals can make their way to the outside.

Every year the administrative sphere prepares a hundred million sheets of documents, i.e., approximately one page per capita per day. At least ninety percent of the papers are useless—they are simply not read by anyone.

This apparatus, so unique for its size and feebleness, is today engaged in translating party decisions on restructuring into the language of circulars, directives, and statutes. The results will not be difficult to predict because more than anything else bureaucrats are concerned with self-preservation or, which is the same thing, the preservation of administrative methods of management.

The existing bureaucratic machine does not mix with restructuring. It can be smashed (which happens with revolutions from below), it can be abolished (revolutions from above), but it cannot be restructured. In any case, there must be changes of a revolutionary nature. Attempts to force scientific-technological progress and to develop the economy under the stifling control of the bureaucrats threaten the economy with stagnation and the decline of our power.

With respect to the bureaucrats, everything is more or less clear. But what about all the rest of us? The instruments of analysis used in this article are too crude for investigating the way in which stable external circumstances are reflected in man's inner world, in his behavioral stereotypes. This is the main thing, after all. Not having learned to be concerned with what is the state's responsibilities (let the leadership have headaches about this), we have also forgotten how to take care of ourselves. A type of social dependence has formed.

In theory, everyone understands: the assertion that the state grants the people certain benefits is no more than rhetoric. In its offices, it does not produce material values. It is not the state that feeds man but, on the contrary, it is the worker who maintains the state. But in practice—give me a free apartment, give me cheap butter to eat to my heart's content, give me this, give me that, and at the same time remove from my sight the neighbor who ventured to feed himself and now lives better—that son of a bitch—than me.

Social inertia is the reverse side of bureaucratism. From the bureaucrat's point of view, individual or collective income belongs to the treasury, which may return all or part of it to its owners but which may also give back nothing. The hope for good leaders has become the behavioral norm.

The conservatism of the bureaucracy has joined forces with the mood of those at the lower levels, i.e., you and me. There is sentimental reminiscing about the past, longing for the boss and for order, the instinctive preference for what is usual and traditional, and attempts to close with one's breast the embrasures through which innovations are seeping. This is the fear of independence and the expectation of manna from heaven. This is the fear of life, of our grim economic realities. In this situation, one serious failure—economic, foreign policy: what kind is unimportant—is enough to isolate the reformers morally.

Here is where the principal danger to restructuring lies. To lose time is to lose everything. Leisurely haste with change is not suitable if only for purely adminis- trative considerations: any economic mechanism has enormous inertia and repels alien elements no matter how progressive they may be. Therefore, it is useless to introduce new rules one after the other in the existing system. This can only discredit restructuring—years have been spent talking, but no changes are evi- dent.

History will not forgive us if we miss our chance again. We must cross the abyss in a single jump. Two jumps means we fall.

Notes

1. K. Marx and F. Engels, *Sochineniia*, vol. 20, p. 207.
2. Ibid., vol. 19, pp. 18–19.
3. V. I. Lenin, *Polnoe sobranie sochinenii*, vol. 36, p. 297. Subsequent references to the works of V. I. Lenin will be indicated only by volume and page numbers in parenthe- ses.
4. Marx and Engels, vol. 4, p. 299.
5. *Iz istorii Vserossiiskoi chrezvychainoi komissii, 1917–1921: Sbornik dokumentov* (Moscow, 1958), p. 95.
6. Ibid., pp. 114–15.
7. *Iz istorii Vserossiiskoi chrezvychainoi komissii*, p. 386.
8. Ibid., p. 256.
9. *Deviatyi s"ezd RKP(b): Protokoly* (Moscow, 1960), pp. 92–94.
10. Ibid., pp. 97, 98.
11. *Kommunisticheskaia partiia Sovetskogo Soiuza v rezoliutsiiakh i resheniiakh s "ez- dov, konferentsii i plenumov TsK* (Moscow, 1970), vol. 2 (1917–1924), p. 153.
12. Ibid., pp. 161–62.
13. Ibid., p. 176.
14. *Odinnadtsatyi s"ezd RKP(b). Mart-aprel' 1922: Stenograficheskii otchet* (Mos- cow, 1961), pp. 535, 529.
15. *Dvenadtsatyi s"ezd RKP(b). 17–25 aprelia 1923 goda. Stenograficheskii otchet* (Moscow, 1968), p. 351.
16. F. E. Dzerzhinskii, *Izbrannye proizvedeniia v dvukh tomakh* (Moscow, 1977), vol. 2 (1924–1928), pp. 504, 505, 507.

"He Wanted to Make Life Over Because He Loved It"

An Interview with Bukharin's Widow

An artist I know once told me about the uneasy fate of his colleague Iurii Larin. "He's the son of Nikolai Ivanovich Bukharin," he added significantly, "and his mother is Bukharin's widow."
"Can it be that she is still alive?"
"Yes, she is . . ."

> *"To: Comrade Mikhail Sergeevich Gorbachev, General Secretary of the Central Committee of the CPSU. Notwithstanding the tense international situation, I place before you the question of the party's posthumous rehabilitation of Nikolai Ivanovich Bukharin, my husband and the father of my son. I address this appeal to you not only on my own behalf but also at the behest of Bukharin himself. When he was leaving for the last time to attend the February–March Plenum in 1937 (the plenum was in session for several days), Nikolai Ivanovich, having the foreboding that he would never return and considering my youth at the time, begged me to struggle for his posthumous exoneration. This unbearably difficult moment will never fade in my memory. Tormented by the investigation, by terrifying confrontations that he could not understand, weakened by his hunger strike to protest the monstrous accusations, Bukharin fell to his knees before me and with tears in his eyes begged me not to forget a single word of his letter, "To the Future Generation of Party Leaders." He begged me to struggle for his exoneration: "Swear that you will do this! Swear it! Swear it!" And I did. It would be against my conscience to violate this oath. . . ."*

> *"You demand Bukharin's blood? We will not give it to you. Know this!"*
> From Stalin's concluding address at the Fourteenth Congress
> of the All-Union Communist Party (Bolsheviks) in 1925

Russian text © 1987 by Pravda Publishers and "Ogonek." "On khotel peredelat' zhizn', potomu chto ee liubil," *Ogonek*, 1987, no. 48. Translated by Arlo Schultz.

"Let us drink, comrades, to Nikolai Ivanovich Bukharin! We all know and love him. Out with his eyes, he who dwells on past sins!"

Stalin's toast at a banquet in honor of
military academy graduates in 1935

N. I. Bukharin spent the summer of 1918 in Berlin. He had been sent there to prepare documents connected with the Brest Peace Treaty. At home, Nikolai Ivanovich recounted hearing about a remarkable soothsayer who predicted the future. Out of curiosity, he and G. Ia. Sokol'nikov decided to visit the fortuneteller, who lived on the outskirts of town. The palm reader's prophesy for him was astonishing:

"You will be executed in your own country."

Bukharin was dumbstruck. Thinking he had not heard right, he asked:

"You think Soviet power is doomed?"

"Who will be in power when you die I cannot say. But it is certain that you will meet your end in Russia. . . ."

Somehow Anna Mikhailovna read that Romain Rolland had chosen Beethoven's words, "Joy Through Suffering," as his motto. No, these words did not become the motto of Bukharin's widow, but life showed that in addition to will, she also experienced joy—in suffering. This was when she thought either about her father or about her husband.

A. M. Larina grew up in a family of professional revolutionaries who found themselves at the helm of the state after the revolution. For this reason, she became interested in internal party life quite early. This interest was especially intensified by her closeness to Bukharin. Therefore, all episodes in Larina's life, even the purely personal episodes, were not the embodiment of some light, pure joy, but were invariably burdened by the invisible fetters of the complex social situation of the time: political discussions, disputes, discord, and finally, terror.

The name of Iu. Larin (Mikhail Aleksandrovich Lur'e, 1882–1932) is almost forgotten today, despite the fact that he is buried in the Kremlin walls. Information about him can be found in various kinds of dictionaries and reference works, but this information does not make it possible to understand the character, the personality, or the dimensions of the person whose life was especially heroic.

Anna Mikhailovna recalls her father with tender warmth; he was the dearest person she knew. I will say only a few words about him. Larin was so popular in the first postrevolutionary years that Anya once heard people at a demonstration singing a chastushka [two-, four-line folk verse] that mentioned his name: "We were taught in books the wisdom of Bukharin and to attend conferences from morning to night with Larin."

Before the revolution, Larin lived the life of a professional revolutionary: the organization of cells of the Russian Social Democratic Workers' Party, open and secret surveillance by the police, moving from city to city, arrest, exile, escape.

When the revolution came, he was a member of the executive committee of the Petrograd Soviet, and he took an active part in revolutionary events. As a writer-economist, he wrote a great deal on economic issues, published books, and carried out personal assignments for Lenin. It can be said that Larin stood by the cradle of Soviet economic policy.

In his daughter's memory, Larin lives as an extraordinary phenomenon. "It is difficult to imagine," she says, "how a person who was physically handicapped from birth could have led such a courageous life. Easily recognized by the Okhrana [the tsarist secret police], how could he endure endless persecution? How could he escape from prison? How could he flee when it took him great effort to move about?" He told his daughter how he was carried away from Iakutsk, where he was exiled, in a large wicker basket; how he was literally dropped over a prison wall and was caught by comrades who carried him for a time. It is astonishing that Iurii Mikhailovich was such a prolific writer for he could not pick up a telephone receiver with his right hand without the help of his left. Everything in Larin's life was accomplished only with the greatest exertion of will.

The obituary written by N. Osinsk stated: "He was one of the most outstanding and singular people among us, one of the prominent figures of the October and post-October periods, a person of rare dedication to the working class and the socialist revolution. . . ." At Larin's funeral, Lunacharskii said that Larin's beautiful eyes seemed to shine even in the dark.

Anna Mikhailovna remembers the early years of her life. When she was four years old, she became quite interested in her parents, whom she saw very rarely, and asked where her mama and papa were. She remembered her grandfather's grumpy answer to one such question: "Your parents are Social Democrats. They prefer to sit in prison, to escape to foreign countries to avoid arrest, rather than to sit with you and cook your porridge." The little girl did not understand what Social Democrats were, but there was a prison not far from her home, and her grandfather told her that it was a place for thieves and bandits. Anya was crushed, and did not venture to ask about her parents any more. But she got to see them "close up" and for a long time after their return from emigration following the February Revolution.

"I liked Mama very much," Anna Mikhailovna recalls. "She was beautiful and slender. She had large, kind, gray eyes and long, downy eyelashes. And I decided that Social Democrats were not so bad after all."

A dramatic episode occurred when she met her father. She looked at him in fright: Iurii Mikhailovich thrust his legs forward and flailed his arms unnaturally when he walked. In horror, Anya crawled under the divan and started crying and screaming: "I want my grandfather!" Her mother forced her out from under the divan with a stick and presented her to her red-faced, excited father. But by evening he had already won her over, and they became lifelong friends.

* * *

The moment when I was first introduced to Bukharin sticks in my memory. On that day, Mother had taken me to see Maeterlinck's *Bluebird* at the Moscow Art Theater. All day long I was under the impression of what I had seen, and when I went to sleep the play was repeated in my dreams. Suddenly someone pulled my nose. I was frightened. The cat on the stage had been as big and tall as a person and I screamed: "Go away, cat!" Although asleep, I could hear Mother's words: "Nikolai Ivanovich, what are you doing? Why are you waking the child?" But I was already awake, and the face of Nikolai Ivanovich came more and more clearly into focus. At that moment, I caught my own bluebird, which symbolized the pursuit of happiness and joy—not fabulously fantastic happiness, but earthly happiness for which I was to pay a dear price.

Of all my father's many friends, Bukharin was my favorite. As a child I had been drawn to him by his irrepressible *joie de vivre*, his mischievousness, his passionate love and knowledge of nature (he was a pretty fair botanist and a first-rate ornithologist), and his passion for painting.

I did not look upon him as a grownup at that time. This may seem ludicrous and absurd, but that is how it was. While I called all my father's friends by their first names and patronymics and addressed them as *"vy"* [polite form of 'you'], Nikolai Ivanovich was not so honored. I called him Nikolasha and addressed him only as *"ty"* [familiar form of 'you'] which amused him personally and my parents who tried in vain to correct my familiar treatment of Bukharin until they got used to it.

One of my first meetings with Nikolai Ivanovich is associated with a recollection about Lenin. Lenin once came into my father's study, which was, as usual, full of people. As far as I was concerned at that time, he was an equal among equals. I remember him vaguely. I will not say that he lisped, that he squinted, that he spoke with a sense of "great importance," and so forth, as many have written in their reminiscences about him. But there was one amusing episode that I will never forget as long as I live. Bukharin had just left when I entered my father's study. They were evidently talking about him and I could not understand everything that Lenin said about Bukharin, but I do remember one phrase: "Bukharin is the golden boy of the revolution." This statement by Lenin about Bukharin became well known in party circles and was taken figuratively. I, however, was totally perplexed at what Lenin had said and made my protest to Lenin. "That is not true," I said, "Bukharin is not made of gold. He's alive!" "Of course he's alive," Lenin replied. "I only used that expression because he's a redhead."

I do not in any way wish to simplify or idealize the relations between the leaders of the revolutionary process. There were also occasional disputes between them. Vladimir Il'ich was always very principled in his relationships with his comrades-in-arms. He did not endorse all of Nikolai Ivanovich's views. But from childhood on, I have always remembered the humaneness among Communists— the openness and friendliness, the high integrity and honesty, and the pursuit of the posited goal.

. . . Nikolai Ivanovich telephoned late in the evening of January 21, 1924, to notify us of Lenin's death. I was not yet asleep and I saw two tears, only two, roll from Father's mournful eyes down his deathly pale cheeks. The day of the funeral—January 27—coincided with my birthday and spoiled the holiday for me as a child. Father said to me: January 27 is rescinded as your birthday. It will henceforth be a day of mourning forevermore. From now on, we will observe your birthday on May 27 when nature comes alive and everything is in bloom. The most noteworthy thing is that Father and I went together to the civil affairs registry office [ZAGS] in Petrovka to change my birth certificate. The ZAGS official, who was dumbfounded by Larin's request, resisted for a long time, suggesting that May 27 be observed as the birthday without amending the documents. He finally gave in. And so I was registered a second time, ten years after my birth. This birth certificate was the basis upon which I was issued my passport that to this very day indicates May 27 as my birthday.

I accompanied my father to the Hall of Columns in the House of Unions where the coffin containing Lenin's body lay in state. It was impossible to get through by car, and I helped my father get there on foot. We left in plenty of time so as not to be late. In a room in the rear of the Hall of Columns, we found Nadezhda Konstantinovna, Mariia Il'inichna, Zinov'ev, Tomskii, Kalinin, Bukharin, and others I do not recall. Excitedly, I went up to Lenin's coffin with my father and stood somewhat to one side. I noticed Anna Il'inichna, Lenin's elder sister. She was standing closer to the head of the deceased, as still as a statue.

Lenin's funeral was unforgettable. Much has been written about it. And I was a witness to everything. The overall picture of the round-the-clock procession to the Hall of Columns could be seen from the windows of our apartment at the Metropol. I arose from my bed at night and watched the endless human flow. The frost, the bonfires, the Red Army men in their pointed helmets [budenovki]. I remember all this as if it were yesterday.

Bukharin had known my father back in the days of emigration. They first met in Italy in 1913; both lived in Sweden from the summer of 1915 to the summer of 1916. From 1918 to the middle of 1927, we lived at the Metropol at the same time. Father and Nikolai Ivanovich did not always agree in their views, but this did not prevent them from being friends. Many years later, at the wish of Nikolai Ivanovich, we named our son Iurii in memory of my father.

. . . When Nikolai Ivanovich would leave us, I became very pained and would run to visit him more and more frequently. Father was pleased when I visited Bukharin. It always seemed to Father that his illness cast a cloud on my life, that I was not experiencing all the joys of childhood. Therefore, when I visited No. 205 where Bukharin lived, he was wont to say: "She has gone to perform seasonal work." Yes, Father himself tried to "fix me up" with his friend.

Many times I encountered Stalin when I went to visit Nikolai Ivanovich. Once in 1925, in a burst of childish tenderness, I wrote a message in verse to Nikolai Ivanovich that ended with the words: "I want to see you. I always yearn for you."

I showed the verses to Father. He said: "Wonderful! Since you have written them, take them to your Nikolasha." But I was too shy to go to him with such verses. My father suggested carrying the verses in an envelope on which he wrote: "From Iu. Larin." I decided to go there, ring the doorbell, hand him the envelope, and then immediately run away. But that was not the way it turned out. I was just coming down the stairs from the third to the second floor when I suddenly met Stalin. It was clear to me that he was on his way to see Bukharin. Without thinking at length, I asked him to deliver the letter and Stalin agreed. Thus, it was through Stalin (what a sinister irony of fate) that I sent Bukharin my first childish declaration of love.

. . . Nineteen twenty-seven was a very sad year for me. Bukharin moved to the Kremlin at Stalin's insistence, and it was impossible to visit the Kremlin without a pass. Even though Nikolai Ivanovich got me a permanent pass, I almost never found him home during that time. I changed my route to school and went by a longer route just to walk past the Comintern building, which was opposite the Manege next to the Troitsky Gates, in the hope of running into Nikolai Ivanovich. I was lucky more than once, and I would run joyfully to him. It was a tense time: the internal party debate had reached the boiling point, preparations were under way for the Fifteenth Congress of the VKP(b) [All-Union Communist Party (Bolsheviks)]. Did he have any time for me? Nikolai Ivanovich visited my father less and less frequently but stayed longer. They talked about current party matters. Their views coincided, and that pleased me even from the sidelines. Nothing troubled me at that time. My uneasiness came later, when I was older and Bukharin came under Stalin's fire.

Nikolai Ivanovich would visit us almost daily at our cottage in Serebrianyi Bor. Mother laughed softly at our love and did not take it seriously; Father remained silent and did not interfere in our relations.

In the fall and winter of 1930 and in the early part of 1931, we tried to spend our free time together. We went to the theater and to art exhibits. I loved the time we spent together in his Kremlin office. There were pictures on the walls. Over the divan was my favorite watercolor: "Elbrus at Sunset." There were various stuffed birds—Nikolai Ivanovich's hunting trophies: enormous eagles with their wings spread, a gray raven, a black-reddish redstart, a red-footed falcon, and enormous butterfly collections.

Nikolai Ivanovich loved to read aloud. I recall how we read Flaubert's *Salammbô*. Nikolai Ivanovich was delighted by passionate and courageous heroes and was enchanted by Romain Rolland's *Colas Breugnon*. "Breugnon" was dear to Nikolai Ivanovich because he himself needed free Russian joviality "up to and including impudence."

How contagious was his laughter when we read about the buffoon Breugnon and his friend Paillard, the notary public, who derived "true satisfaction from giving you, while maintaining a strict mien, a monstrous flourish" and teaching a Huguenot psalm to a thrush perched in a cage.

Sometimes in the evening we would take long walks in Sokol'niki [Park]. At that time, Sokol'niki was on the outskirts of Moscow. We would travel there by streetcar. Nikolai used urban transit quite often. Occasionally the passengers would recognize him and say to each other: "Look, look! It's Bukharin!" Or we would hear: "Hello, Nikolai Ivanovich!" A wellwisher would come up and shake his hand. Nikolai Ivanovich would have to continuously exchange bows with people. He was embarrassed by the attention shown to him.

I do not now remember how it happened, but we were returning from Sokol'-niki. We sat down on a bench on Tver' Boulevard behind the statue of Pushkin, which at that time was on the other side of the square. Nikolai Ivanovich decided to have a serious talk with me. He said that he could do one of two things: either join his life with mine or else not see me for a long time and give me the opportunity to build my life without him. "There is still another possibility," he noted half in jest. "To go out of my mind." But he himself rejected this third possibility.

There was no reply from me. I started weeping.

Today it is difficult to explain the state I was in then: I must have been shedding tears of joy, of deep shock, of the indecisiveness that was typical of those young years in my life, and from the awareness of the fact that I was sitting on a bench on Tver' Boulevard not just with some boy my own age but with Bukharin; whatever, the tears gushed forth. Nikolai Ivanovich looked at me in bewilderment. He was convinced that I had already made my choice, otherwise, he would have said nothing. We sat quite a long time in silence. I shivered and he warmed my cold hands with his warm hands. It was time to go home.

The next evening he invited me to attend a performance of *Khovanshchina* at the Bolshoi Theater. I accepted with pleasure. We showed up at the Metropol late in the evening, after midnight. Mother was already asleep. Father sat at his desk and noticed the perplexed look on my face. He invited Nikolai Ivanovich to spend the night, which he did, sleeping on the divan in the study. I did not sleep well and woke up late after our guest had already left for work.

In the morning, Father, who as I have already mentioned never interfered in my relationships, suddenly started talking to me.

"You must think about how serious your feelings are for him," he said. "Nikolai Ivanovich loves you very much. He is a sensitive, emotional man and if you are not serious about him, you should walk away. Otherwise, this can end badly for him."

This conversation put me on my guard and even frightened me.

Our meetings, theater dates, and reading aloud continued. Once, Nikolai Ivanovich started talking about Knut Hamsun's *Victoria*. "There are few," Nikolai Ivanovich said, "who have succeeded in writing such a sensitive work about love. *Victoria* is a hymn to love!"

I do not believe that Nikolai Ivanovich had brought this book with him by accident. He read selectively and read only the passages he wanted to read:

"What is love? It is the rustling of the wind in the rosebushes. No, it is a flame that glows in the blood. Love is infernal music and its sounds make even the hearts of the old dance. It is like a daisy that opens at nightfall. It is like an anemone that opens its petals at a light breath and dies if it is touched. Such is love. . . ."

He interrupted the reading and looked thoughtfully into the distance. Then he looked at me.

What was he thinking about then?

"Love was the creator's first word—the first thought that illumined him. When he said: 'Let there be light!' love was born. Everything he created was beautiful. He did not want to return a single one of his creations to nothingness. And love became the source of everything earthly and the sovereign of everything earthly. But all along its way are flowers and blood, flowers and blood!"

"Why blood?"

"You would like to see only flowers? That is not the way it happens in life. It does not happen without tribulations. Love must overcome and conquer them. And if love does not overcome life's tribulations, if it does not conquer them, then it was not the real love that Knut Hamsun writes about.''It does not happen without tribulations. Love must overcome and conquer them. And if love does not overcome life's tribulations, if it does not conquer them, then it was not the real love that Knut Hamsun writes about."

Then Nikolai Ivanovich read to me a story told by the old monk Wend about eternal love, about love until death; of how illness made the husband bedridden and disfigured, but his beloved wife subjected herself to a severe tribulation. In order to resemble her husband, who had lost all his hair due to the illness, she cut off her locks. Then the wife was stricken with paralysis and was unable to walk. She had to be pushed about in a wheelchair, and this was done by her husband who loved his wife more and more. In order to equalize the situation, he splashed sulfuric acid into his face thereby disfiguring himself with burns.

"Well, what do you think of such love?" Nikolai Ivanovich asked.

"Your Knut Hamsun tells tales! Why go out of your way to disfigure yourself? Why make yourself a leper? Why throw sulfuric acid into your face? Is it not possible to love without this?"

My answer amused Nikolai Ivanovich, and he explained to me that "his" Knut Hamsun used such means to express the power of love and its invariable proclivity for sacrifice. And he suddenly looked at me with sad and excited eyes and asked:

"Could you love a leper?"

I was taken aback. . . .

"Why do you say nothing? Why don't you answer?"

In my excitement, I asked naively, childishly:

"Love whom? You?"

"Yes of course me," he smiled confidently, joyfully, touched by the childish directness with which I still expressed my feelings.

I was on the verge of saying that I could love him (even though there was no need to use the future tense when everything was already in the present), when he said:

"No, don't. I'm afraid of the answer!"

More than once during the long years of suffering, I recalled the fateful question: "Could you love a leper?"

*   *   *

I will tell about the death of my father, because it has a direct bearing on my relations with Nikolai Ivanovich. We had grown accustomed to my father's morbid condition but nothing foreshadowed such a sudden end. On December 31, 1931, he insisted that I see in the New Year with young people. As a rule, I observed the New Year holiday with my parents. But this time I went to visit Stakh Ganetskii, who was the same age as I. No sooner had I stepped across the threshold of the Ganetskii apartment (Iakov Stanislavovich Ganetskii—a figure in the Russian and international revolutionary movement. Since 1917 he had worked in the People's Commissariat of Finance, the People's Commissariat of Foreign Trade, and the People's Commissariat of Foreign Affairs.—F. M.) than there was a telephone call from my father: "Come home at once, I am dying!" At home I was met with a situation that is difficult to imagine: Father, who usually moved about with difficulty ran through the apartment from room to room in a frenzy. What brought him into such a state remains a mystery to this very day. We suspected mental illness. We called Professor Kramer, the well-known neuro-pathologist (Vasilii Vasil 'evich Kramer—one of the founders of Soviet neurosurgery, the attending physician to Lenin in the last years of his illness—F. M.), who came promptly but did not find any mental deviations. The general practitioners' diagnosis was double pneumonia. Father died an agonizing death sitting upright in a chair—he could not breathe at all lying down. It was two weeks of torture. He died on January 14th. When he became gravely ill, Mother notified his closest friends. Rykov and his wife, Miliutin, and Kritsman came. Nikolai Ivanovich was on vacation in Nal 'chik. (I did not get the telegram off to him on time. He was late for the funeral.)

At this critical moment of farewell, Stalin telephoned and asked to speak to Larin. But Father was unable to pick up the receiver. "Pity," Stalin said, "I wanted to offer him a high-ranking post. . . ."

Father was conscious up to the final minute, and Mother informed him about Stalin's call. All those who were present were extremely surprised. Neither by virtue of his character nor by the state of his health could Father have been an official [rukovoditel ']. Nor had Larin and Stalin been close. The call came as the biggest surprise to Miliutin, because a short time earlier it was he who informed

Stalin that Larin was very ill and that he was probably even dying. "Can it be that he forgot?" Miliutin said, shrugging his shoulders in bewilderment.

Poskrebyshev (Stalin's assistant—F. M.) came, and Father asked Mother to see that Stalin received the folder containing the latest economic project.

Then Father turned to me. His question both excited and perplexed me. "Do you still love Nikolai Ivanovich?" he asked, knowing that we had not seen one another since March 1931. I was disturbed by the fact that I would have to answer this question in the presence of Poskrebyshev. I also did not want my answer to be at odds with Father's deathbed wish, which I did not know. But I could not lie and I answered in the affirmative. It seemed to me that Father was just about to say: "You must forget him. . . ." Instead, in a hollow, barely audible voice, he said: "It will be more interesting to live with Nikolai Ivanovich ten years than to spend a lifetime with someone else."

Father motioned with his hand for me to come still closer because his voice was becoming weaker and weaker, and he almost wheezed into my ear: "It is not enough to love Soviet power because you are living rather well as a result of its victory. You must be able to give your life for it, to shed your blood if necessary." With a great effort of will, he slightly raised the wrist of his right hand, which was clenched into a fist and which immediately fell lifelessly to his knee, and hoarsely exclaimed: "Swear that you will be able to do this!" I understood that I had to be prepared to give my life in the event of intervention against the Soviet Union. And I swore an oath. Father's last words were: "Scatter my ashes from an airplane" and "We shall be victorious."

*   *   *

Anna Mikhailovna spent the entire day of November 2, 1987, watching television. She listened to every word of the report read by the general secretary of the CPSU Central Committee at the ceremony devoted to the Seventieth Anniversary of the Great October Socialist Revolution. She was excited and nervous. She was waiting for something that was very important to her. It was important for many, she understood, but not more important than for her. When she heard Lenin's words that ". . . Bukharin . . . is justifiably considered the favorite of the entire party . . ." she sighed with satisfaction. This was the first time in fifty years that Bukharin's name had been mentioned in a positive context. There is nothing more joyous and understandable than the truth.

Anna Mikhailovna continued her reflections.

Nikolai Ivanovich was a complex man. It was impossible to predict precisely what could be expected of him. And he himself did not always foresee his own behavior. He was capable of rash actions. Political calculations were alien to him, and this hindered him as a politician.

Incidentally, Bukharin was capable of responding to unwarranted attacks sharply and even viciously. He was capable of attacking an enemy with the frenzied energy of his political temperament. At the same time, the keyboard of his spiritual strings was astonishingly, even painfully, sensitive. His nature, which developed in the stormy times in which he lived and played a considerable role in, took the emotional strain extremely hard because the "tolerance" was extremely low and his spiritual strings had snapped.

This character trait had negative consequences for the politician: he was not always able to win, even when he was right.

He also had the habit of capitulating on less important issues. At the First Congress of Soviet Writers, he begged the pardon of poets wounded by his critical remarks. These remarks on raising the level of poetic mastery, which had been made with the best of intentions, were just, and, generally speaking, there was no reason to apologize. When at the February–March Plenum of 1937 Bukharin followed Stalin's advice and asked the plenum's forgiveness for his hunger strike declared as a protest against the ridiculous accusations leveled against him, he also gave in to weakness.

This character trait—spiritual sensitivity and emotional oversaturation—frequently brought him to a hysterical condition. He cried readily. I would not say that he cried just on any occasion. The reasons were always serious. In connection with Lenin's death, I saw tears in the eyes of many of his comrades-in-arms, but only Bukharin could sob the way a woman sobs. He traveled through the Ukraine during collectivization and at the whistlestops saw crowds of children with stomachs distended from hunger. They begged for alms. Nikolai Ivanovich gave them all his cash. Upon his return to Moscow, he visited my father and described all this to him. He then exclaimed, "How can one still see such a thing ten years after the revolution?" and collapsed onto the divan, sobbing hysterically. Mother gave him tincture of valerian. When Bukharin learned that the October uprising in Moscow had not been as bloodless as in Petrograd and that approximately a thousand people had died, he began to sob.

The emotional strain made him physically lethargic. He was often ill. This surprisingly strong man, this athlete with the muscles of a wrestler, began wasting away in the grip of powerful nervous tension. His body was losing its resistance.

I do not mean, on the basis of what I have related, to give the impression that Nikolai Ivanovich was a "whining old woman." This was not the case. Emotional oversaturation was one of the facets of his rich but complex nature. At the same time, Bukharin was a revolutionary of great passion with an unbridled temperament. His revolutionary potential was enormous and demanded action. Nikolai Ivanovich advocated the revolutionary transformation of society and its humanization. He did not think this goal could be attained without changing human nature, without raising the cultural level of the lower strata, of those who were considered to be of "lower origin"—the workers and peasants. This characteristic may be considered somewhat banal, but it was precisely this idea that became his passionate, all-consuming dream and virtually the only goal of his social and political life. The new world, as he conceived it, had to be realized whatever it took; but in his opinion this in no way meant "no matter the cost" or at any price. Bukharin was always tormented by moral collisions. He also saw the tragic side of the idea that was so attractive to him. "Some of the gloomiest people have optimistic ideas. There are also happy pessimists." Ehrenburg wrote about Bukharin: "Bukharchik had an astonishingly whole nature. He wanted to make life over because he loved it."

*   *   *

Anna Mikhailovna answered my queries about Bukharin's everyday and home life, how he dressed, whether he was interested in or indifferent to material goods by describing several episodes.

Once, when Stalin was discussing Bukharin's scheduled trip to Paris, he noted:

"Your suit is worn, Nikolai. You mustn't go dressed like that. Get some decent clothes. . . ."

On the same day there was a telephone call from a tailor who worked for the People's Commissariat of Foreign Affairs who wanted to come as soon as possible to take his client's measurements. Nikolai Ivanovich told the tailor that he was very busy and to go ahead and make the suit without taking measurements. "How can it be done without taking measurements?" the tailor said in astonishment. "Believe me, Comrade Bukharin, no tailor has ever made a suit without taking measurements." Nikolai Ivanovich countered: "Take the measurements from an old suit."

But he forgot that such a solution to the problem was impossible, primarily because he was wearing his only old suit. If he gave his suit to the tailor, the newspaper editor (at that time Bukharin was the senior editor of *Izvestiia*— F. M.) would have to show up for work in his underwear. Bukharin found a minute for the tailor's visit. The new suit was tailored for him and he wore it to Paris and back. It was the same suit he was wearing when he was arrested.

Two months after her husband's arrest, Anna Mikhailovna and her son were moved out of the Kremlin to the Government House at Kamennyi Most, which Iurii Trifonov with the light hand of a writer called the "house on the embankment" and which by that time was already half in ruins. A bill for apartment rent was received. Since she had no money to make the payment and since the building belonged to the Central Executive Committee, Anna Mikhailovna wrote a short note to M. I. Kalinin: "Mikhail Ivanovich! The fascist intelligence service has not seen to the material needs of its hireling Nikolai Ivanovich Bukharin. I am unable to pay the rent. I am sending you the unpaid bill."

According to A. M. Larina, Bukharin never had any cash reserves. He donated the fees for his literary works to the party. He refused to accept pay for his work as editor of *Izvestiia*. He received pay that was due him from the USSR Academy of Sciences, of which he was an active member.

On more than one occasion, Nikolai Ivanovich borrowed money from N. N. Klykov, his driver.

*   *   *

Bukharin was popular. In this regard, I want to recall an episode that took place while we were at Teletskii Lake. Once, when Nikolai Ivanovich was talking with two scientists on ornithological topics and astonishing them with his knowledge, the door suddenly opened and an old Altai native entered the room. He looked attentively in all directions, trying to discern which of those present was Bukharin. The Altaian was wearing a quilted jacket, all in patches, and some kind of ragged footwear. In one hand, he carried a small sack and a parcel in the other.

"Is there something you want?" one of the ornithologists asked.

"My came to see thy," the Altaian said to the ornithologist wearing the broad-brimmed black felt hat, which evidently caused the visitor to suspect that he was Bukharin. According to his image, Bukharin necessarily had to wear a hat.

"Yes, to see thy," the Altaian repeated looking at the ornithologist. "I heard that she had arrived and that she was living in this hut."

He spoke exclusively using the feminine gender and was unfamiliar with declensions and conjugations.

"Well I am not the 'she' you want to see," the ornithologist laughed. "You guess where 'she' is!"

The Altaian was surprised. "Not she?" No one but the ornithologist was wearing a hat, and this discouraged him entirely. Thinking for a moment, he looked in the direction of the second ornithologist who was smoking a pipe and pointed at him.

"That's not 'she' either," said the ornithologist wearing the hat and he decided to help the Altaian native recognize Bukharin. There were still three men left, including the two guards.

"Look, there he is!" And the ornithologist wearing the hat nodded his head in the direction of Bukharin.

"Are you she?" the Altaian asked in surprise. "Is thy speaking the truth?"

Nikolai Ivanovich, who was wearing boots, a sportcoat, and a cap instead of a hat, and who was short, did not make the impression the Altaian had expected.

"Bukharin is tall and handsome but what is this?"

The laughter was deafening. The two guards laughed longest of all.

"Just why did you come to see me? I am not a bride and as you see I am not tall and handsome. It's a complete disappointment. . . ."

The Altaian did not know the meaning of "disappointment," but he understood everything about brides.

"My do not need a bride. My have a woman. She baked flatcakes for you." He handed Nikolai Ivanovich the small parcel that contained flatcakes that had been baked from first-class wheat flour, and, it must be said, masterfully. Nikolai

Ivanovich began handing them out to everyone present, which offended the Altaian.

"My woman baked only for thee. We have little flour."

"But why do I deserve such an honor?" Nikolai Ivanovich asked the Altaian.

"Why? My not understand."

"Why, I ask, did your woman bake flatcakes only for me?"

"My said: bake for Mister Bukharin because she loves people."

"*The* people," the ornithologist said.

"*The* people, *the* people. Yes, yes, yes," the Altaian said in confirmation.

"Well, how are you living on the collective farm now?" Nikolai Ivanovich asked.

"I would tell thee but there are many people here."

"Go ahead and talk, don't be afraid," Nikolai Ivanovich said.

"My said everything and so my you understand, how we live [sic]! I say many people. Cannot talk."

Having satisfied his curiosity, the Altaian made for the door. We all accompanied the visitor to the lakeshore where his homemade boat—a sawed-off section of a thick tree trunk with a hollowed-out section in which to sit—was tied up. The Altaian tied the bag of flour to his back and pushed off from the shore after saying farewell only to Nikolai Ivanovich:

"Be healthy, my dear one."

*   *   *

We touched on the topic of "Bukharin and Pasternak." We spoke about the beautiful assessment that Bukharin made of Boris Leonidovich's works in his report at the First Congress of Soviet Writers. We recalled the poet's "Waves," a poem dedicated to Nikolai Ivanovich:

He himself told about the thrall
Of things erected not just for an hour.
He gave an account of generations
That served a hundred years before us.

"He gave an account of generations . . ."—what a brilliant formulation, what a vivid image!

Anna Mikhailovna recalled the trying days before his arrest, when on one occasion the papers had reported that the Bukharin case had been terminated (this was one more trap set by Stalin). Nikolai Ivanovich received a telegram of congratulation from Romain Rolland and a letter of congratulation from Pasternak, which deeply moved him. Later, in the second half of January 1937, after Bukharin's signature as senior editor disappeared from Izvestiia, *Boris Pasternak once again sent Bukharin a short letter, which strangely was not intercepted.*

In the letter, he wrote: "no power can make me believe that you are guilty of treason." He also expressed his dismay over the events taking place in the nation. Upon receiving this letter, Nikolai Ivanovich was moved by the poet's courage but was exceedingly concerned over his future fate.

*   *   *

At my request, Anna Mikhailovna described the last months and days of her life with Bukharin. It was a tragic, complicated time when Stalin revealed the full extent of the despotic essence of his character. He did so especially toward Bukharin. The events developed as follows. Anna Mikhailovna believes that the last months of Bukharin's life up to his arrest were the time when preparations for his physical extermination became obvious and that the countdown started with the trial of Zinov'ev and Kamenev, i.e., in August 1936.

Three and one-half months prior to this, Nikolai Ivanovich and his wife had returned from Paris, where he and two comrades had unsuccessfully tried to purchase for the Soviet Union the archives of Karl Marx and other documents that were offered for sale by German Social Democrats after Hitler came to power. The disappointment he felt after the unsuccessful trip was short-lived and, after his talk with Stalin and the latter's words—"Don't worry, Nikolai, we'll get the archives, they'll give in. . . ."—forgotten, Nikolai Ivanovich went back to living his normal life, working as editor of Izvestiia, *at the USSR Academy of Sciences, and on the new, so-called Stalin Constitution.*

Their son was born, and the forty-seven-year-old father was in a state of joyful excitement. A month after the birth of their son, the family went to Skhodnia where the Izvestiia *dacha was located. Nikolai Ivanovich went on leave in the beginning of August and journeyed to the Pamirs for the purpose of realizing his age-old dream of hunting in the mountains. He was accompanied on his trip by Semen Liandres (who was incidentally the father of the writer Iulian Semenov), a publishing house worker. Shortly before his departure, Bukharin told his wife of the arrest of his friend G. Ia. Sokol'nikov. He assumed that the arrest was most likely connected with the overexpenditure of state funds when the latter was the ambassador in London.*

Bukharin went far into the wilds of the Pamirs where there were neither postal nor telegraphic communications. Anna Mikhailovna impatiently waited two weeks for news. And unexpected, terrible news was forthcoming on 19 August. She read it in the newspapers, which reported the beginning of the trial of the so-called united Trotskyite center and that many of its participants had given testimony against Bukharin. Soon thereafter the procuracy announced the commencement of the investigation of persons mentioned at the trial, including her husband. There were angry resolutions at meetings: "Put them on trial. . . ." A report of Tomskii's suicide was published.

There was no word from Bukharin. But he finally flew in from Tashkent and accidently learned about the deadly menace that hovered over him. He feared that he might be arrested right at the airport. Upon seeing his wife, he exclaimed: "If I could have foreseen such an eventuality, I would have run from you into cannon fire." "Where to?" the depressed driver asked. Bukharin feverishly explained that he had to go someplace where he could make a private telephone call to Stalin. "Let come what may," he decided and went to his apartment in the Kremlin. The guard on duty saluted the member of the Central Executive Committee as if everything were normal. "Perhaps he doesn't read the papers," Bukharin thought to himself. He made an urgent telephone call, from his own apartment, to Stalin. A strange voice answered: "Iosif Vissarionovich is in Sochi." "In Sochi at such a time?" Bukharin thought to himself. Bukharin considered it pointless to call Iagoda. He did not realize that Iagoda was living out his last days in the NKVD and that he would be judged together with Bukharin in the same trial. So it was that he sat days on end in his office waiting for a call. Once Karl Radek, a member of Izvestiia's editorial collegium, called to inquire why Bukharin was absent from work. Nikolai Ivanovich replied: "until a retraction of the scurrilous libel is published, I won't set foot inside the editorial offices." In the middle of September, he had another telephone call requesting his appearance at the Central Committee for a talk with Kaganovich. "Why Kaganovich?" Bukharin wondered. He decided to call Stalin again and once more received the same reply: "Iosif Vissarionovich is in Sochi." When he returned from the Central Committee, he related something unimaginable: they had arranged a face-to-face confrontation between him and Sokol'nikov, a childhood friend, and the latter had given testimony against him and lied. On September 10, 1936, the newspapers carried an announcement by the USSR Procuracy that the investigation in the case against Bukharin and Rykov had been terminated—a tactical step by Stalin to prove the "objectivity" of the investigation. Bukharin was by nature credulous and Stalin, exploiting this character trait, pretended to love him while preparing the destruction of Nikolai Ivanovich behind his back. This point was confirmed once again on November 7, when, using the ticket sent him from the editorial office, he decided to observe the nineteenth anniversary of the October Revolution in Red Square together with his wife. Their place in the stands, Anna Mikhailovna recalls, was very close to the Mausoleum, and Stalin noticed Bukharin. Anna Mikhailovna suddenly saw that a sentry was heading toward them, and she became very agitated. She thought he was coming to arrest Bukharin. But the sentry saluted and said that Comrade Stalin requested Nikolai Ivanovich to ascend the Mausoleum, that his place was there. Bukharin ascended the Mausoleum but did not have a chance to talk to Stalin because the latter was standing at a distance and was the first to leave. The ensuing month was relatively quiet. Nikolai Ivanovich did not rule out the possibility that he might even be invited to resume his work in the editorial office. He tried to keep busy: he read, excerpted German books, worked on a large article on the ideology of fascism. By the end of November, the nervous tension was so great that he was no longer able to work. He dashed about the apartment like one who was at the end of his tether. He kept looking at Izvestiia to see if another editor was signing the paper. But the signature was still the same: Senior Editor N. Bukharin. He shrugged his shoulders in bewilderment. In the first days of December, he was informed by telephone that a plenum of the Central Committee was to be convened. Nothing was said about the agenda. Upon returning home from the plenum, Bukharin said to his wife:

"Let me introduce myself! Your humble servant is a traitor, a terrorist, and a conspirator." Ezhov, the new people's commissar of the NKVD, fiercely attacked Bukharin, accusing him of being the organizer of a conspiracy and an accomplice in Kirov's murder. "Shut up!" Bukharin shouted right in the auditorium when he heard such a monstrous and absurd accusation. His nerves could not stand it: "Shut up!" Everyone turned around, but no one said a word. Stalin said that there was no need to hurry with the decision but that the investigation was to be continued. Bukharin went up to Stalin and said that the work of the NKVD should be checked up on and asked whether the slanderous testimony could be believed. Stalin replied that no one was denying Bukharin's past services and then went to the side, not desiring to continue the conversation. Nikolai Ivanovich spent most of the next three agonizing months in a small room in his apartment, in what was formerly Stalin's bedroom (at his request, Bukharin exchanged apartments with Stalin after the tragic death of his wife Nadezhda Allilueva). The objectives of the so-called investigation and the person behind it became increasingly apparent. Nevertheless, Bukharin sent Stalin several letters addressed to "Dear Koba," arguing his innocence and denying the libel. Anna Mikhailovna was almost always at her husband's side with the exception of those minutes when she attended to their child. Once she saw Nikolai Ivanovich holding a pistol in his hand and she screamed. "Don't worry, I couldn't do it," Nikolai Ivanovich said. "I thought of how it would be if you saw me not breathing. . . ." He got up, took a volume of Verhaeren down from the shelf, and read: "The blood oozes from the deathly torments of evenings crucified by the purpleness of the dawn from the distant skies. . . . The blood of sad evenings oozes from the swamps, the blood of silent evenings, and in the flat watery mirror everywhere is the crimson blood of crucified evenings. . . ." Shut up in in his apartment, Bukharin grew thinner, aged, and his red beard turned gray. Another summons: a face-to-face confrontation with Radek. Another useless explanation to Stalin. Everything led to the denouement of a long-contemplated sentence, even though in relatively lucid moments Nikolai Ivanovich hoped for life. "And what if they send me to hell and beyond? Will you go with me Anyuta?" Once Anna Mikhailovna went out into the street to get a breath of fresh air and bumped into Sergo Ordzhonikidze. He stopped. Anna Mikhailovna was speechless. Sergo looked at her with such sorrowful eyes that she cannot forget the look to this very day. Then he shook her hand and said two words: "Be strong!" He climbed into his car and drove off. Ordzhonikidze's days were numbered. Bukharin decided to write to Sergo. In his

letter, he asked that his family be taken care of in the event of his arrest. Again the doorbell rang: a notification of the convening of a plenum of the Central Committee of the All-Union Communist Party (Bolsheviks). This was the "February-March" plenum. Agenda: the question of Bukharin and Rykov. Bukharin decided not to attend the plenum and declared a hunger strike. In a letter to the Politburo: "I declare a hunger strike to the death as a protest against the absurd accusations. . . ." The doorbell rings: three men with an order to evict him from the Kremlin. Telephone call from Stalin: "What is the matter with you, Nikolai? People come to evict you from the Kremlin and you tell them to go to hell." On February 16, Bukharin said goodbye to his father, to Nadezhda Mikhailovna, his first wife, who was also later subjected to repression (she had written a letter to Stalin saying that she did not wish to be a member of the party at a time when monstrous, unsubstantiated accusations were being made against Bukharin and had returned her party card to him personally), to his child, and began his hunger strike. He became pale and haggard and had shadows under his eyes. He asked for a sip of water. Anna Mikhailovna squeezed an orange into it—just a drop. The glass went flying into the corner: "You are forcing me to deceive the plenum, I will not deceive the party." Anna Mikhailovna felt that she was dying with her husband. In a soft, faint voice: "A wonderful moon sails over the river. . . ." He sang one couplet. . . . The death of Sergo. . . . Bukharin's verses: "He was pure granite. . . ."

The plenum is postponed because of Ordzhonikidze's funeral. Then a new agenda with the question of N. Bukharin's anti-party behavior in connection with his announced hunger strike. The decision is made: to go to the plenum, not to terminate the hunger strike. Only two ventured to shake Bukharin's hand: Uborevich and Akulov, a secretary of the Central Executive Committee. Stalin: "Against whom did you declare the hunger strike, Nikolai? The Central Committee of the party? Ask the plenum's forgiveness. . . ." "Why should I if you are planning to expel me from the party?" "No one is going to expel you from the party." Bukharin believed Koba one more time and asked the forgiveness of the plenum of the Central Committee.

*   *   *

I remember as if it were yesterday the evening of that fateful day of February 27, 1937, when Poskrebyshev, Stalin's secretary, telephoned and stated that Bukharin had to appear at the plenum.

The tragic moment of parting cannot be conveyed. The spiritual pain that lives to this very day in my soul cannot be described. Nikolai Ivanovich fell to his knees before me and with tears in his eyes begged forgiveness for ruining my life. He begged me to bring up our son as a Bolshevik. "He must be a Bolshevik," he repeated. He begged me to fight for his exoneration and not to forget a single line in his testamentary letter.

"The situation will change. It will definitely change," he stated. "You are young and will live to see it. Swear that you will preserve my letter in your memory."

I swore. He rose from the floor, put his arms around me and kissed me, and said in a trembling voice:

"See that you don't become embittered, Anyutka. There are lamentable misprints in history, but the truth triumphs!"

Agitated, I felt a chill inside me. We understood that we were parting forever.

Nikolai Ivanovich put on his leather jacket, a cap with earflaps, and headed for the door.

"See that you don't tell lies about yourself, Nikolai!" This is all I could say to him in farewell.

He had a sacred belief in the ideals of the October Revolution and wanted me to view this black page in history as temporary, hoping for purification and justice. This is why he willed me to rear our son as a Bolshevik. It was for this reason that he addressed his letter "To the Future Generation of Party Leaders."

The letter was written by Bukharin several days before his arrest. He was psychologically prepared to be arrested and to have to part with his life. He had finally lost all hope of being exonerated and decided to declare his nonparticipation in the crimes to future generations and to request his posthumous rehabilitation in the party. At that time I was twenty-three years old, and Nikolai Ivanovich was convinced that I would live until such time as I could submit the letter to the Central Committee. Being certain that his letter would be confiscated in the event of a search and fearing that I would be subjected to repressions if it were found, Nikolai Ivanovich asked me to commit it to memory. He read his letter to me many times and many times I repeated after him the lines he had written. And how angry he became when I made a mistake! When he was finally convinced that I had firmly and finally memorized the content of the letter, he destroyed the handwritten text.

He wrote his last message to the people, to the party, on a small table on which Lenin's letters to him lay—he reread them all in his last days. . . .

Publication prepared by Feliks Medvedev

Khrushchev

Strokes on a Political Portrait

FEDOR BURLATSKII

Khrushchev and his time. One of the indisputably important and perhaps most complex periods in our history. Important because it has things in common with the nation's present restructuring, with the present democratization process. Complex because it concerns a decade that was initially called "glorious" but was subsequently condemned as a period of voluntarism and subjectivism. It was the time of the Twentieth and Twenty-second Party congresses, which became the reflection of bitter political struggles that determined the nation's new course. Under N. S. Khrushchev, the first steps were taken toward restoring Leninist principles and purifying socialist ideals. This was also the time when the transition from the Cold War to peaceful coexistence began and a window was once again opened to the modern world. At this sharp juncture in history, society took in a full breath of the air of renewal and choked, . . . whether from an excess or a shortage of oxygen.

For a long, a very long time, people were not wont to speak about these stormy years. It was as if someone's hand had ripped a whole chapter from our chronicle. For almost twenty years, Khrushchev's name was taboo. But life takes its own course. In M. S. Gorbachev's report on the seventieth anniversary of the October Revolution, we heard the long awaited word about that period: what had been done then, what had been underdone, or what had been done the wrong way. [We heard] about what had survived to the eighties and what had been eroded and lost during the period of stagnation.

Wherein lay the complexity and contradictoriness of the individual with whom we connect one of the turning points of contemporary history? Without attempting to answer all of the important questions [about Khrushchev], I merely want to share my personal reminiscences and certain judgments

Russian text © 1988 by "Literaturnaia gazeta," published by the USSR Union of Writers. "Khrushchev: Shtrikhi k politicheskomu portretu," *Literaturnaia gazeta*, February 24, 1988, no. 8 (5178). Translated by Arlo Schultz.

The author worked in the central apparatus of the party in the 1960s and accompanied N. S. Khrushchev on many of the latter's trips abroad.

winnowed by the comparison of today and yesterday.

Who finds whom—does history find the individual or does the individual find history? I have reflected a great deal and have written about such dissimilar and contradictory twentieth-century political figures as Lenin and Stalin, Deng Xiaoping and Mao Zedong. . . . But I still cannot answer my own question on this score with complete clarity.

Recall Bulgakov: is it possible to speak of the freedom of human will if we are not in a position to have a plan for at least a thousand years? Or: a brick does not accidently fall on a person's head—everything is predetermined. The belief in predetermination was also suggested to us in our youth. Of course it was given a scientific name: conformity to the laws of nature. Perhaps this came from Hegel: everything real is rational. This means that what has been was to have been. And only with age and experience did we begin to understand the multivariance of history. It contains different possibilities. Different figures participate in the game. The pawn reaches the final row and becomes a queen. Or the queen falls into a trap and becomes the pawn's victim. . . . Here I am not going to discuss the problem of "the people and the individual." Ultimately, the social and moral impulses emanating from the people determine the face of the era. But in certain periods, an enormous imprint can also be made upon it by a major historical figure. Whatever the case, one thing is obvious: a political figure, especially a national leader, is not only the instrument of history but also has a most direct influence on events and fate.

Why was it that after Stalin, Khrushchev, and not someone else, took over the leadership of the nation? It appeared that Stalin had done everything to "purge" the party of all his enemies—real and imaginary, "right" and "left." In the fifties, one of his aphorisms—"If you have a person, you have a problem. No person, no problem"—was widely repeated. The result would seem to be that the most faithful, the most reliable remained among the living. How did Stalin fail to discern in Khrushchev the person who would dig the grave of his personality cult?

In his final years, shortly before his end, Stalin brought about the disgrace of Molotov and Mikoian, and was probably preparing for them the same fate as that of other leaders who were destroyed with their aid and support. The creation at the Nineteenth Congress of the Presidium of the CPSU Central Committee, which replaced the structurally narrower Politburo, was a step in the direction of "picking off" the next generation of comrades-in-arms who had stayed around too long. But Stalin, paradoxically, "did not sin" against Khrushchev.

Was this the blindness of old age? Probably not. Niccolo Machiavelli, that brilliant exposer of tyranny, once said: "Brutus could have become Caesar if he had played the fool." Khrushchev somehow managed to pretend to be an entirely tame person without any special ambitions. It is said that during the long winter gatherings in the evening at the nearby cottage in Kuntsevo, where the boss had lived the last thirty years, Khrushchev had danced the horak [a Ukrainian folk dance]. At that time, he went around dressed in a Ukrainian *kosovorotka* [shirt with the collar fastening at the side] and acted like a "real cossack" with no pretensions to power, and one who was ready to carry out the will of others. But even then Khrushchev harbored protest deep within himself. And this poured forth the day after Stalin died.

Khrushchev came to power by accident and not by accident. Not by accident because he expressed the direction in the party that under other conditions would probably have been advocated by such largely dissimilar figures as Dzerzhinskii, Bukharin, Rykov, Rudzutak, and Kirov. They were advocates of developing the NEP and of democratization and were opposed to forcible measures in industry and agriculture and especially in culture. Despite Stalin's fierce repressions, this current never died. In this sense, it was natural that Khrushchev came to power.

But, of course, there was also a large element of chance. If Malenkov had reached an accord with Beria, if the "Stalinist guard" had closed ranks in 1953 and not in June 1957, Khrushchev would not have become the leader. Our history itself could have taken a slightly different channel. It is difficult for us to make this assumption, but in fact everything hung by a thread.

Nevertheless, history made the right choice. It was the answer to the real problems in our life. The increasingly impoverished and essentially half-destroyed countryside, technologically backward industry, the most acute shortage of housing, the population's low living standard, the millions incarcerated in prisons and camps, the country's isolation from the outside world—all this required a new policy and radical change. And Khrushchev came along—just like that!—as the people's hope, as a precursor of the new era.

At that time we were deeply aroused by everything connected with the Twentieth Congress of the CPSU. How did Khrushchev dare to deliver such a report on Stalin, knowing that the great majority of delegates would be opposed to the exposures? Where did he find such courage and such confidence in his ultimate success? This was one of the rarest cases in history where a political leader put his personal power and even his life on the line in the name of higher social goals. There was not a single figure in the post-Stalin leadership who would have dared deliver such a report on the cult of personality. In my view, Khrushchev and only Khrushchev—so bold, so emotional, and, in many respects, so rash—could have done this. One had to have Khrushchev's nature—desperation to the point of adventurism; one had to go through the tests of suffering, fear, and time-serving in order to risk such a step. His own evaluation of the moment in a meeting with foreign visitors is unquestionably interesting:

> I am frequently asked how I dared to deliver that report at the Twentieth Congress. How many years we had believed this person! We had supported him. We had created the cult. And suddenly to take such a risk. . . . But since they had elected me First Secretary, I had to, I was obligated, to tell the truth. To tell the truth about the past no matter what it cost me, no matter the risk. It

was Lenin who taught us that the party that is unafraid to tell the truth will never perish. We learned lessons from the past and would like the other fraternal parties to draw lessons as well. Then our common victory will be secure.

But, of course, there was more to it than the sense of duty that the First Secretary talked about. I had occasion to hear Khrushchev's reminiscences about Stalin more than once. These were long reminiscence-monologues that often went on for many hours, resembling a conversation with himself, with his conscience. He was deeply wounded by Stalinism. There was a mixture of everything here: the mystical fear of Stalin, who was capable of destroying any person for a single wrong step, gesture, or look; and the horror that the blood of innocent people was being spilled. Here also was the feeling of personal guilt and the protest that had welled up over the decades and burst forth like steam from a boiler. . . . Typical in this respect was a speech he made at a Kremlin banquet for participants in the Conference of Representatives of Communist and Workers' Parties in 1960.

The older generation, naturally, remembers this characteristic personality, but the younger generation has probably never even seen portraits of him. At that time he was already over sixty, but he looked very strong, lively, and cheerful to the point of naughtiness. His broad face, his double chins, his enormous bald head, his large turned-up nose, and protruding ears could belong to any peasant from a central Russian village. This impression of being a man of the common people was strengthened by his stout, plump figure and his long hands that were almost continuously gesticulating. And only his eyes, his tiny, shrewd gray-blue eyes that variously radiated kindness, imperiousness, and anger, only his eyes, I repeat, showed him to be a thoroughly political man who had gone through fire and water and was capable of making the most abrupt changes.

This is just how I saw him then and how I remember him, even though I was most of all attracted by his speech. What I had heard was repeated to me in my presence in another, more intimate atmosphere, in the presence of only a few people. But what is surprising is that he repeated this story almost word for word.

When Stalin died, we members of the Central Committee leadership went to his nearby cottage in Kuntsevo. He lay on a couch. There were no doctors near him. In the last months of his life Stalin rarely summoned doctors. He was afraid of them. Maybe Beria had frightened him, or perhaps he personally believed that doctors were conspiring against him and other leaders. At that time he was treated by a major on the security staff who had at one time been a veterinarian's assistant. It was he who telephoned us to announce Stalin's death. . . .

We stood beside the dead body, saying almost nothing, each one thinking his own thoughts. Then we started going our separate ways, driving away by twos. The first to leave were Malenkov and Beria, next—Molotov and Kaganovich. It was then that Mikoian said to me: "Beria has gone to Moscow to take power."

And I said to him: "None of us can feel secure as long as that swine is around."
And it was then firmly imprinted in my mind that the first thing that had to be
done was to remove Beria. But how to begin the conversation with other
leaders? . . .

The time came and I began to visit Presidium members one at a time. The
most dangerous of all was my visit to Malenkov. After all, he had been friends
with Lavrentii. Well, I went to him and talked about this and that and said that as
long as he is at liberty and holds the security organs in his hands, all our hands
are tied. And we never know what he is going to do next. And, I said, for some
reason he is moving a special division up to Moscow.
And I have to give Georgii his due. He supported me on this point and
overstepped his personal relations. He was evidently afraid of his own friend.

Malenkov was then the chairman of the Council of Ministers and conducted
sessions of the Presidium of the Central Committee. In a word, he had something to lose, but finally he said: "Yes, that is true. It is unavoidable. Only it
must be done in such a way that things don't get worse."

"I next visited Voroshilov. There sat Klim Efremovich," [Khrushchev] recalled. "I had to talk with him for a long time. He was very worried that
everything might go wrong."

"Am I not speaking the truth, Klim?"
"Yes, yes, you are," Kliment Efremovich agreed loudly. "Only there must
be no war," he added for some reason not entirely to the point.

"Well, as regards war, that is a separate matter," the First [Secretary] noted.

So I went then to Kaganovich, laid it all out before him, and he asked me:
"Whose side is the majority on? Who is for whom?" But when I spoke to him
about all the others, he also agreed.

And so I came to the session. Everyone took their seats, but Beria was not
there. Well, I thought, he has found out. It will cost us our heads. No one knows
where we will be tomorrow. But then he showed up carrying a briefcase. My
first thought was "What does he have there?" I also had something in store for
such a contingency. . . .

Here the speaker slapped the right pocket of his wide jacket and continued.

Beria sat down and asked, "Well, what's on the agenda for today? Why are we
holding this surprise meeting?" I nudged Malenkov with my foot and whis-

pered, "Open the meeting and give me the floor." He turned pale. I looked at him and saw that he was unable to open his mouth. Then I jumped to my feet and said: "There is one question on the agenda. The anti-party, divisive activity of imperialist agent Beria. There is a proposal to expel him from the Presidium, from the Central Committee, to expel him from the party, and to try him in a military court. Who is in favor?" I was the first to raise my hand. All the others followed suit. Beria turned green and reached for his briefcase. But I knocked the briefcase away with my hand and picked it up. "You're joking," I said. "Don't try it!" I myself pressed the button. Two officers from Moskalenko's military garrison ran into the room (I had arranged this with them beforehand). I gave them the order: "Take this skunk, this traitor to the Motherland away to the proper place." Here, Beria began muttering something or other. . . . But this was the hero who hauled others over the coals and stood them up against the wall. You know the rest.

"And so I want to drink," at this point he picked up a glass, "to such a thing never being repeated anytime, anywhere. We ourselves washed away this dirty spot and will do everything to guarantee against such phenomena ever happening again in the future. 1 want to assure you, comrades, that we will create such guarantees and that we will all walk forward together toward the summit of communism!"

I had occasion to hear how Khrushchev understood his role in our country's history. He said that Lenin had gone down in history as the organizer of the revolution, the founder of the party and the state; that Stalin, despite his mistakes, had been the man who secured the victory in the bloody war against fascism. Khrushchev believed his own role was to give peace and well-being to the Soviet people. He spoke of this more than once as being his principal goal. The problem was, however, that he did not have a clear conception of the means for attaining these goals. Despite all his radicalism, he rejected the criticism of Palmiro Togliatti, who advised looking for the roots of the cult of personality in the existing system, even though Togliatti naturally did not suggest that socialism be replaced by capitalism but was thinking of actual change in the regime of personal power.

The thirst for newness and an active nature were Khrushchev's integral traits: the broad program for restoring agriculture, the creation of the regional economic councils [sovnarkhozy], intensive housing construction, the technical retooling of industry. The passport system in the countryside, pension security for peasants, higher pay for low-income categories of working people. Drafting of the new party program, modernizing fixed capital, changing the principles and style of relations with the West. And even the famous corn saga. . . . The search for his own ways and solutions and his irrepressible social temperament were reflected in everything. Khrushchev's time was permeated with spiritual renewal even though this process bore the eternal stamp of the past era and was contradictory and frequently rather ineffective.

It was Khrushchev who at his own initiative advanced the task of creating firm guarantees against a return of the cult of personality. He waged an uncompromising struggle for this within the country and in the international arena regardless of the possible cost such a struggle could have to relations with countries belonging to the socialist camp.

Khrushchev attached principal significance to the ideological side of things, to the necessity of exposing the cult of personality all the way, and of telling the truth about the crimes of the thirties and other periods. But, unfortunately, this was only half of the truth, the incomplete truth. From the very beginning, Khrushchev stumbled on the problem of personal responsibility because there were many in the party who knew about the role he had personally played in persecuting cadres both in the Ukraine and in the Moscow party organization. If he did not tell the truth about himself, he could not tell the whole truth about others. Therefore, information about the responsibility of various individuals, to say nothing about the responsibility of Stalin himself, for the crimes that had been committed, was one-sided and often ambiguous. It depended on the immediate political situation. For example, while exposing Molotov and Kaganovich at the Twentieth Congress of the CPSU for beatings administered to cadres in the thirties, Khrushchev said nothing about the participation of Mikoian, who was subsequently to become his staunch ally. When speaking of the thirties, Khrushchev carefully skirted the period of collectivization, since he was personally involved in the excesses of that time.

Khrushchev tried to develop a consensus among all the members of the Presidium of the Central Committee on Stalin's cult. At his direction, all representatives of the leadership who spoke at the Twenty-second Congress had to indicate where they stood on this question. However, as it turned out, after the congress many of them who had fulminated against the cult easily revised their positions and essentially returned to their old views.

The question of [establishing] guarantees against a repetition of the cult of personality and its negative consequences anywhere took up a large part of the process of preparing the party program. I had occasion to participate in this work. I remember, in particular, the drafting of a note to the Presidium of the CPSU Central Committee on the transition from the dictatorship of the proletariat to a state of all the people, which was of great significance since the stereotype of the dictatorship of the proletariat was used in the thirties to justify the repressions. The note was sent by O. V. Kuusinen, and it caused a furor among many leaders. I was sitting in Kuusinen's office when one of the members of the leadership screamed at him over the telephone: "How could you encroach upon Leninism's holy of holies—the dictatorship of the proletariat?" Only as a result of the energetic support of Khrushchev did this idea become part of the party program.

One of the practical conclusions, if one speaks about the past, was also

associated with the more consistent implementation of the principle of replacement of cadres. This question generated the most disputes. The idea of cadre
rotation, which emanated directly from the First Secretary, underwent a number
of modifications. At least ten different formulations were developed to give it
adequate embodiment. Khrushchev wanted to create at least some guarantees
against the excessive concentration of power in the same hands, against leaders
staying in office too long, against the aging of cadres at all levels starting with the
primary organizations and ending with the upper echelon. The part that concerned the primary organization did not generate any particular disputes. But
there was basic disagreement regarding rotation at the top. Even he, with all his
authority, stubbornness and persistence, had to retreat on this point.

The initial draft limited tenure in the top leadership to a maximum of two
terms. This evoked a storm of protest from the younger leaders. They considered
it extremely unfair that representatives of the older generation, who had already
been in power for a long time, were trying to deny them the same opportunity. In
the next draft, two terms were replaced by three, but this draft was also rejected.
In the final text, the whole idea of creating a new procedure for cadre replacement
was no longer recognizable.

The problem of [establishing] guarantees against the regime of personal power
encountered an insurmountable obstacle—the limited political sophistication of
Khrushchev personally and the erstwhile generation of leaders. This was a largely
patriarchal culture that was drawn from traditional ideas of forms of leadership
within the framework of the peasant household. Paternalism, intervention in any
affairs and relations, infallibility of the patriarch, intolerance of other opinions—
all this comprised the typical set of centuries-old ideas concerning power in
Russia.

The events that took place at the subsequent June Plenum of 1957 were
illustrative in this respect. As is known, representatives of the old "Stalin guard"
at the plenum tried to oust Khrushchev on the basis of a so-called "arithmetic
majority." A vote at the Presidium of the CPSU Central Committee removed him
from his post as First Secretary. However, this decision was overturned thanks to
the efforts of Khrushchev's ardent supporters. Marshal G. K. Zhukov played an
enormous role in crushing the Stalinists. During a session of the Presidium of the
CPSU Central Committee at that time, Zhukov reportedly hurled a historic
phrase in the face of those people: "The army is opposed to this decision, and not
a single tank is going to move without my order." This phrase ultimately cost him
his political career.

Soon after the June Plenum, Khrushchev secured the removal of Zhukov from
the Presidium of the CPSU Central Committee and from his post as USSR
Minister of Defense. This was done in the spirit that was traditional for that
time—when the marshal was abroad on an official trip. He was not given even the
minimum opportunity to explain, just as no explanation was given to the party and

the people for the banishment of the most distinguished military leader of the Great Patriotic War. And the reason for banishment was once again traditional: the fear of a strong person.

A certain weakness of Khrushchev as leader also played a part in this. He had long had the reputation of a person who was "down at the heels." It was noticed during his period in Kiev and later in Moscow that he had difficulty picking the right people. He was always more inclined to rely on flatterers than on true supporters of his reforms. Therefore, he surrounded himself with people, such as N. Podgornyi, for example, who took one look at him and were ready to carry out any of his orders. He was little impressed by strong, self-sufficient personalities and people with an independent character. Khrushchev had too much self-confidence to seek support in others. This became one of the reasons for his fall. People who did not basically share his reformist views and considered him a manifestation of incompetence or even eccentricity got rid of him at the first convenient opportunity.

To be sure, at one time Khrushchev was drawn to the more intellectual cadres in the party apparatus. Suffice it to recall his attitude toward D. Shepilov, whom he moved up to the posts of secretary of the Central Committee and minister of foreign affairs. However, Shepilov's behavior at the June 1957 Plenum of the CPSU Central Committee turned Khrushchev against "intellectuals" for good.

Khrushchev's hastiness and penchant for interfering in any matter and resolving questions quickly played part in his relations with the intelligentsia. Here he was frequently the plaything of advisers who were not disinterested or who were even covert opponents preparing his fall. I well remember that his visit to an art exhibit at the Manege was inspired by a specially prepared briefing memo. It said little about problems in art but cited real or contrived statements by writers and artists about Khrushchev, calling him "Ivan the Fool on the Throne," a "cornball," and a "windbag." Wound up to the limit, Khrushchev set out for the Manege with the idea of giving the artists a dressing-down. In this way, Khrushchev's secret enemies inveigled him into the Pasternak affair, managed through him to get A. Nesmeianov removed as president of the USSR Academy of Sciences at the behest of Lysenko, and set him at odds with many representatives of literature, art, and science.

The ancients said that a man goes farthest when he does not know where he is going. But then his steps are meandering and uneven—he lurches forward and falls backward. That is how many of Khrushchev's economic and social reforms looked.

Economic policy remained one of his most vulnerable areas. He saw the task to lie essentially in changing the methods of economic management at the apparatus level—in the State Planning Committee [*Gosplan*], in the regional economic councils [*sovnarkhozy*], and ministries, but he did not understand the significance of deep structural reforms that would change the working and living conditions of the actual producers—workers, peasants, and the science and engineering intelligentsia.

This approach had a particularly adverse effect on the preparation of the Party Program of 1961. The biggest dispute was generated by the proposal to include in the program numerical materials on the economic development of the nation and the course of economic competition in the world arena. A. Zasiad 'ko, chairman of the State Scientific-Economic Council of the USSR Council of Ministers, brought this proposal to one of the sessions. The report he delivered within the framework of the working group struck all participants as frivolous and unscientific. Statistics on the growth rates of the Soviet and U.S. economies were in fact taken from thin air—they represented wishful thinking.

But Zasiad 'ko himself easily put an end to the discussion that had heated up. He opened the first page of a roughly eighty-page typewritten, blue-covered book and pointed to the resolution "Include in Program" and the familiar signature of the First Secretary. Thus, the party program included statistics indicating that we would overtake and surpass the United States in the eighties. The aspirations were high but, as the saying goes, in addition to ambition you also need ammunition.

Of course, we must try to imagine the general spirit of the time. Even though there were few who believed Zasiad 'ko's figures, we were enthusiastic and optimistic. And these feelings were not based on thin air. Everyone was convinced that the adopted program would usher in major structural reforms and changes—otherwise why adopt and approve the new program? And even the departure of Khrushchev did not stop them. In September 1965, a plenum of the CPSU Central Committee on the economic reform was nevertheless held. However, Brezhnev's negative attitude toward it brought the preceding era to naught.

Matters were still worse with respect to reforms in the state administration and the structure of the party leadership. Who "palmed off" on Khrushchev the idea of dividing the party regional and district committees into industrial and agricultural committees? I am intuitively convinced that this was done not without malicious intent in order to undermine his authority among party leaders once and for all.

These mistakes were blamed on Khrushchev at the October 1964 Plenum of the CPSU Central Committee, at which there was a strange symbiosis of political forces—from advocates of consistent movement along the lines of the Twentieth Congress to conservatives and closet Stalinists, everyone united against the leader who had "advanced" the majority of them. Subsequent events left no doubt that Khrushchev was removed not so much for voluntarism as for the irrepressible thirst for change. The slogan of "stability," which was advanced by his successors, inhibited urgent reforms for a long time to come. The very word "reform," like the mention of the Twentieth Congress, became dangerous and cost many advocates of this course their political careers.

Time has not dispelled the innumerable myths surrounding Khrushchev's name both at home and abroad. Sharing the fate of other reformers, Khrushchev did not win objective recognition in the mass Psyche. The people that had at one time elevated Ivan the Terrible and condemned Boris Godunov could not accept after Stalin a public figure devoid of mystical magic, who was earthy and sinful, who was prone to err. During the "thaw," Sholokhov ascribed the phrase to Stalin: "Of course there was a cult, but there was also a personality." This was a hidden reproach to Khrushchev as a less significant figure. It was a reproach to a person who, like Shakespeare's Claudius, took the crown that was lying under people's feet.

At the same time, Western countries placed Nikita Khrushchev on equal footing with John Kennedy and Pope John XXIII and attributed the deterioriation of the international climate in the late sixties to the departure of these leaders from the political arena for various reasons. Many books analyzed "Khrushchevism" as a new current in socialism.

It could be said that a prophet is not without honor save in his own country, but this would not be precise. The question is deeper and more complex. Ernst Neizvestnyi, with whom Khrushchev conducted his cavalry polemic at the Manege, probably came closer than others to evaluating Khrushchev. The monument created by the sculptor on Khrushchev's tomb—a bronze head on a background of white and black marble—aptly symbolized the contradictoriness of the "thaw" and its main hero.

Now, almost a quarter century later, when we compare the period before and after October 1964, we see the strength and weakness of Khrushchev. His main service was that he destroyed Stalin's cult of personality. This proved to be irreversible despite all the cowardly attempts to restore the pedestal to the previous place. They were unsuccessful. Thus, the plowing went sufficiently deep, and the plowman's toil was not in vain. A courageous decision to rehabilitate many Communists and non-Communists who had been subject to repressions and who had been executed during the cult of personality restored justice, truth, and honor in the life of the party and the state. A powerful blow, even though not effective and skillful, was struck against supercentralism, red tape, and bureaucratic conceit.

During Khrushchev's time, the foundation was laid for a breakthrough in the development of agriculture: procurement prices were raised, the tax burden was dramatically reduced, and new technologies were used. For all its shortcomings, the development of the virgin lands played its part in supplying the population with food. Khrushchev tried to orient the countryside toward foreign experience and the first agricultural revolution. And even his passion for corn was dictated by good intentions, even though it was also accompanied by naive extremes. A bad role was also played by gigantomania in the countryside and the curtailment of private plots.

I remind you that major advances in science and technology that made it possible to create the foundation for attaining strategic parity are linked to Khrushchev's name. Everyone can still see the meeting between Iurii Gagarin and Khrushchev that marked our country's entry into space. Peaceful coexistence, which was proclaimed at the Twentieth CPSU Congress, after the shock of the Caribbean crisis [i.e., the Cuban missile crisis], became an increasingly strong platform for agreements and businesslike compromises with the West. The roots of the Helsinki Final Act, which confirmed the borders drawn by World War II and declared a new international relations, economic cooperation, and the exchange of information, ideas and people, date back to the time of the "thaw."

At that time, the party addressed many social problems. The population's living standard in town and country has been gradually raised. However, the planned economic and social reforms did not come to fruition. The tragic events in Hungary in 1956 dealt a serious blow to reformers' hopes. But a considerable role was played by Nikita Sergeevich's lack of concern over problems of theory and political strategy. "Khrushchevism" as a conception did not modernize socialism. To use the image the First Secretary's principal opponent, Mao Zedong, was so fond of, Khrushchev walked on two feet: the one boldly strode into the new era while the other was hopelessly stuck in the mire of the past.

Answering the question of why the 1960 reforms were unsuccessful, it can be said that conservative forces were able to win out over the reformists because the management apparatus and, indeed, all of society were not yet ready for radical change. But this answer is too general. We must try to ascertain what it was the conservatives capitalized on.

In my view, one of the mistakes was that the search for conceptualizing reforms and ways of implementing them was based on traditional administrative and even bureaucratic methods. Khrushchev customarily ordered ministries and departments, i.e., the very administrative apparatus that was to curb its own power, to "critique" various problems—economic, cultural, and political. The apparatus, however, always found a way to protect itself against oversight through direct, indirect, and ambiguous decisions.

More or less successful reforms both in socialist countries and in capitalist countries have usually been articulated by a group of specialists, for the most part scientists and public figures, working under the direction of the nation's leader. So it has been, for example, in Hungary, Yugoslavia, and China. In Japan, I have met with Professor Ohita, who is considered the author of the Japanese "miracle." The reform plan in the Federal Republic of Germany was formulated by Professor Erhard, who subsequently became the nation's chancellor.

Second, "the people were silent." Now, on the basis of the experience of *glasnost'*, we can see with particular clarity how little was done to inform the people about the past, about real problems, about projected decisions, to say nothing about involving the broadest social strata in the struggle for the reforms. How often did I hear at that time: "In what way was Khrushchev better than Stalin? Under Stalin, there was order, bureaucrats were imprisoned, and prices were reduced." It was no accident that after the October Plenum of the CPSU

Central Committee, almost all of society breathed a sigh of relief and hoped for changes for the better.

And the final lesson. It concerns Khrushchev himself. He was a man who had a natural political acumen, who was bold and active, and who did not resist the temptation to glorify himself. "Our Nikita Sergeevich!" Was this not the beginning of the fall of the acknowledged fighter against the cult? Bores drowned him in a sea of flattery and adulation, receiving high awards, bonuses, and ranks in return. And it is not by chance that the worse things went in the country, the louder and more triumphant was the chorus of bores and flatterers about the successes of the "great decade."

*   *   *

The ancients said, "A man's character determines his destiny." Nikita Khrushchev became the victim of his own character and not only of his milieu. Hastiness, rashness, and emotionality were his insuperable qualities.

One of Khrushchev's assistants told me about an astonishing conversation that took place between his chief and Winston Churchill. This was during the visit of Khrushchev and Bulganin to England in 1956. He recalled that they met with Churchill at a reception at the Soviet embassy This is what the old British lion said: "Mr. Khrushchev, you are undertaking major reforms. And that is good! I would only like to advise you not to be too hasty. It is not easy to negotiate an abyss in two jumps. You might fall in." I would venture to add on my own: nor can the abyss be negotiated when you do not know which side you are planning to jump to.

Part Five

SOVIET HISTORIANS RESPOND

That fundamental change had come to the Soviet historical profession as a result of the ferment that took place during 1987 is reflected in a roundtable discussion convened in January 1988 by A. A. Iskenderov, the newly appointed editor of the premier Soviet history journal, *Voprosy istorii* (Problems of History). The publication of the proceedings of the remarkable discussion, the highlights of which are published here, agitated Soviet historians as well as the journal's readers.

The very names of the historians brought together by the editorial office of *Voprosy istorii* signaled to those in the know that the roundtable would be lively and candid. Some of the participants are well-known mavericks whose careers had been compromised in one way or another during the past two decades. Most of them command respect at home and abroad. All but a few are considered by their colleagues in the Soviet Union to be historians of integrity.

Addressing the fact that the Soviet historical profession had lost its credibility as well as the interest of its readers, those historians assembled by Editor Iskenderov spoke frankly about their discipline's shortcomings. In particular, they criticized "vulgar patriotism" in historical writing and the distortion of ethnic relations, suggesting that the latter played no small role in the nationality conflicts that have erupted recently. Academician B. A. Rybakov, who for years dominated the field of ancient Russian history, came under fire for his faulty scholarship, imperious behavior, and intrusive monopoly on publishing. Several respected speakers underscored the sterility of Soviet historical writing. They raised an emotional plea for history with alternatives, for history that would eschew the unsatisfactory practices of the past and that would once again excite readers.

More importantly, speakers also addressed the reasons for the unsound state of the profession. Here they directed their criticisms at the lingering influence of the personality cult and the Stalinist *Short Course* on scholarship, and on the fact that political leaders had and still have scholarly authority. Participants in the roundtable demanded establishment of an autonomous profession, insisting that all the archives be opened and that access to them be simplified. P. V. Volobuev, one of the mavericks alluded to earlier, got to the heart of the matter by raising the "moral question," chastising the profession for its failure to treat the most basic issue of good and evil in its work. The speakers agreed that the influence of the *Short Course*, restricted access to source materials, and avoidance of moral judgments have produced an insipid history with "blank spots," a history of wooden, passionless heroes, a history that is largely dishonest. Not surprisingly, discussion of the impoverishment of Soviet textbooks raised the issue of the popularity of publicists who have captured the imaginations of readers as well as the popularity of writers of historical fiction such as V. Pikul'.

When all is said and done, and when placed within the broader context of the startling events taking place in the Soviet Union today, as this anthology goes to press, the roundtable discussion demonstrates that the reformers have not only gained the ascendancy by 1988, but have also gone far in their quest to set up an autonomous discipline with professional standards. Critics of the ferment are growing more and more silent. The need to include moral judgments in history is now clearly recognized as essential. Although it remains to be seen how the moral dimension will ultimately reshape this party science that by definition is not neutral, it is hard to imagine topics that cannot be treated openly in a sophisticated, professional manner. Compared with the state of the profession before 1985, the Soviet historical discipline has become unrecognizable. It is also taking the first critical steps in becoming part of a broader international community.

Historical Science under Conditions of Restructuring

A Roundtable Discussion

On 8 January of this year, in the editorial offices of the journal *Voprosy istorii*, an exchange of opinions took place, during which the state of and prospects for developing the historical sciences along the lines of *perestroika* were discussed. Questions connected with determining the role and place of historical science in the profound transformations taking place in the life of Soviet society were reviewed. . . .

Published below, in somewhat shortened form, are the participants' remarks. The meeting was opened by A. A. Iskenderov, editor-in-chief of the journal and corresponding member of the USSR Academy of Sciences.

A. A. Iskenderov: *History and society*

. . . At present, historical science is living through a difficult period. It is encountering a rather contradictory situation in which, on the one hand, there is unusually intense public interest in history, especially of our own country. On the other, the prestige of historical works is sharply declining, and they are more and more frequently coming under criticism. How do we resolve this contradiction? To what degree do the present forms of organization of the scholarly process, the methods of administration, and the very character of historical research respond to [society's] growing demands? By what paths and means can we make it possible for historical science to meet fully its enormous social duty? All these are not idle questions; they acutely agitate the public, which wants to know the truth about our history.

Current among a significant portion of the population are ideas about many extremely complex questions relating to our history. Unfortunately, these develop not so much as a result of familiarity with the works of professional historians,

Russian text © 1988 by "Pravda" Publishers. "Kruglyi stol": Istoricheskaia nauka v usloviiakh perestroiki," *Voprosy istorii*, no. 3, 1988, pp. 3–57 (excerpts). Translated by Stephen P. Dunn. The complete text of the Roundtable appears in the Spring 1989 issue of *Soviet Studies in History* (vol. 27, no. 4).

but rather as a result of highly disputable versions, assessments, and ideas advanced by the creators of certain belletristic works and films, as well as by authors of articles and materials which the mass media have lately been publishing in great quantity. Historians themselves are primarily to blame for this because they have failed to respond actively enough to the interest in history that is now being manifested in our society. Further, they sometimes adopt a temporizing position, drawing away from the debate that is having increasingly wide public repercussions.

In the ''stagnant'' years, there flowed from the pens of historians, frankly speaking, dull works that remained silent about, and often consciously distorted, historical truth; they lacked original thoughts and conceptions, and instead of profound analysis of little-studied, acute problems, they thrust upon the reader ready-made sociological formulas that failed to present the genuine content of historical processes in all their enormous variety and contradiction. All this gave birth to dogmatism and conservatism in historical thinking and led to the appearance of ''blank spots'' in history, impoverishing it, depopulating it, making it uninteresting and empty. But perhaps most alarming of all was that this sanitized history seemed to be in conflict with society: the living connection between periods of time was broken; the present and the future were deprived of historical continuity and roots, without which reliable prospects for progress in the economy and in cultural and intellectual spheres are lost.

Of course, we cannot agree with all the critical remarks and assessments that have been uttered in the press and are directed at the present state of historical science. Moreover, one could reproach some authors for their unjustified haste and excessive emotionalism in posing and interpreting serious historical problems, including crucial events in our history. Profound understanding of historical processes, their thorough analysis and rethinking do not allow for hullabaloo and sensationalism. At the same time, new assessments and reevaluations of some state and political figures are sometimes based not on new documentary material but on subjective inferences, making the solution of problems difficult, and replacing one extreme for another. Our attention is drawn to historians who pose as champions of historical truth and who claim that practically the only genuine fighters for the renewal of our historical consciousness are those who, in fact, completely reject the history of Soviet society, insisting, essentially, on a ''destructive conception.'' With this approach to our own history, one could only write it anew.

The new stage into which perestroika has entered demands of historians serious and constructive effort, real steps toward creating honest and truthful historical works marked by a responsible attitude toward our past, present, and future. We are all, apparently, agreed that perestroika in historical science is so far spreading slowly and has not yielded the desired results. This is explained, in my view, not only by the fact that we have failed to work out a clear-cut, integrated, well-considered conception of perestroika in the field of historical science that embraces all the links of a complex research mechanism. The point is that we have not yet genuinely treated history as a science. For the most part, perestroika has taken hold only in the organizational-administrative sphere; it has not profoundly affected the scholarly process itself or radically changed its character. But perestroika in historical science primarily means new ideas and conceptions, new approaches and assessments, new scholarly directions, and new works written in the spirit of the times and responding to the demands from our society for growth.

It is important to dig deep and uncover, objectively, the causes that, in their time, gave rise to stagnant phenomena and negative tendencies in historical science, causes that are rooted both in the science itself and the organization of the research process, and in the political and ideological situation that existed until recently in this country. Such an analysis has not yet been carried through to the end. . . .

In this connection, I would like to draw the attention of the participants in the present meeting to the following group of questions.

The first is the problem of man, or the human factor, in history. However strange it may seem, historical works, especially those on the history of the Soviet period, assigned the poorest and most colorless descriptions to people, the *narod*—the decisive force in history. We literally forgot the famous words of the founders of scientific communism to the effect that history must be viewed from two sides—as the history of nature and the history of people. And "both these sides are indissolubly connected; as long as people exist, the history of nature and the history of people will depend on each other." Karl Marx wrote that society is "the product of the interaction of people."[1] It is the demonstration of this interaction that is missing from historical research. People, historical personalities, are in second or even third place, or simply crowded out. Tons of products produced, millions of kilowatts of electric power generated, thousands of kilometers of railroad tracks laid pushed man with his vital problems and ideals into the background. . . .

The inattentiveness to man is shown by the fact that in our works there are almost no data about Soviet people who perished during the famine of 1932–33 and in the years of repression, etc. If there are data, they are incomplete or inexact. It is characteristic that there are no published data about our losses in a single one of the major battles fought during the Great Patriotic War. To this day there are no exact, completely reliable data about those who perished during the siege of Leningrad. Contradictory data are cited in the literature. . . .

The second problem I would like to cite is the study of ethnic relations, both in the historical aspect and at the contemporary stage. In spite of the fact that there have been quite a few works published on this theme, the problem of ethnic relations has not been given genuine, deep and serious treatment. As it turned out, these issues were treated as anniversary themes, and therefore they were described solemnly, in ceremonial and basically laudatory style. Here, perhaps more than in any other branch of historical literature, complacency ruled, and this resulted in serious, negative phenomena. If we speak of *glasnost'* in historical science, it was most of all lacking in the treatment of these issues.

Now the question of historical education and training is very pressing. It is no secret that in recent years the level of historical education in this country has fallen sharply. Moreover, the very character of the study of and training in history has changed. Here, as in many historical works, ready sociological outlines and scholastic theorizing increasingly crowded out history, with all its complexities, variety, interesting personalities, etc. Engels once said, not without irony, that "the materialist understanding of history, too, now has a multitude of friends for which it serves as an excuse *not* to study history."[2] Probably everyone involved in teaching or inculcating history should reflect on these words.

In conclusion, are we not forgetting at times that historical science never was and is not neutral? It always was and remains a party science. Behind all historical theories, behind any of its moral, religious, political, and sociological constructions stood and stand the interests of some class or one or another social group. The clash of ideas in the field of historiography is, in essence, nothing other than a struggle for the minds of hundreds and hundreds of millions of people throughout the world, for the confirmation in their consciousness of objective scientific ideas regarding the historical development of human society. This has been true in the past and especially most recently. Therefore, we must not allow an erosion of the ideological and political bases on which historical science has stood and always will stand. . . .

The success of scientifically-argued criticism will be more significant the more concrete and differentiated our approach to various currents of non-Marxist historical thought becomes. This demands a more attentive attitude to those of its representatives who, in definite if extremely limited measure, reflect the new trends connected with the social progress of humanity and the struggle for its survival. . . .

Of course, we would like to hear critical remarks from you addressed to the journal *Voprosy istorii*, advice and suggestions which would help it significantly to improve its work and to make the journal more interesting, responding to the high intellectual needs of the contemporary reader.

M. P. Kim: *Look to the future, remembering the experience of the past*

For more than two years the party has been elaborating the conception of perestroika—a complex system of theoretical conclusions and positions, strategic programmatic ideas. . . .

Unfortunately, historians cannot yet say that they have thought through and implemented perestroika on the historical front. In some measure this can be explained by the fact that our profession is oriented toward the past, toward events that are removed from the present by a temporal framework. But the necessity of restructuring historical science, of creating a new system of views about the history of our Fatherland is sensed more strongly with each passing day. The swifter the practical movement and the more grandiose its tasks on the path to the future, the more important it is to remember the stages of the struggle already traversed as well as past achievements, to know history and to take account of its experience. Turning to the past is useful and necessary. But while doing this we must not look only at the past, with our backs to the present and the future. In this position we will not move forward. The past should be behind us, but we will constantly refer to it in order to draw out the lessons of accumulated experience. I am a specialist on the contemporary history of the USSR and wish to share some thoughts about the condition of and prospects for its study.

Lenin's postulate remains valid: for a scientific formulation of the theory of contemporary historical processes and the problems of the foreseeable future we must rely on a thorough analysis of present-day reality and a sophisticated study of historical experience. It is quite understandable why the Communist party demands of historians new interpretations of history in general and that of Soviet society in particular.

. . . The general task is now clear—to write the truth, to explain it correctly and in an objective, scientific manner, to study and to tell readers what was, and how it was, and to correct our disjunctions, mistakes and miscalculations.

It is necessary to reveal the questions historians consciously bypassed, left in the shade, outside of research, and we must correct what we have omitted in the field of theoretical generalizations and evaluations. Our misfortune is that in the study of history and the development of historical science we did not consistently use Lenin's theoretical heritage. We did not develop it in a genuinely creative fashion. We are familiar with the now widely asserted accusation against historians that they for many years played but a single role—commentators on authoritative utterances and evaluations, without disputing them or discussing them, but accepting them dogmatically. In admitting the truth of this accusation, we need to explain why this happened. There existed a tradition by which the leaders of the party disposed of enormous scholarly authority to go along with their political authority. Marx, Engels, and Lenin not only were organizers and practitioners, but thinkers of genius. Their authority as theoreticians of socialism was unshakable. After the death of Lenin, the tradition of seeing in the leader of the party a great theoretician remained, but the leaders themselves changed and manifested theoretical weakness. They not only were unable to develop further Lenin's theoretical heritage, but frequently consigned to oblivion much of what was worked out by him. Not being outstanding theoreticians of Marxism-Leninism, they nevertheless were authoritative individuals, and their utterances became obligatory for all communists, including scholar-historians. It only remained to historians to comment on these utterances. Such a practice was widely followed, most of all when Stalin headed our party. He had a simplified idea of the historical process, depicting it schematically, abstractly.

In the period of the Stalin cult, in that ideological-political atmosphere when heterodoxy was cruelly persecuted, historians were obliged to comment on his utterances. And Stalin, as we know, claimed the role of theoretician in all fields of scientific thought, for example in the field of linguistics, although, from all indications, he understood little about it. In the field of biology, he defended the ideas of T. D. Lysenko. All this created an extremely unfavorable situation for social scientists, including historians. For example, Stalin's utterances negatively affected the problem of the periodization of socialism.

I have already spoken on the question of the scientifically optimal periodization of socialism in our country.* Periodization is not a mechanical division of the historical process, but its division in accordance with the qualitative characteristics of individual stages. The scientific periodization of the post-October period of our history has enormous significance not only for today, but for historical perspectives as well. In this field quite a few erroneous propositions have accumulated. In 1939 Stalin said that our country had entered the period of, or was within range of completing, the building of a socialist society and of the gradual transition to communism. This violated the Marxist-Leninist understanding of the development of socialism and communism by steps and stages. N. S. Khrushchev declared at the end of the 1950s that we had embarked on the period of the all-out construction of communism. This also was an expression of theoretical ignorance. The Third Program of the Party, adopted in 1961, which transferred the task of all-out construction of communism to the plane of immediate practical action, was obviously premature. The timetable for our country's transition to communism by 1980 was clearly utopian. Serious scholars, including historians, understood this; existing reality did not give them reason to agree that in the course of twenty years (from 1961 to 1980) we would build the bases for communism. However, you and I voted for these propositions in the program and theoretically justified and popularized them in our works. Such was the political situation then; that was how it was done in science.

. . . Socialism was consolidated in our country for the first time in the world. Theoretical generalizations about past experience in the development of humanity could not provide answers to many practical questions. We had an abstract idea about real socialism. We also evaluated the conditions of capitalism incorrectly, which also developed and in many fields outdistanced us—in engineering, technology, the natural sciences, medicine. We forgot that Lenin taught us to borrow everything valuable from capitalism. We began to compare ourselves not with capitalism, but with our own past, with the prerevolutionary period. But after all, Lenin more than once emphasized that socialism will win out over capitalism first of all with higher labor productivity.

---

*See *Soviet Studies in History*, vol. 27, no. 1 (Summer 1988), pp. 62–91, and pp. 57–59 of this anthology.—D. J. R.

Social scientists interpreted the development of socialism in our country in an oversimplified way. It was depicted as a greenhouse plant that had no internal contradictions or deficiencies. We attributed all our shortcomings only to legacies [of the past], but at the same time socialism itself gave birth to deficiencies, contradictions, and problems. The nationalities question, for example, in the form in which we inherited it from prerevolutionary Russia, has been solved in our country. But many problems demand further study and generalization. We must study more deeply the dialectics of the relationship between the national and the international; in historiography we still interpret the process of the cultural convergence of nations and peoples without the necessary depth. . . .

Iu. A. Poliakov: *The past must be not only described but also explained*

Perestroika in historical science is moving slowly, but I disagree with those who don't see any forward movement at all. The process of perestroika is complicated and multifaceted: in some areas it is proceeding quickly, in others slowly, and in some areas there is no movement whatsoever.

We may assert with confidence that historical science is not keeping up with the interest that the public has manifested in our country's past. We have observed an unprecedented interest in history in the last year. Against the background of this interest, our professional weaknesses stand out.

More than that, the gap between the growing interest in history and the inability of professional historians to satisfy it has become more marked. . . . Our activity is completely insufficient; it is not adequate to the growing attention being paid to history. The groundwork is probably being created now for fundamental new works on various problems of history, but their publication is a matter for the future.

How do I see the basic directions of perestroika in historical science? I would put democratization in first place. Perhaps this is one of the chief conditions for further successful growth in the field. Perestroika is proceeding slowly here. To be sure, some administrative changes have been observed in the Academy of Sciences; in particular, a new system for electing leaders of institutes and sectors is being introduced. It is in principle democratic, yet we have also seen its deficiencies. . . . Too often among us offices, titles, orders and medals, ranks and prizes are valued more highly than books, discoveries, ideas and—alas— abilities. Hierarchical fame is fine for an academic directory, but for real scholarship it means nothing. Academician and corresponding member—these are concepts by no means administrative, but scholarly. There has arisen—and the public has already drawn attention to it—a contradiction between the thousand academicians and corresponding members and the tens of thousands of scholars working in research institutes, which are primarily what move science. We must coordinate their activities, not counterpose them to each other, but in such a way that academicians and corresponding members become not administrative but scientific leaders. Scholarly prominence should be secured with scientific authority, not with a title.

The question of democratization is the first task of perestroika, including in the field of historical science. The creation of a different moral-psychological climate in the institutes and faculties is also connected with this. Perhaps this is the most difficult aspect of perestroika. I think that the harm brought by the Stalin period is felt even today in enormous measure. An atmosphere was created then, which, to put it mildly, was not the healthiest for the development of science. We unjustly forget 1949 when, under the banner of struggle against cosmopolitanism, representatives of the social sciences, including historians, were subjected to a mass "working-over." I am speaking of the moral and ethical side of this dressing-down. It was disgusting when a student dumped on a teacher, when colleagues did not simply criticize their friends, but flung at them political accusations like "a politically defective book," "a politically mistaken utterance," etc. Now we do not hang labels of that type, but our climate, our ethical ideas and relations, leave much to be desired.

Perestroika in historical science presupposes, in my view, rejection of some firmly rooted stereotypes. We must, for example, get away from singular points of view on events and figures from the past and become accustomed to the presence of diverse views and approaches that are based on Marxism-Leninism. We must learn to reflect the multidimensionality of history. History is past life— and the diversity and variety of life are endless. The researcher should attempt to show in his or her work all the complexity of human relationships. We have described the past in black-and-white tones at a time when we must show history as vital and polychromatic.

The organizational side of perestroika also is significant. Clearly, we should not forget about this. Zealous administrators will always be found for whom perestroika is primarily the creation of new subdivisions and the closing of old ones. They were and, apparently, will be fascinated by this. We must approach organizational matters cautiously, intelligently, seeing in them not a goal in itself but the means for solving scientific tasks . . . we should remember that moderation, expediency, and justification are required.

In the final analysis, the main thing is our work's content. In the field of the history of Soviet society, we are now at the stage of ascertaining the truth. The words "the truth of history" have now become one of the most popular expressions. We have departed from the truth in past years—not only as it applies to the history of Soviet society, but also to the history of antiquity, feudalism, and capitalism. . . . Now we verify the truth, sometimes with exaggeration and with an attempt at sensationalism. . . . We must not only verify those tragic and dramatic events in our past but also explain their causes and roots. This is rather complicated and difficult. In particular, the question of why economic and moral laws were broken, why the law itself was broken, demands not a simple, and still less not a formal answer, but a deep penetration into history. If we only list defects all the time without explaining them, quality turns into quantity. Much has already been said and written about "blank spots" and "black holes." The very important thought has been expressed that they are different and must be understood differently. Yes, that's so. "Blank spots" are the former "forbidden zones" and the biographies of persons who became victims of Stalinist repressions. They are also subjects which no one has forbidden but which are considered either unfashionable, uninteresting, or not very promising. They remain unstudied, or little studied, but over the years we see their significance more clearly. No one now disputes that history must be better "populated," to show its active people as fully and broadly as possible. But this is hard to do. The melancholy listing of persons, like a list of the residents of a large communal apartment, will not enliven or deepen our works. "To populate" history means to show three-dimensional people—political and military leaders, people in science and the arts—to show them in movement, their doubts and passions, victories and failures. And it is imperative to find ways to study and reveal the life of plain people with their thoughts and views. To show them not only on the tractor and at the workbench but in their everyday life.

I am alarmed by the attempt, undertaken mainly by some journalists, to depart from the class approach. There are, for example, arguments over the idea that society should be a unit, and that whoever disturbs this unity (thinking of prerevolutionary society) "acts in a criminal way." But what about the main Marxist thesis about the significance of the class struggle in history? Consciously or unconsciously, the class struggle is presented to the reader as a harmful phenomenon. That kind of judgment, it seems to me, can cause our science great harm. . . . At the same time, one must not contrast what is universally human to what is determined by class. Such human qualities as virtue, courage, honor, valor, compassion, are completely compatible with our socialist morals.

It is necessary to provide room for the growing roles played by scholarly journals, including *Voprosy istorii*. At least two circumstances in lesser measure dictate this necessity. First of all, with the rapid development of views, their collision, and the appearance of new assessments and new documents, a well-run scholarly journal has especially great significance. When many dilettantes have begun to dapple in history and at times have very actively propagandized views that are far from scientific but are eye-catching and superficially attractive, it is important both to promote and defend scientifically based theories just as actively.

In the second place, whole thematic areas are fading and losing their scientific value; new subject areas are appearing, and new scientific directions are opening up; research tasks are being posed in a new way. Under these conditions, it is absolutely necessary not only to illuminate what is new in what is being proclaimed from academic departments and discussion lecterns, but also to organize and unite scholars capable of creatively developing Marxist-Leninist science. This is the exalted duty of a scholarly journal. . . .

All of us hear complaints from readers that the majority of historical books and articles are dry, banal, and therefore uninteresting. These reprimands are justified. The style of a historical work is a reflection of professionalism. Poorly written works are an obstacle to the popularizing of historical knowledge among the general public and lower the prestige of historical science. The journal should take account of this criterion in evaluating published materials. It should repeat to authors the well-known adage: "Either you write better, or better you don't write. . . ."

I. Ia. Froianov: *Our priority must be morality**

I am pleased to take part in such a representative, responsible gathering, called, I think, to facilitate radical changes in historical science. Our "roundtable" must be seen as a step in that direction.

Much is being said now about the unfavorable situation in Soviet historical science: newspapers, established journals, radio and television are constantly reminding their readers and listeners about problems existing today in the field of history, particularly that of our own country. This is no accident. Modern Soviet historians owe a great debt to the people. I would even put it more pointedly: our opportunistic approach and destruction of historical truth and servility have undermined the once high prestige of our historical science. The time has come to restore it. This will be a very difficult matter for us. Perestroika, which has embraced the most important spheres of Soviet society, has not yet genuinely touched our discipline. Until now, we have in fact been discussing the tasks of perestroika at a time when we should already be solving them. However, in order to solve those tasks successfully, it is necessary to see the defects and barriers standing in the path of renewal. I think they are rooted in the past, and by no means in the last twenty years. Back in the thirties, an unfortunate situation arose as a consequence of which it became customary to tie the history of Russia to the history of the West European countries. Any lack of correspondence in the historical processes in Russia and in Western Europe was looked at not in Russia's favor and was described as the latter's lagging behind in its historical development. One would think that the history of peoples is a competition of runners, who take off simultaneously from one starting line. The foolishness of such an attitude is evident. Nevertheless, it remains in force even today, and it has brought and will continue to bring great harm to historical science. It has diluted the uniqueness of Russian history. It has made our history faceless, it has put historians themselves in an exceptionally complicated position, forcing them to seek artificial arguments, which could only negatively influence the moral basis of their work. Opportunism prevailed. History as a science in the true sense lost

---

*The Spring 1986 (vol. XXIV, no. 4) issue of *Soviet Studies in History* comprises translations of Froianov's works.—D. J. R.

its high calling. Let me cite an example that is close to my scholarly interests. To this day, the deviation of Rus' in the pre-Mongol period from "general European" developments is interpreted as a manifestation of its backwardness. Attempts by some researchers to show the uniqueness of Russia's historical past provokes the accusation, strange as it seems, of a lack of patriotism. Striving to exaggerate at any cost the antiquity of the history of their own country was a tribute to this "patriotism." Some influential historians, for example, Academician B. A. Rybakov, groundlessly date the origin of the Ancient Russian state 500 years before the formation of Kievan Rus' in the ninth century. Our ancestors built their state with great efforts, driving back the Scythians, the Sarmatians, the Huns, and the Avars, and finally, after 1,500 years of building it, they lived for 1,000 years under feudalism. Isn't this to the honor and glory of the Russian people?

And, most unfortunately, our press widely popularizes such pseudopatriotic conceptions. By this we are setting a dubious example for the historians of other peoples in our country, who are also attempting to make their ethnic history more ancient. As a result, the ground is being prepared for nationalism. The simple and clear idea expressed first by M. V. Lomonosov has been consigned to oblivion: "Not time but deeds make great peoples." As concerns great deeds, the Russian people and the other peoples of the country should not be concerned with them. The fact that Russia was the first in the world to achieve socialism says much, primarily that our people had those qualities, worked out in history, that allowed them to lead a movement of the peoples of the world in the struggle for renewal and social progress. All this demands a rethinking of the role of our country in the world historical process, beginning with antiquity and finishing with modern times. With such an approach, some contradictions between our history and that of Western Europe will no longer seem as backwardness but as something positive.

Another fact which takes on negative significance under present conditions is our adherence to the traditional problem areas of historical research, which in the final analysis led to stagnation in the study of history. . . .

We need to pay close attention to new directions in historical science, such as historical demography, historical psychology, historical sociology, and we need to be closely engaged with such important themes as, say, the position of women and children, the evolution of the family, crime, the development of literacy among the population, church questions, the history of entrepreneurship, the health of the population, nutrition, and a number of others. The working out of these problems will bring historical science closer to our country's needs today. Let me recall that Russian historical science in the nineteenth and the beginning of the twentieth century was notable for its connection with real life. Thus, the peasant question in the mid-nineteenth century brought forth massive research on the history of the Russian peasantry, the peasant commune, and questions having to do with land reform—research devoted to agrarian representation and self-government in the sixteenth and seventeenth centuries. Similar examples of the ties of historical research with contemporary times could be multiplied. Unfortunately, we have lost these wonderful traditions. Linking the past with the present, however, is quite necessary. For example, the history of the traditions of democratism, collectivism, and community of the Russian people has great significance for understanding present processes of democratization of Soviet society.

A study of reforms undertaken in Russia from the eighteenth through the early twentieth centuries could be conducted in the familiar context of contemporary perestroika; a study of the commune and economic management during serfdom in the context of the productivity of creative and routine work; a study of the antialcoholism movement in Russia in the nineteenth century in the context of the present antialcohol policy.

However, whatever problems we pose, no matter how we try to solve them, we will always depend on the morality of the scholar-historian. Can we consider moral a situation in which a point of view that does not coincide with the opinion of an "official" historian is considered dangerous? Is it moral when a negative assessment of some work, expressed in central publications, is looked at almost as a catastrophe, as well-nigh a political mistake by the author of the work, as testimony to incompetence?

What can we call the existence of "unshakable" truths preached by "generals" from history? It is no secret that cliquishness, attempts to monopolize scientific ideas, and claims resulting from this to a dominant position in science have been widespread among us. This is especially so of historical science in the Academy of Sciences, and was in no small degree facilitated by its perennial presumption of priority in regard to scholarship conducted in post-secondary, supposedly second-rate institutions. There is even such a concept picked up from military, in this case it's better to say garrison, terminology: "The Academy of Sciences is the general staff of science." Well, what has been written and pronounced by the "general staff" is correct. Therefore, when some sort of complicated historical situation arises, the Division of History of this "general staff" acts as supreme arbiter, and frequently as judge. We have yet to calculate how many scholarly careers have been ruined by this arbitration.

Recently, much has been said about coordinating scholarly research. However, coordination is often turned into an instrument by some people for asserting influence in science, and in the final analysis—for suppressing new ideas. . . . As a result, university scholarship was in a subordinate and even frustrating position. Therefore, optimal coordination of historical research can be assured only on the basis of parity between academic and university scholarship.

And one more thing. Soviet historical science is wrongly divorced from world historical science. The information the Soviet press provides about what is being done by foreign colleagues is scanty and extremely irregular. Soviet libraries, even in Moscow and Leningrad, receive a miniscule part of what is being published abroad. Because of old instructions, many innocuous publications land in special keeping, even bibliographies and reference books.

In conclusion, I would like to express several ideas in regard to the work of the journal *Voprosy istorii*. I will begin with the fact that in recent years the prestige of the journal has fallen markedly. This is all the more distressing because in another time (immediately after the Twentieth Congress), the journal *Voprosy istorii* was actively engaged in the process of sanitizing the spiritual and moral life of society, cleansing historical science of Stalinist dogmas. A. M. Pankratova and E. N. Burdzhalov did much in this regard. However, the subsequent slide of our society toward stagnation was, of course, reflected in the journal. Retreating from the positions taken after the Twentieth and Twenty-second congresses, *Voprosy istorii* became a mouthpiece for the views and ideas of conservative forces. Until very recently, it was practically impossible to publish in the journal articles reflecting nonstandard ideas and thoughts. More than that, the journal was a weapon for "the ideological working-over" of unwelcome scholars. The method of selecting members of the journal's editorial board was therefore no accident. The journal stopped supporting progressive and current trends in scholarship. This is understandable, since they were contrary to the views of some members of the editorial board. Reviewing for some historians was taken as complimentary, but for the others, as abusive.

In view of what has been said, there is a critical need to renew the editorial board on a democratic basis, so that representatives of the Academy of Sciences' institutes and of post-secondary sciences serve on it with equal rights, based on reasonable consideration of the geographical principle.

We should constantly inform readers about how perestroika is proceeding in the Division of History of the USSR Academy of Sciences, at the historical faculties of leading post-secondary institutions in the country, and we should publish unexpurgated reports of meetings of the division. I would even propose to introduce a rubric in the journal with the title, "Perestroika and Historical Science."

I believe that the situation in the journal office and the journal itself is changing, and that it will become the tribune of diverse scientific ideas and approaches.

E. V. Anisimov: *The journal should have its own position**

I think the fate of the journal *Voprosy istorii* is somewhat reminiscent of that of *Novyi mir*. After all, historians responded more or less immediately to the decisions of the Twentieth Congress of the CPSU. However, almost immediately a crushing blow was dealt to them by the resolution of 1957, regarding the

---

*The Summer 1989 (vol. 28, no. 1) issue of *Soviet Studies in History* features E. V. Anisimov's work.—D. J. R.

journal *Voprosy istorii*, from which A. M. Pankratova and E. N. Burdzhalov, and, as it subsequently turned out, all of historical science suffered. We must embark upon perestroika in the journal by returning to this resolution, which has never been repealed or forgotten. I think we need an article similar to the one which Iu. Burtin recently published about the old *Novyi mir*.[3] In my opinion, this is the most important civic and professional duty: to defend, although belatedly, the honor of worthy people and the journal itself, to talk openly about injustice.

On the whole, I think that perestroika in historical science is connected first of all with historiography, the history of our science. We must carry out in the pages of the journal as well as in other publications profound, systematic work on problems of Soviet historiography, without bypassing a single blank spot or kowtowing to the luster of prizes and awards, thereby laying the basis for historical knowledge. The problems are many. I, for example, would like to read an article in your journal about the beginning of the destruction of the school of M. N. Pokrovskii—an important event, a crucial one, as it turned out, in the history of our science. Such a theme as ''Stalin's Role in Historical Scholarship in the '30s-'50s and the Influence of His Ideas on Contemporary Scholarship'' is also important.

We were witnesses to how agitated our society became by publications regarding the hundredth anniversary of the birth of N. I. Vavilov. But isn't it our business to tell what was done in historical science in the '30s-'50s? I think the time has come to request from the authoritative organs that they release and publish materials about the ''academic affair'' of S. F. Platonov, E. V. Tarle, and B. A. Romanov in 1929-1930. In general, we should compile a dictionary of Soviet historians, as the Orientalists are doing, directing attention to those who perished in the war or were repressed. We must hurry, while people who remember this are still alive. My generation of the '40s can no longer tell students with certainty whose names were blackened out on the title pages of books and journals in the '30s, and whose introductions were barbarically torn from books. Materials for a biographical dictionary of Soviet historians must be published precisely in *Voprosy istorii*, to which many of them had contributed. We must touch on the shameful ''affair'' at Leningrad University in 1949, when the remnants of the tradition of the brilliant Petersburg historical school were finally destroyed. We have to write about all this without sensationalism, in a balanced way, but without reservation, with names and facts. This is exceptionally important for all of us.

Much is now being said about the need to create guarantees for perestroika. There are no laws that must not be changed. The only guarantee of democracy is glasnost', so that present and potential informers would have a hard time of it, and they would know that their names were known to everyone. This is necessary for the ''ethical hygiene'' of our cofraternity of scholars.

The journal should undertake a struggle against administrative high-handedness in science, against a monopoly on the right to the truth by one man, one institute, one current. The lamentable abusive episodes that occurred before our eyes should not be repeated. We know how for seven years I. Ia. Froianov's book on the historiography of Kievan Rus' was held up for publication, and with what methods his scholarly conceptions are being fought, calling him a non-Marxist and hanging other labels on him. To this day he has not been given the opportunity to respond to the murderous reviews by V. T. Pashuto, Iu. A. Limonov, and M. B. Sverdlov, which had by no means the innocent character of "scholarly" polemics.

I think that *Voprosy istorii* should rectify this mistake. Only then can the disputes about the genesis of feudalism in Ancient Rus' be productive, and only then will people not be afraid to express their opinion. The principle in scholarship of the right to respond to criticism is sacred, and it should be honored.

It is always difficult for me to answer neophytes or students who ask why Marx's book *Secret Diplomatic History of the Eighteenth Century* has not been published in the Soviet Union. It is not so simple to explain that the assessments of the foreign policy of tsarism and its nationality policy existing in scholarship are very far from genuine Marxist ones.

The well-known intensification of ethnic relations in contemporary society is connected with a serious lag in the scientific interpretation of the historical past of our country's peoples. That is, to put it more simply, the problem of empire in all its manifestations, beginning with the formation of the territory and ending with recurrences of imperial consciousness, should become the center of historians' research, along with other important problems. . . .

No problem was ever solved by silence, especially one so acute as the ethnic one. The Marxist-Leninist approach to it is the only way to avoid apologetics, the settling of old interethnic scores, and jingoism, and then it will not be necessary to choose the words "they won," "they united with," "they came into." It is no accident that as a consequence of our silence, a well-known novelist, describing the conquest of Central Asia, instructs the reader: "It is sinful to forget our ancestors, who in cruel deprivations created the great multinational state." There you have it!

We know from where and when the apology for empire arrived. The beginning was laid by Stalin's work "On Engels's Article 'The Foreign Policy of Tsarism'" [O stat'e Engel'sa "Vneshniaia politika russkogo tsarizma"], written in 1934 and published in 1941. This article "rectified" the Marxist view of the problem. Only by rejecting the consequences of this conception will we be able scientifically, i.e., without prejudice, to begin to unravel this complicated, complex national problem. Won't *Voprosy istorii* begin this important business by publishing Marx's book?

About the journal. It seems to me that we must not forget that the journal is a journal, the press, a living thing. It is inconceivable that articles lie unpublished from one and one-half to two years; we need efficiency and a variety of forms for transmitting material. . . . We've had enough sterile, neutral, cautious information about the Division of History's meetings. It happens that the scholarly community knows from rumors what scholarly disputes flare up there, and they stuff us, pardon me, with a society page taking up half the journal. The editorial board should take a position in these disputes.

It is necessary to respond both to the fundamental problems of history and to those agitating the public today, the current ones demanding the efficient intervention of the historian's authoritative voice. . . . There is noticeable interest in N. S. Khrushchev—let's have appropriate material about him.

It is necessary to renovate the journal's structure. I would like to see the following rubrics appear: "The Individual in History," "Portrait of a Historian," " 'Blank Spots' in History," etc. Let's have these rubrics for a few years and then publish them separately as *Little Library of* Voprosy istorii [Bibliotechka Voprosov istorii].

At present, when it is still too early to expect to see the fruits of the new approach, we must intensify, in the first place, the publication of our legacy: earlier banned, unpublished articles, letters, diaries. In a word, do what the thick journals are doing now.

In the second place, work with the reader. On the whole, we see very well that the publication that does not open its pages to readers, does not argue with them, does not work with them, is a living corpse.

The experience of today's journals shows that the reader is the journal's salvation. He brings materials and ideas, makes the demands of the public felt, and suggests corrections. Of course, we must not be attracted by the market, we must weigh everything; but still, not a single journal should work at a loss. You somehow forget, reading the contemporary *Voprosy istorii*, that it is still an organ of the Ministry of Post-Secondary Education. Perhaps [there should be] fewer society pages about the life of the division, fewer bibliographies, annotations of the contents of foreign journals, and more living material. The journal should become the reading material for students of historical faculties, their teacher, educator, and informant. But now not even professional historians read *Voprosy istorii*. . . .

N. I. Pavlenko: *Let's not turn history into arithmetic*

We are accustomed to thinking that the only trouble we have is with the history of Soviet society and that virtually everything is in order with other divisions of our history, at least before the seventeenth century. From my point of view, in research on the period of feudalism, things are by no means like that. Here, first of all, the sign of trouble is the conception that is acknowledged in general works, textbooks, and so forth. Of course, if we turn to the reports "Historical Science from Congress to Congress," we find in them the complete illusion that the situation is fine. There they use such phrases as "convincingly shown," "convincingly discovered," "clearly described," etc. But all this is far from reality.

This is an indication that the discipline is stagnant.

What does the present conception of the period of feudalism in our history rest on? Exaggerating somewhat, I'll say that it rests on two points—that something developed and something declined. At first feudalism developed. Then this process stopped, feudalism began to decline and capitalism developed. The working people lived poorly and their condition worsened. The class struggle was acute, and became more acute through the centuries. This representation had nothing to do with the facts. For example, our failed bourgeois-democratic revolution didn't occur until the twentieth century. All the same, the class struggle was acute.

What were the sources for this? The first was the *Short Course* [Kratkii kurs]. Remember that the *Short Course* said that historical science, if it wanted to be a true science, should primarily deal with the history of the producers of material goods, with the study and discovery of the laws of production. Moreover, there were a large number of forbidden themes. Who in the '30s–'50s could, without expecting much unpleasantness, study the Narodnik (populist) movement? Who could study the history of the church? This was a semiforbidden theme. Who could study the history of the bourgeoisie, the nobility, etc.?

The basic reason for the stagnation in the development of Soviet historical science is dogmatism. The *Short Course* had a decisive influence here. The desire of some historians to present Lenin as the author of the conception of Russian history in the feudal period is also felt. Dogmatism in this regard went so far that on the basis of statements made by Lenin, these researchers attempted to create a more or less harmonious system of normative propositions on the history of feudal Russia. Lenin, of course, was interested in questions of Russian history in the nineteenth century. Practical necessity forced him as a scholar to turn to this period in time. But can we, on this basis, speak of a system and of a conception?

I fully share I. Ia. Froianov's opinion about the erroneousness of the attempt that has become established in the literature to squeeze the history of our country at any cost into the stream of general Western European history. It is time to admit that our history is unique—that both our feudalism and estate-representative monarchy (if such existed) were special and the role of our state was unusual. Without taking account of the universality and special character of our history, we cannot satisfactorily explain such important phenomena as the origins of serfdom, the formation of absolutism, the development of estates, etc. Without taking account of the size of the territory, the climate, the fertility of the soil, the lack of sea routes that would reliably connect Russia with the West, we cannot explain the backwardness of the country's socioeconomic and cultural development. We cannot ascribe all this as previously to the Mongol-Tatar Yoke, for it was not the only reason for Russia's backwardness.

I would like to direct attention to the primary reason for dogmatic descriptions of the period of feudalism in our historiography. This entire current in historical science is based on the misuse of quotations. Dozens and perhaps hundreds of works are "fed" by some single statement by Lenin about the feudal period—

about capitalist-merchants, bourgeois connections, etc. Take this quotation away from the authors and they would be left without support. There are no relevant facts that could support their interpretation.

A second question. To whom does this conception belong that presently exists among us? I should say that I respect its creators because they were real scholars. I have in mind B. D. Grekov, S. V. Bakhrushin, V. I. Picheta, and Iu. V. Got'e. But they created this conception on the basis of the *Short Course,* during the late '30s. What they advanced, with small modifications, in fact exists even today. I classify among similar negative phenomena the attitude of these respected authors toward prerevolutionary historians. Essentially they, too, were trained before the revolution, then they gradually moved toward Marxism and became Marxists. But among their predecessors were such important scholars as S. M. Solov'ev and V. O. Kliuchevskii. Not everything they did was incorrect, but our historiography rejected them *in toto.* Finally, another important figure, G. V. Plekhanov, not a professional historian to be sure but one writing on a professional level about feudalism, was also rejected. . . .

Many historical works published in the country are not needed. They are written only to satisfy the needs of their authors to write dissertations for the degrees of Candidate and Doctor of Historical Sciences. How many monographs are published among us that, in their shallow and local character, give nothing to historical science? This is easily explicable, for the staffs of scientific institutions are inflated. Thus, in 1949 in the Institute of History, USSR Academy of Sciences, there were about 130 research associates. The Institute of History of the USSR and the Institute of World History created by it presently have several times more scholars. How can we correct this situation, how should perestroika proceed? There are, of course, no ready-made formulas, but I would like to direct attention to some issues. Iu. A. Poliakov spoke correctly about democratization. I think that democratization should first of all concern the institutions of the Academy. . . .

V. P. Danilov: *The third wave*

I will begin with the question of what the significance and essence of perestroika in historical scholarship are. In my view, the foundation of perestroika consists in the rebirth of the scientific character of the study of history as a whole, and the history of our own time in particular. This assertion does not mean that up to now the study of history has been unscholarly. But the most important characteristic of the past twenty years or so was not the study of a living historical process in its concreteness and contradictions, not independent interpretation of its movement from a position of developing Marxist-Leninist doctrine, but dogmatic exposition and confirmation with facts of speculative schemata, divorced from reality and considered obligatory. Scholarly work in the true sense of the term often encountered difficulties that were rarely overcome. Increasingly this work has fallen to "eccentrics" and "failures."

In the past, Soviet historical science experienced two stages of active and successful development: a genuine upsurge, distinguished by the posing of a wide range of problems and a relatively free discussion of them, and significant results. I am speaking of the '20s and the decade following the Twentieth Congress of the CPSU [1956—D. J. R.]. These were two mighty growth waves of scholarly knowledge in history. Under perestroika there is arising a new, third growth wave of scientific knowledge about the historical process. This will occur if the principles of scholarly activity are really implemented in the study of history, including free formulation of the problem, free expression of opinions and their discussion, and open and conscientious criticism as a means of struggle both against ideological "erosion" and against pseudoscience.

The critical evaluation of the condition of the social sciences given in the party press applies fully to historical science and in particular to the activity of scholarly institutions of history—research institutes, journals, etc. It is no accident that searches for new approaches and new solutions under conditions of nascent perestroika occurred outside the institutions concerned with history, even when research associates of these institutions took part in them. Historiography as a whole lagged behind those changes in the historical consciousness of society that came about at a new juncture in our public life. Even worse, it could neither prevent nor in any sense successfully dispel false historical conceptions appearing in great numbers at the outset of glasnost'. . . .

Very characteristic—and dangerous—is the fantasy from Boris Mozhaev's novel *Peasant Men and Women* [Muzhiki i baby], in which the responsibility for the violence to which peasants were subjected during the collectivization campaign of the winter of 1929–30 is transferred from the real culprits (Stalin and his immediate circle, especially Molotov and Kaganovich) to Trotsky, Zinov'ev, Kamenev, Iakovlev, and Kaminskii, of whom the first three from 1927 on had no relation whatsoever to the making of political decisions, and Trotsky was even deported from the USSR in February 1929. Perestroika did not give rise to these fantasies. Perestroika and glasnost' only made them manifest.

What is the source of the appearance and dissemination of false ideas about the past? The first cause of this, in my opinion, is the dissatisfaction of society with its present position and development. Dissatisfaction, particularly in conditions of ideological stagnation, often creates interest in the past in search of beauty and of enemies who destroyed this beauty. An idealization of the past, nostalgic feelings for such a situation, arise almost automatically. But false ideas and fantasies have roots that are connected with the development of historical scholarship. From the mid-'60s to the mid-'80s, Soviet historical science passed over the most pressing problems, which were arousing public interest. In general and as a whole, this twenty-year break in active research and discussion of contemporary history did not pass without a trace. In the public's historical consciousness, i.e., in the ideas of the public about its own past, large and dangerous gaps have arisen, and false connections and images have been formed.

Overcoming false ideas, in my view, is one of the primary tasks of historical science. The solution is by no means reducible to the dissemination of historical knowledge (although, of course, this is needed). Historians should turn to research on those problems which, until now, they have not bothered with at all, or studied formally, without going beyond the bounds of the outline which has been presented to them. In this connection I would like to direct attention to one common feature of all systems of widespread false ideas. They are all in one way or another connected with the possibility of choosing another path of development, with the question of alternatives, with the hope that if we had taken another road, "everything would be well." It is characteristic that attention is concentrated on three main problems: the Revolution, NEP, and collectivization. Each of them demands an answer about their meaning and significance, about the tasks that were posed and the results that were achieved. To put it another way, the public needs an analysis of historical alternatives. . . .

There is always the problem of choosing a concrete method for realizing one or another historical process, the choice of paths, forms, and times for solving one or another task objectively facing the public. . . . History presents people with the possibility of a choice of paths and means for further development (within the bounds of definite objective conditions) and therefore demands of the historian an analysis and evaluation not only of the existing variant, but of the variants that did not come to pass. Otherwise history would acquire some sort of mystical character, and the study of it would lose meaning.

The present acuteness of the problem of historical alternatives does not surprise me. Our country was the first socialist country; it overcame unprecedented difficulties and bore enormous sacrifices. The question of the choice of Russia's socialist path should be at researchers' center of attention.

The special interest of the public is now being drawn to the question of alternative solutions at the end of the '20s and the beginning of the '30s. They are all connected, in the final analysis, with the choice of paths for the socialist transformation of agriculture, and more concretely with how to form cooperatives from peasant farms. The economic reconstruction that has begun in the country, the wide use in this connection of family and individual brigades, and also of various forms of cooperatives bring us back to the NEP and the process of forming cooperatives among peasant farms in the '20s, not only as the precondition for collectivization, but as an alternative to its implementation in the Stalinist variant. The renewed study of the conceptions of cooperative development of A. V. Chaianov and a number of other theoreticians and practitioners of the cooperative movement in the '20s played a large role in this.

Research on the Bukharin alternative will have fundamental significance for an understanding of the problems of postrevolutionary development as a whole. There is a pressing social need for this. The universal attention which was drawn to the question of the rehabilitation of Nikolai Ivanovich Bukharin is indicative.

For me there is no doubt that in studying the history of the building of socialism in our country one of the primary tasks now is the scientific analysis of the Bukharin alternative to the Stalinist variant of solving those problems our country faced at the end of the '20s. It is usually spoken of as the only other option, that the choice was only between two variants—Stalin's and Bukharin's. I think that there were not two but at least three variants of a possible solution to those problems, including the variant worked out in the First Five-Year Plan. All of them were really implemented and directed toward industrializing the country, and toward implementing the socialist reconstruction of society, i.e., toward solving those problems facing society at the end of the '20s. The possibility of a choice then was not exhausted by the three variants named. The solutions hinted at by Trotsky and his followers should be studied, if only to rid ourselves finally of ascribing to them the variant implemented by Stalin. . . .

G. V. Klokova: *You can't educate creative people from a dogmatic textbook*

One of our most pressing problems is the study and description of the historical consciousness of society today. I would say, first of all depending on the knowledge of teachers and students, that an enormous role is played in historical consciousness by stereotypes and myths, consciously implanted with the help of the media. A distorted perception of history, especially the history of the twentieth century, has been created.

We should understand the nature of this distorted perception of history, since it was fostered in schoolchildren at an early age and reinforced in adolescence through school textbooks. It reflected certain political circumstances characteristic both of the period in which the personality cult dominated and in the period of stagnation [the Brezhnev years—D. J. R.].

I would like to direct the attention of historians to the fact that we have no precise knowledge and analysis of the character and degree of dissemination of distorted views among the population, including schoolchildren and schoolteachers. If we consider the union republics and the perception of interethnic relations, then we get a depressing picture. Perhaps the journal will coordinate the efforts of historians, sociologists, psychologists, and statisticians, in order, by representative sampling, to get data about this and analyze them.

It has been said here that we should carefully preserve our ideals in order not to weaken them in teaching history. But let us look at how the education of our youth is going. A textbook is always the reflection of the dominant conceptions and approaches to historical science. When it departs from real life, gives a lacquered picture, and presents the figure of silence, it harms education and forms a "dual morality" among students. Young people react to this by retreating from social problems. Those negative processes that are going on among part of the youth, including the creation of some informal groups, are payment for the fact that young people were offered a distorted, incorrect treatment both of the present (although what is happening is openly spoken of at home and everywhere) and of the past. It is very important to take account of these processes.

Historical myths are disseminated not only by historical science and its teaching in the post-secondary institution and at school, but also by the position of public-affairs writing and *belles-lettres*, which also reinforces a distorted perception of history. We must not ignore the fact that some literature, particularly the novels by V. Pikul', replace genuine history and implant ambitious, jingoistic myths, and the broad masses are susceptible to this demagogy.

It is important to understand how historical consciousness is formed and what it presently is in reality. This is one of the paths to knowing the realities of life. An analysis of the current situation shows that young people deny a formal declarative attitude toward the past and the present. They reject negative phenomena and express an urge for historical knowledge, for historical truth, for a class evaluation of what has taken place in the country, and for a definition of their place in the gigantic plans for accelerating and restructuring all aspects of our life. . . .

To solve the problem of history texts, it is necessary as quickly as possible to announce a competition for the writing of new textbooks, especially on the history of the twentieth century; to assure while writing them cooperation among scholars, methods-specialists, and teachers as equal coauthors. The new textbook should reflect perestroika in historical science, reject oversimplified models, silence, and direct distortion of history; it is important to strengthen discussion of the general and the particular, social experience, and the role of historic personalities. As a pedagogical tool, the history textbook should take account of pedagogical regularities and the peculiarity of the psychology of mastering history, the formation of historical consciousness and the students' historical thinking, and strengthen the moral and analytical aspect of the exposition, as well as its vividness and clarity. . . .

A. P. Novosel'tsev: *The source is the basis of the historian's work*

The question of perestroika in historical science agitates us all now. There are various assessments of what it means, but probably those people are right who believe we should not be talking of rewriting all of history (for example, of the USSR), but of reconsidering our views on some problems, removing the so-called blank spots, removing the unfortunately numerous defects that exist in solving both large and small questions. We must work on this now.

Both in the press and at our "roundtable" special attention is being given to modern history, where, for completely understandable reasons, both unresolved problems and complications with their solution are more numerous. But are things so good with other epochs, in particular with problems of the ancient history of our country and the history of the Middle Ages? There are different opinions here. At one of the sessions of the Bureau of the Division of History of the USSR Academy of Sciences, the question was raised of writing a new work on the history of our country that would meet the tasks of reconstructing our historical science. Academician B. A. Rybakov then hurled the marvelous retort: they say we have to reexamine many problems in modern history, but there is a large period—"from the mammoths to Peter I"—that need not be touched, since supposedly everything is in good shape there. I agree with Rybakov about the mammoths. But as concerns our history of the period of Peter I and for the thousand years preceding it, matters are by no means so good.

Ours is a multinational country, and a number of the peoples who inhabit it have very ancient histories, in past epochs often little connected with the history of its other regions. The history of the Transcaucasus in antiquity and in the early Middle Ages, for example, has greater similarity with the countries of Asia Minor than, let us say, with Kievan Rus'. The historian must take account of this circumstance. It is hardly correct to connect the history of the Caucasus in the Middle Ages with the history of Russia more closely than the real sources on Russian-Caucasian relations allow. They are at times extremely complicated and by no means developed in a straight ascending line.

Probably everyone knows that the greatest number of disputes over the history of our ethnic republics arises precisely over problems of ancient history and that of the Middle Ages. I would venture to assert that many of them result from the fact that historians in the center falsify a number of problems in Russian history.

I would like to direct attention to some questions of the history of Ancient Rus'. In recent times, I. Ia. Froianov has been the main target of criticism in our literature. In fact, there is much that is debatable and, in my opinion, wrong in his views. I have written about this, although I should openly admit here that the form of my polemic with him has not always been sufficiently scholarly. Meanwhile, there is a historian whose works contain quite a few inaccuracies and mistakes, but this goes virtually unmentioned in the press. I am speaking of B. A. Rybakov. He, for example, archaizes the time of formation of the Slavic peoples (he dates it to the middle of the Second Millennium B.C., whereas linguists and historians have proved that this took place one thousand years later). In his work of recent years, he denies the role of Novgorod in forming the Ancient Russian state. . . .

However, the main thing that I would like to direct attention to now is Rybakov's attitude toward the use of sources. For any historian, the source is the basis of his work, and one must approach it cautiously, not distorting its meaning. Rybakov's approach to the source is rather free-style. . . .

In many of the works of our colleagues from the republics we encounter attempts to archaize history at any price. Let's ask ourselves the question: aren't the attempts of a number of historians in Azerbaidzhan and Central Asia to find Turkic people in antiquity on the territory of their republics connected with analogous attempts to find Slavs in the Second Millennium B.C.? And if we can pose this question to such a famous academician [as Rybakov], why can't we do the same with local scholars?

I would like to touch on the problem of the genesis of capitalism in Russia. Here some historians have also clearly manifested a tendency to make this process more ancient, predating it to the seventeenth and even the sixteenth century. Citing one or two places in Lenin's works by no means rids us of the theoretical confusion with which the attempt to absolutize some local phenomena of Russian history in the seventeenth century is connected. While working on a multivolume work on the genesis of capitalism I became convinced that the conceptions of our historians who search for capitalist relations in Russia in the sixteenth–seventeenth centuries directly influence the formation of analogous views of Transcaucasian historians. This was at the beginning of the '70s, and the situation has not changed since then. For example, a number of historians in Azerbaidzhan find evidence of developed capitalism in the nineteenth century not only in Baku, but in other regions of Azerbaidzhan. Some historians in Armenia and in the North Caucasian autonomous republics, for example, are not far behind in this respect. We must not forget that our historiography is a unit, and historians in outlying places study with scholars at the center, borrowing, unfortunately, more than just their achievements from them. . . .

K. F. Shatsillo: *We must react more quickly to the demands of perestroika**

Today's "roundtable" in the editorial office gives rise to a feeling of satisfaction. Of course, historians are very conservative, not so much from their convictions as from the character of their work. They probably cannot compete with literary people, but they should react more quickly to the demands of perestroika. We must not twiddle our thumbs. During such radical change in the development of historical science and public life in our country, the journal should play a special role.

What can we say about perestroika in historical science? In the first place, it is going forward very slowly; everyone is waiting for someone else to come forward and restructure. It is my profound conviction that no one is coming forward and no one will restructure. We must do this ourselves, beginning with ourselves. I recall Chekov's words about how he squeezed the slave from himself in drops. The time has now arrived for us when we have to squeeze from ourselves in drops the slave in scholarship. We should not retreat from our class positions, but we must also not confuse—to paraphrase Saltykov-Shchedrin—the concept of "science" with the concept of "his Excellency," not to speak of giving preference to the latter. What, concretely, should we be talking about? About the fact

---

*Shatsillo's work has appeared in *Soviet Studies in History*. See the Winter 1981–82 issue (vol. XX, no. 3).—D. J. R.

that each author in each article should proceed from an existing alternative. But we, as a rule, maintain that that's the way it was and it couldn't be any different.

Now about "blank spots" in history. They are, rather, dark spots. Name me even one work that deals with the nationality question at the end of the nineteenth and the beginning of the twentieth centuries. You can't find one. And this is in a situation in which there is a clear formula from Lenin: "Russia is a prison of nations." We don't study this problem; but people do speculate on it. Or look how we write about foreign policy in the nineteenth–twentieth centuries: according to a formula that was very wittily defined by one British historian—"what one clerk wrote to another." Can we understand the Bosnian crisis of 1908–1909 by limiting ourselves to "what one clerk said to another," without taking account of the fact that the crisis arose when, behind the backs of the premiers, the military prepared for war? No. Accordingly, we must study the history of the armed forces in Russia. Who studies it? The Institute of Military History is supposed to, but it doesn't study anything other than the Great Patriotic War. And to study the history of the armed forces in Russia, you need to work in the archives. Will you find many references by our historians to the archives? No. They are limited only to diplomatic correspondence.

Now another problem, which also arises in the course of restructuring of historical science and inevitably must either aid it or hinder it. This is the relationship of the historian to the archives. It is shameful to say, but we live in a country that does not have a law establishing a definite time limit documents may remain restricted, a law which every civilized country has adopted and implemented. After this period has expired, the departments must be obliged to turn over all materials to the archives for public use. The Presidium of the USSR Academy of Sciences must raise the question with the Presidium of the USSR Supreme Soviet of adopting such a law. There should exist no special collections at all in the archives.

The Ministry of Defense, the Ministry of Foreign Affairs, and a host of other departments do not give their files to any archives.

There are astonishing cases—the Central Party Archive of the Institute of Marxism-Leninism, for example, has the P. V. Struve papers. Why are they being kept in the Party Archive? Why are a little more than half of the documents of the Extraordinary Investigative Commission of the Provisional Government kept in TsGAOR? And where are the other documents?

Consulting archival documents is the historian's professional duty. The historian should base his work on the fundamental layers of historical material. If he does not do this, it is a mistake to call him a historian.

We in the Institute of History of the USSR of the USSR Academy of Sciences recently had a meeting of the Academic Council at which some unexpected facts were reported. It turns out that many archives have been opened, but historians are not going there. People have forgotten how to work in archives. I can say from my own experience that it is difficult to work in the archives. In the first place, this is a task with many unknowns, and in the second place, you get exactly what Maiakovskii said—it's necessary to turn over millions of tons of ore in order to find something interesting. . . .

D. K. Shelestov: *From Polyhymnia to Clio!*

I cannot remember another such time like the past year and a half or so. One well-known political figure whom you know once remarked that historical parallels are dangerous. The judgment is not new and is in general justified. Nevertheless, what is happening now in some respects is reminiscent of 1917, when the whole country decided to speak out. And should this surprise us? Figuratively speaking, April 1985 began the clearing of the path to October 1917, with its great ideals and goals, embodying them on a new spiral of our development today and tomorrow.

As public life is radically becoming more active, there is at the same time a growth of interest in history and in all of Clio's activities. Having been for more than a third of a century one of the apprentices in this "hot shop," where modern times are forged out of the still molten lava of history, I cannot help rejoicing at the growth of this interest and seeing drama in the unfolding criticism of our professional activity. Why hide it, it was frequently connected with the betrayal of Clio in the embraces of another muse—Polyhymnia, who composed, if we believe the ancient Greeks, rousing songs with her head veiled.

At the same time, I will not hide the fact that the growing storm of critical remarks in the press at first called for caution. Not because of a fear of "washing scholarly dirty linen in public," but because—I am convinced of this today as well—a genuine reinterpretation of the historical past can be accomplished above all by historical science itself, assuring a scientific dialectical-materialist vision of sociohistorical development.

It's not enough to rejoice in the growing mass interest in history; we need to see something else—its sometimes peculiar character. One of the testimonies to this is the unexpected hullabaloo in connection with the republication of the works of S. M. Solov'ev and V. O. Kliuchevskii. Passions were so strong that one writer published a letter in a newspaper begging that her children "not be impoverished" (spiritually, of course) by being refused a subscription to Solov'-ev. We can imagine the laughter of the author of the twenty-nine-volume history of Russia, the reading of which, straight through, as they say, from cover to cover, is not, perhaps, within the capacity of every historian.

But irony is inappropriate here. And the incident, if you think about it, is not so unexpected. As a reflection of some complicated phenomena of our present spiritual life, it in its own way illuminates the shortcomings of mass historical education, the decline of broad reader interest in contemporary scholarly historical literature, especially that devoted to the study of the Soviet period. . . .

V. P. Volobuev: *Establish new approaches in historical science*

The preceding speakers have made quite a few interesting comments on the theme under discussion. The problem is really exciting, considering, on the one hand, the enormous interest in history, and on the other, the slow pace of perestroika in historical science. I would like to emphasize that interest in history is growing from above and from below. The reasons for this are evident: not only, finally, to learn the whole truth about our history, past and present, whatever it is, but also to draw once and for all lessons from the bitter experience of history, so that departures from the ideals of the Great October [Revolution] and from Leninist principles of leading the party and the country can never again be repeated. An appeal to the positive experience of our history, to the social creativity of the masses, has considerable significance.

Perhaps for the first time in my memory, I'm hearing speeches about the moral side of the historical activity of classes, parties, individual historical figures. We are so accustomed to operating with abstract conceptions about the regularities of social development, of social progress, that we have completely lost sight of categories like good and evil, the price of progress, and so forth. We are expected, without taking the place of figures in the cultural realm, to show in our works what role moral values and ideals played and play now in the historical progression of humanity and of individual peoples.

The heritage of stagnation is a heavy burden for all of us. The speeches of party leaders and also of public-affairs writers, and, in part, historians, give an analysis of the causes and basic manifestations of the phenomena of stagnation in the social sciences, including history. As applied to historical science, this analysis should be continued and deepened. Along with dogmatism, vulgar sociologism, and economism, we must name at least three more causes. First, the embellishment of our history, even its idealization, as an obligatory research method was extended from the Soviet period to practically all of the periods of our country's history, including medieval history. It suffices to recall how unwillingly we speak of Russia's backwardness, including in the pre-Petrine period, although Peter I's transformations also seem not to have had causes. False patriotism foreign to Marxism was widespread among us, prompting us to ignore Russia's former backwardness compared to the progressive countries of the West in many fields of social life and to "lift" our history to their level.

Second, a fallacious methodological principle—the attempt to adapt our Russian model of historical development to the Western European one—was established. This has been manifested in the treatment of Russian absolutism in the period of feudalism and in the more recent period; in the genesis of capitalism; in the inflated assessments of the level of development of Russian capitalism and imperialism. A direct consequence of this methodological approach was, in particular, the prohibition of research on the multiformational nature and typology of Russian capitalism, since it "spoiled" the picture and distanced Russia from the Western European model. Many historians literally were afraid to face the special nature of the historical process in our country. But it is long since time for us to reject the Eurocentric vision of world history, including ours, and finally begin, in Marxist fashion, to research what our historical path has been and why our road was that way and not another. I. Kliamkin was right when he said that our road is one of the most difficult in world history.[4] But it is ours, it lies on a common line of world development, although distinguished by significant peculiarities. We are seemingly embarrassed by this special character and willingly or unwillingly accept the Western European path of development as a standard. We must not forget that it was our historical road that led us earlier than other peoples to socialism. And as concerns the relative ease of other models of development, apparently that's only the way it seems.

Finally, we have simplified to the extreme, and thereby distorted, the understanding of the action of social regularity, introducing into history teleology, iron determinism and automatism foreign to Marxism. The idea of alternatives, of a people's choice (as classes, parties, peoples) of one or another path of historical development is making slow and difficult progress among historians. Here are two examples. No later than January of last year, a majority of the members of the editorial board of *Voprosy istorii* on the first reading rejected my article devoted to the alternatives of historical development in our country in 1917 and in the Soviet period. The reason for this was precisely that an attempt was made to reveal the real alternatives of that time and the struggle of living social forces for the selection of one or another alternative. In the no. 6, 1987, issue of *Istoriia SSSR* two reviews of the book by I. K. Pantin, E. G. Plimak, and V. G. Khoros, *The Revolutionary Tradition in Russia* [Revoliutsionnaia traditsiia v Rossii], appeared. By itself this is a normal phenomenon. But then the editorial board considered it necessary to give an abstract, and in it the three authors were severely criticized for arguing that in 1917 there existed an historical choice in Russia: socialism or capitalism. The presence of this choice was rejected on the grounds that socialism was historically necessary. But, according to the Marxist understanding of history, historical necessity is realized as a probabilistic process. In order for it to have been realized in October 1917, great efforts by the Bolshevik party and the people were required in the struggle for a socialist choice. Had it not been for this, another alternative not corresponding to the interests of the people could have been implemented.

What do we need first of all on the historical front? We need to activate decisively the process of perestroika in historical science, drawing into it a wide circle of the scholarly public, who are either biding their time or sabotaging it. In this regard, the seventieth anniversary of the October Revolution clearly showed the weakness of our historical front and of the leading historical institutions. I had occasion to read the letters of readers to the weekly *Argumenty i fakty* during an interview I gave to a correspondent of this popular publication. I was surprised by the historical illiteracy of wide circles of readers and their thirst and yearning for historical truth. The question—"When will historians do right and give an accurate picture of our glorious but difficult and often tragic history, especially the history of the Soviet epoch?"—is practically the main refrain of the majority of letters. At the same time, the aggressive rejection by some readers of the attempt to restore historical truth is also evident, particularly when Stalin is talked about. We historians bear a large share of the responsibility for the historical illiteracy of the people, inasmuch as since the April 1985 Plenum of the Central Committee of the CPSU, we could have done significantly more for the historical education of people if we had been more efficient. . . .

I will cite some problems of our history, which, in my view, demand new approaches and conceptual solutions. A new approach is needed to the second, revolutionary-democratic stage of the liberation movement in Russia, in particular the reasons behind the search for a noncapitalist path for Russia. It is necessary to master the conception of a "second echelon" of capitalist development relative to Russia, and the dilemma of the catch-up models of its development in the nineteenth century and before. This will lead us to a correct understanding of the historical legacy inherited from old Russia by the Soviet regime.

While studying the history of the first and second bourgeois-democratic revolutions (1905–07 and February 1917), we should study anew the persistent search by the revolutionary masses for new forms of democracy and popular self-government.

I have already had occasion to speak on the problems of the history of the October Revolution (see *Voprosy istorii*, 1987, no. 6); therefore, I will note that the anniversary report by M. S. Gorbachev, "October and Perestroika: The Revolution Continues" [Oktiabr' i perestroika: Revoliutsiia prodolzhaetsia], illuminates new aspects of this problem area and dictates the need to deepen the elaboration of this, the cardinal event of the twentieth century.

In this regard, the question arises of reinterpreting the intraparty struggle of the '20s and of providing a truthful illumination of it free of the previous cliches and stereotypes. Here we cannot rely entirely upon historians of the party, for this is a problem of general history.

Finally, the people want to know our opinion about the history of Soviet society. Important questions arise: was our historical road the correct one; did it lead us to the shining temple on a green hill? There are those who doubt this. But for us there can be no doubt whatsoever that the people's choice in October was correct and that we took Lenin's path to socialism. But what happened then? While remaining within the framework of socialism, weren't we turned away from Lenin's path at the end of the '20s? This question is raised by part of the public, and there is still no answer to it. . . .

V. I. Startsev: *More attention to historical documents*

I would like to talk about something that has not yet been spoken of today, and that is about sources, which lie at the base of any historian's work. We must begin again to publish sources in order to match the wave of publications we had in 1957–63. Without this we will not be able to solve many of our problems. Researchers should get broad access to materials in central institutions, so that these materials are not the domain of one or two historians. Moreover, these materials must be published, and in the spirit of glasnost'. At present the publication of the Special Journals of the Council of Ministers of the tsarist government has begun, but with great difficulty. We are accomplishing this work slowly, much more slowly than was done by the tsarist ministers, but at least we have started it. We also have to show what our People's Commissars were doing as well, how they worked, beginning with at least the first years of the Soviet regime. Of course, the journal's role and the opportunities in this matter are limited. For a start, the journal could publish a few very interesting materials, introducing a rubric "Published for the First Time." We sometimes criticize journalists for their statements and assessments, but we can't help seeing the usefulness of their statements. An example of this is the publication of a document about the rehabilitation of A. G. Shliapnikov (he was rehabilitated in 1963, but the public wasn't told of this). Materials have been published in *Moscow News* [Moskovskie novosti] about changes in how the cases are presented for the rehabilitation of "the daughters of the Arbat," including documents. This means that the press has also begun to publish sources. So far the journal is behind in this respect. . . .

The journal could devote attention to the moods of various strata of our reading public. In connection with this, I would like to mention the following fact. I have had to speak a great deal in the last year. During my addresses I received about a thousand notes from the audience. To make an analysis, even statistical treatment, of this material would be very interesting.

In the week of December 20, 1987, I had occasion to speak in Murmansk, in the House of Political Education, before propagandists in this transpolar city. One propagandist asked me if I knew Anisimov. I said that I knew him, that I had even approved his acceptance to graduate school. "It would have been better if you hadn't done that." "Why?" "Well, isn't he against Pikul'?! He unmasks Pikul'. Can one really do that?" "If," he said, "it wasn't for Pikul', who would read your history, who would bother with it? You owe it to him that the people got interested in history." As one Leningrader justly noted, a lot of people have become interested in history through those very gutters through which Pikul' is dragging our entire history. The phenomenon of Pikul' would not have occurred if we had something to resist him with.

I would like to raise yet another problem—the struggle against monopolies in historical science. Of course it exists, and we should recognize this. This has already been spoken of. Let me add yet another example. Out of fear of the Memory [Pamiat'] Society, Academician I. I. Mints forbade study of the theme of Freemasonry in our history. A full set of *Ogonek* [Little Flame] for last year was graced with many wonderful entries. But I must exclude from the list one item in the first issue of the journal because of an erroneous assessment of Freemasonry at the beginning of the century. There were Freemasons; they have existed for a long time, and the last émigré Russian lodge closed in Paris only in 1970.

So, out of fear we will not deal with this theme at all, and not say what in fact happened? We do not have a Society of Historians. But such a society should exist; then it would be easier to battle against monopolies in the field of historical science. For this, we have to give academic and post-secondary scholarship equal opportunities, and attract representatives of the latter more widely into research work and publishing activity.

I would like to express the wish that the "Prosveshchenie" and "Vysshaia shkola" publishing houses be more discerning about what they publish. These publishing houses now issue third-rate stuff, with which we have to educate our teachers. Scholarly journals should remember the mass of teachers who are confused and do not know what to do, who are overburdened and do not have the opportunity to become familiar with the newest achievements of our scholar-historians. We also have to produce historical works directly addressed to teachers of history. They are waiting for this from us. I transmit this request in the name of Leningrad teachers, and this has been spoken of in the Post-Graduate Institute for Teachers. . . .

N. N. Bolkhovitinov*: *On professionalism and perestroika in historical science*

I wish to dwell on two questions—professionalism and perestroika in historical science.

I am a long-time subscriber to *Voprosy istorii* (at least since 1957), and I note with regret that the professional level of the journal in recent years has become unacceptably low. When you open any issue of the journal, you find at best one or two articles worthy of attention. The editorial office says the journal's portfolio is filled for three years. Do we have to publish everything? In the best foreign journals (for example the *American Historical Review*), only twenty to thirty articles out of two to three hundred (!) submitted for consideration to the editorial board are published. We must dramatically raise demands on published materials and print only original research articles and notes in which there is something new. It would also be desirable to print articles by foreign authors, accompanying

---

*N. N. Bolkhovitinov's works appear regularly in *Soviet Studies in History.* See, for example, the Fall 1986 (vol. XXV, no. 2) and Winter 1980–81 (vol. XIX, no. 3) issues. —D. J. R.

them, if necessary, with commentaries by Soviet specialists.

The critical and informational part of the journal is in need of radical improvement. Complimentary reviews, entirely lacking criticism, predominate. In this case, it is necessary to curtail their size sharply and print them in the section "Briefly About Books," or simply put them in the notes. On the other hand, we must extend to authors the opportunity to respond to the reviewer and launch a debate. It is also desirable to print readers' letters regularly.

The section "Historical Science Abroad" is particularly poorly represented in the journal. It must be said outright that it does not at all reflect the condition of historical science abroad, especially Western. Notes on articles and reviews of foreign books are random. We should systematically inform readers at least of the contents of the basic American and Western European historical journals and the most important monographs.

It is very sad that the journal *Istoricheskii arkhiv* [Historical Archive], which had just begun to publish unknown documents, ceased publication in 1962. I would like to support the suggestions made earlier about the systematic publication of new archival documents in the section "Published for the First Time." The journal should not be afraid to pose controversial discussion problems, present materials about difficulty of access to archives, the unsatisfactory situation in regard to acquisitions and the activities of the libraries (the Lenin State Library of the USSR, the Institute of Scientific Information in the Social Sciences of the USSR Academy of Sciences, and others), and the creation of a nationwide Society of Historians. The journal should comment on those articles and novels which capture the attention of the whole country. It is highly desirable to publish opinions of specialists and historians about the novels of V. Pikul', to pick apart one of his actual novels. It would also be desirable to include materials about the most topical articles now being published in *Novyi mir*, *Znamia* [Banner], and other leading sociopolitical and literary journals.

I cite as an example the article by I. Kliamkin published in *Novyi mir*, which attracted universal attention—"Which Road Leads to the Temple?" [Kakaia ulitsa vedet k khramu?].[5] The article is brilliant, but it states that there were never any alternatives in Russia, either in the past or at present. Here it is said that if there were no other alternatives, perestroika would be of no use, because we could not build another structure. We know that we cannot build another structure; we know that this structure must be rebuilt. While I value this article highly, I want to say that it can be argued with, not to speak of the fact that the professional historian will find inaccuracies in it. If the journal *Voprosy istorii* drew attention to this, it, of course, would not be quarreling with its nearest neighbor. If what is said is accurate and correct, it will find its reader, and this will exert influence. Perhaps it is worth thinking about a "roundtable" of historians and literary people, about a meeting of the editorial boards of *Voprosy istorii* and *Novyi mir*, the more so since they are neighbors.*

Speaking of the necessity for perestroika in historical science, participants in today's discussion have given examples only from the history of our country. I would like to mention world history. Until recently, it was believed that everything was more or less okay with the study of the history of France or the United States. The works of V. P. Volgin, V. M. Dalin, and A. Z. Manfred, not to speak of E. V. Tarle, became widely known. In the '30s, significant successes were already achieved in the study of the French Revolution at the end of the eighteenth century, the two hundredth anniversary of which the entire world will mark in the coming year. But is everything having to do with this question in as good a shape as we are accustomed to thinking? Back in the '30s, a conception of the Great French Revolution already evolved which celebrated unambiguously the Terror and the Jacobin dictatorship. J. P. Marat, M. Robespierre, and L. Saint-Just are represented as knights without fear and without reproach. It is understood that in those years it was practically impossible to object to the thesis about the intensification of the class struggle and of the complete and absolute justification of the Jacobin terror. A different situation evolved after 1956. Serious Marxist works were published abroad by A. Sobul (France), J. Rude (England), and W. Markow (GDR). Finally, in Leningrad, V. G. Revunenkov published a series of books about the French Revolution in the eighteenth century and the Jacobin dictatorship, which for a long time the Moscow School of French history hushed up, or even subjected to devastating criticism. Only in 1984 did it become possible to give a more or less objective evaluation of the works of V. G. Revunenkov, to mention the scale and negative consequences of Jacobin terror, although even Marx and Engels had written about this. "I am convinced," Engels stated, "that the blame for the rule of the Terror in 1793 falls almost exclusively on the frightened bourgeoisie, who represented themselves as patriots, on the petite bourgeoisie, shitting in their pants from fear, and on a band of scoundrels who took care of Number One during the Terror."[6]

By no means is everything well with the study of the history of the United States. With surprising ease, many of our Americanists write whatever is needed, timely and advantageous at any given moment, and not what is actually the fact. It is hardly necessary to show what harm will be caused if the Americanists incorrectly inform the public and the leadership about the real situation in the United States, the role of the working class, trade unions and the Communist party, and create a one-sided "image of the enemy," and so on. It is especially sad when this involves professional historians, who are called upon, above all, to observe objectivity and honesty. Although many dozens and even hundreds of Americanists have already been sent on trips to the United States, only extremely rarely is their research based on serious and comprehensive study of archival materials.

---

*Bolkhovitinov's advice was taken. See *Voprosy istorii* (no. 6, 1988), pp. 3–114. —D. J. R.

An inadmissible number of inaccuracies and mistakes are found even in the works of our leading Americanists. In this regard, I do not remember a single critical review or discussion of this problem. . . .

The general decline in the quality of works in history and the loss in them of real professionalism is clearly manifested in the fact that historical dissertations are now being written with equal ease not only by trained historians, but also by workers in various ministries and departments, journalists, engineers, and medical personnel. . . .

Great harm to history has been caused by the rigid limitation on the size of dissertations and monographs . . . and what if Marx brought his *Capital* to our publishing houses, or presented it for defense as a doctoral dissertation? It is not hard to imagine what answer he would have received from the All-Union Certification Commission and the USSR State Publishing Committee.

A. P. Tiurina: *The slowing of scientific research on the agrarian history of the USSR*

. . . Characteristic of the '60s and '70s was a decline in scientific research on the agrarian history of the USSR. This conclusion has to be drawn despite the presence of an enormous number of works on this topic. Unfortunately, the real situation in agriculture was not studied deeply, and only the existence of particular laws was confirmed. All the contradictions and negative phenomena in agriculture were as a rule hushed up or attributed to unfavorable weather conditions. From the Ninth Five-Year Plan there began a drop in the growth rates of net production in agriculture, and other alarming miscalculations were evident, in particular the economic impoverishment of agricultural enterprises, the alienation of the peasant from public property, growing social apathy, and negative moral phenomena. However, none of this was reflected in the literature, since it was prepared along the lines of "everything's good, but there are instances of individual defects." This approach deformed research methods, severely narrowed the problem areas of research, greatly simplified the evaluation of events, and at times led to naked opportunism. In speaking of this, I am still not inclined to lay the blame for the situation in agrarian science on scholars of agricultural history. It must be said outright that there was no demand for objective knowledge; on the contrary, this fell in with the command-bureaucratic methods of leadership of society and science, with authoritarian opinions and assessments. Precisely for this reason the researcher's access to the archives was closed, and the publication of statistical data on economic and other problems declined sharply; materials acquired through sociological surveys were classified. This was the reason behind the descriptive nature of many works and the lack of proof of the propositions advanced. . . .

V. D. Nazarov: *Preserve and develop the best traditions of historical science*

I would like to talk about four major but equally significant problems. The first is the responsibility of *Voprosy istorii* as the main historical journal during perestroika. It must be noted first, however, that in the '60s and '70s the journal reflected the condition of the discipline, and there were pluses and minuses in its activity. It sponsored a number of important discussions that facilitated research. At least within the framework of the period I study, and in particular the first peasant war in Russia, the journal published interesting articles on the history of the class struggle of the Russian peasantry in the seventeenth through nineteenth centuries. It seems to me that as a whole the sections designed for the mass reader justified themselves, in particular the thematically organized series, and also the publication of historical sources. I want to be understood correctly. It is necessary—and this should become a norm of scholarly discourse—to criticize that which deserves criticism, which hinders the advance of scholarship, but it is also necessary to preserve and develop the best traditions, including those of *Voprosy istorii*. . . .

Now the second problem—concerning the condition of historiography and the need for historians to "repent." We probably need a new rubric with the conditional title "Looking at Oneself," in which "blank (apparently more accurately, 'black') spots" in the history of Soviet historical science would be discussed. We have just spoken of the "affair" of the Leningrad historians, but we should also talk about the "affair" of the Moscow historians that followed the Leningrad one. And about the repression of M. N. Pokrovskii's students, the historians from the Institute of Red Professors, and the situation in 1948–49. . . .

Now the third complex of problems—raising the professional level of historians, about which N. N. Bolkhovitinov has already spoken. But perhaps it is worth talking right now at least about the preservation of the former rather high level of professional knowledge and competence. After all, in recent years historical science experienced powerful pressure from a multifaceted and varied dilettantism, and this, unfortunately, lowered the demand for quality work. Who, if not *Voprosy istorii*, will be the first to raise the level of published works? Here the selection of themes is important, their novelty, originality, approaches, completeness, and argumentation. I will name only some, in my view the most pressing subjects: the history of interethnic, inter-national contacts and mutual ties in the period of feudalism, the history of invasions or subjugation, of military inclusion of various peoples and their territories into the Russian state, the history of foreign policy, its complicated interconnection with domestic policy, and the fate of the ruling class in the history of feudal Russia. In treating this important complex of problems, we perhaps lag significantly behind Western scholars, in particular those of the United States and the FRG. . . .

Finally, we long ago destroyed the true proportions between scholarship as such, the sphere of scientific popularization and the field of artistic representation in history. The popularity of the historical novels of V. Pikul' is explained, in particular, by our neglect of political history, of personality in historical development, and of a high-quality popularization of historical knowledge. Taboos won't help the matter. In addition, such novels awaken interest in history, although they spoil both thought and taste. There are, in my view, outstanding works—by D. Balashov, for example. In any case, it is the business of historians to criticize what is bad and untrue in historical fiction. But first of all we have to raise the demands made on ourselves: we must more actively and systematically participate in educational and popularizing activity. The main task is to raise the quality of research, to make it more pertinent, and to make it more illustrative and clearer.

V. P. Alekseev: *The timeliness of what is not timely*

I would like to touch on a number of problems that, at first glance, have a rather academic character but at the same time are extremely topical in a historical sense and closely bound up with the most pressing tasks of the present day—educational, managerial-economic, and ideological. The initiative of the journal *Voprosy istorii* made us somehow systematize and organize a number of propositions and ideas, and we may now try as far as possible to formulate them briefly. Here are the problems which, from my point of view, await further treatment.

1. Historical ethnography. Notwithstanding the existence of the large Institute of Ethnography of the USSR Academy of Sciences, which carries out significant work in almost all branches of ethnographic science, a decline in research efforts and in interesting publications can be observed in the sphere of historical ethnography. . . .

2. Historical demography and paleodemography. The term "historical demography" embraces much more broadly than "paleodemography" all periods of human history before the present, and, strictly speaking, historical demography includes paleodemography as a branch. . . .

3. The history of technology. I will say conditionally that this problem is dealt with in detail in the Institute of the History of Natural Science and Technology, USSR Academy of Sciences. Quite recently, for example, an enormous volume was published devoted to the history of technology up to the beginning of this century. But I have in mind not the history of technology as such, but the history of technology as one of the most important components along with man himself, of the history of productive forces in the history of society. . . .

4. The origin and history of agriculture and animal husbandry. This problem is very closely connected with that of the origin of production, and the conception of "a Neolithic revolution" is now very popular. . . .

5. Historical psychology and paleopsychology. We are again speaking about a

problem at the interface of the sciences, and a historian-specialist who thinks in an orthodox way can express him or herself in highly skeptical terms relative to the necessity of treating such a theme. But the rarity of this theme in Soviet historical literature, although veiled in a number of brilliant works both by deceased and living historians, still is striking. Perhaps I am wrong, but it seems to me that this rarity is due to neglect of the full sense of the principles of historical materialism. How socially significant, psychologically penetrating, and brilliant as literature are the portrait characterizations and sketches by Karl Marx relating to the historical actors of various epochs, how many remarkably precise observations on the collective psychology of various social groups we find in the book by Engels *The Origin of the Family, Private Property and the State* [Proiskhozhdenie sem'i, chastnoi sobstvennosti i gosudarstva]. How clear and exhaustively precise, for all their brevity, are Lenin's characterizations of many figures in Russian culture! And the fundamental works by G. V. Plekhanov and A. V. Lunacharskii devoted to special study of the social psychology of Russian and European society in the epoch of feudalism and capitalism and to the uncovering of the sociopsychological forces and preferences in the revolutionary periods of medieval and recent history! The Marxist science of society has registered significant achievements in the field of historical psychology, and our modern historiography draws on these achievements very little and incompletely. . . .

What measures can we take to strengthen the cultural role of our science and its influence on youth and broad circles of readers both in our country and abroad? Four measures would seem to me more or less effective, although this question raises a whole group of fundamental problems, and further considerations will touch on part of them.

The first and basic question, probably going beyond the potential of the Division of History of USSR Academy of Sciences, is the character of the teaching of historical science in our country. We are speaking of the extremely rare opening of specialized departments in historical faculties of universities. The traditional division prevailing in the overwhelming majority of cases is a department of history of the USSR and a department of world history. Only Moscow, Leningrad, and a few other leading universities in the country can boast of the necessary variety of specialized departments, and then in an extremely relative sense. Departments of economic history, military history, and of comparative cultural studies are lacking, but these are enormous branches of historical science. Two or three existing departments of archaeology and ethnography bring together scholars from different disciplines. One department of physical anthropology exists in the Soviet Union—within the biology faculty of Moscow State University. There are no departments of historical anthropology at all. The most widely given reason for this unimpressive list is that there are no specialists. But there are none because they haven't been trained for decades. Moreover, those few trained lack the opportunity to utilize their skills in the teaching process in a systematic way; there are no special courses which make up for the lack of specialized departments.

The second problem, which is extremely important, is the publication of a popular historical journal. We do not need to speak of the crucial need for such a measure—this is obvious. But why has it not appeared to this day?

The third problem is presenting historical information on television. Geographers have prepared broadcasts about expeditions, the zoologists have an excellent broadcast about animals, and many leading scholars and engineers frequently talk about the newest technology and demonstrate it, giving information about the most important discoveries in natural science. Yet history, which interests any literate person, is not represented equally. . . .

Finally, the fourth thing that I would like to mention is the result of many years of expeditions and trips to meet our own and foreign readers. As our Soviet reader loves serious literature translated from Western European languages, so the foreign reader, being interested in the Soviet Union, demands information of equal value. . . . I think that the translation of serious monographs by Soviet historians into foreign languages and their distribution abroad would be an extremely effective measure in this direction.

O. A. Rzheshevskii: *Treat the events of the last war correctly**

I would like to dwell on a number of questions dealing with the Great Patriotic War of 1941–45, which has been studied extensively. . . .

What has been written is frequently subjected now to just criticism. But on the whole, these works contributed greatly to understanding the treatment of the problem, and they corresponded to the level and possibilities of that period in which they were written. However, the new situation, created as a result of the changes in recent years, allows us to approach this most complicated problem in a new way and to present fully and objectively the history of the tragedy and triumph of our people in the war years. . . .

In preparing this work we should, obviously, look in more detail at the question of the Soviet-German Nonaggression Pact, signed on 23 August 1939. . . .

*   *   *

The results of the discussion were summed up by A. A. Iskenderov, who noted that the exchange of views had been fruitful. An open and professional discussion had been held, which, despite a certain emotional tone and even sharpness in some evaluations, would be useful both to historical science and to the journal.

---

*For a criticism of Rzheshevskii's sloppy scholarship see the guest editor's notes, pp. 69–79, in the Winter 1985–86 (vol. XXIV, no. 3) issue of *Soviet Studies in History.* —D. J. R.

The participants in the meeting raised many important and interesting problems that must be dealt with both in the pages of the journal and in scholarly studies. Many of the themes raised in the course of the exchange of opinions deserve to be the subjects of special "roundtables."

Notes

1. K. Marx and F. Engels, *Sochineniia*, vol. 3, p. 16; vol. 27, p. 402.
2. Marx and Engels, *Soch.*, vol. 37, p. 370.
3. See *Oktiabr'*, no. 8.
4. See *Novyi mir*, 1987, no. 11.
5. Ibid.
6. Marx and Engels, *Soch.*, vol. 33, p. 45.

Index

Academy of Sciences of the USSR, 21–22, 27–28, 138, 254; organizational problems, 20–21, 25–26, 138, 150, 249–50, 255, 260
Adibekov, G. M., 83–85
Afanas 'ev, Iurii Nikolaevich, 33–34
Alekseev, Valerii Pavlovich, 278–80
Anikeev, V. V., 12, 99–100
Anisimov, Evgenii Viktorovich, 255–58, 272
Antonov, Aleksandr Stepanovich. *See* Tambov (province)
Archives and libraries: publications from, 85, 138, 272, 274; problems of access, 17, 27–28, 69, 71, 73, 75, 81, 100, 159, 267, 274, 276; value of, 98–102, 139, 148, 158, 267
Arosev, A. Ia., 112
Asiatic mode of production (theory), 6
Astrakhan, Kh. M., 160

Babeuf, Gracchus, 169–71
Baeva, L. K., 161
Baikal-Amur Mainline, 191
Bakhrushin, B. D., 260
Balashov, D., 278
Barsukov, N. A., 82, 97
Bek, Aleksandr Al 'fredovich, 44
Beria, Lavrentii Pavlovich, 230, 231–33
"Blank spots," 56–57, 60–61, 75, 150, 245, 251, 259, 267. *See also* Soviet Union (1917–), history of: problems in
Bogomolov, Oleg Timofeevich, 97
Bolkhovitinov, Nikolai Nikolaevich, 273–76
Bolshevik party. *See* Communist Party of

the Soviet Union; Old Bolsheviks
Bondar ', Vasilii Iakovlevich, 86, 96–97
Brezhnev, Leonid Il 'ich, 56–57, 237
Bukharin, Nikolai Ivanovich, 189, 210, 214, 223–24; Party activities of, 104, 149, 181–82, 218–19, 223, 224–25, 226, 262; personal relations, 213, 214–17, 222, 224, 225, 226; personality of, 212, 214, 215, 219–20, 221–22; publications of, 182, 209, 226–27. *See also* Larina, Anna Mikhailovna; New Economic Policy
Burdzhalov, Eduard Nikolaevich, 255
Bureaucracy, 60, 61–62, 204–208, 256, 276; and reform, 7, 235, 238. *See also* State authority and the economy; Trade unions

Carr, Edward Hallett, 14
Carrier, Jean Baptiste, 169–70
Chaianov, Aleksandr Vasil 'evich, 262
Cheka, 148, 175. *See also* Dzerzhinskii, Feliks Edmundovich
Cherkasov, Nikolai Konstantinovich, 194
Chernobaev, Anatolii Aleksandrovich, 112
Chivilikhin, Vladimir Alekseevich, 197
Churchill, Winston S., 240
Civil War, 71–72, 99, 124–25, 149, 154; participation in, 124–25, 143, 172. *See also* October Revolution; Peace of Brest- Litovsk; War Communism
Civil War and Intervention in the USSR, 149
Collective farms, 167, 175, 222. *See also* State farms
Collectivization, 186, 188, 189; alterna-

About the Editor

DONALD J. RALEIGH, professor of history at the University of North Carolina at Chapel Hill, has been editor of the translation journal *Soviet Studies in History* since 1979. He is the author of *Revolution on the Volga: 1917 in Saratov*, published in 1986, and is now at work on a study of the Civil War in Saratov Province. Raleigh's translation of *Russia's Second Revolution: The February 1917 Uprising in Petrograd*, by E. N. Burdzhalov, appeared in 1987. His edition of *A Russian Civil War Diary: Alexis V. Babine in Saratov, 1917–1922* was published in 1988.